BITTERSWEET

BITTERSWEET

by Leslie Li

CHARLES E. TUTTLE COMPANY, INC.

Boston • Rutland, Vermont • Tokyo

First published in the United States in 1992 by the
Charles E. Tuttle Company, Inc. of Rutland, Vermont & Tokyo, Japan,
with editorial offices at 77 Central Street, Boston, Massachusetts 02109.

The author would like to acknowledge the following publications which proved
most valuable in writing this book:

Li Xiuwen, *My Life with Li Zongren*. Lijiang Publishing Company, 1987.
Li Tsung-jen with Tong Te-Kong, *The Memoirs of Li Tsung-jen*. Westview Press, 1979.
Pruitt, Ida, *A Daughter of Han: The Autobiography of a Chinese Working Woman*.
    Reprinted by Stanford University Press, 1967 (© 1945 by Yale University Press).
Lary, Diana, *Region and Nation: The Kwangsi Clique in Chinese Politics 1925–1937*.
    Cambridge University Press, 1974.
Sitwell, Osbert, *Escape With Me: An Oriental Sketchbook*. Oxford University Press, 1939.
Ebrey, Patricia Buckley, *Chinese Civilization and Society: A Sourcebook*. The Free Press
    (Macmillan Publishing Co., Inc.), 1981.
Rossbach, Sarah, *Feng-Shui: The Chinese Art of Placement*. Arkana (Viking Penguin),
    1983.
Kwok Man Ho, Martin Palmer and Joanne O'Brien, *Lines of Destiny*. Shambhala
    Publications, 1986.
Turnley, David, Peter Turnley and Melinda Liu, *Beijing Spring*. Stewart, Tabori &
    Chang, 1989.
Wolf, Diana, *Chinese Writing: An Introduction*. Holt, Rinehart & Winston, 1975.
"Background for War," *Time* Magazine, June 26, 1939.
Excerpt on p. 209 from *Collected Poems* by Elinor Wylie. Copyright © 1932 by
    Alfred A, Knopf, Inc. and renewed 1960 by Edwina C. Rubenstein. Reprinted by
    permission of the publisher.
Excerpts on pp. 106, 107, 219, 259 from *The Tao of Power* by R.L. Wing. Copyright
    © 1986 by Immedia. Used by permission of Doubleday, a division of Bantam
    Doubleday Dell Publishing Group, Inc.
Excerpt on p. 214 from *Tao Te Ching* by Stephen Mitchell. Copyright © 1988 by
    Stephen Mitchell. Reprinted by permission of HarperCollins Publishers.
Excerpt on p. 236 from "Interior of China Forms Vast Army," by F. Tillman Durdin,
    January 22, 1939.

Library of Congress Cataloging-in-Publication Data

Li, Leslie, 1945–
    Bittersweet / by Leslie Li.
        p.   cm.
    ISBN 0-8048-1777-4
    1. China—History—20th century—Fiction. I. Title.
PS3562.I155B5   1992
813'.54—dc20
                                            92-15385
                                                CIP

Jacket design by Linda Koegel
Tapestry by Amy Zerner
Photograph of tapestry by Julia Walker
Photograph of author by Gustavo Gonzalez

PRINTED IN THE UNITED STATES

To my mother and father
Genevieve and Yau Luen
and to my son
Anton
the links that connect mine to
the Chain of Life
whose pulls in opposite directions
— past and future —
provided the creative tension
that made this book possible.

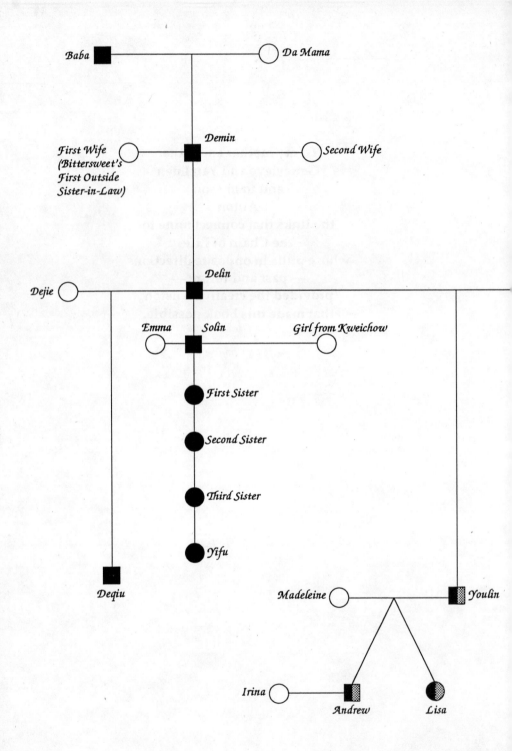

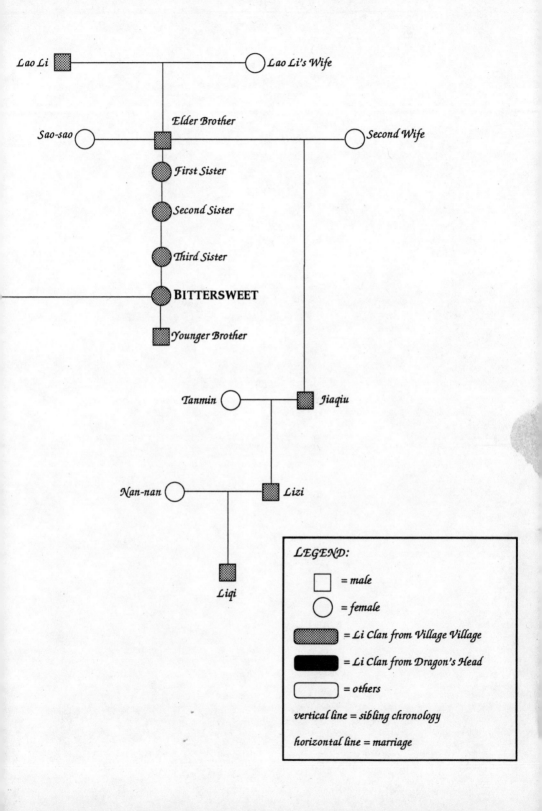

LEGEND:

☐ = male

◯ = female

▨ = Li Clan from Village Village

■ = Li Clan from Dragon's Head

▢ = others

vertical line = sibling chronology

horizontal line = marriage

PREFACE

In 1986 I traveled to Guilin, China, the city of my forebears, to visit my then 96-year-old grandmother, Li Xiuwen, and to Beijing to honor the memory of my grandfather, Li Zongren (Li Tsung-jen), vice president and acting president of China from 1948 to 1949.

Much of the subsequent six years, which included a second trip to Guilin in 1990 to help celebrate my grandmother's 100th birthday, I spent researching and writing an historical novel inspired by my grandmother's (and to a lesser extent, my grandfather's) long and full life.

The century in which Li Xiuwen lived (she died June 18, 1992) is surely one of the most tumultuous in all of Chinese history. It encompasses the demise of imperial rule, the torturous beginnings of republican government, the ravages of warlordism, the Sino-Japanese War, the Communist-Kuomintang Civil War, the Great Proletarian Cultural Revolution, the sporadic Beijing Spring and, most recently, its bloody culmination, the June 4th Massacre in Tiananmen Square.

Though my grandfather was an important military and political figure in modern Chinese history, actively participating in most of these events rights up to his death in Beijing at the height of the Cultural Revolution, it was my grandmother, "mere" witness though she was to China's social and political upheavals and "helpless" victim of its unbending patriarchy, who survived — more accurately, *prevailed over* — them all, employing Taoist, Buddhist, and Confucian stratagems as the situation warranted. It was she who preserved family ties and traditions, customs and culture, and carried them intact as she crisscrossed China in search of a haven safe from invasion and revolution, eventually transferring them to our suburban New York home.

And it is her tale, modified in the protagonist Bittersweet, that is told in these pages — a tale that is as relevant to our age — when questions of loyalty and betrayal, war and peace, individual freedom and collective responsibility, power and empowerment, have taken on even greater proportions and thus meaning — as it was in Bittersweet's time.

While I have introduced several fictitious characters and events into the story for the sake of the narrative, the factual portions of *Bittersweet* are noteworthy for their cultural and historical significance and would have been impossible to relate were it not for the generous assistance of certain persons, organizations, and publications. First and foremost, I am indebted to my father for his painstaking translation of my grandmother's autobiography, *My Life with Li Zongren*. I am also grateful to the East Asian Institute of Columbia University for having inaugurated the Chinese Oral History Project whereby, over three years of his fifteen-year stay in the United States, my grandfather Li Zongren was interviewed extensively by professor of Chinese history Tong Tekong. The result, *The Memoirs of Li Tsung-jen*, along with conversations I had with my parents, relatives, and those who knew my grandfather well, added a broader social context and an historical dimension to my personal knowledge of the man.

I owe a huge debt of gratitude, one that I can never repay, to my mother for her unflagging support during the years I spent researching this book and for keeping my writing of it a secret so that I could work in a "fruitful void" without pressure or expectation. I am also grateful to Mariangela Causa-Steindler, Johanna Boetz, Kathryn Kass, Patricia Dodd, Jean Davis, and John Hines for their unstinting friendship and unwavering faith that my "negative capability" held creative potential.

Lastly, I am deeply indebted to Peter Ackroyd, Linda Licklider Smith, and Roberta Scimone of Charles E. Tuttle Company for offering me the inestimable opportunity of seeing *Bittersweet* in print based on the existence of only its first few chapters; to Debra Spark for her thoughtful and thorough editing; and to every member of the Tuttle staff for the energy and enthusiasm which they brought to each phase of *Bittersweet*'s genesis from manuscript to finished book.

Finally, in thanking these people, organizations, and publications, I in no way wish to evade responsibility for errors which critics may discover in these pages.

BOOK ONE

"Life must go on. The generations stretch back thousands of years to the great ancestor parents. They stretch for thousands of years into the future, generation upon generation. Seen in proportion to this great array, the individual is but a small thing. But on the other hand, no individual can drop out. Each is a link in the great chain. No one can drop out without breaking the chain. A woman stands with one hand grasping the generations that have gone before and with the other generations to come. It is her common destiny with all women."

Daughter of Han
Ida Pruitt

Chapter 1
Small Happiness
(1889)

Lao Li's wife slipped out the back door of her house. She paused on the threshold, tilting her head to one side, listening for the snores of her husband. Hearing the sounds, deep and rhythmic, she grabbed the shovel in the lime shed, scurried along the back wall of the *hutong*, turned the corner of the narrow alleyway and leaned against the rain-splashed bricks.

She had done a terrible thing, and now, in the darkest part of night, she was trying to make amends before the gods grew even angrier with her. Weren't the claps of thunder from their hands? Weren't the bolts of lightning that they threw down, illuminating her crime, proof of their anger? Then again, Lao Li's wife thought, they had sent the wind and rain to muffle the sound of her shovel. They had sent a moonless night to help conceal her crime. And so, now, as she dug behind the house, the blade of the shovel sliding easily into the rain-softened earth, she alternately begged forgiveness of the gods and thanked them for their mercy. Once, she cocked her head, fearing a baying of dogs which might rouse the villagers, then she remembered the dogs had disappeared years ago during the famine and had never reappeared. She resumed her digging.

She thought: I've committed an unthinkable crime, but it has brought this downpour. It has brought water for the fields so the rice seedlings will sprout and bear grain. Surely, it's a portent from the gods that the birth of the child is good. Surely, my dereliction will be forgiven.

She dropped the afterbirth into the hole she had made and covered it over, patting down the earth with the flat of her shovel. Then she turned the effigies of the household gods, whose faces she had averted so they wouldn't see what she was doing. Now that they faced forward in their niche in the wall, they could see how she had righted things. She kowtowed three times before them, begging forgiveness and

1

munificence; she was but a weak and worthless woman who hadn't the heart to kill yet another child.

Five years ago, she had borne a second son, but he was small and frail and would not suck milk. Instead, he cried until his stomach was distended with gas, and he used up what little energy he had helplessly flailing his thin limbs about. On his third day of life, when he was too weak even to cry, she had placed a pillow over his tiny face until what little life he possessed was extinguished. Two years later, during a time of drought and sure famine — her son and three daughters pulling on the hem of her blouse, saying that they were still hungry though they had just eaten all there was — she had another girl. Even before she cut the umbilical cord with her teeth — for in her labor she had forgotten to bring the jagged piece of mirror she had used with her other children — she had smothered the child.

"Did you know?" people had said at that time. "Lao Li's wife gave birth to a girl yesterday. Stillborn." Thus word of the latest infanticide passed from house to house. Each villager, on hearing the news, had nodded slightly and made sucking noises, tongue pressed against teeth.

What else could have been done? A family needed sons to work the land, to pass on the family name, to care for the parents in their old age. A daughter was just an extra mouth to feed, difficult enough in good times but, in bad times, an unbearable burden. A daughter would leave her family to marry into another just when she became useful. What good was she, then, to her own family who shouldered the expense and effort of raising her, only to lose her when she was finally worth keeping?

Lao Li's wife had always known her duties, and she had always performed them. When Fourth Daughter was born in the lime shed in the middle of the night in the middle of the season for transplanting the rice seedlings, she had not hesitated to do the proper thing and kill the child, nor did she now have the slightest aversion for the task at hand. But such a voice! Such powerful lungs on the one that she had just brought into the world!

When she reached for the pillow, her blouse parted and the newborn's mouth grabbed onto one of the breasts and sucked on it with all the fury of her hunger and beginning life. When Lao Li's wife tried to pull her breast away, the baby reacted by clinging tighter,

2

grasping the swollen nipple with toothless gums and pulling furiously.

The mother's breasts grew full to meet the infant's demand. Such a glutton, Lao Li's wife thought in amazement, feeling a sensual rapture she had never known, not even with her first-born son whose exuberance to be alive had not matched this little girl's by half. As her breasts swelled with milk, Lao Li's wife felt her resolve ebb. She reached for the nail she had brought with her to cut the umbilical cord, but it was old and rusty, the point blunted by time and use, so she gnawed at the rope of flesh until she had cut through and could knot the cord, could tie up her daughter's life, now separate from her own. She rose unsteadily to her feet and doused the child with water from the bucket she had carried to the lime shed when she had felt the first contractions. Now, she washed off the white birth curds that clung to the infant's body. Wrapping the girl in a cloth and then setting her and her afterbirth inside her own blouse, Lao Li's wife, dragging the shovel after her, made her way to the bedroom. Only after she had finished digging at the end of the bed did her husband wake and sit up.

"Well, then — what is it?"

"Have you no eyes?" she asked him. She held up the afterbirth, then dropped it into the hole she had made — into the family nest where the afterbirth of only newborn sons was buried. Burying the afterbirth in the family nest kept sons safe within the house. "As you wanted. A son."

"Is he fat and fair?" the man croaked feebly. He was not old, but he was sickly. His wife had always done the farm work while he, shielded from the hot sun with an umbrella she had made out of banana leaves, oversaw her labors. At least, he did so when he felt well enough to walk out to the fields.

Lao Li's wife lifted the cloth from around the dimpled cheeks of the child's buttocks, careful to expose no more than this.

"Ah!" her husband crooned. "Fat and fair! Fat and fair! We shall call him Tian, for after so many bitter years, I am finally tasting the sweetness of having another son." Satisfaction curving his lips into a smile, the new father resumed sleeping while Lao Li's wife started to undo what she had done.

Now that the afterbirth was buried in its proper place — outside the house, for a daughter must leave the house to marry — she caught sight of herself in a puddle that had formed on the ground. In the wind and rain, her hair had come undone from its knot and now hung in limp, long clumps around her face; her soaking trousers and blouse clung to her torso like duckweed at the bottom of a stream. "My reflection frightens even myself," she whispered with alarm. "I look like someone drowned in a well come back to life, a victim of the fox fairy's nasty tricks."

The thought gave her an idea. Bowing quickly to the effigies of the household gods, she scurried back to her house and into the bedroom where her husband slept. Standing at the foot of the bed, waving her arms over her head and rolling the pupils of her eyes up into her forehead so that only the whites showed, she began to wail and gnash her teeth until her husband sat straight up in bed, his eyes wide with fear.

"Ai-yah!" he screamed, clutching the covers to his chest. "Are you possessed?"

The frightful moaning and shrieking soon brought the children into their parents' bedroom, and as soon as they saw their mother, they began to weep and pull at her clothes so she might stop and come to her senses. After a while, she made circles around herself, as if she were trying to find something she had lost; then, whimpering, she slunk out of the house and back to the lime shed.

By mid-morning of the following day, the whole village knew that Lao Li's wife, who had just given him a second son, had been possessed by an evil spirit.

"Do you remember Old Wong's wife?" one villager asked another. "She could no longer bear the beatings he gave her. She jumped into a well and drowned, putting a curse on the whole family. Of course, they said it was the fox fairy made her do it."

"You have it all wrong. It was the word beatings Old Wong's mother gave the poor woman that came down heavier and more frequently than the husband's stick. Anyway, Lao Li couldn't lift a straw. Then again, his mother died years ago. There's no mother-in-law for his wife to fear."

"For sure it was the hedgehog spirit," a third villager said. "He always appears at rice transplanting time."

And so the gossip spread as to what had possessed Lao Li's wife the night before. But by the child's third day of life, there was more to tell: Lao Li was not the father of a second son but of a fourth daughter. On

4

the third day, his wife had unswaddled the child in front of him and tearfully explained to the stupefied man that his son was in reality a mere girl.

"It was the fox fairy who took possession of me," she wept, "causing me to grieve and groan and putting a cloud in front of my eyes. For these last few days, he has blinded me. Only today has he blown away the cloud and shown me that I have not succeeded in giving you a son but failed by giving you yet another daughter. Forgive me, and take pity on the little slave, your daughter."

It was Lao Li's turn to weep, to gnash his teeth in disappointment and unhappiness. He fell upon the ground and pounded it with his fists. The neighbors, who had gathered in a circle around Lao Li and his wife, listened to her explanation and his ensuing cries. They could do nothing but shake their heads and mutter to themselves.

"What I named Tian will now be called Ku," Lao Li moaned. "What I called Sweet will now be known as Bitter."

Still beating the earth so that he raised heavy clouds of dust, the farmer called down curses on the fox fairy that had possessed his wife, causing her to see what wasn't there. The fox fairy was normally a trickster fairy who didn't necessarily harbor evil intentions, but this time he had played all too heartbreaking a prank.

When her husband finally lay spent and still, his wife, devoid of any emotion, said, "Our fourth daughter is a bitter disappointment, it's true, but she has health and vigor. Didn't you yourself say that she was fat and fair? Look at the plumpness of her buttocks. Look at the dimples in her thighs."

The neighbors craned their necks forward to get a better look at the newborn girl, then they nodded their heads. What Lao Li's wife said was true.

"Look at the brightness in her eyes," Lao Li's wife continued. "Look at her hair, black as night, stiff and shiny as a pig's bristles so that it stands straight up from her scalp like rice sheaves in a field." The villagers murmured in agreement, even in approval. Though she looked at her husband, it was to them that she truly addressed her words. It was their consensus, after all, which was important. But Lao Li's wife knew that she must not overplay her hand or overpraise her daughter. "Of course, these attributes belong to a mere girl. As for me, I am but a poor farmer's wife, a weak, worthless and stupid woman — no match at all for the fox fairy." The more she shook her head and wrung her hands, the more her audience nodded in agreement and clucked their tongues, feeling sympathy for her on the one hand and relief on the other that they had not been the victims of so cruel a deception.

When the crowd dispersed, for there was work to be done, Lao Li's wife set her daughter in a sling which she lashed about her neck and waist. She started to walk off towards the paddies where her son was waiting for her to guide the plow. Observing this, Lao Li rose to his feet, but he was neither convinced nor appeased. "Bear a son and money flows into a house. Bear a daughter and money flows out," he called after his wife. She walked on. "How wrong I had been to choose Sweet as her name," he cried, "when bitter is all I feel to be cheated of a son, when bitterness is all yet another daughter will bring into our lives."

At this, his wife turned around and looked at him. Her gaze was direct, her feet set apart and planted firmly on the ground. "In life, we are told we must bear the bitter and the sweet. The sweet is easy to bear. We don't question it. The bitter we say we cannot bear, and yet when it comes, we bear it." She looked down at the infant dozing placidly on her breast. "We will call her Bittersweet."

So while their son and other three daughters went by their position in the family as was customary — First Son, First Daughter and so on — Fourth Daughter was given a name which she was called by both her family and the rest of the village.

One day several weeks later, when the seedlings had all been transplanted and were beginning to bear their first pearly kernels, Lao Li's wife stopped work to get a drink. As she looked over the dipper of water she held to her lips, she noticed that her husband was no longer on the ridge between paddies where he normally stood, sheltering himself from the hot sun under his banana leaf umbrella. That in itself wasn't odd, for he never stayed for more than an hour or so at a time. What worried his wife was that he had left his umbrella behind.

She dropped the dipper back into the bucket and started for the house. The mud of the paddy oozed between her toes and sucked at her broad, flat feet. Normally, she loved this connection with the earth, the feel and grip of it, but this time the mud felt like the ground was giving way under her feet. When she finally reached the bedroom, Bittersweet was gone. Only a shallow depression remained where she

6

had been sleeping peacefully. The sight made Lao Li's wife's heart contract. She ran out to the path at the back of the house and followed it till she came to the stream that flowed from Dragon's Head, the next village over. She ran upstream along the bank, knowing that the water was too shallow here, that the riverbed was deeper farther upstream, and that she must hurry to where it was deep enough that a tossed bundle would sink to the bottom and not float away in the current.

She came upon her husband at the river's edge, just as he was tying the four corners of a blanket together to make a neat sack. When he saw her, he stood up, the sack dangling from his outstretched arms.

"You must be tired," she said as calmly as she could. "Set down that heavy load."

"That I will," he called out to her, holding the bundle farther over the water.

"Spare the child!" she begged.

"So that our other children might starve along with her?" he said. "And you and I with them?"

"Starve?" she cried. "Have you seen the size of the rice in their sheaves? Like kernels of corn. Have you forgotten the rain the night Bittersweet was born? She is an auspicious child, I tell you. Drown her, and you drown our good fortune."

"What if the rice is the size of corn kernels and the harvest is a bumper crop?" her husband countered. "Only more reason for the bandits to descend from their lairs demanding protection money, or for the imperial army to ask to be quartered in our village, and after them the warlord armies and then the Kwangsi New Army, as it calls itself, to take the last of what the others have left behind."

He lowered the sack so that water skimmed its bottom.

"You are right, old sot," his wife said, now calling him "old sot" as a term of endearment. At other times, she used it as a reprimand when she was begrudging him the bit of fiery *san hua* brandy that he loved so much — a terrible extravagance for a poor family, but one which the farmer justified by insisting it was medicinal, the only cure for the pains in his stomach. "You are right, old sot," she said again. "I bore the sorry creature. I should have done away with her then. But I tell you, we are flinging away our fortune along with her, and the knowledge will torment you for the rest of your life. But then, what do I know, ignorant woman that I am? I'm no fortuneteller. If I were and found that Bittersweet's fortune was good, as I am sure it is, then her life would be spared and fortune would flow into our house. But if I found her destiny was bad, then I would drown her myself to prevent it from flowing out, and you would have no part in it. Of course, I am no fortuneteller. . . . "

"We'll *get* a fortuneteller," her husband suddenly decided, lifting the bundle up and thrusting the squalling child at his wife.

Since Village Village was too poor to support a fortuneteller, Lao Li had to send his wife to Dragon's Head to arrange the time, date and price of the soothsayer's visit. She came back with a report on the old woman: she was a wizened old hag with skin the color and texture of dried tobacco. She required a cane for support and saw with only one eye. "But," she had said, pointing at the sightless gray ball in its socket, "this one eye is better than most people's two since it can see the future." The woman, Lao Li's wife continued to explain, wanted five cash for her services, but Lao Li's wife had been able to bargain her down to three cash and a bowl of sweetened rice.

The result was this: on the thirtieth day after Bittersweet's birth — the day when parents of a boy baby hold a completion-of-the-month party to display their new source of pride and wealth, when they pass out red eggs and receive good wishes and packets of food or money from their neighbors — the fortuneteller arrived in front of the outer gate of Lao Li's house.

When the fortuneteller had eaten her last spoonful of sweetened rice, she asked to know the eight characters — two for the year, two for the month, two for the day, and two for the hour — of Bittersweet's birth. When Lao Li's wife told her these things, the old woman consulted the astrological charts she had brought with her. She nodded her head, mumbled to herself, and further wrinkled her already wrinkled brow.

"Well? Well?" Lao Li inquired impatiently.

"Bring me the infant in question," the fortuneteller said, for she was something of a physiognomist as well. "I will read her lines of destiny."

So the mother brought the old woman her newborn daughter who, just awakened from her nap, grabbed playfully at the stranger's hands.

"Strong fingers with tapered tips," the old woman murmured. "Limbs well-rounded. Skin smooth and oily and full of color." She looked up at the parents and smiled a three-toothed grin. "Your daughter's a water-shaped person."

"That's good, isn't it?" Lao Li asked, bobbing his head happily.

8

"Hush," his wife hissed. "Let the fortuneteller continue."

"Ah, ah!" the old woman gasped with each new discovery. "A water-shaped person with some gold in her nature."

"Gold!" cried the father. "That's bound to be good!"

"She has a square-shaped head and white skin," the fortuneteller continued. "As the saying goes, 'Water was born from gold, he will be famous and wealthy; to know is to be round, to be active is to be square.' A person with a round body and a square face such as your daughter can look forward to good fortune."

Lao Li's wife shut her eyes in gratitude while her husband shuffled about in his excitement.

"What did I tell you? What did I say?" he babbled. "A child of good fortune, and now it's been proven."

"There could be a problem," the old woman said.

Lao Li stopped shuffling. His wife held her breath.

"Sometimes the gold nature is too heavy for the water shape to support. Your daughter may have a round body, fair skin, and a square face, but if she has a sharp, high-pitched voice, she will be neither wealthy nor famous. She will have few children or none at all, so when she begins to talk, take note of her speech. But if she has the correct balance of water shape with gold nature, as I think she has from the portents contained in her eight characters of birth, then she will sit calmly, act slowly and methodically as one does when one has a square nature. Wealth and fame will naturally follow."

Refusing the offer of a second bowl of sweetened rice, the fortune-teller made her way into the courtyard where Lao Li's wife pressed two more cash into her parchment-dry palm. It was a small amount to pay so that her child might live. The old woman had given the right fortune, whether it was the one ordained by destiny or not.

Still holding Lao Li's wife's hand, the fortuneteller fixed the mother with her one good eye. "Your daughter, by the eight characters of her birth and the lines of destiny of her body, has the potential of immeasurably good fortune," she said, withdrawing her hand from Lao Li's wife's fingers. "It was to my honor and credit that you called me here to tell it. But privilege brings with it responsibility, and responsibility carries in its wake privilege. They are the two sides of the same coin. Be vigilant in your daughter's upbringing. Instill in her correct behavior and dutiful obedience. And when it comes time for her to marry, marry her to someone whose eight characters of birth and lines of destiny are as auspicious as her own. Only in that way will the good fortune of her destiny become the good fortune of her life."

Lao Li's wife thanked the soothsayer over and over again as she saw her out of the courtyard and onto the road back to Dragon's Head. When the old woman was but a tiny black speck in the distance, she uncupped her palm and stared wondrously at the two cash that the old woman had replaced there.

"Thieves! Bandits! Who has dared enter my house to drink half my jug of *san hua*!"

She refolded her fingers over the coins and thought, how my old sot exaggerates. For these two cash, I sold Old Wong a mere thimbleful. Half a jug, indeed! Then she hurried into the house, pocketing the coins as she went.

Years passed, one after the other, summer following spring and winter following fall. Some were fat years when the sun and the rains came at the proper time for large harvests; some were lean years when rain wouldn't fall and the sun scorched the earth. In the dry times, the villagers spent their days digging canals. Then, they rode the "wooden dragon," a machine with wooden scales that pushed water from the sluggish stream to their fields. Men pedalled the "dragon" and its scales moved, filling the canals with water. It was impossibly hard work, and, at night, women comforted their husbands by rubbing pig's grease into the knotted muscles of their necks and shoulders, though the women themselves, and the children, too, had carried bucket after bucket of water from stream to field.

But the fat years were not so fat that the armies of the emperor — or this warlord or that, or these bandits or those — made off with what surplus there was or "borrowed" from the farmers' grain and oil jars. And the lean years were not so lean that the villagers couldn't remember a worse one and, having survived a worse one, they knew they would survive this one, too.

And as year followed year, Bittersweet grew from infancy into childhood under the benign and watchful gaze of her parents. She soon became her father's favorite as well as her mother's. Unfit for work in the fields, her father had the best opportunity to observe and appreciate his daughter's intelligence and playfulness. He noticed that as soon as she had graduated to being fed at the table, she wanted to wield chopsticks herself, to imitate her family whose faces disappeared behind upturned bowls with the click-click-click of bamboo sticks against crockery, then reappeared glistening with steam and satisfaction. When she tried and failed, and tried and failed again, ending up with rice everywhere but in her mouth, she still refused to be fed by others.

"She's stubborn," her mother said, remembering the soothsayer's admonition about dutiful obedience.

"She's persistent," Lao Li corrected his wife, then set about fashioning a short pair of chopsticks — crisscrossed and tied together at the middle with a string — that might reward his daughter's perseverance.

Chapter 2
The Miracle
(1893)

By her fourth year, Bittersweet was already too spirited for her father to look after her. Finger games and short walks with him no longer satisfied her, so she habitually led him to the rice paddies where her mother and thirteen-year-old brother plowed and planted the flooded fields. Might, she suggested, she do what they were doing? Later, she would plead for the pins, needle, and thread that her nine-year-old sister used to mend the family's cloth shoes. She would pull her father's hand, so she could follow her seven-year-old sister who gathered rushes and duckweed at the river bank. Her six-year-old sister was finally put in charge of looking after Bittersweet. By the time she was five, Bittersweet was carrying dry grass and firewood to the stove and watching the fire to make sure it didn't go out.

One morning, in the autumn of her fifth year, Bittersweet wasn't the first to appear at the breakfast table. Her mother found her still in bed, pale and feverish, with glassy eyes and a dry, cracked tongue.

"Let me change with Second Sister and share First Sister's bed tonight," Third Sister moaned to her mother. "Bittersweet was turning so much, I didn't close my eyes once last night."

Lao Li's wife tried to feed her youngest some rice gruel. She even sweetened it with some juice pressed from a piece of sugar cane, but Bittersweet merely turned her head away. She let her mother dribble some cooled, boiled water between her lips, but even then she would drink no more than a few spoonfuls. Lao Li's wife felt her daughter's forehead, then her armpits.

"If you had taken better care of her," her husband grumbled. "If you had listened to me," his voice dwindled to a hissing whisper, "and done the correct thing when she was born."

His wife knew that it was fear that made him talk this way. He was terrified that he might have unwittingly tampered with Bittersweet's proper fate. Knowing this, Lao Li's wife ignored his words.

"Are you surprised that now the gods are exacting their due?" he continued, almost in tears. "You should have killed the girl years ago, cleanly and quickly. Instead you hired a fortuneteller and, worse, you believed the quack. A child of good fortune! Ha! Just see the misfortune her reading and your stupidity have brought down upon this house."

Lao Li's wife tucked the covers tightly around the little girl, then added one from her own bed. If only she would sweat, Lao Li's wife thought, to show that the evil spirits inhabiting her body were leaving. But Bittersweet was hot and dry as tinder. Unable to do any more for her, she left her with Third Sister and called the others to work, for it was the autumn harvest, and no one and no time could be spared from the fields. Even Lao Li took up his customary place to watch his family at work.

At noon, they stopped briefly for rice noodles in soup, the midday meal which Third Sister brought out to the fields and First Sister prepared. Lao Li's wife went home and tried to make Bittersweet eat, but again the child refused. By nightfall, the child was ghostly with fiery red spots on her heated cheeks. That night, Third Sister slept in her parents' bed, and Bittersweet slept alone. Lao Li's wife lay awake, hoping to hear the child moan, or cry out, or thrash about in her sleep, but silence was all she heard until she herself drifted into a single hour's sleep before dawn pulled her from bed.

The next morning, the child still would not eat, and now she would not even drink the spoonful of water that was slipped between her lips. Her eyes were glazed over; her cheeks were ashen. Lao Li's wife went, sadly, back to the fields.

Early in the afternoon, she looked up to see her husband. "Where are you going with Old Wong's donkey?" she asked. She was crouched over some rice seedlings that she was trying to unearth so she could transplant them in a freshly flooded paddy. On the ridge above her, Lao Li was pulling at the decrepit donkey with one hand and shading himself with his banana leaf umbrella with the other.

"Get on with your work, wife," he answered. "Stop wasting your time and mine."

"Where are you taking Old Wong's donkey?" she repeated, placing one hand on the small of her back before standing with a grimace, for she had been bent in half since arriving at the field.

"Rumor has it that there is a doctor in Dragon's Head. A pediatrician."

"Dragon's Head is too far, old sot, for you and that wheezing bag of bones you're leading," she replied, though she took heart when she heard him mention a doctor. "Besides, I thought you had enough of shamans and their oracles."

"This one, I hear, uses medicine, not incantations, in his cures. Medicine that he mixes and grinds in the correct proportion of roots and bark, of snake blood and gall and dried pangolin hide. He is learned, they say, and has studied in the district capital."

"Get on with you, then," she said, squatting down again. "You keep me from my work. I trust you're taking along a flask of water to quench your thirst and a *mien bao* to ease your hunger?" she asked over her shoulder. He said nothing and she laughed as he and the mule hobbled along the dirt road, for the sight eased the anxiety she felt for her sick daughter.

At the hottest time of day, when the sun shone straight down and the karst hills offered no shade, Lao Li, red with dust and sunk low on the donkey's sway back, rode into Village Village. He was followed by a simply dressed, dignified elder, sitting on a young mule.

No sooner had the pediatrician dismounted than Lao Li's wife ran from her house into the courtyard. She welcomed the distinguished guest with the customary greeting, "*Ni chi le fan le ma*? Have you eaten yet?"

The physician answered that he had, knowing by the hour of the day and the exigencies of transplanting time that the family had already eaten and were giving him precious time that should be spent in the fields. To be courteous, he accepted a glass of water that had been boiled with some wild fruits to make an acceptable tea. With the farmer, his wife and their children trying to read his every gesture and expression, the doctor felt Bittersweet's forehead, peered into her eyes, scrutinized her tongue, and placed his index and middle fingers on her wrist. He opened a bag containing many small cloth sacks and chose six of them. He unfastened their strings, spilling the contents, one by one, onto a small brass scale. There were red wrinkled berries, black chips that looked like slivers of slate but crumbled too easily, white oblongs that looked like goose feathers but were as hard as bone. All these he crushed, mixed together, then divided into four piles, wrapping each pile in a square of paper.

"Morning and evening, twice a day, for two days," he instructed Lao Li's wife. "Boil a pot of water and simmer the contents of one of these packets till the water is reduced by half. Have your daughter drink the cooled liquid. By the morning of the third day, her fever will have broken and she will be well."

For the next two days, Lao Li's wife did exactly what the pediatrician from Dragon's Head said. She boiled the herbs in water and fed Bittersweet the cooled bitter brew. But by the morning of the third day, the fever had not broken. If anything, Bittersweet seemed worse.

Lao Li's wife tucked a large cloth around a pile of fragrant hay stored in the lime shed. She lay Bittersweet on the makeshift bed and smoothed out her child's clothes and her blanket. Then she sprinkled a circle of lime around the shed. Her other children stood outside the circle, silently watching their mother.

That night, as if to match the mood of Lao Li's house, a dry wind came up, blowing puffs of reddish earth in dancing spirals; evil spirits whistled around the corners of the house, setting ill-fitting doors whining and clacking.

"What was that?" Lao Li's wife whispered, sitting up in bed.

"The fox fairy," Lao Li murmured, affecting sleepiness, though he, too, was awake and thinking of his daughter, "trying to lure you outside again. Go back to sleep, woman, and let me go back to mine. It's only the wind."

"The wind doesn't make a sound like that," she replied, listening more closely. "Or the fox fairy, either."

"You should know. You've been bewitched often enough."

"Sh-h-h! Listen! It's more like a moan," Lao Li's wife insisted, throwing off the blanket. "Animal-like."

"Then, it's Widow Zhou and her heifer. The cow's about to give birth any moment now. The Widow's singing to her to help her through the night."

Lao Li's wife slipped into her cloth shoes and buttoned her frayed blue tunic at her collarbone and ribs. When she opened the door and let a dust-laden gust of wind inside, her husband pulled the covers around him more tightly. The latch didn't catch when she went out, so he threw the covers aside with a grumble and closed the door securely after her; he'd take no chances, just in case the fox fairy and other mischievous spirits *did* exist. He peered out into the night through a tear in the oiled paper window.

Holding the oil lamp at arm's length in front of her, Lao Li's wife tried to pick out the animal sound she had heard in the whistling wind.

She followed it to the lime circle she had drawn that morning. The sound was louder now, a wail more than a moan, and coming from the lime shed. What loathsome creature was making so horrible a noise? What spirit from the other world was in there with her daughter? And what was he doing to her to try to make her leave this one?

Slowly the woman advanced, placed her free hand on the doorknob, and swung the door open. She shaded her eyes, more against the image she feared than from the glare of the lamplight.

"Ma-a-a-a. . . . "

The woman passed the oil lamp from her right to her left hand and held it higher to see if the change in lighting would change what she saw; Bittersweet was sitting up on her straw bed, her clothes askew, her hair plastered with perspiration to her forehead and cheeks.

"Ma, I'm hungry. I want some rice."

The mother fell to her knees, touching and feeling her daughter to make sure she was real. Then, shrieking with joy, she gathered the child into her arms and ran back to the house.

"Husband! Old sot! Wake up! A miracle! Bittersweet is alive! Our little girl is alive and well!"

By midmorning of the following day, the entire village knew that a miracle had taken place at the house of Lao Li; his youngest daughter who should have died, lived.

"It was the good medicine of the pediatrician from Dragon's Head," Lao Li's wife explained, receiving the good wishes and congratulations of her neighbors.

"Nothing less than a miracle," the Widow Zhou remarked, who had her own good news to tell that morning; her heifer had given birth to a healthy calf.

"No, no," Lao Li's wife was quick to say, eager not to draw the attention of the gods, whose jealousy might then undo the work of the good doctor, or draw undue attention and thus jealousy from her neighbors. "She's merely a girl, after all."

"Didn't the one-eyed crone from Dragon's Head who reads hands and faces read your daughter's at her birth?" the Widow continued. "And didn't she tell you that Bittersweet possessed good fortune? Extraordinarily good fortune?"

"What could be better fortune than having your life spared not once, but twice?" Widow Zhou's hired hand added.

"Yes, what further proof do you need that your littlest one is blessed with a good destiny?"

But since Lao Li's wife continued to praise the good doctor and his cure as responsible for the "miracle," her neighbors changed their tactics, wagging their heads to ward off an anticipated rebuttal while approving of her modesty, saying, "You must have lived a very kind and tolerant former life. That is the reason for your daughter's recovery." So the villagers went from endowing Bittersweet with a special destiny that could triumph over death to endowing her mother with a particularly blessed past life. And no matter how persistent the girl's mother was in refuting both claims, consensus in Village Village was that nothing less than a miracle, due to the child's own present good fortune and her mother's past lives, had saved Bittersweet's life.

When four years after Bittersweet's miraculous recovery, Lao Li's wife, who was sure her childbearing years were behind her, gave birth to a son, Bittersweet was acknowledged to be the cause of yet another miracle. During Younger Son's completion-of-the-month party, the villagers dropped by to congratulate Lao Li on his good fortune.

"So late in your wife's life to bear another child," they exclaimed. "And a son at that. A stroke of unusually good luck."

So saying, they cast their eyes about for a glimpse of the source of that good luck, as if by setting their sights on her, they, too, could be charmed. Mothers brought their young daughters to Lao Li's house expressly to touch the hem of Bittersweet's homespun trousers or the cuff of her padded cotton jacket, so the little girls in their arms might have better luck than their mothers and, when they married, conceive a son. After all, it was never too early to wish or plan for a desirable outcome.

Lao Li's wife dared not admit that her fourth daughter was a child of good fortune, even something of a talisman, for she knew modesty was a virtue and envy was easily kindled in a small village where everyone knew everyone else and everyone else's business. She also knew that life was unceasing flux, that too sweet a fate would only turn back on itself and eventually turn sour. So she reminded herself at the height of her happiness as she played with her new son, "It is better to have too little than to have too much. Although one might not get very far that way, one is traveling in the right direction. The man who wants to go farther and farther east eventually ends up west."

But in her own heart, she attributed not only her family's personal good fortune, now that they had a second son to work in the fields and to carry on the family name, but also the village's good fortune, to Bittersweet and the lucky star under which she had been born. The year Younger Son was conceived, the rains came at their proper time, and the year after that, the armies bypassed Village Village as too poor, the pickings too slim, to bother with. Thus there was extra rice and tung oil in the storage jars and a string of cash or two in the secret places of every house. No one went hungry, and the elders talked about living out their remaining years in peace.

Lao Li's wife didn't want to waste the good fortune that Bittersweet possessed. She knew that although one is born with good fortune or bad, good fortune can be frittered away and bad fortune can be minimized through good works. She and her husband had to maximize Bittersweet's good fortune by raising her well, by being watchful to see where her talents lay, and by then developing them. Otherwise her good fortune might disperse like chaff winnowed from the grain by the wind. She also knew that the Widow Zhou was thinking of selling her old heifer, now that her calf was a strapping three-year-old ox. She knew, too, that her husband would consider any amount too great to pay for the creature.

One evening after dinner, Lao Li's wife was nursing her infant son and watching Bittersweet who, in turn, was watching her sisters mend the family clothes. Bittersweet was mimicking their movements with an unthreaded needle on a bit of cloth she had wrapped around her corncob doll. Her mother noticed how long and nimble her fourth daughter's fingers were, that they were more graceful and supple than her sisters'.

"What would you think," she began, as she always did when she had mulled over a question, had come to a conclusion, and wished to convince her husband of its good sense, "about taking Bittersweet out of the fields, so she can spend her time taking care of the housework, like the darning of our clothes and the mending of our shoes? She's industrious and she learns quickly."

Her husband puffed on his long-stemmed pipe for a few breaths, then said, "Who would set the rice seedlings in straight rows? Or bring water to the rest of you from the stream? Or gather greens for the pigs? Do you expect Third Daughter to do all this alone?"

He pretended not to notice how deftly Bittersweet's fingers moved the needle. Not once did she cry out "Ai-yah!" for having pricked her finger as Third Daughter often did.

"Second Daughter can help her," his wife answered, "as she has done in the past."

"She is needed to transplant the rice seedlings, to gather and distribute the night soil, and to harvest the rice when the grain is full in the sheaves."

"First Daughter is close to marriageable age," his wife reminded him. "She should be doing more of the housework, cooking, and sewing her dowry. At the same time, she could teach Bittersweet sewing and embroidery. She shouldn't be putting in so much time in the fields."

"If not she, then who?" her husband asked. "Or do you plan to do what she does in addition to taking your place behind the plow?"

"Elder Son will do what First Daughter has done till now, and when Younger Son is older, he will do the same."

"Pray tell, who will pull the plow that you guide if not Elder Son?" Lao Li asked, realizing before he had finished his question that his wife had set a trap.

"Not who, but what," his wife answered. "Rumor has it that the Widow Zhou wants to sell her heifer."

Lao Li spat then stuck his pipe back into his mouth, biting down hard on it in his anger at having been tricked. "For more money than it's worth. She wants five strings of cash for that hide-bound bag of bones!"

His wife clucked her tongue and replied, "That was at the time of the Lantern Festival. Here we are close to the Pure Brightness celebration. Her heifer is that much older and therefore worth that much less. She will take four strings."

One week after Pure Brightness, Lao Li and his wife were the owners of the Widow Zhou's heifer for the sum of four strings of cash. To finalize the transaction and to dispel any resentment which might have arisen for having obtained the beast for a lower price, Lao Li's wife gave the Widow her old grinding stone. It was a small sacrifice since Lao Li's wife had recently replaced her stone with a newer and larger one. Its predecessor was still usable but rather small, and there was a crack in the stone. Still, Lao Li's wife reasoned, what was offered for free need not be examined too closely, as long as it served its intended purpose. Besides, the Widow's own stone was in much worse shape.

19

The acquisition of the heifer brought about a shift in the daily duties and responsibilities in the Li household. Elder Son was no longer yoked to the plow but worked side by side with Second and Third Daughters in the planting, transplanting, fertilizing, and watering of the rice paddies. First Daughter's place was now in the home where she acquired the skills necessary to be a worthy daughter-in-law and good wife while she passed these skills on to her littlest sister.

Now that Bittersweet no longer worked outdoors, her complexion grew lighter and finer. Her hands, previously calloused and thickened by hard labor, grew smooth and soft. She stood straight and tall since she no longer had to squat in the fields but sewed in a straight-back chair. Now that she was only indirectly involved in the life of a farmer, she didn't simply measure the flow of time by the cycle of the seasons. She had a second standard by which to mark time's passing. She had the celebrations.

In particular, Bittersweet looked forward to the New Year, for that meant the spinning of new cloth for the sewing of new clothes and the embroidery of different patterns on them — perhaps one of the eight precious things, or eight Buddhist symbols, or twelve symbols of authority. She joined the other villagers in singing the same songs that had always been sung in Village Village and that every generation knew. Year after year, she laughed at and followed the New Year's dragon — whose great head of a lion and scales of a fish she had helped cut from cloth and sew together — as it writhed and danced down the streets and alleyways. The boys in the village lit strings of firecrackers, competing with each other to see whose were longest or loudest. The bolder among them threw the firecrackers high into the air above the girls who had gathered to watch the festivities. When the girls scattered, Bittersweet was among them, laughing and holding her hands over her ears, her glossy braids, tied with red ribbons specifically for the occasion, flying as she ran. The boys laughed and then singled out some of the girls for particular reasons. One year, Bittersweet blushed just to hear them mention her name. Before she had needed the loud sound of the exploding firecrackers to make her flush. It seemed, to her, an important realization.

And she came to this realization at a time when she was old enough to help her mother and Second Sister prepare the family meals: the rice and the sweet or white potatoes and the one dish of green vegetable that was served three times a day. Once a year, on New Year's Day, after a good harvest, they would kill a pig or chicken and add bits of meat to the vegetable dish. Because the villagers believed that vegetables were cold-producing foods, every house had a mortar and pestle for grinding hot chilies into a paste. It fell to Bittersweet to crush the chilies to make the *la jiao* that balanced the cold-producing vegetables with red heat.

Sometimes when the farm work was light — after a harvest, or just before — the men went to the stream to catch frogs and fish. When they returned, Lao Li's wife would tear off the frogs' legs, slice up the bodies, then sauté the succulent flesh with garlic. Meanwhile Bittersweet would salt the fish and pack it away for when farm work was heavier and the men needed more nourishment. When that time came, she would fry up some soybeans with dried fish and bring out a jug of rice wine for her father. Only when the men folk had finished eating did the women and girls sit down to finish what they left behind — usually rice or potatoes and a few pieces of vegetable.

After burping and inserting a wooden toothpick between his oily lips, Lao Li would often rise from the table and announce, "A farmer's life is hard and bitter."

Though a farmer's life wasn't easy, Bittersweet was unaware of any hardship. She remembered and looked forward to the joyful times, the festivals at the end of the year when the villagers hired professional musicians who played their instruments and sang their songs for three days on end. For those three days and three nights, the villagers looked on, the men smoking their pipes of homegrown tobacco, the women chewing on sugar cane or sewing. The more Bittersweet enjoyed the festivals and celebrations, the more she understood that such happiness would soon end. One day, she would no longer be a child but a woman. She would marry. She would move away from her parents whom she loved and who loved her. She would move out of the home that she had always known. She would live in the home of her husband's parents. As she respected Elder Brother, she would respect her older brother-in-law. As she cooperated with Younger Brother, she would cooperate with her younger brother-in-law. As she obeyed her parents, she would obey her parents-in-law. But a member of her new family, this she could not be. She would remain an honorary member until the day she died; then her name would be inscribed on the ancestor tablets; then she would be a full member of her husband's family. As for remaining a member of her own family, this she could no longer be, for she would have married out of it.

Neither in nor out, Bittersweet thought, neither here nor there. She considered the place without position, the ground without footing, that a married woman occupied, but she resolved not to fret about it. She had seen a strange symbol on the door of the tiny Taoist temple in the village: a circle, half black, half white, and each half a fluid, curving, almost moving, shape. She imagined that to be a wife was to be neither in the black half, nor in the white half, but moving with the line that separated and yet connected the two. Imagining this, she was able to calm herself.

The year that Bittersweet was more a woman than she was a child, Elder Brother took a wife, a thin, tall girl from the next village. She had a loose-jointed walk and a high-pitched nasal voice. The following year, First Sister found a husband, a farmer who owned both a donkey and a water buffalo, but who was tightlipped and just as tightfisted. Fast upon First Sister, Second Sister married a duck farmer who was a widower, and though he had a three-room cottage, he also had two children for whom he needed a mother, so he could attend to his ducks. Third Sister was already betrothed, her wedding just a few weeks away. As the only daughter left in her parents' house, Bittersweet played with Younger Brother, when she wasn't doing the housework. And there was, of course, her sister-in-law to talk to.

But the two girls had very different characters. Bittersweet was a farm girl — direct and straightforward, sometimes even outspoken, which made her mother concerned. Bittersweet's sister-in-law, Sao-sao, who came from a prosperous farming village, looked down on Village Village and its simple residents. She complained that in her family, they had two young oxen, whereas Bittersweet's family had only one old heifer; in her family, they ate meat at all the major festivals, whereas Bittersweet's family ate meat only at New Year's. Sao-sao also affected town ways, or what she thought them to be: a nasal whining voice, a barbed and poisonous tongue, and the rickety walk of a fragile lady of leisure, though she was but a farmer's wife with all the associated duties and responsibilities. Clearly, Sao-sao wasn't the person with whom Bittersweet could share her thoughts and desires as she grew from girlhood into womanhood.

Since childhood, Bittersweet knew, as a child knows about the most important things in life without being told in words, that it was for a son to take a wife and bring her back to his parents' house, carry on the family name through many sons, work the land, and provide for his parents in their old age. She knew that it was for a daughter to find a husband and move into his parents' home, bear him many sons, and take care of his parents when they were old. So it had always been. So it would always be. The path of life before her was clear, and yet it was not. Why, she wondered, must she leave home? Why must she marry? Why must she serve and obey total strangers? But she expressed none of this. She even tried not to think of it.

Still, as soon as Third Sister married and moved away to a neighboring village, the matchmaker of Village Village began inquiring about Bittersweet's age. Knowing of the good fortune predicted at the girl's birth and the miracle of her recovery from sickness and near-death, and thus of the prospect of making a good match (and the long strings of cash that would come from such a match), she clucked her tongue against the roof of her mouth and approached Lao Li's wife.

"*Shemma*! Sixteen already? Why, she should have been married a year ago at least. There's no time to waste. No telling when sweet fortune can turn sour, particularly if a girl waits too long to marry. Now I've heard that there is a tailor's son two villages to the north. . . ."

But Lao Li's wife only smiled tolerantly and said, "We're in no hurry to see Bittersweet wed. Besides, the only acceptable husband would be a man whose fortune is as well-favored as her own. If her destiny was made in heaven, so must her marriage be."

The matchmaker was persistent, but to the names, descriptions, and future prospects of the eligible bachelors she whispered in Lao Li's wife's ear, she received the same apologetic smile. When Bittersweet turned seventeen, the matchmaker increased her visits and brought with her a longer list of young men.

"Ai-yah!" she exclaimed, finally throwing up her hands. "With your other daughters you were less picky, and they succeeded in finding husbands by the age of sixteen. Soon Bittersweet will be eighteen. Then all you'll find is a dwindling selection of young men to be so picky about."

"What are you doing?" Sao-sao asked Bittersweet one morning after breakfast. Sao-sao was on her way out of the house to feed the chickens. Still, the question was odd as she could easily see that her sister-in-law was weaving cotton cloth on the loom. Not far from where Bittersweet was working in the shade cast by the overhanging roof, Lao Li sat on a stool, smoking his pipe, "supervising" his daughter's handiwork.

"I'm weaving another bundle of cloth for my dowry," Bittersweet answered, moving the shuttle quickly and deftly.

"By the time you marry, you'll have enough bundles of cotton to clothe every inhabitant of Village Village," Sao-sao tittered.

"I'm in no hurry," Bittersweet answered without interrupting her work. "Until a young man's fortune matches my own, I'm content to live in my own home, among my own people."

Sao-sao glared at Bittersweet, then narrowed her eyes. The irony in the remark had not eluded her. Sao-sao had not found a place in her parents-in-law's hearts. She considered the work they required of her as beneath her, even demeaning. She constantly complained to their elder son, making him fretful and anxious. Instead of winning over her family through consideration and cooperation, she had alienated every member of the household — and none more so than Bittersweet — with her laziness and her petty dissatisfactions. The family was civil to her, if somewhat distant, tolerating her for Elder Brother's sake and the sake of family harmony. They pretended not to hear when Sao-sao, feeling especially peevish, would whine, "Such a family of peasants that I have married into. How I wish I were back in my own home, among my own people."

One day, however, Bittersweet could no longer hold her tongue and had answered back, "How I wish you were, too!" Since then, the two barely spoke to each other and avoided each other when they could.

"My, my! So much cloth!" Sao-sao sang now, clearly recalling Bittersweet's earlier remark. "My mother-in-law certainly strains the family budget to provide you with such a fine dowry, finer than any of your sisters had, finer even than the one I brought with me into this family."

The shuttle stopped abruptly at its highest point on the loom. Bittersweet let it fall with a loud clack. "The harvests of the past four years have been very good. In the past six years, all my sisters, and my elder brother as well, have married. There are less people in the family to care for, and more money to care for them with. If I am fortunate to have a fine dowry, it is at the expense of no one else."

Sao-sao smirked and said nothing but swung her head toward the chicken coop with such vehemence that her long braid snapped the air

24

like a whip. Lao Li sucked on his pipe and nodded thoughtfully. "If only your elder brother had your temperament and stood up for himself against his wife's words," he murmured. "But you are a woman, Bittersweet. You must be more moderate in your remarks. For peace in the family, you must watch your tongue."

"Baba, if I lost my temper with Sao-sao, it's not my fault alone," Bittersweet replied. "She provokes me with her jealousy. Do you want me to remain silent?"

"Sometimes silence produces better results. Sao-sao is not only jealous, she's egotistical. Something tells me that your words may be the last but that her actions may be more lasting."

Bittersweet laughed at her father's remark, then waved it away. Lao Li commented no further but clamped his pipe stem more firmly between his few remaining teeth.

It was market day. Elder Brother and Sao-sao were tying up the bags of unhulled rice to sell in Liangjiang, the central village in the district where goods and produce were bought and sold three times a week. They balanced their bamboo poles — the ends weighted with sacks of unpolished rice — over their shoulders. Just then, Bittersweet ran out of the house to where her mother was seeing the couple off.

"Ma, may I have a few cash to give Elder Brother so he can pick me up more cotton thread? I need just another spool to finish the bundle of cloth I'm weaving."

Sao-sao's normally tight mouth spread into a sly smile.

"You'll have to ask Sao-sao for the cash," her mother answered. "She's in charge of the family budget now. She's better with the abacus than I am." Seeing her daughter's face sadden at the news, she went on to explain, "She's better at balancing our expenses and our receipts."

"I will not ask Sao-sao for the money," Bittersweet said.

Her mother looked alternately at her daughter and her daughter-in-law. The spines of both women were rigid with pride. Leading Bittersweet out of hearing distance of Sao-sao, she addressed her daughter, "Do you think that she will refuse you, her own husband's flesh and blood?"

"I would prefer her outright refusal than the pleas she would exact from me before she gave me the few cash," Bittersweet answered.

"I wish you and your sister-in-law got on better," her mother sighed.

"Sao-sao is not a bad person, perhaps a bit inflexible, but not bad. It was her idea, in fact, to take over the family accounts to spare me the burden."

Remembering the altercation at the loom, Bittersweet started to say something, but she stopped herself. So her father had been right, she thought, glowering at the ground so she wouldn't have to see her sister-in-law's triumphant smirk. She'd had the last word, but Sao-sao was seeing that she paid for it.

"I'm no longer a young woman," her mother continued, "or haven't I changed over the years?" She searched her daughter's face.

Bittersweet looked at her mother. For the first time, she saw her, not as the woman who bore and raised her, but as she really was: a woman with deep wrinkles, as much from worry as the sun, lining her face; with hair that was more white than black, more thin than full, fastened into a nub of a bun. She was a woman hunchbacked from carrying six children in her arms; from lugging sacks of rice; from the weight of the plow strapped to her back before the days when it could be strapped to Elder Brother or the heifer; from the stoop work in the rice paddies.

"You will marry and go to live with your husband and his family," her mother told her, "just as Sao-sao left her family to live with Elder Brother and us. It is fitting that Sao-sao should take on more and more of the household responsibilities, so I may have less and less of them in my old age. Should I have told her when she asked that I would not hand over the family accounts to her?"

Bittersweet dropped her eyes and shook her head slowly. She heard a voice behind her ask, "Did I hear you say marriage and a husband?"

The matchmaker, who had become Lao Li's wife's shadow of late, hurried up to the mother and daughter, looking into their faces for some sign that they would soon be more receptive to her nagging questions. "Have you finally come around to the right way of thinking? I have just come back from Dragon's Head. There is a family by the name of Li. . . . "

"It is bad luck for a man and woman with the same surname to marry," Lao Li's wife said immediately.

"Perhaps the character for their surname denotes distance or perhaps it means rites and rituals," the matchmaker said quickly. "There are several ways to write Li. Why do you assume that theirs is the same Li as yours, signifying plum?"

Lao Li's wife said nothing. She would not admit that she knew nothing of reading or writing, even though almost everyone else, and certainly all the women, of Village Village, were in the same predicament. The matchmaker herself was illiterate but for a few characters necessary for her trade.

"Speaking of characters, the eight characters of the young man in question match your daughter's perfectly."

"And who is this young man?" Lao Li's wife allowed.

"The second son. . . ."

"Ah, not the first," Lao Li's wife said, quickly dismissing this possibility, "who receives most if not all of the family's patrimony."

"These are enlightened people," the matchmaker protested. "No one is favored. Everything is shared equally among the three sons. The land cannot be divided. That way the family wealth stays intact."

"Is that so?" replied Lao Li's wife, trying not to show that she was impressed by the information. "Three sons, are there? More importantly, how many unmarried daughters are there, and how many daughters-in-law?"

"Four daughters. One daughter-in-law. Only the first son is married."

"Ai-yah!" Bittersweet's mother exclaimed, shaking her head in dismay. "Six women at home, including the mother! Six women and four men to serve! And you call that a favorable match? Sounds more like slavery to me."

"The daughters will marry and move away," the matchmaker reminded her.

"And the remaining son will take a wife to replace the daughters who move out," Lao Li's wife retorted.

"The father is an educated man," the matchmaker smiled encouragingly, changing the subject. "A teacher."

"Bah! A teacher," Lao Li's wife replied, impressed nonetheless. "It isn't the father but the father's son you are insisting my Bittersweet marry. What does he do?"

"Ah . . . that," the matchmaker hedged, pulling at the few long wiry hairs that grew from a mole at the side of her chin. "From what I understand, he's a military man."

"Bad iron?" Lao Li's wife shrieked. "You would have my daughter marry a common soldier? Away with you, matchmaker, till you learn your profession properly!"

Lao Li's wife grabbed Bittersweet by the arm and started leading her toward the house, where Elder Brother and Sao-sao were finally starting on the road to Liangjiang market. If they delayed much longer, the sun's rays would strike as hard as blows upon their backs.

"Good Li *Tai-tai*," the matchmaker pleaded, running after the woman, "you didn't let me finish. Not a soldier. A cadet at the new military academy in Kweilin. When he graduates, he will be an officer, with a commission. Do you think I would suggest a mere soldier for your lucky star?" She stopped, winded, and clasped her hands, holding them out, imploringly.

"An officer! A soldier! It's all the same in the end," Lao Li's wife said, quickening her pace as she led Bittersweet toward the house. "Bad iron! A life of troop movements and army camps, of danger and, in times like these, almost certain death. No, no, my daughter will not marry this soldier candidate of yours only to end up a widow soon after the marriage."

"But Li *Tai-tai*," the matchmaker cried after them. "His eight characters of birth, they do not lie. They complement your daughter's like meat dumplings and New Year's Day. . . ." Her voice trailed off, now that the mother and daughter had entered the house, closing the door behind them. "Humph," the matchmaker said to herself, "good fortune or no, if she keeps on refusing eligible bachelors for her daughter, she'll have an old maid on her hands."

With that thought to sustain her, the matchmaker decided to see a family down at the other end of the *hutong* where an easier match was sure to be made.

Chapter 3
The Wedding
(1908)

Summer passed, slipping into fall, which even more quickly became winter. Winter passed, too, and at the end of it, another year's harvests were celebrated with feasting, firecrackers, the paying of one's debts, and the sewing of new clothes for New Year's Day. The rice harvests had been abundant, and none of the armies, marching to Kwangtung Province, had "borrowed" provisions as they came through Village Village. All the villagers had little to complain about and should have been content. Lao Li and his wife, however, were not; there were still no signs of life stirring in Sao-sao, no promise of the all-important son.

Lao Li's wife, who longed as much as her husband to have a grandson, could no longer keep herself quiet. Finally, she found an opportunity to bring the matter up with her elder son. "Your wife is an able cook," she told him after lunch one day.

Elder Brother smiled at the compliment. His mother was usually circumspect with his wife, and his wife, in turn, was often quite peevish with his mother. They rarely had good things to say about each other.

"It's a pity she doesn't eat more of her own good cooking. She is too thin, and her hips are so narrow, not deep and wide like the prow of a boat, where it would be easy to conceive and carry a child."

Her son's smile faded. "It's not so much a question of ability," he said, "but willingness. She says she doesn't want to bear a son in a crowded house."

His mother looked perplexed. "Crowded? Your three eldest sisters have married and moved out, and even when they still lived at home, the house was adequate." Lao Li's wife narrowed her eyes. "Her own family has five sons, five wives, and three daughters all living in a house no bigger than ours. Yet she calls *our* house crowded!"

Elder Brother turned away slightly to avoid his mother's gaze. "She says we must wait . . ." He looked towards the corner where Bitter- sweet was stacking the rice bowls she had just washed, raising his voice

29

just enough that she might overhear. ". . . until Bittersweet marries. As soon as she finds a husband, then we can have sons."

A loud crash startled both Lao Li's wife and her son.

"What was that?" Lao Li's wife asked. "Bittersweet?"

"A rice bowl," the girl replied, stooping down to collect the fragments. "It slipped out of my hand . . . like Elder Brother's words slipped out of his mouth."

"Be careful that you don't cut yourself," her mother cautioned.

"It's only pottery," Bittersweet answered, coming closer to her brother and mother. "The pieces aren't as sharp as certain remarks."

Elder Brother stiffened, but he couldn't keep his eyes on his little sister's. He looked at his mother apologetically. She, in turn, looked at him with tenderness and pity. "The corn needs grinding," he muttered finally. On his way to yoke the heifer to the grindstone, he passed his wife in animated conversation with the matchmaker.

"Tsk, tsk, tsk. Of course, you're concerned for your sister-in-law. No woman wants to die an old maid. Nineteen years old and still not married. Not even betrothed! Your mother-in-law is all patience, but what must she truly feel? Tell Bittersweet not to despair."

Lao Li's wife, who had followed her son to the door, stood on the threshold, her arms folded across her chest. The matchmaker nodded her head, acknowledging her presence. Lao Li's wife nodded back.

"Well, I must be off. Tell her also that I am available for consultation. Tell her that I don't hold any grudges. Tolerance and forbearance are among my greatest virtues. Remind her of the saying that she seems to have forgotten: 'A young man should have a wife; a young woman should find a husband.'"

"All in good time," Lao Li's wife told Sao-sao when the young woman came up to her to repeat what the matchmaker had said.

"But time is running out," her daughter-in-law insisted. "Bittersweet is nineteen years old. Do you want her to die an old maid . . . and me a childless old woman?"

"Sao-sao!"

She turned at the sound of her name, a name which meant sister-in-law and thereby indicated her lowly position in the family hierarchy. Bittersweet stood in the doorway, her hands on her hips.

"You don't have to be concerned for me. I have no intention of becoming an old maid."

"Becoming? My dear young . . . ," Sao-sao emphasized the word *young*, ". . . sister-in-law, you already *are* an old maid, like it or not."

Hearing that, Bittersweet marched up to Sao-sao and poked her in the side of her head with her fingers so that the woman almost lost her balance. Sao-sao screamed, then began weeping into her hands as if she were being tortured.

Craning her double-chinned neck in all directions so that the loose skin flapped like wet laundry on a clothesline, the matchmaker heard her cries and came scurrying back. "What's going on here? Who's making such a racket?"

Bittersweet ignored the matchmaker and instead turned to Sao-sao and said, "Roll, rotten egg! Roll out of this courtyard!"

Sao-sao fled around the back of the house, screaming for her husband to save her.

"Yes, call Elder Brother to protect you," Bittersweet muttered under her breath, looking after Sao-sao as she fled. "How I feel sorry for him — that he must depend on heirs from a broomstick like you!"

"Ai, ai!" the matchmaker said, putting her arthritic hands up to her head in dismay. "Such words! They're stinging my ears! Perhaps it was to the pediatrician's detriment that he saved your life. Ah, well, at least he can rest at peace in his grave to know that you've spurned his grandson's marriage proposal."

Bittersweet stared at the old woman. "Are you saying that the old herbalist who cured me as a child is the grandfather of the second son of the Li family of Dragon's Head?"

"That he was but is no longer," she replied, casting her eyes on the ground. "He died over two years ago. Some say it was of a broken heart to know that his grandson, your suitor, was choosing the military rather than the academic life." The matchmaker let her hands drop from her ears and shook her head. "I should not like to get into an argument with you, Bittersweet, or be the object of your anger."

"Are your ears still ringing from my harsh words, matchmaker?" Bittersweet asked, breaking into an apologetic smile. "Then here's something to soothe them. Go to Dragon's Head and tell the Li family that I will marry their second son."

"Bittersweet!" her mother cried.

"If he is as you say," the girl continued, still addressing the matchmaker, "a man who possesses fortune as good as mine and whose destiny is complementary to mine, then who am I to quibble with fate?"

"But . . . but," the matchmaker stuttered, looking alternately at the girl and her mother. "It is unseemly, Bittersweet," she hissed, part scolding, part whisper. "Only your parents can choose for you. And your parents have said that a young man who is a soldier. . . ."

"It is my destiny to marry the young man from Dragon's Head. Didn't you say so yourself?" She turned to her mother. "Let destiny run its course, then. Who am I to try to stop it?"

"And who am I to question it?" her mother said, trying to sound lighthearted to hide her concern. "But isn't it also bad luck to marry a man with the same surname as yours?"

Bittersweet thought for a moment, then told the matchmaker, "Tell the young man's family in Dragon's Head that the Lu girl from Village Village accepts his proposal of marriage."

The matchmaker gasped, but seeing the determination on Bittersweet's face and the apparent resignation on her mother's, she assured them both that she would, that very afternoon, carry those exact words to the Li compound in Dragon's Head.

Later that afternoon, Bittersweet, on her way back from the house of Old Wong, where she had gone to return a sickle, came across a young boy leading a water buffalo to the rice paddies. Five children trailed after him. When he saw Bittersweet, he hooted and sang, "The old maid of Village Village changed her name from Li to Lu, and engaged herself to the bad iron of Dragon's Head! The old maid of Village Village changed her name from Li to Lu, and engaged herself to the bad iron of Dragon's Head!"

The youngsters with him began to chant, too, giggling and laughing and running around the water buffalo. When Bittersweet made a motion to rush at them, they screeched and howled with the pleasure that comes to frightened children who fear no real harm. Then, Bittersweet slapped the rump of the buffalo to hurry it, and her tormentors, along.

Even later that day, Bittersweet, on her way to the stream to do the family wash, passed the Widow Zhou. "You should be ashamed of yourself," the old woman called. "Arranging your own marriage! And without your parents' consent. Have you no shame, no sense of face?"

"I agreed to the matchmaker's proposal today at noon," Bittersweet answered. "By the sun in the sky, it's not even four o'clock, yet news of my impending marriage has already returned to its source."

"Proper conduct and dutiful piety are the traits of a virtuous daughter," the Widow Zhou reminded her, placing a crooked finger in front of the girl's nose. "Who ever heard of a young woman choosing her own husband? And a young man that her parents have refused at that?"

But Bittersweet stepped away from the wagging finger and the wheezing accusation. "Widow Zhou, I am merely following my destiny. The carpenter's gouge does not go against the grain of the wood. The cormorant fisherman does not direct his bamboo raft against the current of the stream. Who am I to go against my fate?"

The Widow Zhou, finding nothing to oppose in Bittersweet's rebuttal, went on her way, muttering to herself about unfilial sons and undutiful daughters.

During the year of preparation before the wedding ceremony, the attitude of not only the Widow but also most of Lao Li's neighbors softened. Who were they to denounce Bittersweet's decision, especially when her parents had come to accept it?

Her parents said "It is her destiny" so often that the villagers came to believe this. The impropriety and disobedience that they had once accused Bittersweet of was forgotten. In fact, they began to praise Bittersweet for submitting to her fate so graciously.

Bittersweet sat on the side of her bed, looking out through the small unpapered window of the room that she and Younger Brother had shared ever since Third Sister's wedding day. Elder Brother and Sao-sao now occupied the room that First and Second Sisters had shared when they lived at home.

Bittersweet looked towards the fields where Younger Brother was working alongside Elder Brother. Though she used to play with Younger Brother, teach him finger games and word puzzles, cut his hair, and show him pretty stitches in cloth, she no longer did any of these things with him. They no longer interested her. She found she didn't laugh as much, or joke as much, or even get angry with her little brother as much as she used to. Lately, she preferred to be by herself, and when she was with the other members of the family, she said hardly a word.

Looking out the window, she realized she was actually looking in, going over memories of her past, imagining what her future would bring. Tomorrow was her wedding day, and today, her female relations were throwing her a songs-blessing-the-bride party. For weeks she had looked forward to this party — the one time in a woman's life when she could, in song, say exactly what she felt, exactly what was on her mind, and not lose face or be accused of impropriety.

"Your complaints at this party," her mother had explained, "can be likened to straw dogs in ancient times. They are considered sacred right up to the ceremony. But right after it, they are garbage for the pigs. So will your words be, if you choose to voice them."

Though freedom was common enough in a child's life, the songs-blessing-the-bride party was the one time in a *woman's* life that she would be free — free from responsibility for her actions and thus free from blame. Thereafter, duty and responsibility would fill all her time, and obligation would replace freedom. Now that the songs-blessing-the-bride party was upon her, Bittersweet felt overwhelmed by the singular moment of liberty that awaited her. Her one last chance at freedom, and yet she was afraid to take it! It was that temper of hers! Her unruly character. It had been fine when she had been younger. A year ago it had had its place, indeed it had always made her father chuckle and shake his head — less in disapproval than admiration. Now having a temper was unworthy, undignified, immature. Clearly, a vice. Everything in her life, since the announcement of her betrothal, was awry. She didn't know what to think anymore. She hardly even knew who she was these days. When she looked into a tranquil pool or burnished the piece of bronze she used as a mirror, she didn't recognize herself. It was true, what Younger Brother said: "You're not the same. You're different. You even *look* different."

Early that morning, her maternal aunts had come to the house to painstakingly, and for Bittersweet, painfully, widen her brow to show that she would soon be a married woman, no longer a *xiaojie* but a *tai-tai*, by plucking the hairs along her brow so that her hairline receded practically back to her crown. Each hair was plucked individually by tying a previously plucked hair around the root of the one to be extracted, and then pulling quickly and firmly.

"I am a woman, no longer a child," the poor girl had cried out, as the process began. "What have I done in a past life that the present one should be so painful?"

Each time Bittersweet cried out, one of her aunts had scolded her with maxims like, "There are pleasures in marriage, and there are pains, too. You must accept with grace and docility not only the pleasures but also the pains. Only then will you be happy in marriage." By the time the hair-plucking process was half done, Bittersweet no longer cried out, not even once, though now and again, she wept quietly. When the plucking was done, the aunts dabbed the blood away and exclaimed how well Bittersweet looked with the high brow of a matron. Then, they unbraided what remained of her hair and combed the three sections so that they fell in a single black sheet down the length of her back. "We must separate the sections," they said, "just as you must separate from your father and mother, your sister-in-law and your brothers. We must separate each single strand of hair, just as you must separate your life as a child from the life you will live as a woman and wife."

As this was said, her oldest aunt took up the smooth sheet of Bittersweet's hair and, coiling it into a knot, fastened it at the nape of the girl's neck with a single silver hairpin. As she inserted it, the aunt murmured, "A good lock has no bar or bolt, and yet it cannot be opened. A good knot does not restrain, and yet it cannot be unfastened."

The hair-plucking had been so painful, and yet these words were even worse. "What have I done?" Bittersweet wept. "What I have done cannot be undone!"

Her aunts clustered around the miserable girl, chiding her gently, saying, "What? Tears just a day before your wedding? You should be happy. You are fulfilling the first step in the duties of every woman. You are following the pattern laid out for every woman since the beginning of time."

Bittersweet touched her brow where, only this morning, hair had grown, then she touched the bun at the nape of her neck. Yes, she should be happy, she told herself. Because the harvests had been very good for the past two years, she had accumulated a large dowry: a wardrobe for each season, twenty bundles of hand-woven cloth, trunks, suitcases, and furniture for the bedroom. With the extra income from the plentiful rice they had sold at Liangjiang market, her parents had planned a lavish wedding for her, spending as much on it, much to Sao-sao's chagrin, as on those of her three older sisters combined. The shoes she had sewn for her family-in-law — embroidered ones for the women, plain ones for the men — were the best she had ever made, and she would not feel inadequate when she presented them to her new family. But try as she might to convince herself, she was not happy.

So she gazed out the window, thinking. Her mother and father were taking their places in the courtyard, sitting in straight-back chairs like the very Emperor and Empress of China. Like judges at an execution, Bittersweet thought. "There are two times in every woman's life when her station could be said to equal that of the rulers of the land," her father had told her. "At her wedding, and at her funeral." Perhaps because there is so little difference between them, Bittersweet thought. It was only when her female relatives entered the courtyard for the second time that day that Bittersweet rose to her feet, lifted up by decorum and duty. They had come for her; she had to stand. The songs-blessing-the-bride party was about to begin.

Her two eldest maternal aunts entered her room and, pulling her this way and that, inserted thin silver hoops into her ear lobes, dressed her in the hand-embroidered black tunic and skirt with the red lining, and slipped her feet into the cloth shoes whose soles she had quilted herself. Then, giggling and whispering words of encouragement and advice, they ushered Bittersweet into the courtyard to present her to her parents as their daughter for the last time. Almost all of her female relatives were gathered there. However, Sao-sao, she noticed, was conspicuously absent. Bittersweet smiled inwardly. Her sister-in-law dared not show up on this day of reckoning, when the bride-to-be could say whatever she chose, whatever she had kept locked inside her, or die with it unspoken.

"Here is your good and obedient daughter," sang the "leading lady," Bittersweet's cousin, who was a fixture at all the festivities held in Village Village, since her facility at composing songs and singing was known for miles around, "with whom you took so many pains to raise properly. May her new parents love her and look after her as you have done."

"Your daughter's intelligence is matched by her industry," warbled an old aunt who began immediately where the leading lady left off. A single great gold-rimmed tooth glinted in her mouth. "No reason will her in-laws find to complain about her; and in her care, their household will run as smoothly as a stream in spring."

"She must obey her husband and bear him many sons," piped up a second cousin whose face, pitted like a peach seed from childhood smallpox, now screwed itself up like a prune. "She must serve her

parents to the best of her ability and act in harmony with her brothers-
and sisters-in-law. Then, surely, she will have a happy and prosperous
family life."

All during their singing, Bittersweet worried that she would forget
the words to the song that she had learned. While theirs were im-
promptu, hers was fixed by time and tradition, and to make a mistake
in the words or the notes was to anticipate mistakes in her duties as a
wife. Her throat tightened when she looked at her mother, who took
a handkerchief from her sleeve and began to dab at her eyes. The
women's songs stopped. It was Bittersweet's turn. She raised her voice,
but only a thin, raspy, barely audible sound came from her mouth —
this from someone who, as a child, had had a strong, resonant voice,
a voice which needed no prompting, particularly when her temper had
been piqued. Nonetheless, she began:

> At one, I sat on my mother's knee;
> At two, I crawled around her feet;
> At three, I learned to walk and run;
> At four, I watched the fire that boiled the water for tea;
> At five, I picked buckets of greens to feed the pigs;
> At six, I washed the vegetables in the stream;
> At seven, I held the bag of cotton thread for Mother;
> At eight, I learned to thread the loom;
> At nine, I learned to weave cloth;
> At ten, I wove with flax and silk;
> At eleven, I wove cloth without a single knot;
> At twelve, I was praised for my weaving skill;
> At thirteen, I knew how to make cloth shoes;
> At fourteen, I knew how to embroider well;
> At fifteen, my hair was combed into the young maiden's style;
> At sixteen, the matchmaker came to our house;
> At seventeen, my father began accumulating my dowry;
> At eighteen, my mother bought the bridal bed;
> At nineteen, my parents completed buying my dowry;
> At twenty, a young lady left home to get married.

As she sang, her female relatives passed around bowls of fried beans
and pots of steaming tea and munched and sipped thoughtfully.
Bittersweet suddenly remembered that she hadn't eaten all day and

felt as unsteady on her feet as if she had drunk hot wine. To no longer be a member of her family, she thought, her lips trembling as she sang, and to not yet be an honorary member of her husband-to-be's family! To think she would have to die to be a *full* member of his clan, for only then would her name be written in gold characters on the red ancestor tablets. Her eyes filled with tears. Perhaps to have remained an old maid would not have been so bad after all. At least she could have remained with her family who loved her. She began:

Eldest Brother bought me an umbrella.
Second Brother bought me a pair of embroidered shoes.
Third Brother made me a gold hair pin.
Fourth Brother sewed me a set of clothes.
Fifth Brother bought me a mirror.
Sixth Brother bought me a bronze washing bowl.
Seventh Brother bought me a suitcase.
Eighth Brother bought me a purse.
Ninth Brother bought me a horse.
Tenth Brother bought me a saddle.

As the words poured out, so did her tears. Some of her aunts tried to hush Bittersweet. They clucked their tongues at her, more in sympathy than in scolding, and said that marriage was a joyful occasion. Bittersweet looked at them in astonishment. "Since marriage is such a happy occasion, why are there those among you whose eyes are nearly as red as mine?" she asked when she finished her song. "Why do your breasts heave and shudder as though a violent storm was inside? What do you know as married women that I on my last day as a maiden do not?"

Fortunately for the married women, the songs-blessing-the-bride party was over, and they could gather around Bittersweet's parents, offering their congratulations, while ignoring the bride and her impossible questions. Lao Li and his wife accepted their good wishes automatically, mechanically. Though her mother smiled, Bittersweet, craning her neck, noticed that she could not stop dabbing at her eyes with her handkerchief.

The following day, Bittersweet awoke with an even greater foreboding. A red sedan chair sat inside the courtyard next to the gate, ready to take her to her new home. She stared at it listlessly until the gate

swung open and admitted her maternal aunts and female relatives —
all but Sao-sao — the exact same guests as the previous day. Like
locusts over a field of ripe wheat, they hovered over and around her,
dressing and grooming her, combing and perfuming her hair, inserting earrings into her earlobes, placing her feet into embroidered shoes.
She let them do this, for to object was futile and childish; to aid them
would be to indicate that she was eager to leave home. Then they
herded her into her mother's room where the woman was waiting with
a silent dignity that Bittersweet had never before seen in her. The
bride's farewell party would now begin.

All eyes turned to Bittersweet. For the songs-blessing-the-bride
party, she could rely on traditional songs that had been sung for
centuries; but for her final farewell, only songs of her own making,
from her own heart, could be sung. And so the songs she sang — of
her reluctance and unwillingness to leave home, of her regret that she
had not yet returned the love of her parents or the consideration of her
brothers and sisters — were more simple yet more eloquent than any
traditional songs could have been.

According to custom, the guests sang advice back to the new bride.
Some mentioned the good, some the bad, times in marriage; some
spoke of the times of togetherness and some of the times spent apart;
others of the moments of happiness and contentment; and still others
of the periods of sadness and despair that made up a married woman's
life. But Bittersweet's songs had been so plaintive that they'd touched
the hearts of her guests and unlocked memories long repressed or
forgotten. Words that began as suggestions and admonitions to the
bride became the life stories of the singers themselves.

"Bear your husband many sons. I gave my husband six, and he
cherishes me still," the leading lady warbled, puffing out her chest like
a proud pigeon.

"One day, my husband told me he was going to the river," another
sang, "only to return five years later, carrying with him as many fish
as I had sons." Everyone present, knowing that she was childless,
shook their heads in sympathy.

"My mother-in-law did the unthinkable," sang the third, "and
helped me deliver each of my three children. For that, my husband
soundly admonished her, and he hasn't forgiven her to this day."

"My husband married another woman and lives with her, though he already has me at home. What have I done in this or in my previous lives that he should ignore me this way?"

"Be thankful that he merely ignores you," responded Bittersweet's pipe-smoking aunt, squinting through the smoke. "My brother-in-law was so cruel to my simpleton sister that spirits came and possessed the poor girl and made her pull her hair out and speak wild oaths at night."

The strange words dried Bittersweet's tears, and she looked about her mother's room at these women whom she thought she knew but who, she realized, were strangers. There they all sat, some proud, some happy, some despairing, some vengeful, but all of them emptied of sentiments they had long carried tight in their breasts. Now that they were relieved of them, even the saddest among them appeared freer, lighter, even strangely content.

"A bride's farewell party is her last chance to sing what is on her mind," the leading lady said, turning to Bittersweet, "words that she never dared say for fear of losing face, or of being thought unkind. If she has any complaints against any of her family members or anyone else, then she must tell them here and now, or forever hold her grudges inside of her, for she will not have this opportunity again. Well, Bittersweet? Do you have anything to say?"

Bittersweet looked first at her mother, then at the assembled women. "At the beginning of this party," she sang in a hesitant voice, "I had no bad words. I was afraid that, meeting friends later on, I'd feel embarrassed, and so my songs were songs of praise. But listening to all of you sing has opened my heart of grievances as well as of praise. It is customary, I know, for the bride to scold her matchmaker for separating her from her family and making her leave home, otherwise the bride would be considered an undutiful daughter, one eager to leave her family and home. But I bear no grudge against my matchmaker. How could I, when I, not she, chose my husband? No, all the grievances I bear are directed to one person and to one person alone."

And with that, Bittersweet unlocked her heart and vented her wrath against the absent Sao-sao, enumerating and describing her sister-in-law's every indifference and avarice, her every jealousy and cruelty. And when she was finished, she felt better, even grateful to Sao-sao for not attending the party, for her sister-in-law's absence had not only freed Bittersweet's tongue, it had sharpened it.

When she was through, her two maternal aunts rose and walked over to her. Bittersweet looked at her mother for what she knew would be the last time as her daughter, in a house that soon would no longer be her home. Lao Li's wife was looking at Bittersweet in the same strange way, as though she saw someone she didn't quite recognize, or as though Bittersweet was no longer there. Then her aunts lowered the red veil over Bittersweet's face and led her into the courtyard where Elder Brother was waiting for her beside the sedan chair. By the unyielding stiffness of his arms and the rough way he lifted her into the chair, she knew that he must have heard her complaints against his wife. No doubt Sao-sao, too cowardly to listen for herself, had sent Elder Brother to spy for her. Well, it's over and done, Bittersweet thought to herself, seeing only red, feeling only the fastidious hands of her female relatives patting her bridal dress into place. What was done could not be undone.

As she settled herself within the cushioned chamber, there was the blare of trumpets, the boom of drums, the whine of the *pipa*, and the crackle of exploding firecrackers. Music broke the rural silence of Village Village and continued until Bittersweet's sedan chair, carried on the shoulders of Elder Brother, Younger Brother, and two male cousins, reached Dragon's Head and the house of the Li family. The musical din stopped; the bridal party stopped. Bittersweet's chair was lowered to the ground and she landed with a thud. Surely, this was Elder Brother's doing. Only now that the music had ceased could she hear how quick and shallow her breathing was, how fast her heart beat. The red veil over her face grew brighter: the red cloth doorway of the sedan chair had been parted. A big dark oblong appeared, and she felt her knees once again being inserted into the crook of a pair of elbows. Her feet were then placed on the ground rather roughly, and she was pulled forward by her own outstretched arms.

Bittersweet turned her head slightly as she walked with tentative steps. She was trying to catch the sounds of strange voices whispering, evaluating, suggesting, commanding. From this day forward, these would be the sounds of her everyday life.

"See how she advances with halting steps, her head unbowed. She's a proud and wary one."

"She halts before the unfamiliar. That is only prudent. And her head is not lifted, merely set straight in front of her. She's practical and direct."

"Take care! You're right in front of the threshold!"

"Ah! Did you see that she took care not to step on but over it? It won't be this bride who will dispel the growing good fortune of the Li household."

"Yes, but did you see her feet? Long as a bamboo raft and broad as a houseboat."

"Good for stability when planting in the rice paddies and carrying produce to market."

"You saw the feet but I saw the shoes — thickly embroidered in three colors of thread. Large of foot, nimble of finger. Here is a farmer's wife who will earn her keep."

"Not so fast. There is still her cooking to sample."

Bittersweet could tell that she had left the courtyard to enter the house, for she no longer felt the afternoon sun on her head and a cool draft fluttered the hem of her skirt. She was led in a circle about the room — once, twice, three, four times — her hand placed on someone's arm: her husband's. While they walked, more firecrackers exploded outside, the musicians blew and strummed and banged vigorously, and people outside the circle talked and laughed approvingly. Then, she and her husband — for now he was her husband, having completed and closed the circle four times — stopped walking; the music stopped playing; the firecrackers stopped exploding. A glass of tea was placed in her hand and, carefully, so as not to lift her red veil, she drank in big gulps, for her throat was parched, more with the chaos of emotion than the heat of the day.

She heard the slurping of her new family and their guests as they drank, and she received their toasts to her and her husband. She acknowledged them, as was custom, in silence, her head bowed in modesty and restraint. And then it was all over — at least her part in the marriage ceremony. Her brothers and male cousins would return to what had been her family and home. Of her relatives, only her two oldest maternal aunts would remain behind, to lead her into the bridal chamber, to sit there with her while her husband's family and the other wedding guests celebrated in the next room well into the night.

In the bridal chamber, Bittersweet allowed her aunts to remove her heavy headdress and the red veil it had held in place. She blinked her eyes and looked around the room. She recognized the bed that her father had bought for her dowry. She ran her hand over the chest of drawers that smelled of sandalwood and pulled open one of them to touch a length of cloth inside. It was one of many she had woven for her wedding day. They were all familiar things, but they were all in an unfamiliar place. With a sigh, she sat back down on the bridal bed, into whose red coverlet she had embroidered the ideogram for "double happiness" in gold thread. Just to see the symbol made her sad, for she was anything but happy, let alone doubly so.

"Some tea, Bittersweet?" one of her aunts asked.

On the writing table, also part of her dowry, was a pot of tea and some cups, as well as a wine pot filled with wine and some cups.

"Nothing. I want nothing," Bittersweet answered.

That's not true, she thought, sitting back down on the bed, her back rounded in despair, while her aunts sat like sentinels on the two chairs that guarded the writing table. I want to go home. I want to go back to my mother and father, my brothers. Even Sao-sao would be preferable to this.

Just then, she heard a burst of laughter, followed by lengthy applause. She scowled. How could they even think of being happy, she thought, let alone show it, when here I am, miserable, and alone, and angry.

She jumped to her feet, her hands clenched in determination. Her aunts rose immediately after her, bumping into the table and rattling the tea and wine cups in the process.

"Bittersweet?" said one. "Where are you going?"

"You can't go in there!" insisted the other. "It's unseemly! Improper!"

"I'm not going in there. I'm going *home*!" She opened one hand, then tightened it around the doorknob. But when she heard another burst of laughter and then an enthusiastic monologue interrupted with more laughter, she relinquished the doorknob and all thoughts of escape.

"It's your husband, Delin," one aunt told her gently. "He's making a speech. He's making a speech about the happy life the two of you will have together." She looked at her sister for encouragement.

Bittersweet sank down upon the bridal bed of happiness. What does my husband look like? she wondered, almost sick with apprehension. What is his character like? Will he be good to me? How will my in-laws take to me . . . me, an outsider in their house? How will they treat me? What will they require of me? Why isn't my mother, who has always been by my side, here with me, to counsel me, to console me? How hard her life has been! How she has suffered and struggled to run the family farm and raise the six of us! And now I am married, destined to serve my mother-in-law, a woman I've never even met, when I haven't even begun to serve my own mother who has always loved me!

With that, Bittersweet began to cry with bird-like sobs into the pillow case which, like the coverlet, was embroidered with "double happiness."

The sound of heavy footsteps caused Bittersweet to sit up in bed. She blinked, her eyes bleary with sleep. The fat red candle that her aunts had lit upon entering the bridal bower had melted down to half its height, and the women themselves were dozing.

Bittersweet swung her legs around and planted her feet flat on the floor as the door opened and her husband entered the room. The click of the lock woke the two aunts who, each with an "ai-yah!" of surprise and failed duty, leapt up, then began to fight with each other over who would pour the wine. To their astonishment, the groom took the wine pot out of their hands and poured some of the warm liquid into the two cups. Then he walked over to Bittersweet, gave her one of the cups and, raising his own in front of his face, said, "Let's both drink to our happiness."

Bittersweet, still stunned by her husband's entry as well as the unusual act of his pouring the bridal wine for her, looked up into her husband's face for the first time. Her heart, so tight for days, unclenched. He was smiling, and his face was flushed from the heat of the many cups of wine he had already drunk with the wedding guests. He wasn't tall, but neither was he short, and he seemed taller for his bearing, proud and straight. His demeanor, however, and his eyes particularly, suggested a gentleness and a kindness. So this is my husband, Delin, Bittersweet thought.

He sat down beside her on the bed and together they drained their wine cups. She had never sat with a man, let alone a man who was a complete stranger, and she thought that she should feel odd to be doing so, and yet she did not feel odd in the least. To sit with her husband seemed like the most natural thing in the world.

Delin stood up, thanked the aunts and told them that they could retire to their rooms. All the other guests had returned home, and the house was quiet and locked up for the night. When the two women had gone, he refilled both cups with wine, and they again drained their cups in silence.

"This has been a very important day. You must be very tired."

Bittersweet shook her head. "On the contrary. It's strange, but I feel totally refreshed."

Delin smiled. "Or is what you feel total relief, now that you've seen your husband? Surely over the past year I must have been a kind of ghost to you."

"The way you speak," Bittersweet said, scrutinizing her husband's face, "it isn't a farmer's speech. You use the words of someone who is educated. You have the manners of a town dweller."

"My father is the village tutor. I received my education first at home at my father's knee, then later at the county school in Lingui, and now at the military academy in Kweilin."

Bittersweet looked down at his heavy leather shoes and nodded her head. Good iron is not used to make nails; good men do not become soldiers, she recalled. Then she looked up into her husband's face. The adage might be true in general, she decided, but in this case, it was certainly wrong.

"And you? Do you know how to read?"

Bittersweet shook her head and laughed. "What good is it for a girl to know how to read?"

But her husband did not join her in her laughter. "It's only a blind man who doesn't know how to read," he said. "When I write home from officers training school, how will you know what news my letters contain?"

Bittersweet couldn't answer and looked into her lap.

"If you don't know how to read, you have to have someone else read for you, someone who might read what isn't written, someone who might cheat you. If you don't know how to read, you're dependent on those who do. You must hire them to read for you and write for you, and then they will know all your secrets."

Bittersweet looked up, but, to her dismay, she could say nothing.

"It isn't too late for you to learn to read and write. If you're willing to learn, I will teach you."

"It is unthinkable . . . ," Bittersweet began, staring wide-eyed at him. For a man to allow a woman to learn to read and write was silly. But for a man to actually teach a woman to read and write. It was unheard of! A woman's duties were to cook and clean, to take care of her husband, to serve his parents, and to give him many sons. "Yes," she answered, nonetheless, raising her wine cup in acceptance. "Yes, I'm willing to learn."

"Good. I will give you your first lesson tonight."

Bittersweet smiled in surprise. "On our wedding night?"

"What better time to learn so important a skill?" He rose from the bed.

Bittersweet rose immediately after him.

Delin led her over to the writing desk, sat her down, and put the wine pot, teapot and cups to one side. Then, he poured a few drops of tea onto the inkstone, chose a badger brush from the teak canister and swirled its tip in the liquid till it turned an opaque blue-black. "It's customary to start students off learning to read and write with numbers: one, two, three. But the first word I am going to teach you is Li."

"Our family name?" Bittersweet asked, looking up at her husband.

"Ah, yes. Your name is Li, too, though, I understood that in order to marry me without bringing bad luck to the union, you changed your name to Lu."

"Just for the one occasion," Bittersweet told him.

Delin smiled. "If you learn to write the word Li, it won't be difficult for you to write all the other Chinese characters, for Li contains every stroke that is common to them all." Unfurling a role of rice paper from the writing desk drawer, he drew the character Li, naming each stroke as he set his brush to paper. "Horizontal stroke, which must look like clouds forming a thunderhead. Vertical stroke, like a thousand-year-old vine stem, still stout and strong. Sweeping left stroke, looking like a sharp sword. Sweeping right stroke, looking like a wave rolling up suddenly, before cresting. And hook, so named for the barb at the end of the stroke, sharp enough so that a fish that swallows it will not be able to wriggle free." He extended the brush to Bittersweet. "Here, you try."

Though she proceeded slowly and cautiously, Bittersweet's Li looked nothing like her husband's. Nevertheless, he complimented her and encouraged her to try again. This Bittersweet did, with somewhat better results.

She knew that their surname represented the plum blossom, the first bloom of spring, flowering even in late winter snows. Now, as she wrote the ideogram, she could actually visualize the tree that bore the flowering branch. She could see in the separate strokes the roots, the trunk, the limbs — and beneath the roots, a swaddled child.

"Ah! Good. Better," he praised her new efforts. "Now I will give you a name."

Bittersweet stared at him with admiration and astonishment. She had always been called Bittersweet by her family and close friends, for the disappointment of her birth and then the good fortune that followed. But it wasn't a name; it was a nickname, a reminder of her tenuous beginnings and the fortuitous destiny that might be hers, if she practiced appropriate behavior, if she performed good deeds. She'd always been known as Bittersweet, or by her position within the family hierarchy: Sinu, meaning Fourth Daughter; or Xiaomei, meaning Little Sister. Now that she was his wife and belonged to his family, he would give her a name of his choosing.

Delin took the inkbrush out of her hand and wrote an ideogram that took many more strokes than Li. When he was finished, he set the brush down.

"Xuewen," he announced.

"Xuewen," Bittersweet said, testing the sound of it.

"Here, you try," Delin encouraged, inserting the brush back into her hand.

Wen was quite easy to write; Xue was much more difficult. But Bittersweet kept trying. Without any prodding from her husband, she drew the three ideograms of her new name over and over, repeating each syllable as she wrote each ideogram, "Li . . . Xue . . . wen. Li . . . Xue . . . wen. What," she asked her husband, "does Xuewen signify?"

"Xue means to study. Wen means language, or literature."

"To study language or literature," Bittersweet said, smiling with the pleasure of understanding. "My name's very appropriate, isn't it?" Fearing she'd been immodest, she added, "And with your help, I shall try to live up to it."

She unrolled another swath of rice paper, for she had written her characters so large, as beginners will, that they filled the previously unrolled swath. She began to write again. As she wrote, she said the characters, as though she were drunk on the sound of them, "Li Xuewen . . . my very own name." She looked up at Delin. "In marrying you, not only did I acquire a husband, I also gained a teacher."

Delin laughed. "As your husband, I hope I may teach you more than just reading and writing," he said gently, leaning toward the fluttering candle, practically a pool of wax on the writing table, and blowing out the flame. "That's enough study for tonight. It's late. We must go to bed."

In the early morning darkness, Bittersweet noiselessly took off her bridal clothes at one side of the bed, while Delin undid his cadet's uniform and unlaced his heavy leather shoes on the other. She undressed hurriedly, hoping that the many buttons on her husband's jacket would slow him down and that she would be in her nightdress and under the covers first. She faced away from him, pulled the silken quilt up over her shoulder, and snuggled down into the embroidered pillow, seeking warmth and safety. Her heart was still pounding as when her husband had offered to teach her to read and write, and she realized she was gripping the pillow under her face, its surface cool against her hot cheek. Her old maternal aunts had hinted that strange goings-on awaited a new bride in her wedding bed, but refused to be specific. They merely nodded their heads slowly in what Bittersweet took to be both certitude and consolation.

Bittersweet gave a sudden start as she felt two decisive hands take her by the waist from behind. But instead of grabbing the pillow for protection, or fighting him off as she thought she might do out of fear and disgust, she found herself whirling around in her husband's arms, so she could clasp him tightly to her with her four strong limbs.

Chapter 4
In Her Mother-In-Law's House
(1909)

The next morning, Bittersweet's two aunts led her from her bridal bedroom into the kitchen. All three women carried gifts of embroidered shoes and bolts of handwoven cloth that Bittersweet had made for her dowry. First Outside Sister-in-Law had already filled the water barrels and was stirring a milky broth in which pig's feet floated.

"Let me help you," Bittersweet offered.

The frail, young woman smiled, wiped sweat from her brow with the back of her hand, and waved her fingers in refusal.

"Not today. There will be lots for you to do in the future. Why don't you pay your respects to Father- and Mother-in-Law? They're waiting for you in the parlor."

Through the wide doorway, Bittersweet saw her father-in-law pacing nervously, while her mother-in-law was on her knees arranging the gifts destined for Bittersweet's family. Behind the two, pointing at Bittersweet and whispering in each other's ear, were five of her new brothers- and sisters-in-law. Only First Brother-in-Law — First Outside Sister-in-Law's husband and Delin's elder brother, Demin — was missing, since he had left at daybreak for the fields. Scanning the five youngest members of her new family, Bittersweet understood why First Outside Sister-in-Law looked so thin and tired. Now she knew why her mother said, "When you marry, marry into a family with few children. If there are many children, then make sure that they are sons who will stay on rather than daughters who must leave when they marry and who will resent you for coming to take their place." She understood why her mother had brooded when she agreed to marry Delin, a man with two brothers and four sisters, all but one of them children. Only First Brother-in-Law could do the work of the fields, and only his wife could do the work of the house. Delin's younger brother and little sisters were too young. True, they could be expected to help, yet they provided that much more food to cook, clothes to wash, mess to clean up.

49

Such a big family, Bittersweet thought, and completely dependent on only twenty *mou* of land, the same amount as my own family and yet there are half as many of us. And here I am, the newest member, diminishing what little there is.

Clumsily, she took the gifts from her aunts and, kowtowing before her mother- and father-in-law, placed the shoes and fabric at their feet. "You must have worked very hard to make so many gifts for us," her mother-in-law said in a deep and gracious voice. "Come, children, approach Ninth Sister-in-Law and bid her welcome." Bittersweet was Ninth Sister-in-Law because ninth was Delin's rank in his clan.

Only when they fell upon the shoes that she had embroidered for them did Bittersweet raise her eyes to look at her mother-in-law. The woman had an open, unlined face and a proud, straight bearing, unlike Bittersweet's own mother whose face was lined and whose spine had curved under the yoke of constant want. Her mother-in-law's kindly eyes had the double fold so prized by men who considered themselves connoisseurs of women, and the bridge of her nose was thin and high.

"Return to your bridal room and eat the noodles of happiness we've prepared for you," her mother-in-law said. "After, your younger brother will come to take you and Delin to visit your family and to help carry these reciprocal bridal gifts to them."

Bittersweet was halfway through the doorway when she gasped in alarm, turned around, and ran back into the living room to kowtow to her parents-in-law. Then she scurried into the bedroom where she found her husband, seated before a table set with two bowls piled high with steaming noodles and topped with pig's feet. As she ate, her two aunts scolded her for gobbling her first meal as a married woman.

"Let her eat, let her eat," Delin cajoled the aunts. "I hope my wife will always have such a hearty appetite." Bittersweet looked up and, catching his glance which spoke of another sort of appetite, she blushed and looked down into her bowl. "You see how just a few words from me and she not only slows down, she stops eating entirely," he teased.

Outside, they heard the front gate creak open, then slam shut, and then there were voices raised in greeting in the courtyard. "It's Younger Brother," Bittersweet cried excitedly, peering out the fretwork window. "Let's go!"

On their bridal walk to Village Village, Bittersweet tried to match the steady pace and dignified carriage of her husband, but she was bursting with impatience to reach home and had to restrain herself from running ahead of him. Her mother and father, her brother and Sao-sao, her three married sisters — all of them would be there to see her — a *tai-tai*, a married woman — and the man who had made her so.

When Bittersweet, Delin, her brother, and her two elderly aunts entered the village and approached the house of her birth, the winding cobblestone alleyways were lined with neighbors propped up against their doorways, talking and pointing, inspecting the second son of the Li clan of Dragon's Head. She glanced anxiously at Delin out of the corner of her eye and saw that, far from being intimidated, he was quite composed, that he actually enjoyed all the attention.

"Why didn't you come in sedan chairs?" a voice called out.

Bittersweet glanced to the right and recognized its owner as the village butcher, one of the men who had once asked for her hand in marriage. He was still wearing the blood-stained apron of his trade.

"Dragon's Head is not so far from Village Village," Delin answered, coming to a halt in front of the man. "I enjoy walking. It's good exercise. Sedan chairs are too confining. I think I may never ride in one again."

The villagers laughed and nodded their heads in approval, but the butcher's face grew as red as his apron. He would not be put off. "Dragon's Head, eh? They say that Dragon's Head can be compared with a lotus. A lotus has only eighteen petals. Dragon's Head can support only eighteen families."

The villagers laughed, then they strained their necks forward to hear how Delin would reply.

"It's true that Dragon's Head is a poor village," he answered. Then, looking at Bittersweet, he said, "But today it's made richer by a fair lotus blossom from Village Village."

A hush fell over the crowd, and all eyes turned to the bride. Unused to public scrutiny and to such compliments, Bittersweet blushed in confusion and dropped her head to her chest. Though she wasn't plain, she knew she was no beauty. And yet today, her husband's words were like the sun, and she a tightly closed bud that, upon receiving the warmth of his praise, was opening into a beautiful flower. She raised her eyes and looked at Delin.

"A lotus grows in muck and mud!" the butcher taunted.

"Surely you aren't saying that Village Village is muck and mud?" Delin replied.

The villagers were all hooting now, teasing the butcher. Humiliated, his face working in uncontrollable spasms, he made ready to run away, but Delin caught him by his apron and, pointing at it, said, "Thank you, my friend, for participating in our marriage celebration. You alone among all your neighbors have worn red for the occasion — for our health, happiness, and good fortune."

Immediately, the villagers' derision became appreciation, and the butcher's contorted face relaxed. "A marriage, especially one between our two villages, is an event to be celebrated," the butcher stammered. "Welcome to beautiful Village Village. May you live one hundred years and have one hundred sons."

I have married a remarkable man, Bittersweet thought. Not only is he intelligent, he is also very kind.

When they reached her childhood home, she watched in silence as her husband paid his respects to her family. He had an ease and aplomb that she had never before seen in a farmer's son. With dignity and grace, Delin bowed to her parents and aunts and uncles, nodded and smiled to her older brother and Sao-sao, and drank tea and chatted, neither too casually nor too formally, with his new in-laws. Bittersweet's mother, clearly impressed by her new son-in-law, extended the invitation to sit and stay awhile.

Meanwhile, at the first opportunity, Bittersweet's three sisters pulled her from the living room into the adjoining bedroom, the one that had once been hers and which now belonged to Elder Brother and Sao-sao. "He poured wine for you, and tea?" her eldest sister repeated in amazement when Bittersweet told her what had transpired on her wedding night. "But he is the husband and to be served."

"Nevertheless, he served me wine and tea," Bittersweet answered. "Ask our two aunties if you don't believe me."

"He's promised to teach you to read and write?" her second sister repeated. "But of what use is that to a woman? Still, he has a kind face and a gentle manner."

Bittersweet looked at her second sister, trying to read the feelings behind her words. In her youth, her face had been round, her expression always lively, but after her marriage her face had become thin and dispirited. Bittersweet knew that, though Second Sister spoke now of Delin, she was thinking of her own husband who, fearful of his mother, let her beat his wife with cruel words, let her call her *huai dan*, or rotten egg, and command her to roll out of her house. Bittersweet knew that her second sister returned to their mother's house more often than was seemly and that she went back to her mother-in-law's house only because it was fitting.

"Don't be sad for me," she told Bittersweet, stroking her sister's troubled face. "If First Sister and I have drawn a bad lot in life, there's nothing to do and no one to blame. It's our destiny. Perhaps we're making amends for evil deeds we committed in a past life. We'll be better off in a future one."

"Let's be thankful," Third Sister concurred, hugging Bittersweet, First and Second Sister to her. "For the short time we have together, let's be happy, like when we were children living at home and without a care in the world."

On the second night after their wedding, just after the new couple returned to Dragon's Head from Village Village, Delin turned to Bittersweet and said, "Tomorrow I must return to Kweilin and the military academy." When he saw the expression on Bittersweet's face, he explained, "I'm on extended leave as it is, so I could marry you. My leaves will rarely be three days, a day or two at the most, and then at long and infrequent intervals. But don't worry. My parents are kind. My whole family lives in harmony. And I've asked Father to continue teaching you to read and write. Sooner than you think, you'll be reading my letters and writing ones in return."

Bittersweet's initial involvement with her father-in-law included little more than filling his pipe with a few precious strands of tobacco, boiling water for the many glasses of ersatz tea he drank each day, and cleaning his boar's-hair calligraphy brushes and arranging them in their bamboo canister. To her, the brushes and canister were as beautiful as a vase of exotic flowers. And their beauty only grew when her father-in-law became her teacher.

At the beginning of her lessons with Baba, as he was called by his children and now by his new daughter-in-law, Bittersweet sat far away from her teacher, much farther than her young brothers- and sisters-in-law. In the makeshift classroom that Baba had made out of an unused storeroom, Bittersweet felt clumsy, stupid and ignorant. She was so much older, yet so much less knowledgeable, than her new siblings. But soon her fear of mockery and her bashfulness subsided, and she sat close to Baba, her eyes trained upon his face or upon the characters he wrote on the chalkboard. More often than any of them,

Bittersweet stayed after class to ask questions and show her attempts at writing the words that Delin had taught her.

"I can't say I understand what they mean," Bittersweet admitted one day, as she placed the sheets of paper before her father-in-law.

"'Good men should have great ambitions,'" he read aloud. "'Be determined to help the country. Give up your studies and join the army.'" He cleared his throat. "Hmm. Military slogans. No, I suppose they shouldn't mean too much to you. Nevertheless, your characters are becoming squarer, more balanced."

"When I was a child," Bittersweet said, "I was taught Confucian sayings, like 'Nothing is more important than learning' and 'Try to be virtuous and righteous' and 'The emperor looks highly and respectfully upon virtuous, heroic and learned persons.'"

"The emperor!" Baba boomed, startling Bittersweet so that she dropped her homework sheets. "That sniveling, cowardly . . . What does that sycophant of the imperialists know about virtue or heroism?"

Just then, Bittersweet's mother-in-law entered the room with a glass of boiled water in her hand which she set before her husband. "He's lost the Mandate of Heaven. That's the problem," she said.

"The Mandate of Heaven?" Bittersweet said, looking up from the fallen pages she was collecting.

"Yes," Bittersweet's mother-in-law said, "the seal that gives him authority to rule China. There's always been a Son of Heaven, both father and mother to his people, to rule China. If he was evil and unfit to rule, then the Mandate passed to a new emperor, one that heaven had chosen. But it's the Dowager Empress who had the Mandate last, and she keeps the Emperor prisoner in the Forbidden City or on an island at the Summer Palace. Now no one seems to rule, so the Mandate must be lost."

"Wife, you still believe in ghosts and demons," Baba accused her, "and so you believe in this Mandate of Heaven. China is prey to foreign powers because the Qing government is weak and corrupt, and for no other reason."

"Mandate or corruption," his wife answered promptly, going out the door, "the result is the same: all is chaos under heaven."

Her husband took a sip of water and shook his head in bewilderment. "Bah! Women's logic! The very words resist one another like two lodestones placed side by side."

Bittersweet looked at him through slightly narrowed eyes and smiled. "The book you lent me, Baba? The *Analects* of Confucius?" she added innocently.

"The wisest book ever written," he said decisively.

"In it is written: 'Teach sons, not daughters.' Yet you teach my sisters-in-law and me."

"Yes, well, the China of today is not the China of Confucius. Today there's another sage that everyone is listening to. Better than a sage. A revolutionary. Sun Yat-sen will unify our country and make it strong. Then no one will dare call China the sick man of Asia."

"Who is this Sun?" Bittersweet asked. "Delin talks of him constantly, and words like nationalism and democracy, words I don't understand."

"You might not understand now," her father-in-law replied, "but you will live them one day. It's what your husband is fighting for."

While Baba was teaching her to read and write in the classroom, Da Mama, or Big Mother, as all her children called her, was teaching Bittersweet honesty and industry in daily life. Three times a week, Bittersweet accompanied her mother-in-law to Sankou and Liangjiang markets to sell the rice Demin grew, the shoes Bittersweet embroidered, and the shoe soles Da Mama sewed. At the marketplace, no matter what the distractions, Da Mama's hands worked constantly. When she wasn't selling her goods, she busily twisted a few cotton filaments into thread.

When Bittersweet marveled at Da Mama's industry, Delin told her a story: "My mother raised us boys to be very self-reliant, not to have to depend on anyone. When I was nine, Baba and Second Uncle divided the family farm between them. We had to live on only half the original property, twenty instead of forty *mou*. With each new brother or sister born to my family, less and less rice filled our bowls. One day, my mother asked me to accompany her to her parents' home to borrow some rice. Her father was kind and generous, but her mother was stingy. My grandmother refused to lend my mother the rice, saying that she didn't lend grain without interest and that if her daughter needed to borrow, it was for no other reason than she wasn't hardworking or frugal enough. As we walked home, the rice jar we'd brought was still empty, but my mother's eyes were full of tears. 'Work hard so that when you are grown you won't have to depend on anyone,' she said to me, 'not even your own family.' Though we were poor, still she encouraged us, 'Just because a person is poor doesn't mean that he shouldn't be ambitious.' And when we passed a rich merchant on the road to Kweilin dressed in silk, a man who refused to acknowledge our presence, she would say, 'Just because a person is rich doesn't mean that he can forego kindness and sensitivity.'"

When the old water buffalo died during plowing time, Da Mama yoked Demin in front of the plow and she herself guided him from behind.

"Let us take turns doing it," First Outside Sister-in-Law and Bittersweet cried, seeing Da Mama struggle with the crude implement.

"You two must run the household," their mother-in-law told them.

At first, Bittersweet thought Baba should offer his own help, but she knew this was impossible for she knew that Baba had been studying to take the imperial examinations for the third time when his own father died. His mother died a year later. A filial son, he had put away his books and abstained from farm work for the requisite six years of mourning. After those years had passed, he found he had lost all ambition to be an imperial scholar and was quite satisfied to be the village tutor. As for the farm work, it remained solely in Da Mama's hands until Demin grew to manhood.

"It's quite the same in my childhood home," Bittersweet told First Outside Sister-in-Law after their offer of help had been refused. "My mother runs the farm because my father has a stomach ailment that nothing can cure . . . except a few sips of *san hua* now and then," she added with a smile. "But Baba is not sickly and Da Mama is no longer young, yet the responsibility for the land rests entirely upon her shoulders."

"Our Baba is unaccustomed to working with his hands," First Outside Sister-in-Law explained. "Manual labor is inappropriate for a scholar. When I've seen Da Mama asleep over her sewing at night or bowing under the strain of the rice baskets she carries to market, I've asked her the same question. But she's never given me an answer other than, 'It's enough that my husband is a learned man. I'm a better person for it.'"

"Then we must accept her explanation, mustn't we?" Bittersweet said, unconvinced. "We have her own words for it. But, truthfully, I don't find our father-in-law any more intelligent than our mother-in-law. He might be learned, but she is wise."

· ✦ ·

There were days when Bittersweet would see a neighbor skim the topmost grains from the rice baskets she left near the boundary of the property. At these times, she'd run down the path after the thief, only to be gently admonished by her mother-in-law. "Let it go," Da Mama said. "It's not important. Better that they take a few grains of our rice than we gain their enmity for having shamed them and made them lose face."

Once a blind man came begging at the door and Da Mama gave him a few turnips. When he lifted up his patch to inspect the vegetables with two sound eyes, Da Mama advised an irate Bittersweet: "Forgive the mistakes of others, but correct your own. When you have an open mind and are tolerant, you won't notice the shortcomings of others."

During good harvests and bad, hungry villagers, widows, the elderly, and the childless came to Da Mama's door, since they knew that they would not be turned away without a few cash, or some unpolished rice, or a padded cotton jacket to keep them warm.

"So many of our neighbors to whom you are so generous are at best lazy, at worst evil," Bittersweet blurted out one day when the level of rice in the family bowls was lower than usual. "And yet you don't separate them from the good and worthy, but give to all. Don't you ever worry that your generosity actually encourages the wicked in their ways?"

"Generosity?" Da Mama asked. "Or enlightened self-interest?"

It was true that no one in Dragon's Head had a better reputation for kindness and generosity than Da Mama. Good and evil, lazy and hard-working, all the villagers greeted the woman with praise and reverence whenever they saw her. "Your good deeds, Li *Tai-tai*, will bring many blessings on your children and grandchildren," they'd say, nodding and smiling.

And each time, Da Mama would answer cordially but firmly, "My children and my grandchildren must earn their own blessings and bear their own destinies. My husband and I have only done what we thought was right. If my children and grandchildren choose the right path and work hard for their own future, we will be happy."

"You are too modest, too modest," the villagers would reply.

But Bittersweet's mother-in-law knew — and Bittersweet came to know — that when living close to neighbors in a village as small and poor as Dragon's Head, modesty was far preferable to pride, and a neighbor's blessings could quickly turn to curses.

Indeed, it was Bittersweet who soon soured the villagers' honeyed words and turned them into threats and oaths against the Li family. Not a month after her wedding, Bittersweet found that she did not bleed when she was supposed to. Another moon waxed and waned, and again, she did not bleed.

"Then, surely you are with child," First Outside Sister-in-Law told her. Her happiness for Bittersweet immediately changed to self-reproach. "Here I've been married for almost two years, and still I am childless. It shall be you who gives our parents-in-law their first grandson."

"And you their second," Bittersweet consoled her, "and very soon afterwards."

Though her parents-in-law now regarded Bittersweet with even greater affection — for they had grown fond of her for her service to them, her obedience to Delin, her respect for Demin and First Outside Sister-in-Law, and her harmony with and helpfulness towards the younger family members — the villagers looked at her and her gently rounding shape with apprehension, even, Bittersweet suspected, with misgiving.

"Birth and death are but two sides of the same coin," a village elder warned Bittersweet when her tunic no longer lay flat across her stomach. "When a woman gives birth, she is close to death."

Then, later the same day, the village soothsayer caught up with Da Mama and Bittersweet. "Mark my words," she warned Bittersweet. "You must bring life into this world all alone, with no one to help you. Though you will suffer greater pain than you have ever known, you will have to do everything yourself. I tell you this now: a good wife will remain working in the fields when her labor comes on and have her child there and then. And after she severs the umbilical cord with her teeth and places rice sheaves between her legs, she will stick the little creature inside her tunic to suck contentedly while she finishes the work at hand."

"Hush, old woman," Da Mama hissed, "and leave the poor girl in peace."

"What do they mean, I'll be close to death?" Bittersweet asked when the village elder and the soothsayer were gone. "Why must I be all alone?"

"It is custom," Da Mama answered matter-of-factly, then added in a voice almost lost in wistful sadness, "but then, a woman is always alone."

Bittersweet stared at her mother-in-law who, though much older, still had a swift and vibrant stride and held her head high. Half a head shorter than Bittersweet, she gave the appearance of being tall. "Do you feel all alone?"

"I?" the woman answered, remembering herself. "With my big family?" She laughed.

"Da Mama?" Bittersweet ventured, recalling the soothsayer's words. "Is it wrong not to want to have children?"

The older woman's face contracted suddenly, like that of a sleeping snake touched by a stick. "You must never say that you don't want children. What you feel in your heart is yours to feel, but you must never say what should remain unspoken. Without children, even a girl-child, you have no position in the family. You fear death now, but without a child, you would fear loss of face, even your stature as Delin's wife, even more. It is a woman's duty to bear children. It is she who links generations past with generations to come, so that the chain of life may continue unbroken. No woman may drop out of the chain. You are young. Your body is strong. Don't be afraid, daughter-in-law. You will have an easy labor. I give you my promise."

It was in the fields, at the height of the first of the year's two rice harvests, that Bittersweet felt a sudden dull pain just beneath her stomach. She ignored it and continued to tear the rice plants away from the earth, to tie them into thick bundles and throw them onto the sledge hitched to the family's new water buffalo.

With the second pain, Bittersweet winced and staggered. A cold sweat broke out on her forehead and under her armpits. The baby, she thought, her chest beginning to heave, he's coming. And of all times, when I'm badly needed in the fields. She climbed up the rice paddy bank, pulling on the long weeds to help her. Trying not to call attention to herself, she made her way home, stopping and doubling over when the pain was sharp, scurrying along when it subsided.

I'm not strong enough. I'm not a good woman, Bittersweet told herself, as she fell gasping on her bed. The contractions were coming every few minutes now. The pain, when it came, was unbearable. Anticipating it, knowing it would come, and sooner and longer with each contraction, Bittersweet wadded up a corner of her coverlet and gripped it between her teeth so that she wouldn't cry out. But her resolve collapsed at the crest of each contraction. Pouring sweat, grasping the bedposts with both hands, Bittersweet screamed for human help and god-given mercy. I'm dying, she thought, just like the soothsayer said I would. I want to die, if only to end this pain. Then, she remembered that she had forgotten to bring an old piece of mirror or a nail or a jagged piece of metal to cut the cord that bound mother to child. She had also forgotten to bring a bucket of water to wash the child and a clean blanket to wrap it in. She groaned in despair at her negligence. "If the gods are listening," she cried, "take my life and end my suffering!"

The door shot open with a resounding bang, forcing open her tightly-shut eyes. She lifted her head from the sweat-soaked pillow. They've come for me, she thought, with both terror and gratitude.

"You bring life into the world, and here you are speaking of death!" Da Mama walked towards her, carrying a bucket of boiling water, a cake of soap, the head of a hoe, and a small, clean blanket. "You should be ashamed of yourself."

"Da Mama, you shouldn't be here. You shouldn't have come." Bittersweet's head fell back onto the pillow and she sighed in relief. "Thank the gods you've come. Thank the gods."

"What's this?" the older woman exclaimed, pulling Bittersweet's legs farther apart and peering between them. "A shock of black hair as thick as a bundle of rice sheaves at harvest time. Let's see more. His head . . . that's it . . . push, now. Harder. Ah, a high forehead . . . that means he's intelligent. Again . . . that's it. With all the muscles of your stomach and the force of your will. Ah, broad shoulders, good for the fields. Push, push. Only one more good one and he'll slither out like a wet fish."

With a last push, Bittersweet bellowed till the veins in her neck stood out like blue ropes.

Da Mama laughed. "The ferocity of your cry should kill you if the baby doesn't." And then she showed Bittersweet a little animal with black hair, stiff and prickly as a porcupine's quills. He screamed with the nasal honk of a terrified goose.

"We have a grandson! The Lis of Dragon's Head finally have a grandson!" Da Mama exclaimed, laughing into the infant's wide-mouthed, wrinkled little face.

Together, Bittersweet and Da Mama cut the umbilical cord with the hoe, washed the baby of its birth curds, and wrapped him in the clean blanket. While Bittersweet lay suckling her son, Da Mama used the hoe to dig the family nest at the foot of the bed and buried the afterbirth there to keep her new grandson safe and sound in the house.

While she covered the afterbirth over with dirt, a shadow fell across Bittersweet and the baby. It was a group of elderly neighbors who, hearing Bittersweet's screams then the cries of the newborn, had gathered at the bedroom window. "Ai-yah!" they cried, shaking their fingers at Da Mama. "Not only is your daughter-in-law unclean, but so are you! You're contaminated with Ninth's filth. A curse on you! A curse on you! You shouldn't be allowed to burn incense and candles before the ancestral tablets!"

Da Mama threw down the hoe and approached the window. The elders backed away, fearing contamination. "Before, you blessed me for my kindness to my neighbors. Now you curse me for my kindness to my daughter-in-law, my own family. She was in great pain. Was I wrong to take pity on her?"

Made brazen by their numbers and their righteous indignation, the elders pushed forward, while keeping a respectable distance from the window. "Your daughter-in-law is unclean in giving birth and has made you so. A curse on you if you dare burn incense and candles before your husband's ancestors."

Days later, the villagers of Dragon's Head were not surprised to learn that the son born to the wife of the second son of the Dragon's Head branch of the Li clan had died of the three-day virus. "It was because she defied tradition and permitted her mother-in-law to help her with the delivery," one neighbor concluded. "What did she expect?"

"It was because they refused to pay the soothsayer when the old woman offered to read the infant's eight characters and to forecast his future," a second neighbor added. "Granted, she charged them double the going price, but she was taking a great risk just to step inside a home that had refused to honor custom."

"Too bad, too bad," the kinder neighbors muttered, shaking their heads. "And a big happiness, too."

"It serves them right," others insisted. "By the way, what did the soothsayer forecast?"

"What else? An unfortunate life. But who could have guessed that life would be so brief?"

"Do you really think the girl contaminated her mother-in-law?" they asked one another, thinking of the rice they needed for their stomachs, the jackets they needed to keep warm, the strings of cash they could use on market day. In the end they decided that Da Mama had been absolved by her little grandson's death, and so they felt no reason to abstain from visiting the Li house and asking Li *Tai-tai* for alms, a bit of turnip greens, a few grains of rice, or an old tunic no one else wanted. As for Bittersweet, she, like any woman who had given birth, was unclean and to be shunned for a month.

"One can't argue with one's destiny," Bittersweet told First Outside Sister-in-Law whose eyes were full of sympathy whenever she had to cut a wide swath to avoid crossing paths with the ostracized woman. "It will be you who gives our parents-in-law their first grandchild, as it should be."

Under her breath Bittersweet repeated a couplet over and over. "The river forms a green gauze belt," she said, "the mountains are like jade hairpins." She was trying to give herself courage as she made her way downstream, past the hunched backs of the village women who slapped their laundry on the pale pebbles of the bank, then spread the clothes on the nearby rocks to dry. Some of them, not knowing it was Bittersweet, swivelled their heads and acknowledged her presence with a slight nod. Most of them knew who it was and didn't bother to look around.

Where the river fell over a rocky ledge onto the plain below, Bittersweet set her basket down. Here, she could not see the others and they could not see her. Guardedly she looked about. The limestone cliffs weren't jade hairpins, she thought, but the lairs of outlaws and bandits. And the water that gurgled at her feet was no green gauze belt but the watery grave of unwanted baby girls. She knelt down and slapped a few garments from her basket on the river bank. She was careful not to make too much noise as she feared the bandits that might bear down on her from the foot of the nearest peak, or worse yet, the spirit of a drowned girl-child that might rise from the water. But her fear of a departed girl-child's spirit was nothing in comparison to her sadness at the death of the boy-child she had borne three weeks ago. The memory made her heart sore, and as she kneaded the clothes, she felt as if she was wringing her heart.

For the last three weeks, the laundry she brought to the river consisted solely of her own garments, and not those of her family. Paradoxically, the very lightness of her basket made it that much more burdensome. Jade hairpins, indeed, she thought, continuing her kneading and thrashing. Finally, she gathered the freshly washed clothes into her basket, set it on her hip, and, keeping a respectful distance from the other women on the bank, began to walk back to Dragon's Head. Just one more week, she thought, and I'll be accepted back into my family and community. Just one more week and I'll be able to take back all the laundry and all my other duties from First Outside Sister-in-Law.

In the hope of avoiding any villagers, she chose an out-of-the-way *hutong* to reach home. Though her burden was light, she set the laundry down wearily. She knew it was loneliness that weighted her basket, that forced her to stop and sigh.

An odor of burning incense caused her to lift up her head and sniff. Following her nose to a large gate, she saw a cobblestone courtyard beyond which was an unpainted wooden temple with a curving roof of unglazed terra cotta tiles. Just under the porch roof was a large circle, half of it painted black, the other half white, marking the building as a Taoist temple. When she had lived in Village Village, she had been too afraid to enter the Taoist temple there. Now, piqued by curiosity, and glancing around to make sure there was no one to see her, she hurried across the courtyard and into the great hall.

The temple was empty save for some glowing red candles, burning coils of pungent incense, and a number of hanging scrolls on the walls. Bittersweet walked from one scroll to the next, trying to make out some of the characters. She smiled when she did and pursed her lips when they meant nothing to her at all. She screwed up her eyes and tilted her head in confusion when she saw a scroll marked with a strange stack of four broken and unbroken horizontal lines, one set on top of the other.

"Welcome."

Bittersweet turned around abruptly. When she saw that the voice belonged to a young man dressed in a long black tunic, his hair not in the usual queue but loose and flowing past his shoulders, she took a few quick steps backwards and held her arm up over her face. "Come no closer. I am unclean."

The young man, who held a twig broom in his hands, looked down at his dusty gown and smiled. "Certainly no more than I."

"I mean to say, I am contaminated. I bore a son and my month is not yet up."

"If you bore a son, then you deserve congratulations, and not condemnation."

Bittersweet dropped her arm but she dared not look into the stranger's face. "You mock me. You mustn't mock me because . . . because . . . you see . . . ." Tears prevented her from finishing her sentence.

"I'm not mocking you," he said kindly.

In spite of herself, Bittersweet looked up. His eyes were kind, but his long, loose hair frightened her. She had heard stories about the Long-Hairs — the Taipings — of how they had pillaged China. Had it not been for them, the family she had married into, who were once wealthy peasants, would not now be so poor. It was the Long-Hairs who had thundered into Dragon's Head five decades ago, ravaged the village, ravished the women, and turned the finest house there — a home three courtyards deep — into a pile of smoldering wood and rubble.

"You are a mother. In the Way, we all aspire to be like the Mother, for She is the source of all things."

His words were incomprehensible to Bittersweet, but the manner in which he said them made him that much less frightening.

"You look like a Taiping," she said.

The man laughed so heartily that Bittersweet took another step backwards. "I'm hardly a Taiping. What I am is a seeker of the Way."

"I *was* a mother," Bittersweet admitted, dropping her eyes. "My son died of the three-day virus three weeks ago."

The young man said nothing, but drew his eyebrows down close to his eyes.

"It was his destiny," Bittersweet continued, "and mine. I wasn't strong enough to bear him alone, and my mother-in-law, hearing my cries, came to my aid. When the soothsayer insisted on twice the usual fee to tell my baby's fortune, the family refused. Small wonder that my son died. One cannot escape one's destiny," she said sadly.

"Is that what brought you here?" the seeker of the Way asked.

"My grief over the loss of my baby?"

"No. That it was your destiny."

Bittersweet frowned. The long-haired young man strung words together in such strange patterns.

"I know it was *my* destiny that brought me here," he continued. "There are three ways to change things in imperial China. You can get yourself chosen as advisor to the emperor and present your petition. If he accepts it, fine; if not, it's your duty to kill yourself as a sign of your loyalty to him. Or you can become a rebel and overthrow him as Liu Bang did. Or you can drop out of the system and become a monk or a member of the literati. I dropped out to follow the Way of the Tao."

"There is a fourth," Bittersweet declared. "You can give up your studies and join the army like my husband has. You follow this Tao of yours; he follows the three principles of Sun Yat-sen. The army will change things in imperial China." She felt almost proud of her little speech.

"I agree with giving up your studies. Actually, I wasn't very good at mine," he admitted. "Much to the dismay of my magistrate father. But the Tao says, 'To pursue the academic, add to it daily. To pursue the Tao, subtract from it daily.' See? It says so, right next to tetragram number 48." He pointed to a stack of four broken and unbroken horizontal lines and the vertical rows of characters beneath the figure. Tentatively, Bittersweet approached the scroll. She glanced up and down the many rows of characters, straining to recognize them. Her head dropped forward upon her neck.

"I'm just learning to read and write," she said in a small voice. "My husband is teaching me. But he comes home infrequently and can stay only a day or two, so my father-in-law is teaching me with passages from the *Four Books* and the *Five Classics*."

"I know them well," the young man said, pursing his lips together as though he'd just tasted something sour. "Do you enjoy reading them?"

Bittersweet didn't see what enjoyment had to do with learning to read Confucian texts. It was what her father-in-law was teaching her, and it was her duty to learn to read and write what he had to teach her. She only wanted to learn to read and write so she would know what Delin's letters had to tell her, and so she would be able to answer them with letters of her own.

"If you like, I'll help teach you to read. Your father-in-law may use the *Four Books* and the *Five Classics,* but I'll use," he extended his arm and turned in a circle, "these as a text. The *Tao Te Ching.*"

"I don't know," Bittersweet said after a moment. She wanted to ask him what this *Tao Te Ching* was, what those stacks of four broken and unbroken horizontal lines meant, why he wore his long hair loose, and even what the life of a Taoist priest was like. But she dared not show her ignorance or, worse yet, her curiosity.

"It's really quite easy and, best of all, completely true," he told her. "Just think. Everything that you'll ever need to know in only five thousand characters."

He was so enthusiastic, so joyful, that Bittersweet's first inclination was to accept. "If all you know is five thousand characters," she sniffed, "perhaps you won't be able to help me read my husband's letters." With that, she extracted Delin's last letter home and held it against her heart. There had been a section in the letter that her father-in-law had stammered and mumbled over. When Bittersweet asked him to repeat it, hoping the second reading would be more intelligible, he'd refolded the letter, saying that since it didn't concern her, the passage was of no consequence. What did concern the entire family was the fact that Delin had marched into Kwangtung Province to do battle with a man nicknamed the Dragon, arch-enemy of the governor of Kwangsi, Lu Jung-ting. With Delin's victory, the Dragon Suppression War was over. Lu Jung-ting was now commander-in-chief of both Kwangsi and Kwangtung, and Delin had been named company commander of the Sixth Army. Soon afterwards, civil war broke out between north and south and Delin and his army were sent to Hunan where they liberated the capital city of Changsha. All this her father-in-law had read to her from Delin's letter.

Now, Bittersweet bit her lower lip, then extended the letter to the young man. "Can you read this last section?" she asked him, pointing to it. "I can make out only several characters. Hunan and lilies and bamboo shoots. Hunan Province must grow an abundance of flowers and vegetables."

The priest took the letter from her and began to read: "'I'm considered a hero for liberating Changsha. People run out of their houses, grab my hands or kowtow before me. The innkeeper has invited me and my immediate officers to stay at his establishment. He insists it would be an honor to provide the roof over my head. He has a beautiful daughter who smiles at me whenever she sees me and serves us our meals. She has bound feet, as most Hunanese women do, and they are as small and slender as bamboo shoots. She minces about most appealingly on her golden lilies, as such feet are called — for my appreciation, I think. Like most of the Hunanese women I've seen, she is beautiful, delicate, fair-skinned, exquisitely groomed, and very liberal in social intercourse. Still, with such feet, how can they work as hard as men in the fields, as our Kwangsi women do?'"

Bittersweet felt her heart contract as the young priest read the passage. Rocking on her feet from side to side, she retrieved the letter, folded it clumsily, and slipped it into her tunic pocket. Suddenly, she felt terribly self-conscious in front of the young man. She wrapped one foot around the ankle of the other, alternating feet by turns in her effort to conceal the fact that they were large. They were, in fact, very large, but never until today had she noticed their size nor, before today, had their size seemed a detriment.

"What does . . . what does 'very liberal in social intercourse' mean?" she asked finally in a wavering voice.

"It means a very good conversationalist," the young man answered softly.

"I see," Bittersweet said, then bit her lip.

"In my mind, words are not important. In fact, they can be very misleading. Look here." He pointed to another tetragram and read aloud the characters underneath it. "'Those who speak do not know. Those who know do not speak.'"

Bittersweet smiled and her downcast face lit up.

"So?" the young man asked. "Am I hired? Will you come back for your second lesson?"

"My parents-in-law won't allow it," Bittersweet said, pulling at her tunic and playing with the Chinese frog at her throat. "I have too much work to do at home. Then again, Father-in-Law is teaching me. And Delin, when he comes home. What need do I have of a third teacher? Then again, we are Confucianists, not Taoists. The villagers won't approve. They'll whisper behind my back. How can I be ostracized a second time, just when I am finishing out the term of my first?"

"Can you think of another reason not to come back?" the young man said with a smile that was mocking yet not malicious. "Nothing can make you return if you don't want to. And no one can prevent you from returning if that is what you truly desire."

Bittersweet stooped to pick up her basket. When she righted herself, her eye caught sight of a third tetragram under which was written: "The Tao is a refuge for All Things, The treasure of the good, The protector of the not good." Surprised that she had been able to read it in its entirety, and afraid to consider it as a portent, she took several tentative steps backwards towards the temple entrance. "I must go home. I've stayed too long," she stammered. "Thank you for reading the letter for me. But no, I won't be coming back. There's no reason for me to come back."

Then she turned and went out the door and across the courtyard into the *hutong,* not stopping once till she reached the safety of her mother-in-law's house.

Chapter 5
Return of the Warrior
(1916)

Looking into the polished bronze disc that served as her mirror, Bittersweet fastened the frogs of her tunic. Two days ago, she had twisted and tied the red satin piping into four eternal knots. Then, she had sewn the knots — one at the two sides of her high collar, one under her armpit, one at her hip, the last at her thigh — onto a simple black tunic, transforming it into her very best. She would wear the tunic tonight at Delin's going-away party. When the sun rose tomorrow, he would return to his men and military life, and Bittersweet would again sleep alone.

She unfastened the complicated red frogs and slipped into her old everyday tunic, with its simple knots and loops. The laundry still needed washing, and she wanted to get it done early so that she could stop by the Taoist temple for her lesson with Xiao Tzu. Before she'd stumbled upon the Taoist temple and its young priest, the laundry had been a chore. But now she looked forward to doing the wash.

With her basket of clean, wet clothes on her head, Bittersweet waited outside the temple gates, as she always did when she arrived early and the monks were still finishing up their midday chant. She waited for Xiao Tzu to appear and invite her inside. There, in the empty hall, he would select one of the eighty-one tetragrams from the *Tao Te Ching* that hung in vertical scrolls upon the walls, or one of the sixty-four hexagrams from the *I Ching*, the *Book of Changes*, that were written on the long running scroll that he always took out of a brocade-covered box whose lid was fastened with ivory pins. With each lesson, Xiao Tzu grew more and more pleased with his student's progress, and Bittersweet herself felt that she was learning faster and retaining more knowledge. As explained by the young priest, the words of the *Tao Te Ching* were more memorable than the *Analects* she recited for Baba or the military slogans she repeated for Delin.

If she were a particularly diligent student, as she was today, Xiao Tzu allowed her to gather up sixty-four yarrow stalks and separate them into three bundles. After counting out the stalks of each bundle by threes, she would then tally up the stalks that remained. Bittersweet did this five more times to construct a hexagram or, as Xiao Tzu called it, a "window looking out onto one's immediate future." Today, she matched the upper and lower halves of the hexagram, then consulted the chart to produce hexagram 56 and, with the changing lines, hexagram 46.

Xiao Tzu consulted the appropriate passages in the *I Ching*. "Passage 56 reads, 'Traveling brings progress in small matters. Correct persistence when traveling brings good fortune.' And passage 46, 'Advancement brings exceptional progress. It would be useful to see the leader. Fear not. Movement towards the south results in good fortune.'"

"It's Delin who will be traveling south to Nanning tomorrow, not I," Bittersweet replied. "As for advancement, this summer's harvest was a rather poor one. From twenty *li* around, the villagers come to market and compliment me on my embroidered shoes, but no one has enough strings of cash to buy them."

"Still, this is what the *I Ching* divines for you, not your husband," Xiao Tzu insisted. "If you choose to heed these hexagrams, you should entertain modest goals and dutiful behavior. Wherever your travels take you, your stay will be temporary. You won't be putting down roots. When you find yourself in a disagreeable situation, move on. That's concerning the travel hexagram. As for the advancement hexagram, you stand to gain personal power, social status, and the esteem of others. Don't be afraid to approach persons with authority. Utilize your self-discipline and your strong will to achieve your aims."

Bittersweet dropped a few cash in the collection bowl near the doorway, bade Xiao Tzu good-bye till tomorrow, then trotted down the *hutong* towards home. When she arrived, visitors and guests were already congregating inside the small courtyard. She smiled to see how handsome and confident Delin looked as he sat in the parlor, laughing and chatting with the assembled guests.

In the kitchen where Bittersweet dropped off the wild fruits she had picked near the river to brew a makeshift tea, First Outside Sister-in-Law smiled and told her, "Feed them to the pigs. Your husband has bought real tea leaves for the occasion."

Da Mama, who was frying soybeans in the wok, added, trying to conceal her pride, "And tobacco for the men's pipes. And sugar cane for the children."

In her room, Bittersweet changed into her best tunic and combed her hair into a tight knot. She slipped on the thin silver hoop earrings her mother had given her on her wedding day almost two years ago. They were the very hoops her mother had worn the day she married Bittersweet's father.

Guests and well-wishers crowded into the house in such numbers that Bittersweet and the other women in her family could barely move about to serve them glasses of tea and bowls of fried soybeans.

Still, in the commotion, Bittersweet made out a single, gruff voice among the many guests. "Jumped into a well, she did, ending her life. Better that than bring shame to her family." Bittersweet turned and recognized the owner of the voice. It was one of the neighbors who had cursed her mother-in-law for assisting at her baby's birth. He was talking with the soothsayer who, as usual, was eager to hear what he had to say. "Seems she was seduced by one of the old priests at the Taoist temple. You know the building. On the northern edge of the village. Bad *feng-shui* there. Rumor has it she was carrying his baby, so she jumped into the well to put an end to her shame." He shook his head and sucked loudly on the brown stumps of his teeth. "A pity. She was a real looker and only fourteen."

"Whose well did she jump down?" Bittersweet asked, refilling his tea glass.

"Why, her family's well," he answered, as if there should be any question.

"I only ask because to jump down someone's well is to haunt that person forever. If the poor girl didn't have any hard feelings against her family, she would have drowned herself in the river. And if she had any hard feelings against the Taoist priest, she would have jumped down the temple's well."

"Bah! Women's logic!" the grizzled man guffawed, gripping his glass. "Don't be stingy. Fill it up to the brim."

"Who was the poor woman?" Bittersweet asked.

"Old Tang's third daughter," the soothsayer answered in the man's stead.

"The one they wanted to marry off?" Bittersweet said, pouring continuously so that the boiling liquid overflowed the glass and scalded the man's hand. "Oh, a hundred apologies. The one who refused because the man who had asked for her hand was not only stingy but also four times her age?"

"Three and a half!" the grizzled man bellowed, blowing on his hand, then clenching it into a fist. "And I would have paid a fair bride's price in the bargain. A little wench, she was! Wouldn't relent no matter how hard they beat her."

"Ninth, you've upset one of your guests," the soothsayer admonished, helping him wrap his hand in the dirty handkerchief he'd pulled from his pocket, "and here he came to wish your husband well."

"*Tai-tai*," Bittersweet answered, "he came to fill his stomach with free food and his ears with gossip."

"It's common knowledge that you have strong opinions and a mouth capable of voicing them," the soothsayer said, her voice more ominous than scolding. "If you can't avoid expressing them, you might at least try to make your words a bit more convoluted." She narrowed her eyes and tilted her head. "Just like you make your walk home from the river — so that it passes the Taoist temple."

Bittersweet looked at the old woman. "There's nothing wrong with taking the long way home. I enjoy the exercise."

"Did I say there was?" the soothsayer asked, feigning innocence. "But there are many long ways home, all of them at least as pleasant if not more so. One wonders why you choose that particular one, hmmm? The one that passes in front of a temple where only males may reside, and you an unaccompanied woman, and a married one at that."

"Only males may be monks and priests," Bittersweet replied, "but the followers of the Way may be anyone."

"Taoists!" the grizzled man growled. "All Chinese are Confucianists when successful, and Taoists when they're failures." He laughed, coughed up some phlegm, then spat on the floor.

"Have you become a Taoist?" the soothsayer asked, probing Bittersweet's face. "Are their priests so . . . persuasive? Or just a certain priest?"

Bittersweet was just about to answer when her father-in-law's voice rose above the others. His eyes glistened unnaturally and his bearing, usually rigid and restrained, was pliant as a boy's.

"Uh-oh," First Outside Sister-in-Law whispered to Bittersweet. "Baba's got his 'extra hour of daylight.'"

"A guest has brought him some medicine, as Baba likes to think of it, to ward off the evening chill," Bittersweet answered with a conspiratorial smile.

"It's not evening yet," First Outside Sister-in-Law reminded her.

"No, but now that Baba's had his medicine, we're in for a long night," their mother-in-law whispered.

When the three women laughed, they were promptly hushed by the crowd and Baba's stern look.

With a few puffs on his opium pipe, the usually taciturn village tutor was transformed into a storyteller. It was almost always the same story, but Bittersweet never failed to succumb to its spell. She could listen for hours as he recounted the history of his family.

"It was in the northwestern province of Kansu," he began, a wisp of smoke from his pipe encircling his head like a halo, "in the village of Lungshi, that the seeds of the Li clan were first sown. That subsequent generations were blown southward can be explained by one of the following two legends. The Yellow Emperor Qin Shi Huang ordered the Lin Canal to be built, so there would be a link between north and south China, so military transport and trade would be facilitated. Two generals by the name of Li were sent to Kweilin to supervise the construction of the canal. Smitten by the haunting beauty of the jade peaks and blue-green rivers, they stayed on, and all their descendants after them did the same. The second legend recounts a slow exodus of my ancestors starting in the Chin Dynasty. They wended their way from Kansu, to Honan, to Hunan, finally reaching Kwangsi Province in the Tang Dynasty. It was a trek that spanned a thousand years."

Stimulating his memory and loosening his tongue with another puff on his pipe, he continued. "My branch of the Li clan is singular in that, in every generation, there were fewer members than those in other branches of the clan. Worse still, generation after generation bore just a single son. Fearing that our family line would die out with so few males to perpetuate it, my ancestors performed endless good deeds to bring blessings — sons — into the family. The single-son curse was finally broken when my father's wife bore five sons, the first of whom is telling you this story. But a different curse befell us: the Taiping Long-Hairs ransacked our village, cut off our queues which marked our subservience to the Manchus, raped our women, and, because our house was the largest in the village, burnt it to the ground. My family, a family that had long been prosperous, was now destitute. Never mind that my father told the Long-Hairs that, as a boy, he'd been captured by soldiers of the Manchu emperor and used as a pack animal, forced to carry their weapons. Because of their abduction and ill treatment of him, my father hated the Manchu overlords and clamored for the Qing Dynasty's overthrow. But his hatred of the Qing meant nothing to the Taipings."

Baba's eyes glowered with disgust.

"It was not the Manchu but the foreign devil that I hated. I had heard rumors that they were barbarians, eaters of small children, men who smelled stronger than swine, but I thought it was idle gossip and so I didn't believe it. How could anyone be such a monster? Was not the foreigner still a man? One day, after I'd fulfilled my obligation of mourning towards my deceased father and mother, I read that the English in Hong Kong were looking for Chinese to work on the rubber plantations of Malaya. They needed a scribe to write letters home for the illiterate laborers they hired. This, I thought, would be a perfect opportunity to see a different part of the world and to learn, not from books this time, but through listening, observing, experiencing. Though my family begged me not to go, I answered the advertisement and shipped out first to Hong Kong, then to Malaya.

"What I saw in Malaya still makes my heart turn over," he continued. "The English had promised the workers a ten-hour day, two meals consisting of rice and vegetables, and the equivalent of three strings of cash daily. What the men actually received was one meal of rice gruel, an eighteen-hour workday, a string of cash a day, and inhuman conditions and treatment all the time. If the laborers did not cut the minimum number of trees assigned to them, they were docked pay, or food, frequently both. If they were surly or insolent, they were flogged. At night, they were tethered together with a certain kind of vine. If they struggled against their bonds, their perspiration soaked the vine which shortened as it dried, thus tightening about their limbs and cutting off their circulation. In several cases, a man's hand or foot had to be amputated because the vine had cut through flesh which, in that hot, humid country, soon putrefied with gangrene."

A murmur rose in the room. Some of the listeners shook their heads in disgust or grunted in dismay. All eyes remained on the man sitting in a cloud of opium smoke.

"Before too long, a resistance movement mounted among the workers. They wanted decent living conditions, wages, and food. Because I was educated and articulate, they chose me to be their representative. I went before the Chinese henchmen of the foreigners. These Chinese bullies were put in charge of the work crews and the flogging, so they could show their loyalty to their white masters and their disdain for their own blood. I demanded to meet the foreign devil, to tell him that the workers had demands that must be met. The British overlords accused me of being a rabble-rouser, of inciting the men to rebellion. They terminated my contract and put me on the next boat to Hong Kong without giving me the pay due me. I had to make my way home from Hong Kong by force of my own wits. During those weeks, when I begged for my food, slept in alleyways, and stowed away on a steamer to Canton, my heart grew hard with hatred for the foreign devils."

A low buzz of consensus circulated around the room.

"But imagine my dejection to return to my country, after my personal humiliation in Malaya, to discover that all of China and all my fellow countrymen were being humiliated daily, that, at the least threat, the weak and frightened Manchus were giving away bits and pieces of China, placing the country like a rotting carcass before the circling buzzards of England, Germany, Russia, France, even thanking them for taking the flesh so cleanly from the bone."

"Down with the decadent Manchus," someone shouted, coming to his feet and raising a fist in the air.

"It's not the Manchus you should curse — they're finished anyway — but Yuan Shi-kai," another cried. "That charlatan wants to out-emperor the Emperor and sit on the Dragon Throne for a thousand years."

"No!" someone exploded in fury. "It's as the tutor says. Our wrath should be vented at the evil foreign devils! Down with the infant-eaters!"

"The Manchus, Yuan Shi-kai, the foreign nations with their spheres of influence and their extraterritoriality . . ." The angry buzz and murmur ceased for Delin had begun to speak. "These are all the same side of the coin, all outside forces eating away at our country. What you see on the other side is the fragmentation and lack of unity of China, the isolation and backwardness of our country and her institutions. This makes China an easy target for the Manchus, for pretenders to the throne such as Yuan Shi-kai, and for foreign nations. When there is national unity in China, when there is political stability and economic prosperity in China, the scavengers will fall away from the carcass, and written on the bones of the carcass will be an oracle for China's future.

"I tell you, already there are signs. China is turning over in her sleep — not her grave as the foreign nations hope. A great foreign general,

75

one of the greatest generals in all of history, and an emperor too, once said of our country, 'China? There lies a sleeping giant. Let him sleep. For when China wakes, he will move the world.'"

That night, after the family retired, and while she refilled the lamps that had burned through the evening, Bittersweet thought of how eloquent her husband's words had been. They had touched her heart with a fervor that was passionate, just as the words of the Tao spoken by Xiao Tzu touched her heart with a power that was subtle and deep. In the glow of the oil lamp, Delin's face appeared. Bittersweet gasped when she heard him say her name, the one he had given her.

"I see you so often in my thoughts and dreams, I thought I'd conjured up your image," she apologized. "You spoke brilliantly this evening. Your words are still in my ears."

"One of the duties of an officer is to rouse his soldiers to action," Delin answered modestly. "It is *you* who are to be commended. My father tells me that you're his star pupil." Bittersweet blushed and looked away. The gentle face of Xiao Tzu flashed across her mind's eye, and she shook her head to erase the image. "Don't try to deny it. He says that your progress is unbelievable, that he's never seen anyone learn to read and write so quickly. It's as though you double the hour a day he teaches you through your own diligence."

Bittersweet, fearing that she might inadvertently reveal her secret, remained silent.

"Not like me," Delin admitted. "As a child I was the red chair sitter. We were too poor for me to attend school full-time, so at the age of six I embarked upon the family tradition of half-studying and half-farming with a ceremony called 'enlightenment of the dullness.' But my skull was too thick, and nothing could penetrate it — not even a whack from my father's bamboo rod. While the other children memorized a thousand characters, the *Four Books* and the *Five Classics*, I could only recall a line from the *Young People's Poems* which my mother had memorized: 'Generals and ministers of state come not from descent.' I'd rather have been daydreaming, lying on the back of our water buffalo, my hands behind my head, gazing up at the sky, and imagining that the clouds were bandits, Manchus, Englishmen, Taipings, and Boxers, charging, clashing, retreating, surrendering, all to my command. The only words I retained of my father's weren't those he spoke as a tutor but those he used to describe the history of our clan, the way he did tonight."

"He's very proud of you," Bittersweet said. "And your mother, too —so much so that she has to appease the jealous gods, and our envious neighbors, by emphasizing what a miserable student you were."

"So miserable that I quit school," Delin recalled. "Trouble was, at the weaving center in Kweilin where I was an apprentice, I was no better. I twisted and tangled the threads. I scorched and overstarched the cloth. In my frustration, I applied to the new school in town — Kwangsi Military Officers Training School — and was accepted, to my parents' deep disappointment."

"Perhaps then, but they couldn't feel more differently about your choice today."

"And you?" he asked her, turning up the flame of the oil lamp and looking into her face. "How do you feel to be married to a piece of bad iron?"

Bittersweet looked down and smiled. "If I was tentative two years ago, I, too, couldn't feel more differently about my choice today."

Delin lowered the flame until it was almost spent. He leaned over, his face so close to Bittersweet's that she felt the warmth of his breath against her cheek. He blew out the tiny spark with a sigh. "It's not easy for a soldier to be away from his wife and family for so long. It'll be even longer in the days to come, now that the two Kwangs have declared war on each other." He walked towards their bedroom. "The morning comes early tomorrow," he said, looking over his shoulder at her. Wordlessly, Bittersweet rose and followed him.

Weeks passed without word from Delin. Then, a letter arrived, sent from Kwangtung Province, as were his subsequent letters, though each from a different town or village, each sent at irregular intervals, sometimes two in a month, sometimes nothing for months on end. But Bittersweet's own progress in reading and answering the letters was very regular, despite the fact that, since her husband's going-away party, she had not returned to the Taoist temple and the tutelage of Xiao Tzu. On her walks to and from the river to wash the family's clothes, she chose a different *hutong*, one far from the village outskirts where her former teacher lived and prayed. But in her drawer, under her homework and her class assignments for her father-in-law, she had hidden the eighty-one *Tao Te Ching* tetragrams that she had copied with Xiao Tzu's help. Every night Bittersweet picked a passage to read before going to bed. The words put her heart at ease and assuaged her loneliness, all the more now that her father had died. Younger Brother arrived in Dragon's Head, dressed in white sackcloth, to tell her the news and to take Bittersweet back to her natal village for the funeral. Over two days, she and the family she had once belonged to wept over her dead father's body, walked beside his casket, and saw it interred not far from her old house in an unadorned grave befitting a poor farmer. Then she returned to Dragon's Head and the house of her mother-in-law, for Dragon's Head was her home and she was the second daughter-in-law in Da Mama's house.

"Today's the day that you should try to read every character." Baba held up Delin's latest letter in front of Bittersweet. "Right now," he prodded her. "Aloud. To your mother-in-law and me. Consider it a class assignment."

There was an energy and exuberance in her father-in-law's manner that made Bittersweet take the opened letter from him and begin to read immediately. In it, Delin spoke of battles lost and won, tattered summer uniforms in winter, straw sandals in place of leather boots, and inadequate food. Then, he spoke of the end of the war between the two Kwangs, his own promotion to captain, and finally his wish that Bittersweet, now that the civil war was over, join him in Kwangtung and live by his side. When she finished reading, Bittersweet blinked at the letter, then folded it carefully along its creases.

"Well done," her father-in-law said. "A perfect score, yet you look as though you just failed the course."

"Forgive me," Bittersweet murmured, "but my heart is divided. I'm both happy and sad."

"Your husband asks you to go to Kwangtung to live with him," Da Mama said, scrutinizing her daughter-in-law's face. "Have you no answer for him?"

Bittersweet pressed Delin's letter between her palms. A woman's duty, she well knew, was to serve her parents-in-law and obey her husband. Yet if she obeyed her husband and went to him in Kwangtung, she would relinquish her obligations towards her parents-in-law. And if she stayed in Dragon's Head to perform the duties of a proper daughter-in-law, she would be remiss in her duties to her husband.

"Da Mama, as a daughter-in-law, I dare not be the one to speak," she said with perfect propriety. "The decision to go or stay is not mine, but yours, to make. Whatever you say I will do."

Baba leaned back in his chair and nodded approvingly. Da Mama looked at him, for his demeanor would help her formulate her reply.

"For the past two years, Delin has been away. For the past two years, no one has been at his side to take care of him. We are many in this house. Your younger brother- and sisters-in-law are growing up and can take on more responsibilities. One member less won't make much difference. You should go out into the world. Husband and wife should be together." Da Mama looked at her husband. "If we don't let you go, I don't know when I will hold a grandson in my arms."

And so it was decided. Bittersweet, in the company of a maiden aunt and an aide that Delin had promised to send, would walk to the city of Kweilin, then travel by boat and sedan chair to Xinghui County where Delin and his army were stationed. It would be a journey of three days.

"Xinghui County," Delin wrote in his next letter, "is one of the richest counties in Kwangtung Province. Many of the young men here have left home to seek their fortunes in foreign lands. The lucky ones return home with enough money to invest in business, commerce, and trade, and they don't have to worry for the rest of their lives."

"But what of the unlucky ones?" Bittersweet asked Baba. "Fortune or no, why would any Chinese want to leave home and family to run the risk of danger and hardship in an unknown country?"

"Why, Ninth?" Baba replied. "Because the ruling Qing Dynasty, being weak and corrupt, is unable to stop foreigners from carving up our country into spheres of influence for their own profit and pleasure, all the while denying us the rights and privileges they take for themselves. Why go abroad? Because warlords and their private armies roam the countryside waging war against each other, terrorizing the peasantry and preventing them from growing their crops and making a living. Do you wonder that those who can, those who dare, leave for Southeast Asia, even America, to return home in better times?"

Bittersweet listened patiently, mulling over her father-in-law's excited words. From what she had seen in her twenty-six years, life in Dragon's Head ran like a silken thread, smooth and straight and without knots. Civil war, if civil war there was, didn't happen here, but raged far away in some remote town, upon some distant battlefield. Though the family farm was only twenty *mou*, every single *mou* was theirs. They owned their land and no one could take it away from them.

The day Delin's aide finally arrived, Bittersweet was busy packing with her aunt's assistance and instructions. "You don't have to pack so much," her aunt told her. "City women dress differently than women from the country." Bittersweet didn't reply but unpacked all but her best clothes and shoes. She emptied her pouch of silver jewelry and put every piece on.

The aide's mouth twitched and he coughed politely into his hand. "Very attractive, but so many bracelets and necklaces might be an invitation for a thief or bandit."

Chastened, Bittersweet blushed but, to save face, announced, "I'm wearing them in case we meet soldiers of an enemy warlord. If they take you prisoner, I can bargain for your life."

The next morning, before the sun was fully up and after Bittersweet had said her farewells, the threesome stepped outside the gate and into the shadowy *hutongs* of Dragon's Head.

"No, this way," Bittersweet said, indicating the direction opposite from the way the aide and her aunt were headed. "There's one last farewell I must make."

When they reached the gate of the Taoist temple, it was shut tight. After Bittersweet's third knock, the bolt was pulled back and the heavy wooden doors creaked open. A wizened old priest, upon seeing the young woman, asked her to wait. He scurried away and Xiao Tzu returned in his place. When he saw who his visitor was, he smiled and opened the door wider. Only when he noticed her traveling companions and the suitcases they carried did Bittersweet speak. "The hexagram was right. I'm going on a journey both south and east. To Kwangtung. My husband has sent for me."

"Kwangtung is far," Xiao Tzu replied. "I wish you a safe and pleasant trip." They both lapsed into an uncomfortable silence, having so much more to say. "Do you plan to keep up with your studies?" he asked finally.

Bittersweet nodded. "In fact, the pages of the *Tao Te Ching* that I copied with your help are in one of the suitcases." She looked away. "I couldn't come back to the temple. My duties at home prevented me."

"I would have thought that the many tongues wagging in the village were an even greater obstacle."

Bittersweet looked at Xiao Tzu, her eyes full of gratitude. "I'd better go now before the sun grows too hot for walking. I just wanted to say good-bye."

"*Zai jian*, Bittersweet. Till we meet again."

The sound of her name, the name he had never uttered till now, touched her. One of the many tears she had withheld during her farewells to her family now escaped. Quickly, she pulled on the gates, closing them before he could see.

Chapter 6
City Life
(1917)

By the time Bittersweet and her two companions reached the outer gate of Dragon's Head, the villagers were already on their way to market or milling about their doorways. They all knew why she was traveling that day, and they wished her a pleasant journey. As she answered them with words of thanks and farewell, she realized she was already homesick for the *hutongs*, the rice paddies, the limestone peaks, and the green river of her husband's village, and she was already anxious about being a simple rustic in a big city.

With only a short stop in Liangjiang market for lunch, the small group arrived in Kweilin by early evening. Shops and offices were closing up for the night, and workers and customers were filing out onto the streets. The sheer number of people amazed Bittersweet who stared at them.

"Look!" she gasped, grabbing her aunt by the arm and pointing to the sidewalk in front of her. A few feet ahead, a woman in a sun-faded silk *cheongsam* minced, hobbled, and swayed on stumps of feet. So these were the "golden lilies only three inches long."

"She walks by herself," Bittersweet's aunt sniffed. "She's not from a good family. Women of rich and important families always have a maidservant at their side to support them."

"What are you gaping at?" the woman of the golden lilies sneered when Bittersweet passed her. "Have you never seen a bound foot?" She glanced at Bittersweet's feet, then whispered something to the effete young man who was walking beside her. They both burst out laughing.

"I'd heard that city women with their golden lilies were gentle creatures," Bittersweet said to her aunt. "They're indeed unsteady on their feet, but by their speech and demeanor they're not as gentle as I'd been told. Good family or no, rich family or poor," Bittersweet continued loud enough for the tittering couple to hear, "I wouldn't want to be one of them, to suffer what they have suffered, to have the

82

arches of my feet broken, my toes turned under and bound tightly with strips of cloth so that I tottered and faltered instead of walked. Rich or poor, great or insignificant, a women with natural feet stands on her own. She has no need of a maidservant to support her."

The couple was already out of sight but Bittersweet, knowing they had heard her, felt vindicated.

"But honestly, Auntie, do you really think stumps that size are attractive? How could I carry heavy loads or go out in the paddies to plant and harvest with feet like those?"

The old woman merely shook her head and laughed at her niece's naïveté.

That night, Bittersweet slept on a bed tented with fine mosquito netting in a hotel lit with electric lamps. The following morning she ate small steamed buns filled with sweet red bean paste and drank chrysanthemum tea — both items she had never had before. For the first time, she sat on the deck of a boat not paddled by men but powered by steam from burning coal. The vessel, though it traveled upstream, was swift enough that her face was buffeted by a strong breeze, and she thrilled to feel it and to know that she was venturing out into the world, traveling to be reunited with her husband. The stands of bamboo that lined the shores in thick clumps looked more feathery than any she had ever seen. The children who waded out in the river to wash the family water buffalo seemed unusually playful and spontaneous. The karst peaks that stood like sentinels along both banks appeared mysterious and majestic. And the river itself, with its constantly changing views, was like a variegated silken ribbon that she wound upon her memory.

Finally, cloistered in a covered sedan chair and tired from the long boat ride, Bittersweet dozed intermittently and reflected upon the incredible things she had seen. By far, the most awesome sight was her first glimpse of a foreign devil. She had seen the devil in Canton just before she and her aunt had found three sedan chair bearers to take them to Xinghui.

"Look!" her aunt had whispered, shielding the words behind her raised hand. "A *da bizi*!"

Bittersweet glanced in the direction of her aunt's steady stare and, sure enough, there was a human being — that is, he had all the trappings of being a human if a rather strange one. In the center of his face was a nose so protuberant that her aunt's description of him as a "big nose" seemed understated. He moved his head about with rapid, bird-like movements, the great beak on his face slashing the air in all directions. But even more odd was the depth at which his eyes were sunk in his face. They were like two stones buried in dark caves where light might never reach. When the *da bizi* glanced up and the sunlight finally did reach his sockets, Bittersweet saw that his eyes were a pale blue. His curly hair was yellow as ripe corn, and his skin was the tint and texture of a plump piglet.

"You mustn't stare," her aunt admonished her. "It's rude."

"As is a mouth that's hanging ajar," Bittersweet replied, to which her aunt promptly clamped hers shut.

Finally, the thud of the sedan chair jolted Bittersweet awake. She slid open the door and peered out. "Are we in Xinghui yet?" she asked the bearer. She squinted her eyes against the bright sunlight. When her eyes could focus, she saw three military officers in immaculate gray-green wool uniforms. Two had their backs towards her and a third stood facing her. After blinking several times, Bittersweet recognized this third man as Delin.

"Indeed you are," he said, extending his hand and helping her out of the chair while Bittersweet's aunt haggled with the bearers, and the aide counted and inspected the luggage.

Only when Bittersweet's eyes were fully adjusted to the light did she realize how handsome, poised, and distinguished her husband looked. She glanced down at her black dress, gray from the dust of the road and wrinkled from the long ride and her nap. Suddenly, she was ashamed of the plain, homespun cotton. It hadn't been that long ago that she had swelled with pride over her talent at the loom. Embarrassed, she cupped her hand about her bun and felt for stray wisps.

"You've cut off your queue," she said for want of something to say, conscious that the other two officers were looking at her and realizing, too late, that Delin had cut off his queue over a year ago. In the early stages of the Boxer Rebellion, it had been dangerous to sport a queue, and also dangerous *not* to sport one. Members of the secret Boxer Society had been known to stop unsuspecting men and declare: "Lose your queue, or lose your life!" To the Boxers, queues were the hated symbol of Chinese subservience to the Manchus. If a man allowed the Boxers to cut off his queue, he was safe from further interrogation at their hands, but he had only exchanged one danger for another. Now he had to run the risk of the Manchu soldiers mistaking him for an outlaw Boxer. Some Chinese men kept their severed queue and wore it fastened under their skull cap — or didn't wear it, as the situation warranted — but a mere tug on the long braid revealed any duplicity.

"The Qing Dynasty is dead," Delin laughed, brushing the dust off her clothes. "No self-respecting Chinese wears a queue nowadays. A republican China is being born."

Bittersweet blushed. "Should you be doing this — an army captain — in front of your fellow officers and your aide?" she whispered, mortified.

"It's because I am a captain and rank above those two officers and my aide that I may do so," he answered, with a smile. "Besides, you're *very* dusty!" He opened the back door of an automobile and motioned to Bittersweet and her aunt to get in. The aide slid into the front seat behind the driving wheel while the two officers mounted their motorcycles. "You can enter. It's fine," Delin assured her. "I want to show you our new home."

With the two motorcycles leading the way, the car — starting, stopping and honking its horn to clear the road in front of it of pedestrians, pedicabs, rickshaws, and lumbering oxen — finally arrived at a large two-story house in Xinghui City. It was a house of plastered stone with glass windows, more stout than graceful, but sturdy and well-made. A manservant, dressed in a peasant's tunic, wide pants, and cloth-soled shoes, bowed to Bittersweet as she approached the front door.

"He will help you with the housework, the cleaning, and the laundering," Delin told Bittersweet. "Another manservant will assist you with the cooking and marketing."

She looked up and down the house, then at the manservant who had come to greet her. "But you've spent a fortune on this house," she whispered as her husband led her inside.

"It's merely rented, not bought," he replied, pleased it had made an impression on her.

"Still!" she exclaimed, trying to calculate what it must cost to rent so spacious and comfortable a house. As a lieutenant at officers training school, Delin had earned thirty-four *kuai* a month, of which he had sent home ten *kuai* to add to the family finances. As a captain, could he be making that much more?

"Delin," Bittersweet whispered, the manservant still in attendance

85

upon them, "we don't need two menservants. Surely, one will do. The cleaning of the house and marketing I'll leave up to him, but the cooking and laundering is my work to do."

He waved away her suggestion, thinking she was trying to spare him an expense he couldn't afford. But Bittersweet persisted.

"Today I live in a big house in the big city. But for all my life, I have lived in the country. I'm used to doing the cooking, the laundry and more. What should I do if not what I've always done?"

"I'll grant you your wish of a sole manservant, but you must do what other officers' wives do. That way you'll also have company. I'm at army headquarters so much of the time, and I don't want you to be lonely."

Bittersweet, not knowing what other officers' wives did and not wanting to appear ignorant by asking, nodded in assent.

Soon after her arrival in Xinghui, Bittersweet decided to send for her widowed mother so that she could finally enjoy a comfortable life in the spacious home of her son-in-law. But after only three weeks, her mother was ready to return to Village Village.

"The rice crop is ready for harvesting," she explained. "And though I'm no longer able to help your brothers gather it, I still need to see what our land has given us this year. Poor land though it is, it is our land. The fields are my home."

After her mother left Xinghui, Bittersweet planted a small vegetable garden, for she, too, missed the fields. Now she could serve her husband the very freshest *bok-choy*, *guy-lan*, and tomatoes.

One day, Bittersweet was on her hands and knees, weeding the freshly-hoed earth, when her manservant appeared bearing the news that she had a visitor. Following him into the parlor, she found a woman — with her young maidservant and menservants who were holding six fancy red boxes containing cakes and sweetmeats.

"Tell Li *Tai-tai*, the mistress of the house, that a distinguished visitor is here to see her," the woman ordered Bittersweet.

"I am Li *Tai-tai*," Bittersweet acknowledged simply, wiping her hands on her gardening clothes.

The woman's face fell, but she quickly composed herself with a nervous, tinkling laugh. After mincing across the room on bound feet encased in tiny tasseled brocade slippers, she extended a pink and white hand, soft as a newborn's, and placed it on Bittersweet's. Several rings of brushed gold and polished jade encircled her fingers. Bracelets ran up her forearm from her wrist to her elbow. Her face was a mask of white rice powder, and her lips, which she drew back into an overly-wide smile, were painted blood red. Imperiously, she ordered her menservants to set down the boxes, and then she told all but her personal maidservant (who was barely more than a child) to withdraw.

"Li *Tai-tai*," the woman said, still holding Bittersweet's hand and introducing herself as Mrs. Fan, "I apologize for not having come sooner, but my husband and I have been on the giving or receiving end of parties every day for the last four weeks. Finally, I'm able to welcome you to our city. Now that you're here, I hope we'll be very good friends. If there's anything you'd like to do or have done for you, just send your manservant to tell me. I can accompany you to the opera, to go shopping — anywhere your heart desires. Captain Li is terribly busy, but I would be delighted to keep you company."

She narrowed her eyes, then let her gaze flit over the parlor. Clearly, she was using her observations here as a measuring stick to gauge the number, size, and contents of the other rooms she supposed the house contained. "If you're unhappy with this house, just tell me," she continued, smiling at Bittersweet, who found the woman's perfume so strong she felt faint. "My husband and I have an empty house in town, larger and more opulent than this one. We'd be honored if you and Captain Li decided to live in it."

That evening, when Delin returned home for dinner, Bittersweet told him of the strange visitor who had come to see her.

Delin's forehead creased in displeasure.

"Was I wrong to receive her?" Bittersweet asked.

"Fan *Tai-tai* is the wife of a very rich merchant in Xinghui," Delin said. "It's better that we don't associate with people like the Fans, let alone befriend them. Not only am I a captain in the army," he explained, "I hold an important civil position in Xinghui — acting county commissioner. The activities of all the local merchants fall under my jurisdiction, including those of Mr. Fan. He's one of the several Xinghui merchants who have offered me many 'favors' which I have politely but firmly declined. Since you haven't touched the boxes of cakes and sweetmeats, we'll send them back tomorrow with a note saying that we're allergic to refined sugar. They'll understand the message without either of us losing face."

Delin smiled to himself. "Fan *Tai-tai* is similar to her husband. She was hoping to succeed where he failed. Unfortunately for Fan *Tai-tai*, you are similar to me in your determination not to succumb to her overtures. Such 'gifts' are mere disguises for compromises upon my honor."

Had Delin initially harbored any anxieties that Bittersweet would fall prey to the skillful machinations of city folk, clearly those fears were unfounded. If anything, Bittersweet's avoidance of her new neighbors caused her husband a different sort of concern. As she had promised him, she sampled the teas and outings to which she was invited by the other officers' wives, but she soon tired of them. What did she have in common with these women who spent all their time in the pursuit of pleasure, playing cards and mahjong, eating out in expensive restaurants, and attending Cantonese opera? How could she answer them when they laughed and made fun of her — a captain's wife who did her own laundry and grew her own vegetables!

"What would you have me do?" Bittersweet replied, in frustration, to their teasing.

"Why, enjoy yourself, of course!" they answered. "*We* enjoy *ourselves*. Why shouldn't we, now that all under heaven is chaos? Our husbands, being military men and living on the battlefield, can die at any moment. At any moment, we could be widows. Then, what would we do? We could remarry, but to follow a second husband would bring us shame. And if it didn't bring us shame, it certainly would bring us no honor."

Bittersweet listened, at first in bewilderment to their incomprehensible Cantonese, a dialect that clattered on the palate and against the ear with its seven tones and its many hard consonants. Then, when she could speak enough Cantonese to hold a halting conversation, she listened in silence to their explanations but thought even less of their words. She found that she felt no differently when she accompanied Delin to the many social functions he was required to attend. There she met the husbands of the wives she had found so little in common with, and though she didn't agree with the women's breezy attitude towards life, now at least she understood the reason for it; their husbands were no different. They, too, believed in having fun, attending performances of Cantonese opera, eating in fancy restaurants, and drinking themselves into a stupor. When she asked one of them why he clung to such a life, he answered, "We have no idea if or when we'll die in battle. Chances are it will be when. So while we're alive we must eat good food and drink fine wine. When we die, we want to die with our bellies full."

"If you're so sure you'll die in battle, why did you join the army in the first place?" Bittersweet asked.

"It's either that or die a slow death of starvation on the family farm ravaged by flood or drought, or be forced to join a bunch of bandits or a warlord army. For now at least, we get decent pay. And besides, the ladies prefer men in uniform."

"Thankfully, not everyone shares your reasons for joining the army," Bittersweet said bluntly, turning away. "Thankfully, there are those like my husband who have joined the army to save our country."

The next day, Delin called Bittersweet in to his study.

"You've lived in Xinghui now a little over two years. Have you been happy here?"

Bittersweet told him that she was — happy to keep house for him, to cook his food, and wash his clothes, happy to work in the garden growing vegetables for the table.

"That's your relationship to me. What about your relationship to others — your friendships with the other officers' wives, with the officers under my charge?"

Bittersweet admitted that she had little to do with them, for they had little in common.

"Certain people are saying that you don't behave like an officer's wife, that you avoid the other wives, that you ask questions of their husbands that they have difficulty answering. Such are the things I've been hearing, and it troubles me that you don't have friends to talk to and appropriate activities to give your time and attention to."

"That will soon change," Bittersweet promised him.

"Then you'll accept the invitations of the officers' wives?" Delin asked, brightening. "With the officers, you'll speak about the weather, and smile and laugh at their corny jokes, and disregard their cruder ones? Or, if you can't do that, you'll at least feign incomprehension of their Cantonese?"

"I won't have any time to spend with the officers' wives in mahjong parlors or in teahouses, or with the officers at dinner parties," Bittersweet replied. "You see, my time and my hands will be full . . . with the child that is coming."

"Child?" Delin stammered. "You mean, you're. . . ."

"Yes," Bittersweet said, searching his face for his feelings, "to be born in seven months time."

Though he was a captain and commanded many men, Delin slid from his chair onto his knees. He placed his cheek to her belly and wrapped his arms around her broad hips. "That it be a son. That it be the big happiness of a son," he said, completely forgetting why he had called his wife in to see him in the first place.

Chapter 7
Big Happiness
(1918)

Bittersweet was weightless. The glass cylinder with the sharp needle had infused her with a liquid that released her body from gravity, from all earthly sensation. Now, spirits dressed in white gowns with white masks over their noses and mouths hovered by her bed. She knew they'd tightly tucked in the sheets so she wouldn't float away. I'm in the Land Beyond the Yellow Springs, Bittersweet thought, surprised that she didn't feel sadness to have left the world behind. Perhaps, her next rebirth would place her back on earth as a higher human being. She'd be without her mouth, the one that refused to swallow inappropriate words, and without the temper that helped her form those words. Or, maybe, for her derelictions in this life, she would come back in a lower form. Maybe as a water buffalo. If that were the case, she hoped her master would be Delin in *his* rebirth, for she knew how much he had loved the family water buffalo when he was a child and what care he had given it. Or perhaps she'd come back as a cloud, floating above all things, detached from humans, from all the poor creatures imprisoned by joys and sorrows. Perhaps that's what she was now.

"Forceps," she heard a *da bizi* say. The *da bizi* had tried to conceal his big nose behind the gauze mask, but it pushed against the fabric anyway. Bittersweet giggled, though she knew that was impolite. But for a cloud to giggle was fine, she told herself, giggling again. She winced. Her cloud had come to earth and fallen into the sea. The sea was heaving in a storm; its waves were pounding against a rocky shore, rolling inland then out again, expanding on the shore, then contracting painfully. Quicker and quicker, the waves came and went, contracting and expanding. Then, the storm subsided. A crow was cawing above the thinning clouds, calling forth the sun.

"Son," she heard a Chinese doctor say behind his gauze mask. "You have a fine son."

Bittersweet looked down at the infant lying on her breast; his black-crow-feather hair, wet from her womb, glistened. She placed his cawing mouth to her breast, and her son stopped crying.

"A son," she murmured, drunk with pride and the doctor's gravity-defying injection.

"I'll go tell Captain Li to come in," the Chinese doctor said. "He'll be happy to know."

No, Bittersweet wanted to call after him, afraid for her husband. I'm unclean, contaminated by the filth of birth. Then she remembered that she was in a Western-style hospital in modern Canton and not in her mother-in-law's simple home in rural Dragon's Head.

Delin came rushing into the room, anxiety and happiness struggling for predominance on his flushed face. When he saw Bittersweet suckling the child, he stopped short as if he had just seen an apparition. His visored cap fell from his hands.

"Come closer," Bittersweet said in a faint voice, "and take a look at your new son." The baby was wrapped snugly in a clean white blanket.

"He looks like an ear of corn in its sheaf," Delin said awkwardly, at a loss for words.

The doctors gathered around, their masks lowered about their necks, smiling and nodding in amusement or agreement.

"Is he healthy?" Delin asked, looking at the head doctor, a foreigner. "And strong? And my wife? Is she well?"

The Chinese doctor answered that they were, that his son wouldn't catch the three- or the seven-day virus for they had worn rubber gloves and used only sterilized implements.

Giving birth had exhausted Bittersweet, and in spite of the commotion and admiration of her husband and the hospital staff, she fell soundly asleep, her child still at her breast.

"We'll call him Youlin," Delin said to the Chinese doctor who translated his words for the foreigners in the room.

"Son of Delin," he explained in English.

They all nodded, for it was the perfect name for the child.

"In my home village, a woman who has just given birth is back in the fields a few days later, fortified by several eggs and some glutinous rice," Bittersweet protested, while her husband straightened her blanket and tucked her into her bed at home.

"You'll stay in bed for a month," he told her. "I've hired a nurse to take care of you." Then he called the manservant and told him to buy the ingredients for *gai jow*, or mother's brew, which the cook would prepare to revitalize his wife's health and fill her breasts with milk. "Go to the grocer's and buy a freshly killed chicken, wood fungus, dried lily buds, ginger root, peanuts, and rice wine," Delin said, handing the man a few bills. "Also get some pig's feet, black vinegar, and extra ginger, and tell cook to make some pickled tonic broth for your mistress."

By the end of the month, Bittersweet was fully restored to health, but Delin was called away on military matters. After another few months, when Delin returned, arrangements had been made for Youlin's completion-of-the-month party which, by Chinese reckoning, celebrates a child's first year on earth. Bittersweet was so happy with her child that she cheerfully extended invitations to all her husband's colleagues and their wives, though only months before she cringed at the thought of being in the same room with them.

On the day of Youlin's completion-of-the-month party, Bittersweet stood by Delin's side, receiving the compliments and congratulations of all those gathered in the house. Meanwhile, the nurse showed off the handsome infant in his red silk coat, his tiger's cap, and his soft silk slippers that sported two eyes so that the wearer might never take a faulty step. But Bittersweet's smile faded when she opened the gifts the guests had brought and saw how expensive they were, far too costly for so young a child: ivory Buddhas, arm and ankle bracelets of twenty-three karat gold, jade charms, and lockets to "lock" a baby son into this world so that he might never leave for the spirit world.

"Is it seemly," she asked her husband when he wasn't receiving yet another guest, "that our guests should give such expensive presents to a child just one year old? In Dragon's Head, for a poor family. . . ."

"A baby's completion-of-the-month party is a very special occasion," he hushed her. "Our guests want to celebrate it with good wishes and thoughtful gifts. How can we refuse their generosity?"

"Yes, but. . . ." Bittersweet remembered Fan *Tai-tai*, her entourage of servants, cakes, and sweetmeats, and Delin's reaction to that earlier extravagant gesture.

"We're no longer in Dragon's Head," he reminded her gently. "Our guests aren't poor farmers. What's unseemly in Dragon's Head is appropriate in Xinghui."

Bittersweet looked around at her house. The rooms had been festooned with red good luck banners, couplets, and garlands of flowers.

She looked at the beautiful silk *cheongsams*, the pearl earrings, the gold necklaces, and jade bracelets on the wives of the officers, then at the ruddy, perspiring faces of the husbands who were singing drinking songs and playing finger games to see who must next empty the cup of *mao-tai* without once lowering it from his lips. Bittersweet brought her eyes back to her husband's face, then lowered them, nodding.

"It is so," she said. "We're not living in the country but in the big city. Our guests are not poor farmers but proud military officers and their sophisticated wives." In so saying, and despite the fact that she herself was wearing a silk *cheongsam*, pearl studs in her ears, and an apple-green jade ring on her finger, Bittersweet recognized herself for what she was: a simple farm woman from a village so small and insignificant that it didn't have a proper name but was called Village Village. She was aware of being out of character in fancy clothes, out of place in a great city, and out of touch with her true nature in acting the part of the wife of an army captain and civil administrator.

"Are you well?" Delin asked, for her face had suddenly grown pale.

She made light of his question by waving her hand before her face — all the better to hide her expression. "I still haven't gained back all my strength," she lied, "even though Youlin arrived several months ago. But I'm growing in vigor and happiness every day. Oh, look!" she exclaimed, relieved by the opportunity to distract her husband's attention. "The career tray!"

The manservant entered the parlor bearing a carved teak tray which held child-sized versions of an abacus, symbolizing a merchant's calling; a calligrapher's brush, symbolizing a scholar's life; a scythe, symbolizing a farmer's life; and a doll dressed in warrior's garb, wielding a pike in one hand and a sword in the other. The manservant set the tray on a low table while the guests gathered around it, waiting for the nurse to reappear with Youlin in her arms. Everyone cooed and clapped at the sight of the pretty infant gazing around curiously.

"This is what you should be looking at," his father said, pinching the child's chubby cheek and tapping the career tray to redirect the boy's attention. Out shot the baby's two stubby arms, their fingers working as though independent of the rest of his body. His eyes traveled from object to object on the tray, while his torso strained against the arms of his nurse.

"No cheating now," a guest laughed. "The first object he touches will be his chosen calling."

The manservant, who had seen to it that the warrior doll occupied the center of the tray, while the other items formed a distant circumference, blushed and shook his head, as if to deny any favoritism in the arrangement.

A murmur rose from the crowd.

"The abacus. He'll be a merchant when he grows up."

Bittersweet looked at Delin and saw that his smile had become rigid and artificial. Their son had not even looked at the warrior doll but immediately hooked his tiny fingers onto the abacus which he was now shaking like a rattle.

Fan *Xiansheng* thrust out his chest and his rouged and bejewelled wife also smiled and nodded in self-congratulation. "An astute and wealthy merchant," Fan *Xiansheng* said, adding arrogantly, "like me!" The merchant raised his glass to Delin. It would have been an unpardonable insult for Delin not to acknowledge the toast, but he brought his glass just to the level of his lips and he merely wet his mouth on the rim.

"It's only a game," Bittersweet consoled him. "Something to amuse our guests — nothing more."

She forgot her own heavy heart, for she was far better able to withstand her own unhappiness than witness her husband's. Delin's mouth curved into a grateful smile. "If Youlin had chosen the doll, it would have accorded with the wishes of his father — himself a child so poor he had no career tray to chose from. All I had were my father's stories, my own hopes and dreams for China, and the belief that soldiers and ministers of state are not born but formed by self-discipline and desire. When our son is older, I will tell him stories of war and life on the battlefield. I will select the appropriate studies and the best military school in the county for his education. Youlin will have a second chance at the career tray. He will choose a vocation closer to his father's heart and his country's needs."

The ominous clouds of civil war were again gathering on the horizon between Kwangsi and Kwangtung. To keep them at bay, Bittersweet found herself following her husband and his army first to Huiyang, then to Gaozhou, then to Zhaoqingau. No sooner were they settled in their new home, no sooner had she accustomed herself to a new house and new acquaintances, than they had to move to another town. Travel was slow and arduous and relocating was physically and emotionally draining, especially with a small son. Sometimes, looking about her in an unfamiliar house, with boxes and crates yet to be opened, Bittersweet would despair and grow sullen and withdrawn. Then she would remind herself of her mother-in-law's words — that a wife's duty was to live with her husband, a wife's obligation was to take care of him and make him happy. Then, she would watch her husband and son at play, watch them talking, laughing and challenging each other to word puzzles and finger games, and her mood would brighten. Only when Delin was with his son did Bittersweet see her husband totally free and at peace, and seeing him thus put her heart at ease.

Still, she could not always conceal her unhappiness from Delin. What she thought she often said, and what she didn't say she might as well have said, for it was already written on her face.

"But all this uprooting, all this replanting in foreign soil," she asked her husband one day, as he was helping Youlin set up a line of miniature soldiers, "doesn't it bother you?"

"A soldier has no home," he answered matter-of-factly. "The battlefield is his home."

Bittersweet settled back in her chair where she was sewing new shoes for Youlin. Again, she was embroidering the shoes with eyes, to guide his steps through life. Gazing at her husband, she sighed. How adaptable he was to circumstance. With calm deliberation and poise, he confronts the unknown and the uncertain — even the prospect of death. Her eyes floated to her lap and she vowed to imitate her husband's perfect equanimity.

"You-lin! You-lin!"

Bittersweet ran to the back of the house, then returned to the front, then searched every room before she ran out the front door, across the courtyard, and into the street. She looked up and down the road, shading her eyes with the flat of her hand. There was no sign of her little boy.

"Li *Tai-tai*, I've looked everywhere," her manservant panted, running out to her. "I can't find the young master anywhere."

Bittersweet grabbed her head between her hands. "Do you think it's possible that he's been kidnapped?" she moaned. They both knew that bandits roamed the nearby hills and that kidnappings, especially of children, were not uncommon. Bittersweet's hands slipped from about her face and came together as if she were praying.

96

"No, Madam," he said, hoping to reassure her. "The little master has just wandered off somewhere. He'll wander home soon. The gods will see to it."

"That may be," Bittersweet decided, unfolding her hands and starting down the road with determination, "but they might find a bit of human assistance helpful. No, you must stay home," she ordered when he tried to follow her. "If Youlin returns and finds no one here, he'll be frightened and wander away again."

"But you are a *tai-tai*," the manservant replied. "It's inappropriate for you to walk unescorted outside the walls of your home."

But Bittersweet didn't hear him. With her big feet and her long strides, she was already out of shouting distance, and, even if she were still close, her anxiety would have made her deaf to her manservant, just as she was now blind to the stares of the townspeople as she strode past them on her way to find her husband. When she did find him, he was at army headquarters, in the middle of a chess game with a fellow officer. Several other officers looked on, or smoked, or chatted together. Excitedly, Bittersweet excused herself for the interruption and explained that she wouldn't have come if Youlin weren't missing and, she feared, kidnapped.

Delin listened impassively while she spoke. "The boy has not been kidnapped," he said when she finished. "I guarantee it. After all, who would want to kidnap the son of a mere captain?"

Hearing this, the other officers in the room laughed, but Bittersweet, beside herself with worry, exploded, "How can you joke about such a matter?"

The officers' faces went white and their smiles froze. Bittersweet, though already shamed by her outburst, continued nonetheless, "You don't care about your own son! You care more about your soldiers . . . and your chessboard!" In her fury, she upended it, scattering the chess pieces about the room. Stumbling to the doorway, half-blinded by tears of rage and humiliation, she made her way back home, not stopping once till she was safe within its gates. There in the courtyard, riding on the shoulders of a galloping soldier was Youlin. He was laughing and hitting the man's shoulder, as if striking a horse's rump.

"Oh, Mama!" he cried as he was set down by his human steed. "I went to Daddy's army barracks and watched the soldiers washing the big horses. It was so much fun!"

Bittersweet ran to Youlin and took him in her arms. "I should be angry with you," she tried to scold him between sobs. "*So* angry that you strayed from home." But all she felt was great gladness; her lost son was safe at home.

"Did you just come from the barracks, Ma'am?" the soldier asked.

Bittersweet nodded, still rocking Youlin in her arms.

"Then you witnessed the ruckus."

"Ruckus?" she asked.

"You know how the townspeople feel about the army being stationed here . . . ," he began.

Bittersweet did not, for Delin tried not to bring his military life with him when he came home in the evening. Nevertheless, she nodded so that the soldier would continue.

"Well, today things reached the breaking point. This morning, this woman comes to see Captain Li, charging that two soldiers made lewd remarks and improper advances to her. She brought a couple of her neighbors along and, by their faces, you could see they were ready to fight. But, your husband is *ding hao* — first rate." The soldier shook his head in unbelieving admiration.

"First he's faced with our pay and rations coming from the provincial government, which can barely support itself, instead of from national headquarters like they used to be. You know what that means: deferred pay, barely any rice, and what rice there is is unhulled; no new uniforms so we're walking around in tatters. The men are so fed up, a thousand of them threatened to revolt. But Captain Li calmed them down. Sold some captured guns and ammunition and used the strings of cash to pay the men and buy some extra bags of rice. Now this woman comes along, and tension between the soldiers and townspeople is. . . ." The soldier shook his head, as if amazed that there could be that much tension in the world. "But Captain Li," he continued, "he knows he's got to act quickly, decisively and, most important, correctly. 'Madam,' he says, 'if some of my men have behaved improperly towards you, you're right to report them to me. Such behavior is no small matter. It is, in fact, punishable by death by firing squad.' Then he has a hundred soldiers line up, all dressed in identical uniforms, and asks her to identify the men who insulted her. After she goes down the line of soldiers and chooses two of them, Captain Li asks, 'Are you absolutely sure that these are the men in question?' So she goes back over the line and picks out two more men. Again, Captain Li asks her if she's sure she's picked the men who offended her. When she insists that she has, he says, 'Then how can these *four* soldiers be guilty when you originally claimed that only *two* men insulted you?' That got her! She slunk away real fast, her head hung low, and her neighbors shuffling away with her. Your husband knew exactly how to handle the situation, and because he did, the townspeople lost their pretext to start a riot."

"Mama," Youlin said, stroking Bittersweet's tear-stained face, "don't cry anymore. I'm home now and I won't wander away ever again."

"It's not that," his mother told him, hugging him close. "I was just thinking of how hard your Daddy works, how many problems he must solve, and how much understanding he deserves from us all."

That evening when Delin came home, Bittersweet prepared one of his favorite dishes — a minced pork patty filled with finely chopped black mushrooms and water chestnuts and topped with shaved ginger root. After Delin ate his fill, he looked at his unusually quiet wife, "Wasn't I right? The boy came home, safe and sound."

"You were right," Bittersweet answered, her eyes downcast.

"When you came to my office and told me that our son was missing, do you think I wasn't worried?"

Bittersweet shook her head.

"I'm an officer in the national army. My men look to me for leadership. If I show myself to be indecisive or easily flustered in my personal life, how can they obey my orders when death might await them on the battlefield? When problems arise, I must be calm and deliberate. You should have stayed a little longer instead of running out as you did. You'd have seen that I'd ordered a soldier to search for Youlin — the same soldier who brought Youlin home to you."

"I apologize," Bittersweet said, looking up, her eyes filled with tears. "I apologize for the intrusion, and I apologize for ruining your chess game."

Delin smiled. "You did me a favor," he said. "I was losing."

The storm clouds of civil war continued to gather, and Delin moved his family and the army farther into the mountains to Yulin. But they could not stave off the impending catastrophe no matter how they tried to avoid it, and just as Bittersweet set up her new home, civil war between Kwangsi and Kwangtung broke out. At first, Yulin was untouched by the war, then gradually the glare of exploding bombs lit up the horizon, and cannon, machine gun, and rifle fire drew nearer until it was almost at the edge of town. After several months in Yulin, Delin, who had been promoted to lieutenant-colonel, called Bittersweet to his study and informed her that he was arranging for an aide to escort her and Youlin back to Dragon's Head which, thus far, was peaceful.

"Besides being safer, I think you'll also be happier. It has troubled me, more than you know, that you've had to live a life that has been disagreeable to you."

For a while, Bittersweet was silent. "I am neither sad to be leaving Yulin," she said finally, "nor happy to be leaving the side of my husband. But I have my duty to perform, which is to obey you and to care for our little son, just as you have your duty to fulfill, which is to lead men into battle."

Two days later, Bittersweet and Youlin, together with an aide, began the long journey from Kwangtung back to Kwangsi and the village of Dragon's Head. Bombs dropped in the distance and cannon fire and rifle shot sounded along much of their route. None of the three travelers spoke more than a few words, silenced, as they were, by fear. Bittersweet, however, did sing songs and tell children's stories to Youlin.

"Tell me about the boy and the father and the fish!" Youlin cried. "I want to hear it again."

"Me, too," the aide admitted, for the tale of filial piety was a favorite, a story told to every young Chinese boy.

"Once upon a time," Bittersweet began, "there was a farmer and his little son. The farmer loved his son very much and gave him the best ears of corn to eat and the softest grains of polished rice. And the son, in turn, loved his father very much, as good sons will. One year, a plague of locusts stretched across the land, eating everything in sight, every kernel of corn, every grain of rice. Famine bent people's heads in unrelieved sorrow, and many of them went hungry. It was a particularly cold and cruel winter that year, and the farmer lay wrapped in his blanket on his bed of straw, for he was very sick from lack of food. His son knew that there was no food to be had anywhere, for the locusts had eaten the fields and paddies clean, and the land lay under a thick blanket of snow.

"'If I might just have one fish to eat, I know I would get well,' the farmer, too ill to lift his head from the pillow, told his son.

100

"But when the son went to the river to cast his net, his heart sank: the river was frozen solid. He was almost in despair when an idea came to him. He walked to the middle of the river and lay down, vowing to lie there until the heat of his body melted the thick ice. He lay there all winter long and through the first days of spring. He felt neither cold nor hunger, so great was his resolve, so deep was his love for his father. Then one day, feeling the current flowing under him, he plunged his arm beneath the water. When he brought his hand up, he held a great, squirming fish. He ran home with his catch and cooked it for his father whose strength returned as quickly as he ate it. And so it was that the filial son saved the life of his honored father."

As they passed through many villages by foot, sedan chair, or donkey back, Bittersweet watched as the citizenry — their belongings strapped onto their backs, in wheelbarrows or animal carts — abandoned their homes. They were fleeing the imminent fighting and hoping to take refuge in the homes of friends or relatives. At a fork in the river, the aide suggested walking to the next large town where they could take a steamer to Liuchow. The rowboats they had planned to take were overcrowded with fleeing refugees. When they arrived in Liuchow, they learned that one of the rowboats had struck a rock in the river and capsized. Several of the people on board had drowned — among them were two of Bittersweet's neighbors in Yulin. For most of the second leg of the journey from Liuchow to Kweilin, Bittersweet was pensive. She and her party had decided not to board the rowboat but walk, a choice which had saved their lives. Others had died in their pursuit of safety.

Perhaps they'd have done better to stay at home, Bittersweet thought. War had come to the province, but there are those whose lives are spared by war. To stay at home was at least to die in one's bed. As they were about to enter Kweilin, she dared not think that she was almost back and safe at last. Not till she, Youlin, and the aide passed inside the fortified walls of Dragon's Head, the very walls she had left behind almost six years earlier, did she cease to brood. Not until Da Mama ran out to hold her grandson in her arms for the first time, did Bittersweet dare believe that life might be long and good.

Chapter 8
The Letter
(1923)

In no time at all, Bittersweet resumed the life she had led when she first left her own family to become part of her husband's family in Dragon's Head. But, now, there was one important difference: she was the mother of her husband's son and thus she was accorded the respect and deference that attended such a position. In addition, she had borne the first grandson to the Li branch at Dragon's Head, and so her place in the family hierarchy — though she was wife to the second son — rose above that of First Outside Sister-in-Law, who was still childless. The family fortune — through the generosity of the gods, the abundance of recent harvests, and the taels of silver that Delin sent home — had increased. There were two water buffalos in the stable, a dozen chickens in the courtyard, a litter of pigs in the pen, meat weekly on the dinner table, and real tea served daily. A neighboring farmer with few *mou* to tend was hired during planting and harvest to help First Brother-in-Law, Demin. Demin was now joined by Third Brother-in-Law, Solin. Together they worked the new, larger paddies purchased with the proceeds from the sale of the abundant rice harvests. More land meant diverse crops, and Demin now grew *bok-choy, guy-lan*, tobacco, rape seed, and sugar cane, in addition to the staple, rice.

Now when Bittersweet went to the Taoist temple, the tongue in the village soothsayer's mouth was still, or if it wagged it wagged in approbation. "Li *Tai-tai*, Colonel Li's wife and the mother of the first grandson born to their branch of the clan, is going to the temple to burn incense and recite prayers for the safety of her brave husband," she took pleasure in saying to whomever would listen.

And while the soothsayer wasn't lying, Bittersweet also went to the temple to resume her reading and writing lessons and to share the stories of her peripatetic life with her old friend Xiao Tzu. She described to him all she had seen: how, for instance, houses were built in the city — often with a flat roof, like the lid of an iron pot, instead of a curving roof of overlapping terra cotta tiles, like the scales of a fish.

While they were larger, she explained, sometimes opulent, and more solid in construction, city houses seemed heavy and graceless. Their rooms, though spacious, were lacking in harmony, flaunting size and contents while disregarding proportion based on *chien*, a given measure of width to depth to height.

In these city houses, she told him, city folk lived lavishly, displaying their material wealth and urban sophistication. Still, she'd found them sadly wanting in genuine human warmth and generosity. They didn't have the proper relationship of respect for and submission to the laws of nature and the universe. And their clothes! City men strutted about in hard leather shoes; Western suits with sleeves and pant legs that looked like stovepipes; straw hats that looked like inelegant dinner platters; and, sometimes, felt derbys that looked like deep rice bowls turned upside down. Meanwhile, city women tottered about on their golden lilies in flamboyant *cheongsams* or Western clothes that seemed to cut off circulation. If a city woman didn't have bound feet, she wore Western shoes that forced the arch of the foot up on a raised heel so that, instead of tottering on her heel as a woman with bound feet did, she teetered on the ball.

Bittersweet had heard — though her own modesty and her respect for her Taoist teacher forbade her to mention it — that city men, and some country men, too, considered a woman's bound foot the most erotic and tantalizing part of her body. In the House of the Wide Gates, men would fondle the tiny, senseless stumps — which only the loosest of women would ever let a man see, let alone caress. Men put the stumps in their mouths and licked and tickled them with their tongues. Rumor had it that the height of passion for a certain high-ranking army officer was to bring unshelled nuts to his favorite who would then use her nerve-deadened feet as hammers. Then, she fed the sweetmeats to her lover from between her tightly curled toes. It amazed and disgusted Bittersweet to think that so useless and deformed an object could raise certain men to heights of sensual rapture. It surprised her to overhear the reproaches and encouragements of mothers as they broke the arches or bound the broken insteps of their weeping six- or seven-year-old daughters: "A pretty face is a gift of nature, but a perfectly bound foot is a sign of industry and diligence."

Each new binding was tighter than the previous one, so many girls were forced to crawl on all fours, dragging their misery behind them. She heard girls praying at the temples for the gods to endow them with the strength and forbearance to endure the torments of ever smaller feet, for no eligible and desirable bachelor would even look at a woman with unbound feet unless it were out of pity or disgust.

"My wife's feet are less than three knuckles long," she overheard one man boast to his cohorts. "She threatens to run away when she's due for a beating, but how far can she get on her tiny claws and those withered shanks? When she tries to escape, I catch her in a single bound and give her an extra thrashing for trying. When she particularly displeases me, I stamp on her golden lilies. She knows no pain more excruciating than that."

Hearing this, Bittersweet thought: Women with bound feet are prisoners. Their husbands have made their deformity desirable and their incapacity a virtue. It's no different when a man who cannot find a wife offers a lower bride price for a normal woman and a higher bride price for a retarded one, since a retarded woman will be more obedient. Mulling over the matter in her mind, Bittersweet came to the conclusion that just as bound feet hampered a woman's physical movements, so a bound mind — one denied education and exposure — hindered a woman's knowledge of and effectiveness in the world. Grateful that her father-in-law and her husband were enlightened and had encouraged her to read and write, and that her mother-in-law had encouraged her to go out into the world, she realized that men and women were essentially the same and should, therefore, be equal. Yet this was far from the case, and education was the reason why. Men received an education and so acquired knowledge, and this knowledge set them free; women were denied an education and so remained in mental bondage and physical slavery. And that, she thought, made all the difference.

All these thoughts and observations she shared with Xiao Tzu. They were ideas and experiences that she could freely tell him and him alone, for no one else understood her as well as he did. And he agreed with her, or when he disagreed he did so with gentle humor.

One day, after her return to Dragon's Head, she discovered that he shared many of her opinions, because, he, too, had lived a city life and had experienced many uprootings.

"Shanghai!" Bittersweet exclaimed when she learned the city was Xiao Tzu's ancestral home.

Delin had described Shanghai to her as the most Western of Chinese cities, with tall skyscrapers and sprawling homes that made Canton's buildings look like doll houses. These giant edifices were filled with foreign devils who lived in their own enclaves called "foreign settlements," communities where they lived as if in their own country, exempt from Chinese laws and customs.

"With contempt for Chinese laws and customs was what Delin said," Bittersweet told the priest.

"What your husband said is so," Xiao Tzu allowed. "They live by their own laws, though they live on Chinese soil. They call this right 'extraterritoriality.' It's as though they'd established a foreign colony in China." Xiao Tzu's face twitched, then hardened. "Or rather, they're turning China into a giant colony of their foreign country."

"That will never be," Bittersweet insisted, and, as proof, she read him Delin's latest letter, though she didn't tell him that it had been written months ago, a fact which worried her. Death, she knew, was never far for a soldier. In his letter Delin had written of the death of imperial China, of Sun Yat-sen's nomination as president of a republican China, of his own personal victories on the battlefield, of his determination to rid Kwangsi of its warlord Lu Jung-ting, and of how he and two other Kwangsinese, all of whom had attended the same military academy, had met again on the battlefield and vowed in a blood oath to work together for the modernization of the province and the unification of China.

"I pray with all my heart that your husband's words come true," Xiao Tzu said, "but I only know that when I was a young boy and still the son of my father, as we walked in the great city of Shanghai one day, about to enter a park, we were confronted by a sign written in English letters. There were Chinese characters beneath the English letters and they read, 'No dogs or Chinamen allowed.' The face of the man who was my father turned red with rage. He shook his fist at the sign and told me, 'The *da bizi* with their unequal treaties and their unequal treatment of people different from themselves. One day we will chase them from our land. One day they, too, will know what it's like to feel the master's boot on their necks, they who would treat us like dogs.'"

"The man who was your father and the man who is my father-in-law, had they met, would have had very much in common," Bittersweet said gently. "They both have high Confucian ideals and a great dislike of foreigners."

The phrasing of Bittersweet's words indicated that she wished to know why he was no longer his father's son and was trying to find a polite way to ask.

"I could never live up to Confucian ideals," Xiao Tzu explained. "I was an unfilial son. I questioned Confucian concepts — philanthropy, morality, and propriety. To my adolescent eyes, philanthropy was merely enlightened self-interest. It was still in the service of the self; others were only the vehicle. Morality wasn't an absolute truth but a social invention of those in authority who couldn't find truth in themselves. Because they were untrustworthy, they found no reason to trust others. But even more dangerous than morality was *li* — propriety — all the ceremonies of our culture, all the learned behavior that smothers our brains, clamps shut our mouths, blocks our ears and eyes, all the rituals that require study and memorization and lead to hypocrisy and falsehood."

He pointed to a passage of the *Tao Te Ching* hanging on the temple wall. "Let's just say I've chosen to follow a much simpler Way."

> *Superior Power is never Powerful, thus it has Power.*
> *Inferior Power is always Powerful, and thus it has no Power.*
> *Superior Power takes action and acts without motive.*
> *Inferior Power takes action and acts with motive.*
>
> *Superior philanthropy takes action and acts without motive.*
> *Superior morality takes action and acts with motive.*
> *Superior propriety takes action and there is no response*
> *So it raises its arm to project itself.*
>
> *Therefore lose the Tao and Power follows.*
> *Lose the Power and philanthropy follows.*
> *Lose philanthropy and morality follows.*
> *Lose Morality and propriety follows.*

"Or perhaps," Xiao Tzu went on, "I didn't chose a simpler Way; perhaps, It chose me. Before, I didn't have a path to follow. I walked whatever road I found in front of my feet. One day, I met a man who was seeking the Elixir of Life so that he might live at least 150 years as he heard certain Taoist recluses have done. He needed someone to carry the sack he'd brought along for the magical herbs he planned to find in the mountains above the clouds. I carried that sack, and he is now head abbot of our temple."

"And did he find the Elixir of Life?" Bittersweet wanted to know.

Xiao Tzu laughed. "Better than that. He found Life itself."

It was too much for Bittersweet to comprehend — much less think about — and yet Xiao Tzu's words played over and over in her mind like a refrain. Why shouldn't Da Mama practice enlightened self-interest? Why shouldn't she think of her family first when she gave to the poor, the orphaned, the widowed?

It was good of her to give to them, but it was her duty to see to the needs of her family. What was wrong with Confucian ceremony and ritual? Bittersweet liked to light the candles and burn incense before the ancestor tablets; though, as an honorary, not a full member of her husband's family, she was relegated to the last row of worshippers. What's wrong with hierarchy, she thought to herself. If there was no hierarchy, there would be no order, and without order, all would be chaos under heaven.

"Not chaos," Xiao Tzu differed when she returned to the temple the next time and brought the matter up with him. "No-thing."

"That's even worse," Bittersweet replied. She could not imagine nothing, the complete absence of things.

"But no-thingness is not-thereness, the most useful of things," Xiao Tzu laughed, then recited from the *Tao Te Ching*:

Thirty spokes converge at one hub;
What is not there makes the wheel useful.
Clay is shaped to form a vessel;
What is not there makes the vessel useful.
Doors and windows are cut to form a room;
What is not there makes the room useful.
Therefore, take advantage of what there is,
By making use of what is not.

Really! Bittersweet thought in frustration upon reaching home after her visit with him. Xiao Tzu doesn't know what he's talking about. After all, he subtracts from the academic daily to follow the Tao. No wonder his knowledge is depleted. I enjoy our discussions, but I mustn't take him seriously. What is greater and more honorable, after all, than the Confucian virtues of loyalty to one's clan and of daughterly devotion? Nothing, she answered herself. Then with a start of recognition, she changed the emphasis of the two syllables. "No-thing."

On entering the house, she passed her parents-in-law's bedroom. She noticed that the door was open and that Baba and Da Mama were inside. Seeing Bittersweet, they looked at each other, their glances furtive. Baba turned away and, as if to offset his action, Da Mama turned to face Bittersweet. A strange, almost apologetic look wavered in her eyes. A letter dangled from her hand.

"From Delin?" Bittersweet asked hopefully, then cautiously, "Is my husband well?"

"He is well," her mother-in-law replied.

Baba still turned away from them, his hands clasped tightly behind his back.

"Youlin," Bittersweet said, "did he let the pigs out of their pen again?"

But her naughty son of yesterday, Da Mama confirmed, had been a model son today.

Bittersweet leafed through the past few days. She had accomplished her given tasks as she had always done — better now that she'd returned from Yulin, happy to be rooted in native soil, to be sharing her family's home again. Each of her family members had remarked on the extraordinary care and diligence that she brought to her daily chores. What was it, then, that she had done to elicit her parents-in-law's displeasure? Perhaps she had stayed too long at the temple. Perhaps the soothsayer was up to her old tricks, filling the *hutongs* with gossip.

"I've done something to displease you," she said, dropping her eyes to the ground. "Please let me know what it is, so I may correct my faults and atone for my misdeeds."

When neither Da Mama nor Baba answered her, she dropped to her knees, bowed her head to the floor, and repeated herself. No sooner had she kowtowed than she felt herself being lifted up by the shoulders, and when she rose to her feet, she saw that her mother-in-law's eyes were filled with pity. "You've done nothing to displease us," the woman said. "Not you, but. . . ." Pursing her lips together, Da Mama looked at her husband who still turned away. Finally, stern and erect, he walked out of the room.

"The letter that Delin has written," Da Mama began tentatively, "it comes so many months after his last, and now I know why. At first, I greeted his words with joy — his bravery on the battlefield, his service to the army and to his country. But his letter also brings news that has filled me with pain for I know it will cause you great anguish."

Da Mama extended her hand that held the letter.

"Tell me," Bittersweet said, ignoring the gesture, continuing to look at her mother-in-law's face.

Da Mama took a deep breath and expelled it and with it the words, "Delin has taken a second wife."

The pounding that had begun in Bittersweet's ears the moment Baba had left the room stopped abruptly. Now it was her heart that throbbed. "A second wife?" she said hoarsely, as if she didn't understand what the words meant.

"It's incomprehensible to me, too," Da Mama answered. Her perplexed face suddenly contracted in anger. "It's reprehensible!" she exploded. "Never has such a thing happened in our family. Never! Your father-in-law and I are deeply grieved and greatly angered by our son."

"A second wife!" Bittersweet murmured in disbelief. The knees that had bent voluntarily a few minutes ago now buckled under her. Dropping to them once again, she swayed back and forth, moaning softly, her arms hugging her sides. Da Mama knelt beside her, her hands on Bittersweet's shoulders.

"Never have we had such a situation in our family," she said, her voice full of empathy. "But my husband tells me that this unhappiness is not unique to us. He tells me that for many families it isn't strange at all but even customary for men of wealth and high position to have two, even three or four, wives to serve them. My husband tells me that Delin is doing what is proper for his position. But what will this situation do to our family? The family is *everything*. It cannot be divided."

Bittersweet stopped moaning and weaving about. She blinked the tears from her eyes. "Everything. No-thing," she mumbled.

She was aware of how firmly her knees were anchored into the floor. She felt the broad base of her subordinate position, far more stable and secure than if she were standing. She looked up at Da Mama who had risen to her feet.

"My husband has done what is proper for his position," Bittersweet said, fighting for control of her emotions and her words. "What, then, is my position, given this new situation? Confucius himself said that

109

it is crucial to know one's place in the scheme of things and that to know one's title is to know one's place in the universe and one's relationship to one's fellow man. There is someone else at my husband's side, the place I once occupied, bearing the title I alone once held. What, then, am I to be called? I must find out what my husband thinks of me. I must know how he will treat me. I must discover what my position and my title are, now that he has taken a second wife.

"A family cannot be divided," Bittersweet said, repeating Da Mama's words. Bowing her head to express her submission, she asked, "What should I do? Tell me what I must do and I will do it."

Humbled by her subservience and sharing in her suffering, Da Mama raised her daughter-in-law to her feet. "You must go to Kweiping. You must join your husband. You must take Youlin with you and together you must face your husband. My husband will write to Delin that you and your son are coming. I'll send for Old Uncle Bagong to accompany you on your journey."

"If that is your wish of me," Bittersweet said, bowing, "then my wish is merely to obey. But will Baba agree to it?"

The women looked at each other, knowing they were of one mind but knowing also that their respective positions must be maintained and the proper channels of communication observed. How fortunate I am, Bittersweet thought, to have entered into *this* mother-in-law's house!

"In matters such as this," Da Mama said, "a man listens to his wife. It is a question of face, and his face rests with her. A man cannot overcome his wife with principles because the principles reside with her. The letter will be written. The letter will be sent. Your father-in-law will tell you that you must go."

"Then I accept my parents-in-law's decision for me as my own," Bittersweet acknowledged, bowing lower.

Chapter 9
Concubine
(1924)

Once again, Bittersweet prepared for another uprooting. Her last had been to escape danger. Now she was going to meet a different type of danger, to see what it looked like, so she would know what to do. It was similar to what Delin had said of his military campaigns, "If you know your enemy, you will overcome him; if you know yourself, you will never lose a single battle."

During the day, when she was planning and packing, serving her parents-in-law, and caring for Youlin, Bittersweet's suffering was lightened by activity. But when she was in bed at night, it came fully upon her, pressing down until she could scarcely breathe. Here I am, she thought in the oppressive darkness, leaving my parents-in-law who love me to join my husband whose feelings for me I can only surmise.

Once aboard the steamer that left Kweilin to sail down river to Kweiping, Bittersweet, on the pretext that she needed some air, went up on deck. She left Old Uncle Bagong and Youlin below and out of the sun, since she wanted to be alone where they wouldn't see her long face and red eyes.

But she wasn't alone for long. A woman who was returning from Shanghai to her home in the countryside came up to Bittersweet and, between puffs on her long-stemmed pipe, began to speak of her life in that great port city.

"I can see that you're a farm woman, too," she said rather impolitely, "and I know you'll understand how lonely and alien someone like me would feel living in a city like Shanghai."

When Bittersweet asked, out of politeness rather than interest, why the woman had decided to go to Shanghai, the pipe smoker replied, "I went to join my husband who'd taken a concubine, just like you're doing now."

Bittersweet told the woman that she was mistaken, that she was traveling to Kweiping to visit her mother's relatives. The pipe smoker squinted her eyes and nodded, saying, "Then you'll forgive my mistake, but your manner and your pallor are so like mine when I set out for Shanghai that I naturally assumed the cause was the same. I hope you won't take offense if I tell you a little story."

Before Bittersweet could say anything, the woman was telling her tale:

"A farm boy and girl were wed, and he went north to seek his fortune in the city, promising to send for her when he'd found it. He kept his word and sent for her, but when she arrived she found that, because of his new status as a rich man occupying a high position, he'd taken not one but two concubines. The wife, being a simple country woman, didn't know how to control them or even how to protect herself against their machinations. They made fun of her, played tricks on her and, unknown to her husband, who was often away on official business, even starved her.

"One day, she was invited to dinner by other high officials' wives who inquired why she was so thin. When she told them about her troubles, they gave her this advice: 'The next time your husband is out, take the official seal and sit at the judgment table.' The starving young woman thanked them and promised to do as they advised, saying that she would never have thought of the solution herself.

"The next time her husband went out, she took up the official seal and sat at the judgment table. Then she called the servants and told them, 'Bring the two concubines and beat them with bamboo switches.' Seeing that she held the official seal and sat at the judgment table, they could only obey, and they beat the two concubines till they screamed for mercy.

"Her husband came home and heard the cries of his concubines and the thrashing of the bamboo switches, but he merely sat by the side door and hung his head, for his seal was in action and he, being a man like any other, could do nothing. After his wife called off the servants, he knelt before her and begged to know the reason for her actions. When she told him, he promised to make amends. The quarrel was laid to rest. Her husband respected her. The concubines now trembled before her and served her as was her due. And her place in the household as first wife and her position as second only to her husband was undisputed."

"That's a very clever story," Bittersweet said when it came to an end.

The pipe smoker squinted through the smoke and smiled. "It's an old story. But it contains a moral that's true to this day."

Hearing the delighted squeals of a child, the woman looked around and saw Youlin and Old Uncle who had come on deck. Bagong was explaining to the boy the different parts of the boat and their functions. "I've watched you and your son," the pipe smoker told Bittersweet. "You love him very much. I have no such son. If I did, I would love him as much as you do yours. The official seal, the judgment table of my story, they are nothing compared to a son. A son is worth a thousand seals, a thousand judgment tables."

When they docked at Kweiping, Bittersweet wished the woman well and, together with Youlin and Bagong, disembarked from the steamer. Riding sedan chairs and escorted by one of Delin's aides who had come to meet them at the dock, they arrived in front of a large house where Delin was waiting for them outside the gate. He didn't brush the dust of the road from Bittersweet's traveling clothes as he had years ago when he was a captain. In less than two years, he had risen in rank to lieutenant colonel, then to colonel, and he was surrounded by several subservient officers. Bittersweet noticed, too, that he was even more distinguished and handsome than when last she saw him.

"*Ni hao*," he bade his wife welcome, bending slightly at the waist. Then he took his son into his arms, saying, "Ah, how tall you've grown."

Youlin stared at his father. "Daddy?" he asked, at which Delin and the other officers laughed.

"Then you do remember me!"

"I'm almost seven years old," the boy replied. "I remember everything."

Delin and the officers laughed again.

"You've traveled a long way," Delin said to Bittersweet. "You must be very tired." Bidding his fellow officers farewell and still carrying Youlin in his arms, Delin led the party inside to a spacious parlor. "You'll be wanting some tea," he decided, then called out, "Dejie!"

A beautiful girl, no more than sixteen years old, floated into the room. She was slim and fine-boned with a complexion as smooth and white as rice paper and a tiny face set with regular, delicate features. Her fingers were long and tapered at the tips, and her feet, in Western-style shoes, were so small that they might have been bound save for the absence of the humped arch where they would have been broken.

The exquisite girl bowed to Bittersweet, turned to the ebony sideboard where a teapot and cups had been set, filled a cup with tea, and brought it over to her. Then she went over to Delin and tried to take Youlin from his arms.

"No, no," Youlin cried, pushing her away and kicking with his feet so that she set him down. He ran to his mother's side and glared at the young woman who had tried to hold him. His lower lip extended in an angry pout. Without a word or the slightest expression on her face, Dejie turned and walked out of the room as silently and gracefully as she had entered.

"So, now you have met Dejie." Delin went to the sideboard, poured himself a cup of tea and sat in the armchair next to Bittersweet. He took a few sips from his cup but waited until his wife had drunk from hers, as though what he was about to say would go down easier once she had.

"I married Dejie because I needed someone to care for me and to accompany me to social functions. Now that you're here, I hope that you and she can be good friends. Do you think that will be possible?"

Rather than listen to his words, which he said so matter-of-factly, Bittersweet studied Delin's face. She saw no malice, only gentle candor. How, then, could she answer him? What purpose would it serve to describe her feelings upon learning the contents of his last letter? To counteract the grief and despair she suffered, Bittersweet recalled, with no small amount of pride, that she had never done anything to displease her husband. The one time she had spoken to him in anger had not been for her own, but for Youlin's, welfare, for their well-being as a family. And nothing was more important than the well-being of the family. And so she answered, "It is possible."

Delin smiled and called out, "Dejie!" Upon hearing her name, Dejie reappeared and stood with her hands clasped before her, her eyes downcast. It was proper that the second wife stand while the first wife sat. "We're all one family now," Delin announced. Turning to Bittersweet, he said, "You must call her by her first name — Dejie. Since she is younger than you and must be respectful, she will address you as Li *Tai-tai*. Though her family is of modest means, they're good people and Dejie is a dutiful daughter and a diligent student. If there is anything that you want done, just tell her and she will see to it." His eyes softened with a plea for understanding. "For the past three years, you and I have lived apart. There was no one to take care of me. Dejie has brought comfort and consolation into my life. Now that you and Youlin have come, my happiness is assured."

Bittersweet felt her heart and her tongue pulling in opposite directions. To have been displaced from her husband's affections was her greatest suffering. But to deliberately inflict suffering upon her husband was to wound not only Delin, but herself — to wound her character. And so she answered, conquering the impulse in her heart, "I am as glad for your happiness as I am happy to be here. A family should be together."

At her words, Delin swung Youlin, squealing and laughing, high into the air.

"Cook! Manservant!" Delin cried.

Two men — one middle-aged and wearing an apron on which he was wiping his extraordinarily large hands, the other barely out of his teens — rushed into the parlor, bowing as they came.

"Prepare a banquet," Delin ordered with a grin. "Tonight I'm celebrating the arrival of my wife and son."

Delin motioned to the young manservant to take the mistress of the house upstairs to her room and to send the maid up to help with the unpacking. While Delin chatted with Bagong, Bittersweet followed the boy up the curved wooden staircase of the house. The second floor served as living quarters while the downstairs rooms were used as Delin's offices. A living room and a dining room comprised the center of the living quarters, while on either side were two bed-sitting-rooms.

"This is your room," the boy said, putting down her suitcases in the one on the left. "The one across the hall is Guo *Yi Tai-tai*'s," he explained, indicating it with a toss of his head.

Yi Tai-tai, Bittersweet reminded herself. Not *Tai-tai*. Concubine, not wife.

The bed-sitting-room was furnished with comfortable armchairs with crocheted doilies on the head- and armrests; a delicate side table on which rested a teapot and two cups of precious Jingdezhen porcelain; and a long low table with stout legs that curved like the horns of a water buffalo. The room was large and airy. The light of the late afternoon sun filtered through panes of glass held in place by green and red fretwork, done in the pleasing, asymmetrical cracked-ice pattern. The four-poster was wrapped in sheer mosquito netting like

115

the cocoon of a silkworm, and the *siming* blanket was red and woven with the pattern of butterflies. Great care had gone into the arrangement of the room. It's good that I'm here, Bittersweet thought. I was right to have come.

That evening, she sat in the place of honor, at the head of a table crowded with the choicest banquet dishes — shark's fin, bird's nest, hairy-leg crab, and succulent vegetables. Despite the luxury and variety of foods, Bittersweet missed her bowl of rice, "the sweat of the peasant's brow," which was too common to be served on a special occasion such as this. Delin filled her cup with wine then raised his own.

"To your health, and may you be happy in your new home. *Gan bei.*"

Dejie reached for her wine cup and, raising it before her face, joined Delin in drinking to Bittersweet's health and happiness. Finally, Bittersweet raised her own cup to her lips. Looking over its rim and surveying the richly-laden table, she thought: What if I'd made a scene, ranted about Delin's having taken a second wife? I would have shamed him and made him lose face. For a man of his stature, face is no small matter. Here is my husband who speaks of the battlefield as his home, a man who daily confronts many dangers, even death. Why should I deny him a second wife to take care of him, he who has devoted his life to our country? The Chinese character for peace is a roof, and under that roof, one woman. The Chinese character for adultery is three women. Dejie and I are only two women. The Chinese character for good is a woman and a child. I am that woman and Youlin is that child.

As Bittersweet drank, she remembered the pipe smoker she had met on the steamer that morning who had told her that a wife's power lay in her son. The childless Dejie is only half of the character good, Bittersweet told herself. Her power is further circumscribed by the fact that she is the second and secondary wife. I am the first and primary one. As nothing can change the former, Bittersweet reminded herself, as she tore a bristly claw from a hairy-leg crab and sucked out the tender meat, so, too, nothing can change the latter.

Delin refilled Bittersweet's cup, and though already light-headed, she again drained it. If I were intolerant of the situation and caused trouble for Delin, she thought, people would talk — not against him for taking a second wife but against me for having the audacity to object. And if they talked against me and Delin heard of it, he would lose respect for me. If he lost respect, then he would become indifferent and uncaring, but no one would think any less of him. Instead, they would say that I deserved his disdain for being cruel and spiteful, for making him lose face. With society's full approval, he could abandon me and there would be no one to sympathize with me, nowhere to turn for justice.

When Bittersweet raised her wine cup, first to Delin, then to Dejie, for the third *gan bei*, she made a vow to herself: I will give my husband no cause to be displeased with me. I will strive to live in peace and harmony with Dejie.

That night, as Bittersweet lay under the mosquito netting that made her feel as though she were floating inside a cloud, suspended within a dream, she heard footsteps coming up the stairs—not the soft shuffle of the cloth-soled shoes that she was used to hearing in Dragon's Head, but the hard sound of a soldier's heavy leather boots. For an instant, she remembered her wedding night, how she had fallen asleep on her bridal bed, how she'd been awakened by the thump of Delin's leather boots and his entry into the bridal chamber.

The sound of the footsteps grew louder as they came down the hall, then veered right and faded away. Bittersweet heard a door whine open, then click shut.

Chapter 10
Two Wives
(1925)

"Mama! Mama! Come down! We're going to Xishan!"

Bittersweet stuck her head out the window, looked down onto the front courtyard of her house, and waved to her son sitting on his pony. Dejie was beside him, mounted on her steed and wearing a Western riding habit. "You know I don't ride," Bittersweet yelled down.

Dejie, anxious to be on her way, sat higher in the saddle and cut the air with her crop. Delin, who loved to ride, had taught Dejie the sport soon after he'd met her. As soon as Delin had taught Youlin to ride, the three of them went out on horseback as often as they could.

"Have Daddy teach you," Youlin yelled back.

"I have a better idea," she heard her husband's voice say.

When he appeared, it was with four men bearing an exquisite blackwood palanquin. "Can I tempt you to come to Xishan in this?" he called up to her.

Previously, he had extended the invitation to accompany them on their outings in a two-bearer sedan chair, but the roads, especially up Xishan, were too rough to ride in such a chair. But a *four*-man palanquin!

"I'll just change my clothes," Bittersweet answered.

Dejie pulled at the reins of her horse and he reared.

Quickly, Bittersweet cleared her writing desk of its wet inkstone, calligraphy brush, and fine-grained rice paper. She'd just finished answering Xiao Tzu's letter when Youlin had called her to the window, and she wanted no trace of her activity for the servants to find. Weeks ago, she had succumbed to the desire to write to him, to tell him why she had come to Kweiping, for she hadn't had the opportunity to say good-bye to him in person, nor was there anyone else to whom she could confide her current feelings. She also missed letter writing, for now that she was reunited with Delin, there was only Baba to write to.

While Xiao Tzu's response had assuaged her loneliness, it had also given her some concern. In the last paragraph, before his signature, he had written: "Perhaps it was better that you didn't come to say good-bye, for after the first farewell, when you went to Xinghui to join your husband, I couldn't have borne the news of a second leave-taking. Perhaps you knew, and that's why you didn't come, realizing that the student-teacher bond, from the point of view of this teacher at least, has transmuted into different, deeper ties. I dare say this now, when you're already gone and so far away, when I don't have to see your face and feel your shame at my confession. Forgive me, Bittersweet, but I wouldn't have made such an admission if I didn't feel that in some small way you already knew of my feelings, that in your compassion you would pardon me for them, and that they would, if ever so slightly, give you some consolation in your unhappiness."

After the first reading, Bittersweet had crumpled the letter and thought of burning it, but she couldn't bring herself to do so. Instead, she carried it about until she thought of a proper reply. Now that she had, she could burn Xiao Tzu's letter. And yet still it remained whole in her tunic pocket, next to her heart.

Coming down the stairs, she slipped her reply into the manservant's waiting hands, told him it was a contribution to the Taoist temple in Dragon's Head and to post it right after the riding party left.

"Why, it's got room for two," she exclaimed as she entered the palanquin.

Hearing that, Delin called Dejie from her horse, for it was unthinkable for Bittersweet to ride in the palanquin alone. Dejie flushed, but she acquiesced without a word and climbed in beside Bittersweet, while Delin mounted Dejie's horse. Then off they went.

Dejie's mount was feisty, snorting and whinnying, and Delin was required to rein him in time and again.

"You must have a way with that horse," Bittersweet remarked. "See how much trouble he's giving Delin."

"Thunderbolt's used to me. I've mastered him," Dejie replied. "I wish I could say that I had similar relations with your son."

"Oh?"

"Li *Tai-tai*," Dejie continued, looking out the palanquin window, "my duties are not only towards my husband but also to you and Youlin. I don't think that I've failed you in any way, since I haven't received any complaints from you or heard them from anyone else. If anything you've been fair and kind to me and for that I'm grateful. But try as I might to be kind to Youlin or to play with him, he either runs away from me or ignores me. He talks with the servants and even plays with them rather than talk or play with me. It's also my duty to deal with the servants, who are very fond of Youlin, as am I. But since he doesn't return my sentiments, they, too, have become difficult. Is there nothing you can do to remedy the situation? You're his mother. He'll listen to you."

Dejie turned to Bittersweet who saw by the young woman's face that her distress was genuine. "Youlin is but a child. He thinks and acts as a child will. I hope that you'll be patient with him a little while longer. I will, however, speak to Youlin and tell him that he should be polite to you. I'll do it this very day."

Dejie thanked Bittersweet and resumed looking out the window on her side of the palanquin, while looking out the other window, Bittersweet watched her son trotting contentedly alongside his father. I'm a farmer's daughter, Bittersweet reminded herself, as Delin is a farmer's son. We're both stubborn. Why should the fruit of our union be anything less? She recalled how just days ago Youlin had stamped his foot when she asked him to be courteous to Dejie and, folding his arms across his little chest, had shaken his head no.

"Do you know what that woman told me?" he had said. He never called Dejie by her name. "She told me that if only I would call her Mama, I could have all the money I want."

"What did you answer her?" Bittersweet had asked.

"I told that woman, 'Why should I want your money? My Daddy has money for me, and much more than you.'"

Even Delin was powerless to change the mind of the seven-year-old boy.

There was a knock on the palanquin door.

"Your horse requires its gentle mistress," Delin told Dejie.

With an acquiescent nod to Delin and a respectful one to Bittersweet, Dejie slipped out of the palanquin and remounted her horse while Delin slid in beside Bittersweet. Dejie trotted up beside Youlin, but the boy veered away and rode behind the carriage. Delin shook his head but said nothing. Though he was disturbed by Youlin's dislike of Dejie, he literally couldn't express his discontent in a frown for, a year earlier, a bullet had passed through one of his cheeks and out the other, shattering several teeth and giving him a perpetual grin whether he felt cheerful or not.

"So," he asked, "were you right to come along?"

Bittersweet nodded, then breathed in deeply. The air smelled of freshly turned earth, pine needles, and recent rain.

"Beautiful country," she said.

"Yes," Delin answered, though she could see by his dimmed eyes that, in his mind's eye, he saw the battlefield, exhausted soldiers, screaming civilians. "China *will* be a beautiful country and a free one."

"How did you meet Dejie? Did a matchmaker introduce you?" she teased, changing the subject, incapable of seeing her husband unhappy without feeling unhappy herself. "Did her fortune match yours? Did she ride to your door in a sedan chair with a red silk veil drawn over her face?"

Delin laughed. Every now and then, Dejie swiveled her head around to look into the carriage. When she heard Delin's laughter, her eyebrows drew together, and she reined her horse in close to the palanquin door.

"No matchmaker introduced us, and we didn't have our fortunes told," he said. "Those are obsolete beliefs. You have to admit, the old marriage customs were very foolish. Remember how, at our wedding, we were pulled about like monkeys by our friends?"

Bittersweet nodded wistfully. Indeed she did remember, but she didn't think the old ways foolish.

"Actually, my lieutenant introduced us. We'd gone to inspect the new girls' school in town. Two of the older students were exceptionally beautiful. I'd seen them previously and I had my eye on one of them — Dejie — for a long time. My lieutenant, noticing the longing in my gaze, spoke up, 'Your wife has a young child and cannot follow you in your military life. Why don't you take another wife? It's not fitting that there is no one at your side to care for you.' My lieutenant knew Dejie's family and arranged for us to meet. I had no intention of marrying Dejie at the time, but when I was introduced to her, I changed my mind." Delin chuckled. "It's true, however, that she came to me in a sedan chair, but we had a modern marriage ceremony — a simple wedding party to introduce her to my friends."

Delin noticed that Bittersweet's shoulders were shaking, and her head was buried in her lap. "Xuewen," he said, touching her gently on the shoulder. "Have I upset you? Xuewen?"

Bittersweet lifted her head. Her face was red, but Delin couldn't tell from her expression whether she'd been laughing or crying.

"So you two did have a matchmaker," she said, clapping her hands together. "Your lieutenant. And you say that the old marriage customs are worthless. I bet he got a nice promotion out of it, too."

Delin was puzzled by his wife's outburst, but he laughed along with her. For the remainder of their ride, they chatted and laughed about old times, and never did he guess that Bittersweet's thoughts revolved around more serious matters.

It's true, she thought, it *is* impossible to follow you around in your army life. I have a young son. How can Youlin lead a normal, healthy life if he's uprooted each time the army moves to a new town? He's already started school. Can he just be pulled out of one school to be plunked down in another every time you leave with your soldiers for a new encampment? It's also true that you occupy high positions in both military and civil affairs. How can you go uncared for? You require a woman at your side, one who can attend social functions with you, who can make a dazzling appearance and witty remarks to impress your colleagues. These things I cannot do for you, and so you have found someone else who can. But I *can* give all my attention to bringing up our son.

"With you to take care of Youlin," she heard Delin say, "and with Dejie to take care of me, my happiness will be complete."

Bittersweet looked out of the palanquin window. Mists, like wind-swept veils, were swirling over the face of the mountain, concealing its harsh contours, softening its crags and peaks.

"You'll never have to fear unkind treatment," Delin continued. "Have I ever treated you unkindly? Have I ever broken my promises to you?"

Certainly the mountain is much more beautiful for being partially concealed from view, Bittersweet thought.

"You have not," she answered, her face averted.

"Remember what the fortuneteller said? You will enjoy honor, respect, and good fortune. As my wife, haven't you enjoyed all these things?"

Honor, respect, and good fortune aren't everything in life, Bittersweet thought, especially for a woman.

"I have," she answered, still looking out onto the mist-softened landscape. She continued to look out the window until they rode back down the mountain to Kweiping.

Two Wives

·◆·

In battle, Delin often had good reason to quote the aphorism, "Bad news travels a thousand *li* while good news barely sets one foot out the door." But the good news of his promotion to brigadier general traveled quickly. Soon, many of his family and friends from Dragon's Head came to visit. And soon, many of them required jobs and houses of their own. Bittersweet found her upstairs living room filled with Delin's relatives, while in the downstairs living room, military officials and civil administrators stood, shoulder to shoulder, waiting to see Delin. Bittersweet's days and nights were spent receiving, feeding, putting up Delin's family members, locating rooms for them, seeing to it that Delin wrote letters of introduction and recommendations for them, giving them sound advice, and introducing them to prospective employers. Her success in assisting them brought her Delin's gratitude and more relatives from Dragon's Head.

On the day that First Cousin Li was to come in on the afternoon boat, Bittersweet went to Delin's office to tell him of the arrival. The door was partially open, and before she could knock she heard her husband say, "Commander Chiang, it is a great honor you wish to bestow on me, but one I must politely decline. What you suggest is a feudalistic practice, one that no longer has any place in the new China we have pledged ourselves to create."

She peeked into the room and saw her husband withdraw a red card from his jacket pocket. It was the card with the eight characters of one's birth which, when exchanged, symbolized sworn brotherhood. To be sworn brothers was tantamount to swearing an irrevocable oath of mutual loyalty. Delin bowed and extended it to a seated man who was twisting a cigarette into a cigarette holder. His shaved head was strangely shaped — bulbous at the crown and jaw but narrow in between, so it looked like a peanut. And, she noticed with a start, the man had gray eyes.

The gray-eyed man took the red card that Delin held out and reinserted it into her husband's jacket pocket.

"Now that I have pledged my loyalty to you by giving you my red card, may I have your card?"

Delin's face turned pale, but he reached inside his jacket and, with a stiff bow, reciprocated.

123

"Ah, Brother Li!" the man exclaimed, smiling even more broadly, embracing him, and slapping him on the back.

"Brother Chiang," Delin murmured without enthusiasm.

"Sworn brothers!" the peanut-headed man cried in a high-pitched nasal voice. He shot a fist into the air. "To the death!"

Delin bent at the waist. "To the death."

Bittersweet knocked then opened the door all the way. "Oh, excuse me," she said. "I didn't know you had a visitor."

"Come in, come in," Delin said, a look of relief on his face. "Commander Chiang has graced our home with a visit, coming all the way from Peking where he was conferring with Sun Yat-sen just before he died."

While Delin made the requisite introductions, Bittersweet studied Commander Chiang. He was too thin, too rigid in his bearing for her liking. The dazzling whiteness of his smile was obviously due to the false teeth which made him lisp and spray saliva about when he spoke. But his pale, mouse-gray eyes were his most disagreeable, even ominous, feature.

"You know what they say about gray-eyed people," Bittersweet recalled her mother saying. "They're gray because they're filled with envy. Jealousy's eyes are green, but envy's eyes are gray."

The mainstays of Chinese culture, Bittersweet knew, have always been graciousness in living and harmony in human relationships. As Commander Chiang had offered his brotherhood by extending his red card, Delin could do nothing but return the gesture and the life-long loyalty it implied. Anything less would have been not only a grave breach of etiquette but a gross insult. It would also have been unthinkable, as Chiang, who had initiated the gesture, was Delin's superior. Yet, in her heart, Bittersweet regretted that her husband had given Chiang his red card. Knowing Delin as she did, she was certain that he would abide by the oath of mutual loyalty. While she had only just met Commander Chiang, she was not convinced that he would act in kind.

"I've just informed Commander Chiang that our provincial army will be the first to throw its lot in with the National Army. One by one the other southern provinces will come around and join us in our goal of national unity and a strong China. When they do, we'll be ready to launch a campaign to rid the northern provinces of their entrenched warlords." Delin lowered his eyes. "I'm only sorry that Sun will not see that day nor witness his dream become reality."

"Momentous news," Bittersweet said, dutifully looking downward. "I bring only meager news, of your first cousin's arrival this afternoon from Dragon's Head. Our house is full with other relatives, and I've come to ask your permission to put him up temporarily in the White Swan Guesthouse."

"You see, Brother Li?" Chiang said, turning stiffly to his host. "You've worked hard, earned honor and high position, and now that you have a fine home, many servants to do your bidding, and many well-connected friends ready to advise and assist you, your success has brought more and more friends and relations to your door. You know the old Chinese proverb: 'With more responsibilities, more privileges; with more privileges, more responsibilities.'"

Chiang recrossed his legs and sat back in the armchair. He meant to stay a while.

Bittersweet excused herself to attend to her responsibilities.

"You look tired," Delin remarked when they crossed paths in the hallway that evening. "I'm thankful you have Dejie to help you."

"Ah," Bittersweet said simply.

"What did you two do today?" he asked with some misgiving.

"Hwang *Tai-tai*, the governor's wife, accompanied me to see the rooms for rent on Willow Lane. When I met your cousin at the dock, he told me that he'd decided to stay in Kweiping for several weeks. The White Swan is expensive by the day and rented rooms will be cheaper. The house on Willow Lane is comfortable, the middle section is for rent, and the price the owner — Hwang *Tai-tai*'s uncle — quoted is fair. With your permission, I'll rent it for your cousin."

Delin gave his permission with a nod of his head, but his face contracted in angry disappointment, though his mouth remained in a grin. That Dejie had not been the one to assist Bittersweet in her duties was a dereliction of her own. "Why isn't Dejie accompanying you on your errands?" he asked.

Bittersweet regretted that she had alluded to Dejie's misconduct. She thought of Da Mama's words when Bittersweet had previously caught their neighbors in Dragon's Head stealing rice, so she said, "Let it go, let it go. Dejie might feel embarrassed to be called to account and her embarrassment turn to rancor. What difference does it make if she or someone else accompanies me on my visits and errands? Better that I have a friend who is pleased to give her time than a foe who begrudges me it."

Though Bittersweet had feared she would be the one to break the peaceful accord of two wives living under the same roof, it was Dejie who grew dissatisfied with her position and began to express displeasure. When Bittersweet first arrived in Kweiping, Dejie had dutifully kept her company, run errands, and accompanied her on her social rounds. Intellectually, she understood that Bittersweet occupied the higher position both in the family and in society. But, emotionally, it rankled her when guests addressed Bittersweet as Li *Tai-tai*, the first wife, while they addressed Dejie as *Yi Tai-tai*, the lesser one. For a while, Dejie swallowed her pride and accepted second place.

While she did, the relationship between the two wives was peaceful and harmonious. Bittersweet, against her will, even began to grow fond of Dejie, finding similarities that surprised and pleased her. Though Dejie prided herself on being city born, her father was a tanner who had worked with animal hides for so many years that his skin had turned as brown as the backs of the farmers in Bittersweet's Village Village. Bittersweet remarked upon this fact when Dejie's parents first came to pay their respects.

"Much to the dismay of my daughter," Dejie's father said, hanging his head, "I am but a poor tanner who has been branded by his lowly profession."

"Ah, well, I, too, am a farmer's daughter and proud of it. Working with one's hands is honest labor," Bittersweet answered. "It's nothing to be ashamed of."

But poor old Guo, or *Lao* Guo as he was called, shook his head and admitted, "Ever since she was a child, my daughter has used a parasol against the sun to keep her skin white. And today she wears only the whitest of rice powder on her face. I know she's trying to disinherit her modest background. Our ancestors must be very angry."

Bittersweet felt sorry for the gentle and honest man, but because of Dejie's marriage to Delin, *Lao* Guo was finally accorded the title *Xiansheng*, or Mister, and could cease his labors, the fruits of which had always eluded him. His good fortune was short-lived, however, for he died soon after he first came to pay his respects to Bittersweet. She paid her own respects by attending his funeral.

"He was a lowly artisan — an insignificant tanner," Hwang *Tai-tai*, scandalized by her best friend's behavior, chided her. "*And* the father of your husband's concubine! How could you disgrace yourself by attending his funeral? You, the wife of a brigadier general — one of the Kwangsi Three! Have you no face?"

Bittersweet only answered, "Perhaps he was a tanner, but he was an honest and unassuming man who was always respectful to me. How might I not respond in kind?"

After *Lao* Guo's death, his wife doubled her visits to Bittersweet to continue to pay her respects — and to keep an eye on Dejie. Like her husband, Guo *Tai-tai* was simple and straightforward — and she was troubled by certain "small inconsistencies," as she called them, in her daughter's character.

"Every day I thank the gods," the woman said by way of greeting Bittersweet one morning, "that Dejie is so fortunate to have you as the mistress of the house where she lives. I thank them, too, that she understands full well your primary position and her own subordinate one, and that it's not your temperament, though it's certainly within your power, to make her life miserable, even unbearable. As her mother, I know that Dejie can be petulant and proud at times. And I'm afraid, Li *Tai-tai*, that she may overstep her bounds and spoil her good fortune."

"Tell your daughter that second is a fine place to be," Bittersweet said. "It's not I who say so but the ancient wisdom of the Tao. 'I have Three Treasures that support and protect,'" she recited. "'The first is compassion. The second is moderation. The third is daring not to be the first in the world.'"

But when Guo *Tai-tai* visited her daughter in her room, Bittersweet heard raised voices and slamming doors.

"It isn't her fault," the poor mother assured Bittersweet. "The ground on which my daughter and I stand on are at different levels, she above and I below. I am but an ignorant and illiterate tanner's wife," she apologized, "while my daughter is an educated, modern-day woman — a woman in the Western mode."

"How did your parents feel about your marrying Delin, an army officer and a married man?" Bittersweet asked Dejie one day when they were doing the marketing together. "You must have had many younger beaus who were bachelors."

Dejie smiled behind her hand, concealing the pride she felt at having been the most desirable girl at school and also the hardest-to-get.

"At first I disdained the attentions of a military man — bad iron, according to my parents. I wanted to marry a member of the literati, an educated man, one who'd gone to school in an enlightened country, like England, America, or Japan. My mother always told me that fishermen and military men made bad husbands. Fishermen went out with the tide, she said, sleeping during the day then going out with the night watch. They sold their catch, then drank and gambled and smoked away all their money at the inn. With soldiers, it was similar, only they went to the battlefield instead of the sea. If they were victorious, they spent their pay carousing in the town they'd taken. If they were defeated, they remained on the battlefield as corpses. The wives of military men, she insisted, made good candidates for early widowhood. When my mother learned that I would be Delin's concu- . . . second wife, she forbade me to marry him. But I was persistent, and my parents finally accepted my decision."

"It's to your credit that you saw Delin for who he is," Bittersweet said, recalling her own struggles with her parents to marry the man of her choice.

"After I married Delin, people said I had a third eye," Dejie boasted, forgetting herself. "They said I knew how to recognize a military hero, a man who'd go far and bring me up . . . bring *us* up with him."

Bittersweet was feeling some Hami melons that had arrived that day from the far northwest and pretended not to have heard Dejie's slip of the tongue.

"It's clear that you know how to recognize a military hero," she said, dropping a plump, round melon into Dejie's hands. "Now can you select a good Hami melon for tonight's dessert? Mind that you don't choose a spoiled one — one that has a fine-looking appearance but, when cut open, is hard and dry — not at all what the outside promised."

Dejie searched Bittersweet's face for signs of the innuendo she was meant to hear.

"Then again, you don't want too young a melon. It, too, feels heavy in the hand and sports a ripe green skin, but slice it open and the flesh is pale and acidic. It's not ready for eating and is best left to mature for a few more days when its sourness can turn to sweetness."

With that, Bittersweet lifted the melon from Dejie's hands, set it back in its stall, and left her blinking in irritation, while she wandered down the aisles of produce in search of other good things to eat.

Gradually, what Guo *Tai-tai* had feared for her daughter came to pass. Gentle and mild-mannered, Dejie, as a new second wife, fulfilled all her obligations to Bittersweet. But, as time passed and Delin's prospects and position continued to soar, she began to neglect her duties to the mistress of the house. She no longer accompanied Bittersweet on her rounds of social visits, nor did she help receive and care for arrivals from Dragon's Head, nor run errands for her. While much of Dejie's time was spent accompanying Delin to social and official functions, the rest of it was channeled into "entering society." Like the officers' wives that Bittersweet had found so little in common with in Kwangtung, Dejie enjoyed going on shopping sprees, to mahjong parties, or to the theater and opera. Her companions were, like her, the second wives of high officials or decorated military officers — city women dissatisfied with their secondary status. Some of them had been tricked by their husbands into believing that they were the sole and thus primary wife. Embittered for having been so misled, many of them hoped to unburden themselves of the rancor they felt by infusing it into the newest members of their ranks.

"Why do you attend the same functions as your husband's first wife?" they asked Dejie. "There they treat her like a queen and you like her lady-in-waiting. Is that the position you wish to hold? Have you no face? Refuse to accompany her. What could you possibly have in common with a farm woman like that?"

Soon afterward, Dejie no longer accompanied Bittersweet anywhere. Bittersweet said and did nothing to call attention to Dejie's dereliction. She preferred to employ *wu-wei*, the principle of non-action or tactical inertia prescribed by the Tao. She'd let matters take their own course. Like iron filings to a magnet, the situation would, in and of itself, attract the necessary attention.

When it did and Delin confronted Dejie about the evasion of her obligations to Bittersweet, Dejie replied in an exasperated tone, "When do I have time to fulfill them? My service to you takes up all the hours of the day and night. I accompany you to all your functions. I give speeches in your name. I dedicate schools and hospitals on your behalf. I receive and entertain important visitors when you are away. Do you begrudge me the little time I spend with the wives of other officers? Don't you know that this time, too, is for *your* benefit? To befriend the wives of your fellow officers is to foster good relations between you and their husbands. As for your first wife, she prefers women like herself — simple folk from the country. I sincerely doubt she wants my company."

Delin, who listened courteously to Dejie's explanation up to this point, rose to his feet. His features were brittle. "You will show more respect for my wife," he told her bluntly. "I, too, am 'simple folk from the country.'"

Dejie's face flushed, but she bowed in accordance to propriety — offering the show if not the substance of submission to his will.

As Dejie's ambitions continued to exceed her position, the harmony in the house began to dissolve. Those inside dared not speak of the growing discord or even acknowledge it; still, they carefully guarded it from outsiders' eyes. The situation resembled that of a shadow play: the casual observer saw the outlines and the movements of the puppets behind the screen and heard the words they spoke, but not the intentions of the puppeteers who manipulated the sticks that moved the puppets and put words into their mouths. The screen of propriety that separated the observer from the observed divided what *was* from what *seemed*.

The day finally came when the flood of in-laws and friends trickled to a stream, then to a standstill, and Bittersweet could once more rest from her outside labors and focus her attention on her immediate domestic duties. The visitors from Dragon's Head had either returned home or stayed on in Kweiping. Some who weren't attached married Kweipinese women. Some who were married sent for their wives and families back in Dragon's Head. And some who were already married took a Kweipinese woman as a second wife.

One day, when Delin summoned Bittersweet to his offices, she found him with his first cousin, the one she had found rooms for in Willow Lane.

"*Ni hao*, Ninth Sister-in-Law," he said, smiling and bowing politely. "I trust you are well. And how is that fine son of yours, Youlin?"

When he had first arrived in Kweiping, Bittersweet recalled, there was rice chaff in his hair and instead of carrying a suitcase, he'd slung a fish net, filled with belongings, over his shoulder. In a few short months, he'd acquired enough poise and assurance to be mistaken for a long-time Kweipinese.

"*Ni hao*," Bittersweet said. "Both of us are very well, thank you. And you?"

"Oh," he said with a smile, glancing conspiratorially at Delin, "well enough, but I hope to be even better very soon."

"My cousin has just told me that there is a young lady in Kweiping whom he wishes to marry," Delin explained. He indicated a chair for Bittersweet to sit down, "And that she has accepted his proposal."

"Oh?" Bittersweet said, looking at First Cousin. "Does the young lady in question know that you already have a wife back home in Dragon's Head?"

"Not yet," the man replied, blushing, "but she will, in time."

"And your wife?" Bittersweet asked. "Does she know of this second marriage?"

"My cousin," Delin interrupted her with a cough, "would like to ask a favor of you."

"I hope you will do me the honor of serving as chief witness at my wedding," First Cousin said with another bow.

Bittersweet felt her throat constrict and she inadvertently sucked in air through her mouth. "How is this ceremony to be performed?" she asked finally. "As a first-time ceremony, or as a second-time ceremony?"

"Why, as a first-time ceremony," the man answered, looking at Delin for support.

"How can this wedding be celebrated as a first-time wedding when you are marrying for the second time?"

First Cousin's smile disappeared. He looked pleadingly at Delin who, in turn, averted his eyes.

"But a first-time wedding is so festive, so much more impressive," the young man stammered. "And the young lady I'm marrying thinks that. . . ."

". . . she's marrying as a first and only wife," Bittersweet finished for him.

"First Cousin," the man begged Delin, "speak to her. Say something."

"What do you expect my husband to say?" Bittersweet replied, sparing Delin the need to answer and the accompanying loss of face. "This is our home, not the battlefield. Our discussion touches upon domestic, not military, affairs. In matters such as these, the wife holds sway."

She smiled. "Delin always likes to quote Sun Tzu when it comes to formulating battle strategies and military tactics: 'When the commander is at the head of the army, he need not accept all the sovereign's orders.'" Bittersweet looked at First Cousin pointedly. "Is not my husband, Delin, my sovereign? As his wife, am I not the commander of my household? As such, I need not accept all my sovereign's orders, and Delin, wise sovereign that he is, need not voice them."

Bittersweet rose, and the two men rose with her. "I regret, First Cousin, that though you are a close relative, I cannot comply with your request. I wish both you and your bride-to-be much happiness, but I must decline your invitation to serve as chief witness at your wedding."

The two men inclined at the waist and bowed their heads to her. As she turned to go, Bittersweet caught a glimpse of Delin's face. For an instant, the public mask of the brave brigadier general disappeared. In its place was the expression of the private man who felt both deep regret for Dejie's recent actions and great admiration for Bittersweet's aplomb. He bowed lower than was appropriate for a man to bow to his wife.

Though she declined to serve as chief witness, Bittersweet attended First Cousin's second marriage. She was there as a guest and as a family member, standing in for Delin who had been called to the front. Dejie served as chief witness at the wedding ceremony. As at a first-time wedding, the bride arrived at Bittersweet's home in a sedan chair, but no other ceremony was held, no lavish banquet was served. With the omission of the festivities, the young bride could no longer hide her feelings or maintain her face. As the reception wore on, tears of frustration welled up in her eyes.

"You were to have been the chief witness at my wedding!" she screamed at Bittersweet. "It would have given me great honor if you had accepted. Instead, you refused! You refused because you knew I wasn't being married as a true wife but being taken as a concubine. Are you satisfied that I'm miserable?"

Quickly, Dejie appeared and led the sobbing bride away.

"You should have answered her," Hwang *Tai-tai* came up and whispered to Bittersweet. "How dare she accuse you — you, the hostess and mistress of the house where her reception is being held. And she a mere concubine! As her better, you should have put her in her place."

Bittersweet shook her head and looked sadly in the bride's direction. "How unhappy she is on what she thought would be the happiest day of her life! Should I have made her even more so? It's not for me to put her in her place. Her husband has already done that, a place that she is loathe to occupy. She rails against me, but her anger is really directed against the man who deceived her."

"Li *Tai-tai*, either you are too kind or you have no sense of face," Hwang *Tai-tai* scolded, snapping open her fan to blow away the heat that had risen to her cheeks.

The rest of the evening was an exercise in vicious slander. The first wives stuck together, forming one camp, the second wives formed another, and the husbands of both tried to keep out of the way. The young bride had recovered from her outburst and gathered the other second wives about her. "Because she's had a son by Brigadier General Li, she holds a high place in society, and people have to respect her," she told them. "If she didn't have his son, her husband would have abandoned her long ago, farm woman that she is."

"Throw her out of your house," Hwang *Tai-tai*, whose ears heard everything, advised Bittersweet. "End this wedding reception now! Truly, she's taking advantage of your tolerance!"

Bittersweet calmed her friend, then opened the door to the library where the men had taken refuge. She'd drunk a few glasses of wine in celebration and, after the bride's fit of crying, she'd had a glass of *san hua* in consolation. The taste of the fiery brew evoked memories of her outspoken youth in Village Village, and its alcoholic content loosened her tongue. She marched to the center of the room in the midst of three dozen suddenly silent men, most of whom she had known in Dragon's Head.

"You men have no hearts," she told them. "When you were poor farmers and labored in the fields, you were honest and good. Now you have jobs in the big city — office jobs in the provincial government and in business. You think you're important, and so you've taken second wives to cater to your selfish needs. But the worst of it is that you lied to these young girls about their being your first and only wife. And you deceived your first wives by hiding your intentions to take a second. Are you not men that you must obtain your women through lies and deceit?"

Not long after the disastrous wedding reception, rumor that her husband had taken a concubine brought First Cousin's first wife to

Kweiping. Her arrival polarized the first and second wives even further. Being officers' wives, the women even thought of themselves in militaristic terms as battalions, and the course of their quarreling seemed to follow the events of the civil war. The dream of blissful married life that First Cousin had imagined vanished, replaced by scenes and arguments between his two wives. When he tried to mediate their disputes, he only made things worse. Finally, he decided to send his first wife back to Dragon's Head. But his second wife wanted true revenge. Incited and spurred on by the second wives' battalion (of which Dejie was now a leading member), the formerly sweet, submissive woman returned to the school where she had been a student — the same girls' school that Dejie had attended — to warn her former fellow classmates about deceitful men with wives back home. Enraged by her tale, the schoolgirls insisted on taking the matter before the district magistrate. Was there nothing to be done? they asked him. The woman's husband had lied to her, had deceived her into believing that he was single and that she therefore would be his first wife. The magistrate, who had two concubines and a primary wife at home, told them that nothing could be done. There was no law against taking a second wife, no matter how it was done, by honest means or by deception. Furthermore, the taking of a concubine, in whatever way a man could or would, was widespread and customary. "Besides," the magistrate told the girls by way of ending the interview, "it's too late to do anything about it. What is done cannot be undone."

"A divorce can undo the evil that's been done," a girl student contradicted him.

But a divorce, as everyone, including the girls, knew, was a man's prerogative: men divorced; women were divorced.

"It's custom," the magistrate shrugged, his neck disappearing into his shoulders, as he flung his arms out and turned his palms up in a gesture of utter helplessness. "It's always been so."

The petty fighting between the first and second wives' battalions continued, just as the civil war raged between the two Kwangs. Rumors were rampant that the fighting would soon reach the city gates and had already reached Dragon's Head. Delin, who was commanding the fronts at Nanning and Liuchow, sent his parents to Shanghai for safety. In Kweiping, evacuation orders grew more and more frequent. For Bittersweet, rumor of attack seemed worse than actual attack, impending disaster worse than disaster itself — for the people were constantly fearful, constantly in a panic. Time and time again, Bittersweet and Dejie packed up their belongings to follow the army to a safer town. When they arrived in their temporary haven, they rented a house to live in; if no house was available, they stayed at the army barracks. Living at the latter, Bittersweet soon wondered which was the greater threat: the enemy armies or their own armies who, like common thieves and vandals, terrified and terrorized the townspeople, "borrowing" from the merchants' shops and the farmers' fields.

"Is this how our troops carry out their military duties?" Bittersweet wrote in a letter to Delin. "Their minds must be befuddled by opium. The people here refer to them as 'bulb heads,' for as a vacuum exists inside a light bulb, a vacuum exists inside the heads of our soldiers. A frequent motto here is 'Army's passing, everything's smashing.' And they're not referring to the Kwangtung army. What difference does it make to them if Kwangsi's soldiers are friend or foe, warlord army or revolutionary army, when both our soldiers and our officers take advantage of the people?"

Finally, Bittersweet refused to abide by yet another evacuation order. She wouldn't risk living in another army barracks. She preferred, she said, to take her chances back home in Kweiping where, if she was to die, at least she would die in her own bed. For once Dejie was of the same mind, and the two women returned to their quiet house in the nearly deserted city. There they learned that the rumors that had prompted the evacuation orders had all been false alarms. There, too, they received a long-awaited letter from Delin. In it, he answered Bittersweet's queries:

"What you say about our soldiers is true. But why is it true? For months now, my men have received neither pay nor rations. In one breath, Chiang and the central government tell us that we're all part of one China and that they need us to achieve this goal of unification. In the next, they tell us to win the war against Kwangtung and unify Kwangsi on our own, and not to expect any help from them. I asked Chiang, 'Are we all not part of this unified China you talk so much about — poor provinces as well as rich ones? Or is it only Kiangsu and Szechuan Provinces that qualify for central government assistance? Those wealthy provinces need help least, and yet their pay and rations arrive on time, while we poor provinces must rely on revenues from the tax on opium. And most of the tax never reaches the provincial coffers but winds up in the pockets of the tax collectors who, in addition, skim some of the opium and sell it (to the bulb heads, as you, Xuewen, refer to them). Yet Kwangsi men have been praised as warriors since ancient times. If they're trained properly, if they're treated fairly, there are no better fighters in all of China.'"

In the autumn of 1925, the civil war between the Kwangs ended, peace was declared, and Delin was promoted to the rank of general. After ten years of military and civil strife, Kwangsi was unified and at peace. For days on end, the Kwangsinese lit firecrackers and beat gongs and drums. Colorful parades thronged streets full of joyful, laughing people. Happiest of all were the military and their wives: soldiers and officers no longer had to fear death on the battlefield, and their wives no longer had to fear widowhood at an early age. The first and second wives even called a truce for a time.

With peace came prosperity. New floating restaurants were moored in the river, and theaters and opera houses were constructed or refurbished. Everywhere there was the clicking of chopsticks in restaurants, the whining cry of street vendors, and the high-pitched nasal warbling of opera singers throwing their voices against brick and plaster walls to strengthen and warm them up for an evening's performance. Farms that had lain fallow or been trampled by army boots now bloomed with fresh produce. Merchants and shopkeepers who had closed their doors against both friendly and enemy armies now threw them wide open and rested their soft hands on their protruding stomachs to show that now they could eat their fill.

Delin, relieved of much of his military duties, threw himself into the civil administration of the province. The Kwangsi Three—Pai Chung-hsi, Hwang Shao-hsiung, and Delin — established commissions on finance, education, and public construction. They filled posts with men known for their honesty and capability. A more equitable land tax was instituted. Tax collectors were now appointed on merit.

With the increased revenues, people's livelihood improved. A provincial university was founded in Wuchow and later moved to Kweilin. A military school was established in Nanning to create well-trained, disciplined soldiers. "Bandit pacification" — the offer of military posts to induce bandits to surrender, a practice which only encouraged what the government sought to eradicate — was scrapped, and bandits were sent back to their families who were required to take responsibility for them. Once known as "the province of bandits," Kwangsi lost its tainted reputation. Under the Kwangsi

Three, a handful of roads became a network; the irrigation systems were improved. Forestry, land reclamation, and mining were all promoted. Nearby provinces, which had once shunned their unruly neighbor, now sent delegates to seek advice from and pledge cooperation with the new, youthful administration. Kwangsi, once China's backwater in almost every respect, was transformed from a rebellious, chaotic, bandit-infested province into a model of civil administration.

Just as Delin, Bittersweet, and Dejie were preparing to move to Nanning, Kwangsi's new capital, news came from Da Mama that Baba had died in Shanghai and that she was traveling with her husband's body to Dragon's Head to give him a traditional burial. Though, as an adult, Baba had disavowed certain ways and customs of his youth, his wife had found a source of solace in them, a comfort which she did not find in their strange modern replacements, and so it was the old ways she turned to for the funeral.

"A traditional funeral takes much preparation and many, many days," Delin told Bittersweet. "The provincial government is just being set up in Nanning. How can I discharge both my duties — that of son of my country and son of my father?"

"When I married you years ago, it was considered bad luck to marry a man with the same surname, and so I changed my name from Li to Lu just for that occasion," Bittersweet said after a moment. "Just for this occasion, may I exchange my identity for yours — I, who have so often represented you, your family, and your clan? I know what plans and preparations must be made for a traditional funeral. You know what plans and preparations must be made to establish a new government for Kwangsi."

Wearing unhemmed clothes of white sack cloth and with a length of rope tied around her forehead, Bittersweet was both Delin's representative and chief mourner at Baba's funeral. Bittersweet carried the heredity jar — a small earthenware vessel into which members of the succeeding generation put rice, meat dumplings, and steamed wheat bread. She saw to it that the jar, placed at the front of the coffin, was full to ensure a long line of descendants, plenty of food for Baba on his long journey, and good luck for all those who contributed to the jar's contents. Baba's youngest son — Delin's third brother, Solin — then sealed the jar with a round loaf of bread into which he plunged a pair of chopsticks.

Bittersweet was pleased to learn that many people had been present when her father-in-law died and to see that many more were present at his funeral. It was believed that those who died alone were fated to come back in their next life as single people — people with no descendants. Even more than death, Chinese feared being alone, without any family around them.

As chief mourner, Bittersweet had sewn the little red bag which contained material comforts for Baba's journey: a piece of silver so he could buy whatever he needed; a pinch of tea; a piece of candy; and a piece of salted vegetable to make his food more palatable. She inserted the bag into his mouth, then placed a small bag of food in his hand, so he could feed the dogs as he crossed the great Dog Mountain. Then, so that his body would be still and not get up again — for Chinese loved this world, believed in no greater paradise, and hated to leave it — she bound his feet with a cord.

The night before the day of the burial, Bittersweet and Baba's family knelt around his coffin and wailed in sorrow. Meanwhile, hired musicians blew trumpets, crashed cymbals, and beat on drums to help the spirit leave the body and go its way to the spirit world. So that Baba would be well-provided for in the afterworld, family members burned paper ingots, paper houses, and paper servants they had fashioned and piled into a heap. Then, the ashes were swept into an earthenware bowl. After the coffin was lifted up and placed on the shoulders of the closest male members of Baba's family, it was carried to the *feng-shui* grave that had been prepared midway up a hillside outside the village walls. The location of the grave was propitious, situated as it was in a large vein of the earth dragon, where vital energy abounded. Here, the earthenware bowl was thrown to the ground where it shattered, and the wailing voices of the family rose high to the heavens one last time.

Chapter 11
Dashao
(1925)

For two months in Dragon's Head, Bittersweet lived with her wid-owed mother-in-law, Youlin, Delin's brothers, First Outside Sister-in-Law, and her unmarried sister-in-law, Yifu. Here, she felt as safe as when she had not known war or uprooting, as secure as when she had been a child in her own parents' home. The soaring hills and the meandering green river, the bamboo groves and the osmanthus trees were all the more beautiful to her for her having been away from them for so long. After her first month home, she thought of taking Youlin on a visit to the Taoist temple. She wanted, of course, to see Xiao Tzu again.

In Kweiping, she had written a letter in response to his, admitting that she, too, felt a bond other than that between teacher and pupil — the bond of friendship. So many years had passed, she thought, surely any feelings more tender than those had also passed.

When Bittersweet and Youlin came to the temple gate, her heart sank. While the other *hutongs* and houses in Dragon's Head had been spared any serious damage, the temple seemed to have fared badly. Half of the roof was missing; the other half was blackened by fire. Debris littered the courtyard and a hole, nearly the size of the entry gate, gaped in the wall.

"The wages of war," an old priest explained, smiling and nodding his head in welcome.

When Bittersweet expressed regret at the destruction, the old priest laughed and said, "Why? All the better to see the rising of the moon."

"Was anyone hurt?" she inquired.

"Yes. Killed by a mortar shell that ripped right through his stomach. A young priest. Thank the Taoist pantheon he was killed instantly! There were a few others who were injured, but their wounds have healed."

Bittersweet scanned the courtyard for signs of her old teacher. A few priests were sweeping the cobblestones or burning piles of debris.

"The priest who died," Bittersweet asked, her breathing suddenly labored. "Do you know his name? It wasn't . . . isn't Xiao Tzu, is it?"

"You mean the abbot's prize student? That prankster?" The old priest laughed again. "No, that one wouldn't try to obstruct a mortar shell with his body — he'd turn immaterial first. Xiao Tzu's alive — more alive than most, I'd say," he continued. "But if he's the one you want to help you make your offerings, he's not here but on a retreat with the abbot. They left a few days ago. I don't think they'll be back for several weeks."

"Ah," Bittersweet said in gratitude, then she shook her head to decline the old monk's invitation to assist her in making her offerings. She left, promising to return at a later date. Her relief quickly turned to joy; Xiao Tzu was well and still his irrepressible, spontaneous self. But no sooner did she acknowledge her happiness and its cause than she felt disappointment that he hadn't been at the temple to see her. She wanted to tell him so many things — of her life with Delin and Dejie, of her uprootings during the civil war, even of the factionalism between the first and second wives. She had missed his company and his friendship — more than she cared to admit — and had looked forward to today's visit with an enthusiasm, even an urgency, that she now wanted to deny.

"When are we going to see Daddy again?" Youlin asked one day. He was tearing the barbed tips off the snow peas he'd helped harvest from Da Mama's vegetable garden. Bittersweet and Da Mama glanced at each other. They had enjoyed each other's company these past two months and had tried not to think of the inevitable leave-taking.

"Any day now," Da Mama answered. "Your Mama's place is beside your Daddy, and yours as their son is with them both."

That very night Bittersweet began packing.

"This old mansion used to be the home of the famous warlord and governor, Lu Jung-ting," the rickshaw driver told Bittersweet. "It's fitting that one of the three heroes of Kwangsi should be living in it now."

The house in front of which the rickshaw driver stopped was even larger and grander than her former house in Kweiping. Bittersweet wondered how many sections deep it ran and how many courtyards separated them. Holding Youlin's hand in hers, she crossed the threshold of the *da men* and passed under the moon gate and around the spirit screen, the screen which prevented straight-line-traveling evil spirits from entering the compound.

Delin stood, across the first courtyard, by the front door of the house. "Welcome home," he said. He tousled Youlin's hair, for his son was too big now to swing into the air. Together the three of them toured the first *siheyuan* of several rooms which served as Delin's offices and crossed the second courtyard to the living quarters in the second *siheyuan*. There, just as in the house in Kweiping, Bittersweet's bedroom suite was on the left, while Dejie's was on the right, of the courtyard. The third section of the house comprised the servants' quarters and storerooms. Throughout the house and in the courtyards, people were bustling about.

"Have more relatives arrived from Dragon's Head?" she asked. "And though the house is large, are there enough rooms to put them all in?"

Delin laughed and shook his head. "No, I guess we ran out of relatives before we could run out of rooms. Most of the people you see here are servants."

Bittersweet looked perplexed. "Are there that many of us living here?"

"It has less to do with the number of residents than the number of bars I wear on my uniform." Delin smiled in self-mockery. "Didn't you know? Your husband is a big man in Kwangsi."

Bittersweet smiled in turn, recalling how at officers training school, Delin, though he was one of the smallest cadets, was known as Fierce Kid Li, for he was tireless in military drills and brave in battle.

"Because of my position, I'm expected to have a large contingent of servants to see that my life and my house run smoothly. I could do with fewer, but Dejie insisted. For herself alone, she has two maidservants and a secretary as well as two cooks — one for Chinese and one for Western food. And two tutors — one to learn English and the other for Bible studies."

"Bible studies!" Bittersweet exclaimed. "But only Christians study the Bible."

"A leading example of whom is Chiang *Tai-tai*," Delin replied in a flat voice. "Dejie admires and therefore tries to emulate her. Chiang's wife is known in China as the paragon of the modern woman. She wears Western fashions, attended a women's college in America, speaks fluent English. . . ."

"And follows a Western religion," Bittersweet concluded.

"Now that I hold an important position in both the national army and in the provincial government," Delin continued, eager to change the subject, "it's only fitting that you should have people to serve you, too."

Bittersweet understood that, since her position was superior to Dejie's, she was expected to take a greater number of servants for herself. But if she took on so many that she didn't need or want, it would be extravagant, excessive, and extreme — not the way of the Tao.

"I'll advertise for a maidservant first thing tomorrow," Bittersweet said.

"One maidservant?" Delin asked.

"One," his wife answered.

His surprised expression quickly transformed into one of approbation. "As you wish," he said with a smile. "After all, in domestic matters such as this, the wife always holds sway."

Two days later, a woman in her mid-thirties, broad of face and bottom, with an open expression and a direct, commonsensical gaze, knocked on the *da men* of the Li residence. "My humble respects to the august mistress of the house," the woman said with a deep bow to Bittersweet as she handed her a letter of recommendation.

Though she is a servant, Bittersweet thought, as she led her inside to the sitting room, she possesses the propriety and bearing of an educated person. And how at ease she is in these elegant surroundings — as though she were familiar with luxury. Because a servant who worked for a family over many years came to be considered a family member, Bittersweet conducted the interview with thoughtfulness and thoroughness, seeking clues not only to the woman's professional qualifications but also to her character.

Her given name was Dashao, or Big Few, and she hailed from Liuchow where every Chinese longed to die, for the best coffins were made in Liuchow where the best hardwood trees grew. As Dashao spoke, Bittersweet became more and more amazed at how similar their lives' circumstances were, and yet how different their fates. Like Baba, Dashao's father had been a teacher who had failed the imperial examination towards the end of the Qing Dynasty. Before he died, and before Dashao was fifteen years old, he taught her how to read and write. From her mother, she learned sewing and needlework. To supplement the family income, she became a skillful seamstress. At eighteen, she married an army officer who was killed at the beginning of the war between the Kwangs. His body was never found.

"To lose one's husband to war is terrible enough," Dashao told Bittersweet, "but not to be able to give him a proper burial was a tragedy indeed. At twenty, I was a widow with two infant sons. But the worst was yet to come. One I was to lose to small pox, the other to a bombing raid."

A smile softened her otherwise tough, weathered face. "When I was a child and living in the house of my parents, I witnessed the wedding procession of a well-born maiden to a dead man. They had been betrothed since infancy, but soon after their engagement, he died of tuberculosis. The wedding procession wended its way though the part of town where I lived. Standing inside my doorway peeking out, I saw the bride dressed in the white of mourning. Her sedan chair was settled high on the shoulders of important officials and magistrates — in honor of her fidelity to her dead husband. His sedan chair carried his ancestral tablet. Touched by the pomp and dignity of the ceremony, I vowed that if my husband-to-be died before me, I would be an honorable widow and never marry again. Little did I know that my husband would be taken from me so soon after our wedding. And when he was, I wished I had been so lucky as to marry a groom who was deceased, for then I wouldn't have to be lonely without him. I wouldn't have had children that I had to support on my own. I wouldn't have had to grieve on three separate occasions within the span of five years: first, when I left my family to be wed; second, when I learned of the death of my husband; and third, when I buried my two sons."

"How did you support them and yourself?" Bittersweet asked the unfortunate woman.

"Madam, I worked in this very house," Dashao replied, to Bittersweet's astonishment. "General Lu Jung-ting was warlord of the whole province at the time, and I found employment as one of the many maidservants in his enormous household. I received no pay — just two meals a day and a roof over my head and the heads of my children. When I heard that the wife of the man who had defeated General Lu was now living in his house and looking for a maidservant, I came straightaway."

"You were right to have come," Bittersweet told her. After she explained to Dashao what duties would be required of her and what remuneration she could expect, the matter was settled. Dashao would be Bittersweet's personal maidservant and Youlin's nursemaid.

The relationship proved propitious from the start. Dashao was honest, diligent, and hard-working, and Youlin took an instant liking to her.

"How is it that my son is getting such good grades?" Delin asked his wife not long after Dashao had entered into Bittersweet's employ.

"Your son is naturally intelligent and diligent," Bittersweet answered. "But he also owes his good grades to the intelligence and diligence of another. Dashao compliments him not only on his grades but also the effort he makes to achieve them. And when he has a little friend over, she modulates her praise and also encourages the other boy to do better. That way, she gets the best results from both and avoids instigating a rivalry between them."

"What an extraordinary woman," Delin said.

Bittersweet nodded. "Yes, extraordinary," she said. "To prevent a rivalry between two small boys is no small thing — almost as extraordinary as preventing one between two grown women."

The comment was not lost on her husband. Now that the civil war was long over, the truce that had been called between the first and second wives was revoked, and they again divided into separate camps.

On many days, in Bittersweet's sitting room, over mahjong, Dragon Well tea, and fancy cakes filled with melon rind, the embittered first wives shared tales of second wives whom they'd forced to tears or to return to their families, of beatings and near starvation that had made the young women contemplate suicide and sometimes even commit it. When one tale was told, a second one was begun, surpassing it in imagination and cruelty. On these social occasions, Bittersweet was not only silent but often the recipient of the other first wives' rebukes.

"Aren't you a first wife, Li *Tai-tai,*" Bittersweet's mahjong partner asked, "and a most powerful first wife, that you have no contribution to make to our conversation?"

"That I am my husband's first wife is true," she replied, "but I'm afraid I have nothing to add to this particular conversation."

Annoyed, the other women looked at each other. "You and Dejie are inseparable friends, I suppose."

"We're able to live together in harmony," Bittersweet answered.

"Aren't you afraid that Dejie is taking advantage of you?" Hwang *Tai-tai* asked, genuinely concerned for her friend's welfare. "Don't you fear that all of your husband's money is going into Dejie's purse? If you don't put her in her place, she may soon be vying for yours."

"If she isn't already," quipped another first wife.

"Don't you read the papers?" asked another player, shuffling the ivory tiles. "There are always pictures of your husband with Dejie at his side. Where, then, is your place?"

"Yes, I read the papers," Bittersweet said calmly. Knowing that her inquisitor was illiterate, she added, "*Besides* looking at the pictures. It's Dejie's *duty* to accompany my husband to social and official functions. Being a society matron, she knows how to dress and talk at these occasions, and so she is a credit to my husband and an asset to his career. However, as Delin's first wife, my position is assured. As his second wife, Dejie's position is tenuous — she must always strive to elevate her position in society since she may not raise her place at home. You ladies would do well to remember that. You'd be less dissatisfied."

"You're much too kind, Li *Tai-tai*," the wife who beat her husband's concubine said. "No wonder Dejie calls you the woman from the farm." Several other first wives seated around the mahjong board tittered behind their hands.

"Oh, I don't think I'm the only one they call by that name," Bittersweet replied, taking a sip of tea. Chastened, the women fell silent. After all, many of them had rural origins, too.

"They'd have liked you to cause trouble for Guo *Yi Tai-tai*," Dashao sniffed after the guests had gone and she was clearing away the mahjong board and delicate plates and cups, "just so they'd have a pretext to continue to mistreat their husbands' concubines. When I heard what you said, I knew I was working in the right house."

"What purpose would it serve if I'd agreed with them?" Bittersweet said.

Misunderstanding her mistress's question as one that required an answer, Dashao replied, "The opportunity for people to be scandalized, to laugh and gossip behind your back, to accuse you of pettiness and jealousy. General Li would then suffer shame on your account and lose much face. Everyone would side with Dejie, feeling sympathy for her and ill will towards you."

"I see no advantage to succumbing to my guests' suggestions," Bittersweet said. "Yes, there would be a moment of satisfaction in doing so, but then, after, there would be a lifetime of regret."

"Like I said, Li *Tai-tai*," Dashao sniffed, "I came to the right home."

The more Dashao studied her mistress, the more trusting she grew, and the more forthright she became in exhibiting her extraordinary skills.

"You must taste Dashao's cooking," Bittersweet told Delin one evening after he had dined with Dejie as was customary. "It's common knowledge that men make the best cooks, but Dashao is an exception to the rule."

"If that's an invitation to dinner, I accept with pleasure," Delin replied, suppressing a burp. "Dejie's Western cook prepares such heavy meals."

"Tomorrow evening?" Bittersweet suggested. "At seven."

The next evening, Dashao prepared some of her very best dishes: tortoise eggs; roast turtle; bamboo shoots with shredded Yunnan ham and sea slugs; minced pork and *bok-choy* with mushrooms, served in a bean curd jacket; winter melon soup served in its own rind; and pudding of the eight heavenly flavors. At the end of the feast, Delin sat back in his chair and surveyed the empty bowls and platters. "Not only have you found a remarkable maidservant," he told Bittersweet and, indirectly, Dashao who had entered the room with a pot of fresh tea, "but an exceptional cook."

Dejie smiled and nodded at her husband's remark and, though she hadn't touched her wine cup at dinner, she blushed bright red.

A week after the successful dinner party, while Bittersweet was reading in her rooms, Dashao came in with her feather duster — an unusual occurrence since Dashao never entered her mistress's room when Bittersweet was present, unless she was expressly asked to. Conscious of Dashao's presence but not acknowledging it, Bittersweet continued to read. Obviously, something was on her maidservant's mind and it must be serious: Dashao had not only entered unannounced and uninvited, she was humming under her breath. Finally, when she dusted close enough to Bittersweet to cause her mistress to sneeze, Dashao said without preliminaries or apologies, as was her way, "Guo *Yi Tai-tai* stopped me in the hall the other day."

Bittersweet looked up from her newspaper.

"It was in a corner of the hallway at a time of the day when no one passes. She asked me to work for her so that General Li could eat my good food every day." Dashao slid the feather duster along the windowsill behind Bittersweet.

"And what did you reply?"

"I told her that I was already employed, that I worked for you and my young master, and that I was very happy with my job."

"And did she accept your answer?"

"She asked me how I would have responded if General Li had put the same question to me." Dashao's duster came to a stop. "I told her if General Li wanted to eat my food, then he should be the one to tell me so."

That same day, Bittersweet asked her husband why he wanted to take Dashao away from her. "But who told you that?" he asked, frowning. "I have no wish, nor do I have any intention, to take Dashao away from you and Youlin. On the contrary, I'm delighted that you've found so trustworthy and capable a person to serve you." He smiled. "I still remember that dinner she prepared for us a week ago. As a cook, she's an absolute treasure."

"Dashao was so pleased when you complimented her," Bittersweet said, "and Youlin and I would be pleased if you came to eat with us whenever you liked. I'm sure Dashao would be, too."

Thereafter, once a week, Delin and Dejie joined Bittersweet and Youlin for dinner.

"Ah, unpolished rice," Delin sighed one night after eating a few bites. "I've almost forgotten how good it tastes."

Bittersweet, who had been watching Dejie picking at her food, now found a perfect opportunity to poke fun at her city ways. "Do you really like it? You know, unpolished rice is planted by China's farm women. They don't eat it, however. They sell it at market so that city women can have their fill. If farm women didn't plant this kind of rice, city folk would never know what it tastes like."

"Don't I know it," Delin said. "Don't forget, I was a farmer once myself. You two have married a farmer at heart. It's this nation building that's pulled me out of the rice fields and onto the battlefield. But when peace is achieved, what's to prevent me from retiring from the military and returning to the paddies to plant rice?"

Dejie's mouth was pinched tight in anger. She set her chopsticks down beside her bowl so that no one would see that her hands were shaking. Having achieved her aim, Bittersweet was silent. While she ate the remainder of the unpolished rice in her bowl, she digested her small but gratifying triumph.

Dejie, however, was not one to be defeated so easily. If she hadn't succeeded in making Dashao her cook, Dejie was determined to make her the next best thing: a practicing Christian.

It was the era of the New Life Movement in China, a movement that combined aspects of Christianity and Confucianism. The improvement of personal conduct and the cultivation of virtues such as courtesy, service, honor, and honesty was encouraged for the betterment of society at large. Since the New Life Movement was promoted by Chiang *Tai-tai*, Dejie was quick to support it.

"'Except a man be born again,'" she often quoted Chiang's wife, "'he cannot see New Life.'"

Dejie had decided that Dashao was in particular need of salvation and that constant criticism was the way to help her attain it.

One hot, humid summer's day, Dejie was wearing a long-sleeved *cheongsam,* since modesty — no matter what the temperature — was a strong New Life principle. In the crook of her arm, she carried a big black Bible, St. James version, in English. She stopped Dashao in the hall and said, patronizingly, "I saw you watching that gaudy funeral in the center of town yesterday when you should have been busy running errands for your mistress. Aren't you aware that such expensive celebrations are wasteful and superstitious?"

Dashao shrugged her shoulders. "I like lighting joss sticks and firecrackers and burning spirit money," she admitted. "Now that I work for a wealthy family, there are lots of things it would be improper for me to do but, thank the gods . . ." Dejie grimaced at this heresy. ". . . enjoying funerals isn't one of them. At the temple fairs and outdoor theatricals, I'm forced to sit in a special section reserved for the well-to-do and their servants, far from the stage and the excitement. I must be on my best behavior not to shame Li *Tai-tai* or make her lose face because of me. Sometimes I think I'd rather trade places with the beggar women I've seen at these spectacles," she continued with a sigh. "They have a front row seat, practically up on the stage. They have no face to save and so they can have a grand time, laughing, chattering away, and slapping their knees, without fearing what others will think of them. Even if I'm having a good time, I can't show it."

From then on, when Dashao shuffled, Dejie told her to pick up her feet. If her bun was less than tight, she told her to straighten it. If she cooked more than four dishes and a soup for Bittersweet and Youlin, Dejie — who had rid herself of her Western cook, less out of New Life frugality than for the fact that his cuisine gave Delin heartburn — accused Dashao of being frivolous and wasteful.

One day, Dejie came upon Dashao scrubbing her hands and face, drying them, then immediately repeating the procedure two more times. When Dejie asked why she was duplicating her efforts, the woman said, "Didn't you tell me that I must bathe once a week, wash and boil my vegetables before eating them, and wash my hands and face three times a day? I thought I'd get the last rule over and done with all at once, so I could get on with my chores."

The more Dejie tried to imbue Christian ways or New Life attitudes in her, the more Dashao took pleasure in ruining her plans.

When Dashao scolded the serving boy for being lazy or slow, Dejie folded her hands meekly on top of her Bible and chided, "If you were a Christian, you'd be more charitable in your dealings with others. If you become a Christian, you'll grow a good heart, save your soul, and go to heaven."

"I've seen Chinese who are Christians and Chinese who are not," Dashao answered. "The good actions of one are no better than the good actions of the other. And the same holds true for the bad actions — they are no worse. As for heaven, what do any of us know about what awaits us after death? Who's to say that your Christian heaven is any better than the Chinese spirit world?"

Another day, Dashao was sitting in the courtyard mending a pair of Bittersweet's cloth shoes. To thread the needle, she held it very close to her eyes. Seeing her squinting, Dejie, who was reading from her Bible under the willow tree nearby, remarked, "In the Christian religion, in order to get into heaven, the rich of this earth will have to pass through the eye of a needle, but the poor of this world will wear a gold crown set with as many precious stones as the persons they've converted to Christianity. Those with the most gems in their crowns will sit closest to God the father."

Dashao dropped her hands into her lap and burst out laughing. "No *wonder* you're so anxious to convert people," she cackled. "All I know,

Guo *Yi Tai-tai*, is what is here and now. And what I see is the rich of this world passing across wide thresholds whose doors are held open for them, while we poor must slip around to the back entrance and pound on the door for someone to open up."

But Dejie wouldn't be deterred. "There are rich who believe and there are poor who believe."

"The rich think it's fashionable to dress in Western clothes and eat Western food," Dashao said, wetting the thread on her tongue. "Why wouldn't they think it fashionable to believe in Western religion as well? As for the poor who believe, their faith is seasonal. When the harvest is bad and there's little rice to be had, they believe and the Christian missionaries give them rice. When the harvest is good and their bellies are full, they revert to burning incense in front of the ancestral tablets."

Dejie threw down her Bible in frustration. "You should be ashamed of yourself — sewing in the courtyard for all to see when today is the Sabbath, the day of rest. If you must sew for your mistress, can't you at least sew in the privacy of your own room?"

"What difference does it make," Dashao asked, pulling the thread through the needle and knotting the two ends together, "if I sew here in the courtyard or alone in my room, since your god sees every-where?"

Dejie picked up the Bible with an angry swipe and rose to go inside. "It's better that you're not a Christian," she snapped. "You'd make a very bad one."

"Now *there* we are in complete agreement," Dashao said, slapping her thighs in confirmation. "For one, I cannot tell my hands to be still on the Sabbath any more than I can any other day when there's work to be done. They simply wouldn't listen. For another, Christians, so you tell me, always tell the truth. When I go to market, how could I tell a merchant who wants fifty cash for an article that I have only forty cash, when that's not true? Li *Tai-tai* entrusts me with the family budget. What kind of manager would I be if I spent all that the merchants ask?"

During the time when Dejie was busy trying to convert Dashao to Christianity and the New Life Movement, relations between the two wives were quite harmonious since they were quite removed. Bitter-sweet socialized as little as possible with the first wives and, for the first time since the truce between the two camps was broken, she felt that domestic peace reigned within her household. But good fortune often springs from misfortune, and misfortune often arises from good fortune. Misfortune she might have anticipated from Dejie, but when it came, its source was none other than Delin.

As one of the Kwangsi Three, Delin shared the accolades, as well as the criticisms, of his position with two other men — Pai Chung-hsi, a Mohammedan who, as the silk glove for Delin's so-called iron fist, often served as intermediary between Delin and Chiang; and Hwang Shao-hsiung, the governor of Kwangsi and the husband of Hwang *Tai-tai*. In addition to censure and praise, all three men shared striking similarities. Like Delin's father, Pai and Hwang's were failed imperial scholars who had earned their livelihoods as school teachers. Hwang's grandfather, like Delin's, was a practitioner of traditional Chinese medicine; and Hwang's father, again like Delin's, had advocated a modern China and encouraged his son to question, even attack, the old order. Delin and Hwang were both sons of men whose efforts to restore the past prosperity of their families had met with defeat, and sons of women who had run the family farm while their husbands sought to establish themselves as scholar-bureaucrats.

When Bittersweet first met Governor Hwang, she saw the head-strong young cadet he must have been at Kwangsi Military Officers Training School. Surely, he had been as determined as her own husband to help bring about a new China. As such a man, she thought, he was an appropriate match for his equally determined, equally head-strong, and equally capable wife. Still, their union caused Bittersweet some concern, for she occasionally caught glimpses of Governor Hwang going into or coming out of the House of the Wide Gates. Knowing that he was Delin's trusted colleague and a man who had been instrumental in ending the civil war, as well as the husband of her closest friend, Bittersweet was concerned but nonetheless tactfully silent about the matter. Hwang's wife, however, was not.

"I'm well aware of my husband's visitations to the House of the Wide Gates," Hwang *Tai-tai* remarked one day when she and Bitter-sweet were passing not far from the house of ill repute, "and I encour-age it. I've borne his two daughters and a son who died of the seven-day virus and who nearly took me with him. I've adopted a son who will carry on the family name and care for us in our old age. My position is thus assured. Having done my wifely duty, I prefer to sleep in as narrow a bed as he does a wide one."

Bittersweet

When Bittersweet met Governor Hwang at dinner parties or other social functions, he was often red-faced and bleary-eyed with drink, and she was troubled for her husband and for her best friend. But it was when Governor Hwang began smoking opium, which Delin had always hoped to control in Kwangsi, that her anxiety found voice.

"Governor Hwang seemed a bit despondent the last time he was here," Bittersweet told Delin one day. "He also looks dissipated. Do you think he might be ill?"

"I've been talking the matter over with General Pai," Delin said, his gaze unsettlingly direct. "We both agree on the cause of the illness . . . and the cure. He needs a son."

The skin along Bittersweet's hairline contracted, tightening her face. "But he has a son."

"A secret child. An adopted son," Delin qualified. "He wants a son of his own blood. He and his wife haven't shared the same bed for some time now."

Bittersweet took a deep breath and held it, as if by holding it, she could hold back the request she knew was forthcoming.

"I'm afraid of what will happen to the provincial government if Governor Hwang goes on this way. Everything we've worked for, fought for, died for." His voice hardened. "I'm asking you to help me. I'd like you to find a young lady to be his second wife."

Bittersweet expelled her breath and slumped against the back of her chair for support. "I, who am the best friend of his wife?" she said, barely above a whisper.

Delin pretended not to hear. "There's already an appropriate candidate — a high school student. Governor Hwang has met her, though not formally, and is quite smitten with her."

Bittersweet, who had succeeded in deflecting the barbs and taunts of the first wives, who had shielded herself against the second wives' pettiness and cruelty, now found herself defenseless. Delin's intention was hardly to hurt her as theirs had been, yet he was hurting her nonetheless with his call to patriotism. Again, she was reminded of the fact that, though she was his first wife, she was not first in his heart. Again, she relived the suffering she had endured on learning that Delin had taken a second wife — only this time she was required not only to accept his decision but also to give her blessing to the union, not only to serve as matchmaker for a concubine but also to betray her best friend's trust.

"I believe you know the young lady in question, since you know her mother. In fact, you're on quite friendly terms with Tien *Tai-tai*."

"Tien *Tai-tai*," Bittersweet gasped. "Tien *Tai-tai* is a first wife whose husband has taken a second with whom she does not get along. Do you think she would willingly give her only daughter to a man who already has a wife, to suffer what she suffers?"

"I don't permit myself the luxury of thinking in personal terms," Delin said gravely. "I'm thinking of Kwangsi. I'm thinking of China." He looked at his wife. "Tien *Tai-tai* respects you. She'll listen to you. If you spoke with her, perhaps she could be persuaded."

Bittersweet placed her hands in her lap and looked at them. They, too, she noticed, were unusually big, as her feet were big. A farm woman's hands and feet, she thought. "It is myself I must first persuade."

She looked at Delin. "Years ago, when I joined you in Kweiping, I met a woman on the boat. Like me, she was the first of two wives, but unlike me, she was not joining her husband in the big city, but leaving him in Shanghai to return to his family farm outside Nanning. She was a country woman, and she was an honest and upright woman, so I listened to her. She told me that there are two things that a woman must not do: she must not act as a matchmaker for a woman to marry a second time, for to marry two times . . . for a woman at least . . . is to mix the streams of life, and a sin. 'A good horse does not carry two saddles,' she said. 'A good woman does not marry two times.' The second thing she told me was that a woman must not act as a matchmaker for a girl to become a concubine. To be a concubine is to suffer too much, for she is at the mercy of the first wife. To be a matchmaker for a concubine is to destroy a life."

"That is not the case in my house," Delin said with a bow; in so doing, he both paid Bittersweet great honor and destroyed her argument. "And that needn't be the case in Governor Hwang's. If Tien *Tai-tai* demands good treatment and a high position for her daughter as the governor's second wife, tell her he will give it. If she demands that her daughter be on par with his first wife, tell her he will grant it and even guarantee it in writing. As for Hwang *Tai-tai*, her position is already assured. She has a mind for money and a way with it. What she may not gain in position and respect, she will reap in material rewards. Tell her that her husband will place a large part of his possessions in her name and will do so with pleasure."

After Bittersweet had listened to her husband's words, she could do nothing other than promise to speak to Tien *Tai-tai* and to Hwang *Tai-tai* and to carry out her promise soon.

Because hers was a delicate mission, Bittersweet went to see Tien *Tai-tai* several times. The first time, she merely put the matter to the woman in general terms, without mentioning who it was who wished to marry her daughter or what exactly his professional prospects or marital status were. When Bittersweet had interested Tien *Tai-tai*, she intimated that the man asking for her daughter's hand was already married. Tien *Tai-tai* was aghast, but she didn't stop Bittersweet from explaining.

"The future of Kwangsi depends on the gentleman-in-question," she told Tien *Tai-tai* whose face was white with alarm. "His ability to rule the province will be greatly impaired if he is denied a happy family life and greatly improved if he were granted it."

On the second visit, Bittersweet named Tien *Tai-tai*'s prospective son-in-law. She also spoke of Governor Hwang's close friendship with Delin, of the lofty position he presently held in the provincial government, and of his great prospects for national recognition.

On Bittersweet's third visit, she assured Tien *Tai-tai* that any young woman who married Governor Hwang would be accorded not only excellent treatment and high position but the full measure of respect accorded to a first wife. When Tien *Tai-tai* asked Bittersweet if Governor Hwang was willing to guarantee her daughter equal rank with his first wife, Bittersweet replied that she had his word that he was prepared to do so.

On the fourth visit, Tien *Tai-tai* permitted Bittersweet to bring Governor Hwang to her house. There, before all three women — Bittersweet, Tien *Tai-tai*, and her daughter — Hwang smashed his opium pipe to bits and swore that he would end his dissolute ways and become a whole person, if only Tien *Tai-tai* agreed to give him her daughter in marriage. In the end, and with the requisite guarantees written and stamped with his official chop, the marriage date was set.

In addition to her visits to Tien *Tai-tai*, Bittersweet had the task of informing Hwang *Tai-tai* of the governor's wish.

"You poor dear!" Hwang *Tai-tai* exclaimed after Bittersweet had discharged her hateful duty. "I don't know who's to suffer the worst of it — you, me, Tien *Tai-tai*, or her daughter!" After rubbing her friend's icy hands, she rang for her maid to bring a pot of fresh tea.

"These wretched men and their bloated egos! If we're not careful, we women will get trampled underfoot. We must defend ourselves by sticking together and rising above them. Thankfully that's not too hard to do, for snakes lie belly to the ground."

Bittersweet raised her head. She hadn't dared to look her friend in the face for fear of seeing her own shame and sorrow reflected there. "Then you're not. . . ."

"Angry with you for telling me? Heartbroken that my husband, the old goat, is in love with a child? Before Tien *Tai-tai*'s daughter was born, I'd stopped sharing my husband's bed, finding no joy there. Before I married him, I knew that love was chaff and scattered at the first breeze of married life, and that the solid kernel of what counts in marriage was position and possession. So! My husband wants a son of his own seed, does he? He wants a young wife in which to plant it? I will grant him that, along with the guarantees of first wife status for her. I'll do it all — for an extravagant price. You see, Li *Tai-tai*, I, too, have a dream, one I've been able to conceal and sustain far better than my husband has his. I've held him at bay physically while actively managing his estate and organizing his rise to governorship. You might even say that I orchestrated his taking a second wife so that I might devote all my energies to advancing his career and filling my purse. Let him take her body. I possess his soul."

Bittersweet stared at her friend while Hwang *Tai-tai* ordered the maid to pour the tea and then withdraw.

"Do I disgust you? Do you despise me? Or do you pity me for being heartless?" Hwang *Tai-tai* asked her friend. "Yes, it *is* terrible not to be able to love, but perhaps not quite so terrible as loving and not being able to help oneself . . . as you love."

Bittersweet smiled sadly. "Is that why you and I, despite our differences, are such good friends — *because* of our differences?" she asked.

The two women raised their teacups and drank, studying each other over the rims of delicate porcelain.

"No doubt," Hwang *Tai-tai* answered, then grimaced. "The tea's too strong, don't you think? I must reprimand the maid. Yes, we're polar opposites and thus complementary. Yin and yang. Night and day." She smiled, nodding. "It's no small thing to have a good friend. When I was a young and poor farm girl, I knew it was crucial for survival. Now that I have position and possessions to maintain, I find it no less so, perhaps more. I might scold you for your generosity and kindness to Dejie, but it's because I like you and I don't want to see her take advantage of you. Even more than that, it's because I admire you for what I lack — your tolerance, your forbearance — and I marvel at the results of your patience. Your husband has absolutely nothing to fault you with."

Hwang *Tai-tai* gingerly picked up a melon cake and nibbled on it to dilute the bitter taste of the tea. "So now I'm in your shoes — a first wife whose husband has taken a concubine," she said, narrowing her eyes as if trying to foresee the future and the part she would play in it. "One of our many differences has become a similarity, and so I am forced to appreciate our mutual situation. You've come on a bitter mission. Let me, then, tell you something sweet."

She settled back comfortably, draping her arms, with their many bracelets, over the carved ebony arms of her chair and said, "Many years ago, after my son died, and I almost with him, I went to a doctor who made sure that I would never conceive again. He is a doctor famed far and wide for his ability to prevent conception in women who do not want children and for his ability to increase the fertility in those who do. I have long ears, Li *Tai-tai*, and I have friends with long ears as well. I pay them dearly to make sure what they hear is accurate. One of my ears needed an abortion, and so I sent her to this very doctor less than a week ago. While she was lying there recovering from the operation, she heard him talking in the next room with a concubine he'd just examined who, though she'd been married for years, had not conceived that essential son who would secure for her the position she needed. He told this woman that there was nothing he could do to help her, for she was barren. My accurate ear heard the woman sobbing on the other side of the wall. The sobbing stopped after some moments, and a red-eyed young woman passed the open doorway of the room where my ear lay. My accurate ear also has eagle eyes and what they saw you would do well to know. The red-eyed woman was Dejie."

Bittersweet, who had raised her teacup to her lips, set it back down in its saucer without having taken a sip.

"Ah, you see?" Hwang *Tai-tai* exclaimed, irritated. "She made the tea too strong! The girl deserves a sound thrashing!"

"No, no," Bittersweet protested. She raised the cup once again and, this time, took a deep, long draught. "It's not bitter at all. In fact, it's sweet and clear."

· ✦ ·

The marriage ceremony of Governor Hwang and Tien *Tai-tai*'s daughter was to be celebrated with all the pomp and splendor of a first-time wedding. During the two months preceding it, the governor of Kwangsi regained his health, good spirits, vigor, and vanity, a manifestation of which was a smaller waist size so he might fit into his wedding suit. During this same period, Bittersweet, in her role as matchmaker, spent many hours requesting and negotiating the necessary guarantees required by the governor's first wife. Finally, Hwang *Tai-tai*'s steward arrived on Bittersweet's doorstep and handed her a document bearing his mistress's large and elaborate chop. It stated that Hwang *Tai-tai*, being an obedient wife and a dutiful daughter-in-law, having learned her virtue from her mother and from the *Four Books*, and because she was a moral woman of impeccable principles, hereby acquiesced to her husband's demand that his second wife be granted first wife status. She did so on the condition that first wife status be maintained for herself, and that she, Hwang *Tai-tai*, be granted sole and full ownership of one-half of her husband's real estate. This included half of the prime properties he owned in the center of town, as well as full and sole ownership of two-thirds of his liquid assets, i.e., the entirety of the gold and silver specie he possessed. On the document, a narrow space was left for Governor Hwang's signature and his chop. Not very much room to maneuver in, Bittersweet thought, once the space was filled in.

At the wedding reception, Bittersweet, as chief witness, raised her wine cup along with the scores of other guests. She congratulated the bride and groom and wished them happiness, prosperity, and long life. Though Governor Hwang looked handsome and proud, it was his beautiful young bride, who had conducted herself with the utmost propriety and decorum, that drew all eyes to her.

Is she truly happy, Bittersweet wondered, trying to recall her own feelings on her wedding day.

"Isn't she exquisite?" one guest whispered to another. "She smiles delicately and says nothing. She's been well-coached for her big day — a great credit to her mother."

Bittersweet looked in Tien *Tai-tai*'s direction. The mother of the bride stood in a circle of well-wishers. When she wasn't weeping disconsolately, she was smiling happily. It has always been so at weddings, Bittersweet thought; there are always so many tears to shed, and all for such different reasons.

"A second wife," another guest said behind a raised hand, "but with the guarantee of first wife status."

"Even so, the mother was either very daring or very tolerant to have allowed her daughter to enter such a union. No doubt the first wives feel terribly deceived by such a traitor."

"Two traitors," another corrected, eyeing Bittersweet.

"It's a victory for the second wives."

"You'd think so, but you'd never know it to look at Guo *Yi Tai-tai*. See how haggard she looks! She probably feels cheated that she didn't think to demand first wife status when she married General Li. Did you notice? She didn't drink to the bride's health at every *gan bei*. It's envy that's hollowed her eyes and drained her cheeks of color."

"I hear the Tien girl, despite her innocent and helpless appearance, is very ambitious — ambitious to the point of defying her mother who was against the match."

"You're misinformed. They both jumped at the chance. Who wouldn't marry her daughter to the governor — whether she be his second, third, or fourth wife?"

"I hear the fate of our province depends on this marriage. From the look of things, Kwangsi's in for brighter days. The old cock can't take his eyes off his young chick."

"Which isn't ruffling her downy feathers one bit."

"Yes, and there's an old hen who's trying to smooth hers, I'll bet."

"I wouldn't worry about her if I were you. She knows how to feather her nest."

Again, Bittersweet stood in her husband's stead and acted as his representative, for at the time of the wedding, Delin was in Canton meeting with the gray-eyed Chiang who, by elegant manipulation and intrigue, had replaced Sun Yat-sen. At his death, Sun left behind him plans for an expedition to rid northern China of its warlords and to unite all of China under a single national government. Before Delin left to help organize the expedition, he told Bittersweet that it was thanks to her that he was able to go; he could leave Kwangsi with a clear conscience, knowing that the province was in the hands of a rehabilitated Governor Hwang.

"Kwangsi and Kwangtung are no longer at war. They're cooperating, even collaborating, with each other. A Northern Expedition is finally possible — and with its success, a unified national government and a unified nation. Kwangsi is the first province to join forces with Chiang's central government and his troops heading north. Self-governing provinces only perpetuate endless warlordism and endless provincial wars. I've thrown my lot in with Sun's Three People's Principles and with the central government in Canton, and there it'll stay."

Outwardly, Bittersweet admired her husband's courage and resolve, but, in truth, she was leery. How firmly were the Three People's Principles established in China's new leadership? It was hard to tell, now that Sun was dead and a Ningpo man with gray eyes and a peanut-shaped head had emerged to proclaim himself Sun's successor and China's hope. Rumor had it that Chiang's background and character were questionable. Some said he had been a member of the Green Gang operating out of Shanghai, that his connection with that most notorious *tong* had never been completely severed. While Delin had had absolute faith in Sun, Bittersweet knew he harbored grave doubts about Sun's shrewd successor.

When Delin finally returned to Nanning, after his meeting with Chiang in Canton, he called Bittersweet into his office.

"Kweilin has been chosen as the starting point for the Northern Expedition," he announced, excitedly. "I will lead the Seventh National Army — 40,000 Kwangsinese strong — into Hunan Province."

Yet another civil war, Bittersweet thought, trying to be happy for her husband's sake. But how to be happy? This time the conflict would be a larger one, not between the Kwangs, but between a central government that was being born and provincial ones that refused to die. How could unity be achieved by force? Was it possible? Or did force only breed counterforce, and counterforce eventual disintegration?

"Fighting will begin again," Delin continued. "In the cities it will be fierce, but there's little chance that it will reach the hamlets. My family will be safe."

"I'll begin packing so Youlin, Dashao, and I can leave for Dragon's Head whenever you say," Bittersweet replied, rising from her chair.

"No, not Dragon's Head," Delin said. "I want you to take our son to Hong Kong."

"Hong Kong!"

"Youlin will be entering middle school. I'm concerned about his education. Dragon's Head possesses only a rudimentary village school. In Hong Kong, he'll receive a good education at a private middle school. I've arranged everything — Youlin's schooling, your new home, financial matters, everything. Do you think you can pack in two days? One of my officers will be coming to escort you to Canton, then down the Pearl River to Hong Kong, the day after tomorrow."

Bittersweet, who had had plenty of experience in packing within the span of two hours, let alone two days, assured him that she would be ready. And so, the following morning Delin left for the north, for Hunan, to head the Seventh Army. Dejie accompanied him, Bible in hand. She would be the chief of the Kwangsi Women Students Northern Expedition Corps — the one hundred women who would serve as nurses, information disseminators, and morale boosters, the only women's unit in the country to serve at the battlefront. One day later, Bittersweet, Youlin, and Dashao left for the south and Hong Kong.

Chapter 12
Fragrant Harbor
(1929)

"I see only eight of them. Where's the ninth dragon?" Youlin called from the terrace.

Dashao scurried out of the house carrying his school books and a silk scarf. "You were coughing again last night, and this morning you complained of a sore throat," she said, tying the scarf around his neck. Youlin pulled the scarf off and shook his head.

"Do you want to get tonsillitis for the third time this year?" she asked, winding it around his throat once more and giving the knot a final tug. "Do you want to miss my good cooking and subsist only on *tsuk*?"

"So where's the last dragon, Dashao? I counted only eight."

She smiled and rapped her knuckles against Youlin's forehead. "What do you think you're standing on? Isn't Mead Mountain the curving back of a dragon?"

Before Delin left Nanning to initiate the Northern Expedition, he had rented a villa for his family. It was a spacious two-story house with a separate bungalow in back for servants' quarters, storage rooms, and kitchen. Far from the center of Hong Kong below, Seymour Terrace, as the place was called, was on the top of Mead Mountain. Despite the house's bucolic location, true peace came only with the price of a bodyguard. Kidnappings in the British crown colony were common, and wealthy families hired men to protect their person and patrol their property. Bittersweet had halfheartedly followed suit and hired Wenti, a middle-aged Hong Kong Chinese who could speak some English. He lived in the small gatekeeper's house beside the iron-grilled *da men* and went by the nickname Question since a childhood injury had curved his spine into the shape of a question mark.

"*Hen hao!*" Bittersweet exclaimed, coming out onto the terrace to see her son off to school. "So you've found Kowloon's nine dragons, have you?"

161

"We're studying Hong Kong's history," Youlin replied, smiling at his mother's praise. "Kowloon means nine dragons in Cantonese, and it's a peninsula that sticks out from China. Hong Kong means Fragrant Harbor, and it's the island that lies just beyond Kowloon in the South China Sea. With some other islands, they form the crown colony of Hong Kong which the British won from the Chinese during the Opium Wars." He looked inquiringly at his mother. "Does that mean that we're living in a part of England, Mama?"

"I'm not sure, but it does seem to suggest that Hong Kong belongs to England, even though England is half the world away."

"It doesn't seem right," Youlin muttered, frowning.

No, Bittersweet silently assented, it doesn't.

Because of the threat of kidnapping — even with Wenti as protection — Bittersweet lived on the British island of Hong Kong, in her villa, in self-imposed isolation. Now there were only three in the home. There was no extended family to entertain and feed; no friends and acquaintances to invite over. As for initiating friendships with her neighbors on Seymour Terrace, Bittersweet cared less for them than she had the officers' wives — first *or* second battalion. And it appeared that the sentiments were mutual.

In Bittersweet's eyes, her indigenous Hong Kong neighbors looked Chinese and spoke Chinese, but they did not act Chinese. They could stare right into her face without saying hello. At times, catching a glimpse of her or Dashao or Youlin, they even quickly looked the other way, pretending not to have seen them. When they did see, what they saw was the cost of one's clothes, the number of servants or bodyguards one could afford to hire, and the size and extravagance of one's house and furnishings. Warm human relationships meant little unless it was accompanied by the promise of profit. Like Westerners, her Hong Kong neighbors worshipped newness, speed, power, and technology. Weren't the cars and motorcycles parked in their garages and the washing machines and radios in their homes ample evidence of this?

"Li *Tai-tai*," Dashao said one day, seeing her mistress sitting alone in the parlor and knowing that she was missing her old friends, "now that you have the time and freedom to do so, why not resume your studies and perfect your reading and writing? Not only do you have General Li to write to, but also your family and friends in China."

Bittersweet's pupils dilated at the idea. Why not, indeed?

"Call a rickshaw," Bittersweet told Wenti. "Dashao and I are going to Queen's Road to buy some books and stationery."

In a dark, cavernous stationery store smelling of printer's ink and polished wood, Bittersweet bought rolls of rice paper, calligraphy brushes, inksticks, and inkstone. These were the four treasures of the calligrapher's table, all she needed to write her letters. But there was something else she wanted to buy.

"Do you have a book about Hong Kong?" she asked the clerk. "One that deals with its history and isn't too difficult to read?"

The clerk searched the shelves and returned with a thin volume; it turned out to be the very book Youlin was reading in school.

"My son and I can learn together," she said, clapping her hands together.

While Bittersweet was waiting for her change, she noticed that everyone working in the store was Chinese, but a Westerner owned the place. When he barked something, the clerk rushed up the rolling ladder to find a certain title, or the beads clicked louder and faster on the abacus, or the cashier bent lower on his stool to tally his receipts. Bittersweet recalled Baba's description of the English he had worked for in Malaya. She looked at the faces of the Chinese employees in the Hong Kong book shop. She saw no hatred there, but there was fear. She frowned, puzzled. She had seen very few foreigners on her trip into town. Most of the people she saw were Chinese. How could so many fear so few? How could so few rule so many?

"You're going to hurt your eyes," Dashao muttered one evening, coming upon her mistress reading in the fading light of the evening sun.

"Mmmm."

Dashao turned on the table lamp and peered over Bittersweet's shoulder. "Reading again," she said with a disapproving sniff. "That children's book about Hong Kong."

"Mmmm. That is, no," Bittersweet replied, her eyes still fixed on the page she was reading. "I finished that book last week. This one's about Chinese history. Recent history."

Dashao shrugged her shoulders. She'd accompanied Bittersweet to the bookstore twice in the last week and watched her purchase one volume after the other. What could her mistress find so interesting about what she already knew? Hadn't she lived recent Chinese history? Hadn't she listened to the stories and legends, generations old? Didn't she use her eyes to see and her ears to hear and her mind to separate what was likely and what was not? What more about China did she need to know? Better to go to the temple fairs to listen to the gossip there, or to a teahouse, or to the marketplace, or to a village well — if only there were village wells on Mead Mountain — where the information was alive, uttered by human mouths, and where if you had questions or disagreed with a given answer, you could ask or argue instead of pondering the scratchings of a book. Dashao shrugged again and turned to leave the room.

"It says in this book," Bittersweet said, her finger following the characters down the page, "that hundreds of years ago the Manchus were strong and ruled a Chinese empire that stretched as far west as Tibet and Turkestan, as far east as Formosa, as far north as Manchuria, and as far south as Burma. Foreign trade was restricted to the single port of Canton. Foreign nations wanted Chinese tea, silk, and porcelain, but they had nothing that the Chinese wanted in return — until the British found something they did want: opium which they grew in their colony of India. So that's why. . . ."

Bittersweet looked up, holding the book for a moment to her chest. But Dashao had left the room. So that's why Baba hated the English so, Bittersweet thought, not just for their personal treatment of him, but for their treatment of China as a nation, for their enslavement of the Chinese as a people.

That evening and far into the night, she read, learning that with China's defeat in the Opium Wars the ports of Amoy, Fuzhou, Ningpo, and Shanghai were forced open to foreign trade and that Hong Kong was ceded to Britain. As the Qing Dynasty grew weaker and more corrupt, Tientsin was added to the list. Russia acquired railroad rights in Manchuria and a lease on Port Arthur, while Britain leased Weihai, France Canton, Germany Jiao Shan. Japan obtained Formosa and won control of Korea. While the Taipings tried to overthrow the decadent Manchus, the Boxers chose the foreign devils as the target of their hatred. Sun Yat-sen, on the other hand, had tried to strengthen the country through the unification of the provinces and the formation of a single central government — a quest which Delin was continuing by joining forces with Chiang and launching the Northern Expedition to rout the warlords in the north.

So many ports leased to the foreigner, Bittersweet thought sadly, closing the book, so much of China ceded to the West and to Japan. So these were the concessions acquired by the foreigners and signed away by the Manchus through unequal treaties. These were the foreign settlements where the *da bizi* lived as though on parcels of their native soil. This was the right of extraterritoriality that absolved the foreigner of Chinese law though he lived on Chinese land. The words of her father-in-law and her husband — which had formerly meant nothing to her — now made sense. But such sad sense! And she recalled the words of Confucius: "If you can rule your own country, who dares insult you?" By the same token, she thought, if we cannot rule our own country, any and all dare insult us.

"Where is my grandson?" Da Mama called from the *da men*. "I've come all the way from China to bring him his favorite fruit."

"Red plums!" came a shout from the parlor. Youlin bounded out of the house and ran across the courtyard.

"Oh, *Nai-nai*!" he moaned suddenly, pointing at his throat. "I can't eat anything sour till I'm completely well."

"That's precisely the idea. The faster you recover, the sooner you can eat them."

"Your grandmother is one smart woman," Dashao acknowledged. She crossed the courtyard and relieved Da Mama and her entourage of their luggage. Bittersweet appeared in the doorway.

"And your mother is a very daring one," Da Mama told Youlin, though she was eyeing Bittersweet.

"Both Taoists and Buddhists believe that good and bad exist only in our minds and that the seeds of one are carried in the fruit of the other," Bittersweet told Da Mama in welcome. "Here's proof that they are right. My son's tonsillectomy brings my family to Hong Kong."

Bowing, laughing, and patting each other in mutual affection, Bittersweet playfully urged Da Mama, her fourth sister-in-law Yifu, so nick-named for her love of finery, and her third brother-in-law Solin into the house. With Emma — Solin's recent bride and an Englishwoman he had met while living with his mother in Shanghai — Bittersweet was more restrained, for she was both a *da bizi* and Solin's wife.

Bittersweet bowed and, smiling shyly, extended her hand, inviting Emma to enter. Misunderstanding the gesture, the young Englishwoman took it in hers and pumped it several times, while Solin explained to Bittersweet that a handshake was a customary Western greeting. Dashao, having witnessed the Western mode of welcome, placed her palms together and, lifting them to her forehead, bowed slightly at the waist to Emma — a gesture which seemed to suggest a plea for more gentle yin and less exuberant yang.

Inside, Youlin opened his mouth to show Da Mama where his tonsils had once been. "Yes," Da Mama repeated, "your mother was very daring. An operation such as yours was no small matter."

Three months before Da Mama's arrival, Youlin had succumbed to tonsillitis for the third time within a year. This time it was so severe that he could barely swallow. When his fever hovered over 100 for two days, Bittersweet decided that it was time to take him to the hospital.

"Your son is underweight and underheight for his age," said the examining doctor. "If he doesn't have his tonsils out, he'll always be sickly. If they're removed, he'll be stronger and healthier. It's up to you."

"That isn't so. I cannot make so important a decision without consulting my husband," she replied.

But Delin was on a battlefield somewhere between Changsha and Peking, and the doctor was persistent; the operation must be done as soon as possible, and he must have her answer one way or the other. Bittersweet weighed the consequences of her two choices: if she waited for Delin's decision or refused the doctor's suggestion, Youlin's health was at stake; but if she granted him permission and the operation wasn't successful, Youlin's life was at stake and she would be to blame. She could expect no pity from her husband or from herself. It was as the Buddhists said: if an endeavor is a success, it is due to the efforts of others; if an endeavor ends in failure, the fault lies with you. After a day's deliberation, she agreed to the tonsillectomy and sent a telegram to Delin's field headquarters informing him that Youlin would be hospitalized for an operation, though she didn't specify what kind. A month later, one of her husband's aides appeared on her doorstep inquiring after Youlin's health. He added that her telegram had caused her husband great concern and that Delin was sending his mother and some other family members to Hong Kong to assist with Youlin's recuperation.

"Is General Li scolding my mistress and using you to do so?" Dashao asked the orderly. "Do you really think Li *Tai-tai* should have waited for your arrival and her husband's instructions to determine whether or not her son should have received the operation?" she scolded in return. "You go back to your commander and tell him that my young master is well. He'll be happy to know the good news."

Now that Da Mama and her entourage had arrived, Bittersweet was happy to no longer be head of the household. One of Da Mama's first dictates, as mistress of the house, was that, in honor of her new English daughter-in-law and of Youlin's improved health, the entire family eat out at a Western restaurant. "Eating in a Western restaurant is much more hygienic than eating in a Chinese one," Da Mama explained. Though, the truth was hygiene wasn't her principal concern. During her stay in Shanghai, she had grown fond of certain urban amenities, one of which was eating out in Western restaurants. "Each person has only his own portion on his own plate, and his eating utensils touch only his own food." Yifu, who could never go out often enough, was the first to applaud Da Mama's decision.

When the day of the dinner came, Dashao laughed out loud when she saw Yifu dressed from head to toe in newly-bought finery. "A chicken in a peacock's borrowed feathers is still a chicken," Dashao crowed.

Yifu berated Dashao and complained to Da Mama and to Bittersweet, but Dashao just cackled all the more.

Delin was right, Bittersweet thought, studying her youngest sister-in-law. We'll have trouble with that one. She was only a child when we were poor farmers in Dragon's Head and doesn't remember the hard work and the sacrifices of those days. Life for her started when Delin was already a colonel and the family coffers were full.

"English food!" Emma raved, when she heard they would be dining at an English hotel. "At last, I will know what I'm eating. With Chinese food, one never knows. And considering what the Chinese regard as edible, perhaps it's better that I don't."

In comparison with Yifu, Bittersweet found Emma much more difficult to comprehend, not only because she was foreign and didn't speak Chinese, but because she didn't participate as a member of her Chinese family nor in Chinese life. Nor did she show a Chinese person's curiosity or seem to need *renao*, the warmth and noise of human relationships. She preferred to keep to herself. She liked her privacy; it was a basic right, she said. But Bittersweet couldn't understand this privacy. Emma just seemed stand-offish.

Seated in the opulent dining room of the English hotel, Bittersweet discovered that eating in a Western restaurant was a totally different experience from eating in a Chinese one. Bread was served instead of rice. Meat was not served in bite-sized morsels but in a slab that had to be cut into pieces — with metal instruments called a knife and fork — before it could be put into one's mouth. A dish, called a course, was served only after the preceding one had been consumed. And there was an abundance of crockery and silverware: bowls for soup and for dessert; plates for appetizer, entrée and bread; different knives to cut one's meat and to butter one's bread; different forks for the entrée and the dessert; different spoons for one's soup and pudding and to stir sugar into one's coffee or tea. To complicate matters even further, each set of silverware had to be placed at a specific location around the plate. It was all extremely complicated and inefficient, though it wasn't without a certain theatrical charm.

Not wishing to make a fool of herself, Bittersweet watched Emma and her mother-in-law before taking a single bite. Then, with them, she broke and buttered her roll, skimmed her soup with the proper spoon, cut her meat with her knife, dabbed at her lips with the pink cloth napkin, and wiggled her fingertips in the crystal bowl of warm water in which a lemon slice floated. She sighed, not so much out of satisfaction as out of relief, when the meal was over.

Poor Solin fared even less well. He barely had time to sink his knife into his beef before he was called upon to translate his wife's frequent remarks. But, by the way he blushed and avoided his family's eyes as he searched for Chinese equivalents, Bittersweet knew that his translations were indeed approximations, more diplomatic than accurate.

Only when the meal was over did Bittersweet realize that her first Western meal had consisted of chicken consommé, filet of beef, boiled white potato, boiled beets, whipped cream cake, and coffee.

"An adequate meal," Bittersweet told Dashao when the group arrived home from their foreign expedition, "but still there's nothing like your cooking."

Dashao smiled, displaying her overlapping, gold-rimmed teeth. "I knew that. Did you think I doubted it? My concern wasn't about which cuisine is better, Chinese or Continental, but if this foreign food would upset your stomach or constipate your bowels."

Dashao had decided, not long after Emma arrived in Hong Kong, that she disliked the Englishwoman, and so she also chose to dislike English food. Da Mama guessed the motive behind Dashao's quip and said, "I thought that dinner at an English restaurant was the proper welcome for my English daughter-in-law to Hong Kong. But I must admit that of all Western cuisines, my personal favorite is French food."

In fact, Da Mama so enjoyed French food that she soon devised a ploy to get her family to join her at — or, better yet, take her to — French restaurants. First, she taught mahjong to Bittersweet, Yifu, Solin, and Emma, but she added an extra rule: quarreling or losing one's temper was strictly forbidden, and the penalty for violating the rule was to take the others out for a French meal. Generally, the players formed a peaceful group, but occasionally — perhaps feeling hungry for *coq au vin* — one of them would speak out of turn or contest a move. Then all of them, Youlin as well, would travel down Mead Mountain to one of the colony's French restaurants. On these occasions, Da Mama was the merriest diner of all, but when she thought no one was looking, she would glance at Emma with concern and even anxiety in her eyes.

Though these "foreign expeditions" were an occasional treat for them all, the meals gradually became everyday occurrences for Emma and Solin. At first, Emma was willing to try to eat with chopsticks, but inevitably food would fall before reaching her lips. Instead of taking the encouragement her family offered her or making light of the episodes, Emma grew frustrated. She insisted on eating Western-style with knife and fork and then on eating solely Western food. Eventually, Solin had to ask his mother to increase his allowance, so he could afford the meals out.

"Our household budget doesn't include so many meals at expensive restaurants," Dashao informed him, for she was offended by Emma's rejection of her cuisine.

"But Emma can't eat Chinese food," Solin said, addressing his comments to his mother. "It doesn't agree with her."

"How does she know?" Dashao quipped. "She can never get it into her mouth."

"And why should she?" Solin exploded. "Chopsticks touch everybody's food! They're unhygienic! They spread germs!"

He turned to his mother imploringly. "And she needs a larger wardrobe. I need money for that as well. She insists on having her clothes custom-made."

"I agree," Da Mama replied. "Emma needs clothes, of course, but Western dressmakers charge many times the price of Chinese ones."

"Are you saying that Emma should wear Chinese dresses?" Solin asked with a sarcastic smile. "You yourself took her to be fit for a *cheongsam* at Hong Kong's most exclusive dressmaker and still she looked like she was wearing a potato sack. Emma has a Western body that needs Western clothes."

Da Mama looked into her son's face and finally reached into her purse and handed him several bills. Dashao looked on, expressionless, her arms folded across her chest.

"You can go now, Dashao," Solin told her, counting the bills.

"I can," Dashao sniffed, "but I won't. I'm fine right where I am."

Solin clucked his tongue nastily at her, then turned to his mother with a bow.

"*Duojie, duojie,*" he thanked her, "but this is enough for two Western dresses, three at most. Emma tells me that in London a woman from a good family wouldn't be seen in the same dress or suit in the same week."

"The gods forbid! And I'm sure that Emma's from a good family!" Dashao said, twisting her mouth.

"And so are we," Solin said bluntly. "I won't have her think our family is anything less."

Da Mama reluctantly gave her son several extra bills which he pocketed. Then, Solin bowed to his mother again and, ignoring Dashao, walked out of the room. Dashao watched him without comment. A stick figure, she thought. Like a Westerner, stiff and constrained in his worsted Western suit. Stovepipe sleeves and pant legs! Even though it's spring in Hong Kong and far too warm for woolens, much less a vest and a tie. Rope to hang oneself is what I call a Western necktie.

"Emma needs time to adjust to our ways," Da Mama said, sensing Dashao's hostility. "She's only been in Hong Kong for a few months."

"And Shanghai for over a year," Dashao reminded her.

"She feels that the way we do things is strange."

"She's not the only one. I feel the way she does things is strange, too.

She's not a guest, Da Mama, but a member of the family. She should try to adapt to the family's ways."

Da Mama nodded, more in comprehension of Dashao's feelings than in agreement with her reasoning. After all, Emma treated Dashao as if she were a servant in the Western sense — an employed person to whom one owed only wages and no more. She didn't understand that in China a servant who rendered long and loyal service was considered a member of the family.

"You must be patient with her," Da Mama said. "Her ways are different from ours, but they'll change in time. We must encourage, not criticize, her."

But it was Solin who was changing over time. He no longer joined his family for Chinese meals but ate out with Emma in Western restaurants. He no longer played mahjong with them but bridge with Emma and her English friends who lived in the British enclave on Victoria Peak. And he began to look down on Chinese ways. This Bittersweet, too, noticed and was saddened by, and she blamed it not on Emma but on the fact that they were living in a British colony and subject to British rule. It was this colonial status that alienated Solin from his blood and background, that made him ashamed of being a son of the sick man of Asia.

"Wenti, you've worked for the English before," Bittersweet said to him one day. "What are they like?"

"The English, Li *Tai-tai*?" he said, grinning broadly. "The English are not the Chinese. Where we are self-indulgent, they are austere. They're all born with a curious part of the physiognomy called a stiff upper lip which does not allow them to laugh easily or cry at all. Their mouths simply won't assume the shape. Their voices won't make the sound. Instead of face, they have this lip which they say is their honor, along with their word. This word, once given, may not be taken back, even if offered or altered to suit changed circumstances. It is immutable. One must die for it if need be. But such a limitation allows them a certain amount of wit, which they say we lack altogether. Where they are witty with words, they say we are witty with our hands. And we surely find humor in different things. Miss Emma, for example," he said, scratching his chin. "The other day I accompanied her and Master Solin to town because they needed someone to carry her hatboxes. We saw a rickshaw driver lose control of his carriage, veer suddenly, and careen into a Japanese soldier, pinning the poor fellow to the Japanese embassy wall. The Japanese grimaced in pain, but determined to be a samurai, and racked, as he was, between physical anguish and spiritual ecstasy, he bore it bravely. Miss Emma cried out for me to help the soldier and end his torment. When I didn't and instead burst out laughing at the sight — this love of pain the Japanese have! — she berated me for finding his suffering amusing. She didn't understand that I wasn't amused by his pain but by the sublime suffering he took in it and by the comical way in which it had been induced."

A shriek cut Wenti's laughter short. He rushed into the house and up the stairs with Bittersweet and Dashao, wielding a broom, running behind him. When he flung open the door, he found the young Englishwoman standing knock-kneed in the center of her bed and shaking all over. White with terror, she pointed to the far corner of the room. "That . . . that creature that looks like a miniature stegosaur," she sputtered.

"Mistress no like?" Wenti asked. "Little dragon very pretty." Wenti caught the bronze-colored lizard and held its tiny head tightly between thumb and forefinger, forcing its red mouth open. Held thus, it thrashed its tail about and miserably clawed the air. "Much prized in Chinese medicine," Wenti assured her. "Good for vitalizing the blood."

"Get that frightful beast out of here!" Emma ordered imperiously with the sweep of an arm. "Kill it!"

"Kill it?" Wenti asked dubiously, eyeing the twisting lizard.

Before Emma could stop him, he threw the lizard against the bedroom wall where it landed with a brittle crack. When it fell to the floor, Wenti's heel finished the job. Emma dropped limply to her knees. "I think I'm going to be ill," she moaned, putting her head between her knees.

Dashao swept up what remained of the lizard and tried to show it to Emma.

"Mistress see?" Wenti coaxed. "No more dragon."

But by mid-summer Solin and Emma, who had spent most of their time exclusively with each other or with her young English friends, began to spend more and more time apart, and when they were together, they barely spoke to each other. If they did, it was often with raised voices. Sometimes Bittersweet heard them quarreling and her heart turned over in sorrow. How could a husband and wife speak to

172

each other with such lack of respect? The sound of their words broke the air like smashing porcelain, rent it like tearing silk. These things could not be put back together again, she thought. The scars of anger and bitterness show up on the human heart.

One day, Solin appeared before his mother. His face was pale, his mouth pinched. "Emma wants to return to England to visit her family," he said bluntly, without respectful preliminaries. "Of course, as her husband I'll be accompanying her. I've come to ask you for the money for the trip."

His mother looked at him with pain and compassion. "Such a trip requires much forethought, planning, and preparation. Your wife hasn't been in Hong Kong even one year, and England is far away. To send both you and Emma for a visit will be very expensive. This is a matter of some importance. It will be necessary to consult the rest of the family. We must hold a meeting of those who are here and write to Demin and Delin."

"Damn Demin and Delin," Solin shouted. "And damn the family council! Emma's right! A Chinese isn't an individual unique unto himself but an insignificant part of his family branded with its collective identity. A Chinese doesn't speak his mind but the will of his family. I want my share of the family money. How can Emma look up to me when I must always come grovelling to you for my allowance like a snivelling schoolboy? I want my share and I want it now."

"I know I'm doing the wrong thing to give Solin the money," Da Mama confided sadly to Bittersweet, "but I will do anything to stop them from quarreling. Lately Solin looks at me with such reproach, it breaks my heart. But worse, if he and Emma continue to argue with each other, they'll break the bonds of their marriage and their ties to the family, and nothing must be allowed to do that." She looked at her daughter-in-law as if begging her to understand what was entirely incomprehensible to Da Mama herself. "He says he wants to lead his own life. He says that the family denies him a life of his own and denies him happiness. He says he no longer wants to live with us." Tears gathered in her eyes and she blinked as though by blinking she could clarify the matter. "I cannot understand such words," she said finally. "I cannot understand the feelings behind such words."

A week before Solin and Emma were scheduled to sail to Shanghai, then on to London by airplane, the entire family was sitting and drinking tea in the backyard where Bittersweet grew a vegetable garden and Dashao kept a pen of several chickens and two roosters. Suddenly there was a ruckus in the pen, for the two roosters had begun to fight over a certain hen. Bittersweet, Da Mama, Solin, Wenti, Dashao, and Youlin merely watched, sipping their tea, knowing that roosters will ruffle their feathers for one reason or another, and that when one grew tired, they both would stop.

The hen who had caused the disturbance began to circle the two contenders for her favors — perhaps to get a better view or, maybe, to size up which of the opponents would be the victor. Mistaking the hen for a third rooster who wanted to join the fray, Emma rose from her seat and rushed at the bird, frightening her away and startling the two roosters so that they immediately stopped fighting and scurried away in alarm.

Dashao and Wenti burst out laughing, and the others soon joined them.

"How dare you laugh at me!" Emma cried, tightening her hands into fists.

Everyone stopped laughing and froze in stupefaction.

"*You* are the ones who are ridiculous!" she screamed. "The food you eat is inedible! The clothes you wear disguise and disfigure the human body! A man looks like a woman in them, and a woman a man! Your houses and mores show total disregard for a person's privacy! Your table manners are disgusting — and you're dirty!"

"Enough!" Solin cried, rising to his feet. His entire body was trembling. "I thank heaven that my family can't understand your hateful words, though they have the misfortune of witnessing your barbaric behavior. Do you realize that you are in my aunt's presence? Do you forget that you've been living in her house for over a year? You've insulted my mother. You should fall on your knees and beg forgiveness."

"Fall on my knees," Emma gasped. "*I am your wife.*"

Da Mama rushed over to Solin, begging him to be calm and kinder to his wife. Bittersweet hung her head in shame to have witnessed so brutal a scene, while Youlin stared fearfully at his enraged aunt and uncle. Dashao and Wenti clucked their tongues in sad disapproval.

"What kind of family do you have," Emma asked, "that a husband sides with them against his own wife? You're like any Chinese. Your

174

loyalty is dictated by blood. You treat me like an outsider, while you fear me as a foreigner."

When the boat sailed for Shanghai, Solin wasn't on it. He didn't say when he would be joining his wife in London, and Emma didn't say when she would be returning to Hong Kong.

Though Emma's presence had made life difficult for her in-laws, her departure cast a pall over the Li villa on Mead Mountain. Some weeks later, however, the gloom was brightened by the arrival of an unexpected visitor. Late on a warm, humid summer's night, Bittersweet heard a frantic pounding on the front door. Quickly, she put on her robe and, opening her bedroom door, found Dashao gripping a meat cleaver.

"Put that away," Bittersweet said. "Go downstairs and see who it is. I'll be down in a minute." While she wound her hair into a bun and inserted tortoise shell hairpins into it, she heard muffled words — Dashao's and those of a man. Then she heard footsteps on the stair and a low, weary voice which she recognized instantly.

Bittersweet rushed to the landing where she gripped the wooden railing. A hundred times she had rehearsed the words that she would greet Delin with after so many months, but now that she saw him, her voice would not come to her throat. He was painfully thin. Tension and fatigue had added sharp angles and deep hollows to his cheeks and eye sockets. Even the two dimples that the bullet wounds had left in his cheeks no longer produced the ever-present smile. Instead, there was a tight grimace.

"I'm sorry to come so late at night," he said. "I hope I didn't startle you."

"Time of day or night is of no importance," Bittersweet replied hoarsely. "It's just good that you have come."

Delin looked around as if a modern house such as the one he was now standing in was new and foreign to him. "I arrived in Hong Kong two days ago. I never thought I'd come here." He leaned heavily against the railing. "I never dreamed that the success of the Northern Expedition would only result in civil war."

"Dashao," Bittersweet called down to the foot of the stair where her maidservant stood, "please make a pot of hot tea for the general and bring it to my room. And a bowl of noodles in soup."

To the latter, Delin shook his head and waved his hand, signifying he'd already eaten, or, perhaps, that he was in no mood to eat. "Just tea, Dashao."

Bittersweet led the way to her bedroom where Delin sank exhausted into one of the two stuffed armchairs. Normally, she loved to sit here early in the morning and watch the sun rise over the nine dragons of Kowloon, lighting up the sails of the junks in Victoria Harbor as it came. But Delin closed his eyes and faced away from the window as though the mere sight of the British colony hurt him.

"It's ironic," he muttered, opening his eyes. "The expedition was a Pyrrhic victory. We wiped out dozens of petty warlords — only to create one big national one."

Bittersweet didn't have to ask the identity of this sole warlord. Her husband always referred to him as China's new Son of Heaven. Chiang had destroyed his own generals by the same method he used to defeat the northern warlords. That is, divide and conquer. He pitted one army against the other, eliminating both, thus preventing any one commander or army, other than himself, other than his own, from gaining too much popularity or power. No one should threaten the Son of Heaven's position on the Dragon Throne.

"From the outset of the expedition," Delin continued, bracing himself with frequent sips of tea, "I found myself fighting a war on two fronts: the armies of the northern warlords, and Chiang's purposely erroneous or simply inept commands. Our Kuomintang, or KMT, armies weren't fighting the enemy as much as competing for Chiang's favors, each army weakening the other, eroding our goal of national unity in the process. As the expedition marched northward, piling up victory upon victory, the bonds of our common cause, loosened by corruption, favoritism, and factionalism, snapped and were replaced by regional bonds forged by common origin and experience. The rift with the Communists led by a librarian from Hunan by the name of Mao Tse-tung was widest of all, and Chiang, fearing their growing power and efficiency, turned on them, massacring Communists by the thousands in Shanghai. My colleague General Pai captured Mao's ablest lieutenant, a Shanghainese of Mandarin origin and educated in France named Chou En-lai but, knowing what fate awaited Chou and having gone to school with him, Pai allowed him to escape. After all, what did one Communist lieutenant matter? By the time we reached Peking and the end of our quest, we were separate armies fighting each other off, defending the territories we'd won, and contending for those controlled by others. The strongest army, after Chiang's, was ours, Kwangsi's, and the commanders who had proven most competent were Pai and myself — an enviable position and thus a dangerous one, as we were soon to learn."

He stopped to sip his tea and began again. "In Peking, Chiang secured Sun Yat-sen's position by throwing himself on Sun's casket and sobbing to prove his devotion. The impostor! To the country at large, however, that dramatic gesture proved Chiang's sincerity and worthiness to fill Sun's shoes. Now that the expedition was over, I was anxious to broach the question of disbandment. What need did we have of separate armies, now that we had unified the country? The four group army commanders — Chiang, Feng, Yen, and I — met to discuss the issue, but it soon became clear to me and Commanders Feng and Yen that Chiang was out to dissolve our forces while maintaining his. The disbandment discussions went no further. We each returned to our own armies, knowing that Chiang was out to destroy us. Internecine war was imminent."

Bittersweet poured her husband another cup of tea which he drank to the dregs before continuing. "While Chiang could play divide and conquer with Feng and Yen, he was unable to induce Pai and me to enter his game. And so from Nanking, the new capital, he began waging a propaganda campaign against his 'arch-enemies, the Kwangsi Three.' He issued an official declaration of war against us and our troops stationed in Wuhan. Then, he relieved Pai and me of all our posts and expelled us for life from the Kuomintang Party. Chiang denounced us as feudal regionalists — selfish, secretive, and opportunistic. He accused us of having joined the KMT only to further our own private aims, of having negotiated with warlord armies during the expedition, of having colluded with the Communists, of having systematically looted Nanking, of having disregarded the regulations on disbandment, of trying to form an anti-Nanking alliance in southwestern China, and of being crude, primitive, and old-fashioned. A disgrace to China!"

Delin drew in a deep breath. "Chiang's Nanking forces attacked — 150,000 strong — against our 60,000 in Wuhan. We lost the city and, one after the other, the provinces of Hupei, Hunan, Kiangsi, and Kwangtung. We even lost our home base of Kwangsi. We are generals without an army." His head sank upon his chest.

"You may be a general without an army, but you'll never be a disgrace to China," came a voice from the open doorway.

Delin immediately rose to his feet and to an erect military bearing. "And yet I come to you in disgrace," he told his mother, bowing low.

"You come to me very tired, Second Son," she said, crossing the room to where both Delin and Bittersweet stood. She looked into Delin's downcast face. "I will speak to you plainly, Delin, as I have always spoken to you. For ten years you have governed Kwangsi wisely and without incident. A flower cannot bloom for one hundred days; a person's luck cannot last for one hundred years. For ten years, your life has not been your own. Take this time you now have to rest for a while."

Delin bowed again, lower this time, but his face broke into a smile. "Daddy!"

Dashao gave Youlin a little push of encouragement which sent the boy running across the room into his father's arms.

"So," Delin said, sitting down and seating Youlin on his lap, "do you like your Hong Kong home? And how is school? Is Dashao still seeing to it that you're first in your class? And how's that throat of yours now that your tonsils are gone?" He looked at Bittersweet. "Your mother took on a big responsibility, having them removed without first obtaining my permission."

"I like it here a lot," Youlin replied. "And I'm doing well in school. Uncle Solin takes me swimming. Auntie Yifu takes me shopping. And *Nai-nai* takes me out to eat French food."

Everyone laughed, including Youlin.

"When are you going to take me horseback riding?" Youlin asked his father. "And to a French restaurant for *escargots* and soufflé? Tomorrow? Yes?"

"I can't tomorrow," Delin said apologetically. He turned to Bittersweet. "I can't be seen in public. There are people who mustn't know I'm here. Several colleagues have followed me to Hong Kong where we plan to muster support to win back Kwangsi. When conditions are better," he promised his son, "I'll take you horseback riding and to French restaurants. If you must get in touch with me," he said to his wife, rising, "Dejie and I are staying with friends at the end of Robertson Road. Otherwise, it's better to wait until I contact you."

At the mention of Dejie's name, Bittersweet gave a slight start and the joy she felt to see her family reunited faded. Isn't it so, she reminded herself. The seeds of the bad are already planted in the fruit of the good.

Over the three weeks that followed Delin's night visit, she had no word from him. Then, one rainy evening, when she and her family were seated at the dinner table, they heard impatient knocking at the front door. When Dashao opened it, Delin rushed in, flung off his cape, and hurriedly apologized for interrupting their meal.

"Sit down and join us," Da Mama invited, motioning Dashao to set a place for her son.

"I can't stay. I've come to say good-bye."

Dashao set a bowl of hot and sour soup before him, nudging him to sit down and eat.

"But you can't go!" Youlin blurted out. "You promised to take me horseback riding — and to eat French food."

Delin pinched his son's cheek and forced himself to smile. "I haven't forgotten my promise. I will keep it, just as soon as I return from Saigon."

"Saigon!" Bittersweet gasped, setting down her porcelain spoon.

"You people don't know how fortunate you are," Delin said, "to be able to sit down at a table and appreciate good food in good company instead of eating rotting army rations with only a lazy orderly or an irritable officer for fellowship."

"Why are you going to Saigon?" Bittersweet asked, no longer hungry.

"General Feng was in Hong Kong to see me. Seems he caught on to the Son of Heaven's strategy of playing him off against Yen and decided that wasn't the kind of reward he was expecting for his part in the Northern Expedition. Chiang found out that Feng was in Hong Kong and had met me. He's afraid that Feng and I will become allies and turn against him and his disciples, so he's bribed the Hong Kong authorities to deport me. . . ." Delin chuckled. "As a Communist spy!"

"Then you're in danger every minute that you stay here," Bittersweet said.

"That's why I'm leaving in less than half an hour, taking Generals Wei, Yu, and Xia with me. We'll be traveling under assumed names and carrying false passports. Mine says that I'm a rice merchant!"

"Unpolished rice?" Bittersweet teased, trying to smile.

"What else? Everything's been arranged in advance, down to my 'employer' who will meet me upon my arrival in Saigon."

He reached into his jacket pocket and extracted a thick envelope which he handed to Bittersweet. "Take good care of our son. You'll continue to receive money every month to cover your living expenses. You needn't worry about your welfare."

"It's not my welfare that I worry about," she answered, taking the packet and looking gravely into Delin's face.

"You don't have to worry," he assured her. "I have many friends to help me along the way." Then, he turned to Youlin and hugged the boy to him. "Are you terribly angry that you'll have to wait until I can keep my promises to you?"

"No," came the muffled reply, "but only if you come back soon."

"I'll try." Delin quickly fastened his cape about his shoulders and waved his hand in farewell to his family. Then he passed into the rain and was gone.

A week went by. Then, Wenti began to announce a series of visitors to his mistress. First, there were common police officers, Hong Kong Chinese. Then came inspectors and officials of the colony's government, British *da bizi*. And last came officers of the Chinese Kuomintang Army and officials of the Chinese central government in Nanking. They all knew that Delin was, or had been, in Hong Kong. They all wanted to know where he was now, and they all were worried about Delin's welfare, for rumor had it that the Communists (if the Kuomintang officials were the ones interrogating her, the British if the Chinese were interrogating her, or the Hong Kong Chinese if the mainland Chinese were interrogating her) were offering a large sum for his capture or for knowledge regarding his whereabouts.

"I've told the Hong Kong Chinese and the Hong Kong British. I've told the police and the civil authorities. I've told the Chinese military and the Chinese civilians. And so I will tell you what I have told them," Bittersweet said. "I do not know where my husband is. I do not know where he was. For all I know, he might never have been in Hong Kong."

"Come, come, Li *Tai-tai*," they scoffed. "Do you mean to tell us that your husband didn't come to see you when he was in the colony?"

"As I did not see him, I can only doubt that he ever was here. Perhaps your sources are mistaken."

"We know for a fact that your husband was in Hong Kong and that he left recently."

"Then it should be *I* asking *you* questions about my husband, as you seem to know much more than I do and have all the answers."

"All but one. Where is he now?"

Bittersweet shrugged her shoulders and shook her head.

"Has he written to you? Where are his letters?"

"Why should he write to me?" she asked. "I who am an illiterate Chinese woman."

"Then you don't mind if we offer you our protection and keep one of our men patrolling the premises and checking the mailbox. You never know. You might receive threats. There might be a bomb in a package sent to you. You might be harassed. Your husband is an important man."

"Whether I mind or not, you have the authority to post a guard on my property, don't you? While he might prevent others from harassing me, he will, undoubtedly, disrupt the harmony of my family's life and the rhythm of our days."

"Our sincere apologies."

"You do well to apologize, whatever your sincerity."

"We're glad you understand, Li *Tai-tai*."

"I understand that you are doing your duty." Then, she added, only to herself, "As I am doing mine."

Months went by during which Bittersweet was both relieved and frustrated not to receive any word from Saigon. She destroyed her previous letters from Delin by having Dashao use them as kindling. Finally, one day, Wenti wordlessly slipped a letter from his wide sleeve into hers. When she was in the privacy of her bedroom, she took it out and examined the envelope. No stamp or postmark. Obviously, it had been passed from hand to hand all the way from Saigon. Only when she tore open the envelope and read the letter did she know she was mistaken:

Dear Xuewen,

I write this letter to you from Nanning — yes, I'm back in our native province, safe and sound, though it's only now that I fully believe in my good fortune to be home.

When I first saw you in Hong Kong, I couldn't bring myself to tell you that I'd already been there for months, constantly pressured by the governor to leave, who in turn was being harassed by Chiang to deport me.

Finally, I agreed to leave and obtained a visa for France. But when I sailed out of Hong Kong, my destination was Indochina — close enough to China to learn about developments there, far enough away to be safe.

When we arrived in Saigon, we were standing on deck, looking for our contact 'Mr. Hsin, the rice magnate' when French immigration authorities boarded our boat and forced all the Chinese passengers onto the dock. There, police were waiting with truncheons and whips to herd us into a windowless brick building — so dark inside you couldn't see the fingers in front of your face. The place reeked of urine and excrement. I tripped over something, and only when I righted myself did I see that it was a man and that scores of people were lying on the straw-strewn floor. Just as we were being pushed into a cell, a well-dressed, middle-aged man waved and called to us. It was Mr. Hsin. No sooner did we introduce ourselves by our assumed names than a large wad of bills was transferred from Mr. Hsin's hands into those of the attending police officer, and we were released. After an anxious night spent in a large hotel in the center of town, we stood in line at the immigration office to apply for residence permits. Standing several people in front of me was a young Chinese fellow who kept staring at me. I thought little about him but rather about how much earlier the following morning I'd better arrive if I was going to reach the front of that line.

I hadn't returned to my hotel room for more than a few minutes when a knock came at my door. When I opened it, a French officer standing at full attention saluted me and inquired, "General Li?"

"How did you know my name?" I asked him, knowing it was futile to try to conceal my identity.

"The Chinese government in Nanking received a report about your arrival in Saigon yesterday and instructed the Chinese embassy in Paris to take the matter up with the French foreign office. Nanking has charged you with collusion with the Chinese Communists and with using Saigon as a base from which to sabotage the Chinese

government. They demand your immediate expulsion from French Indochina."

"I've just arrived in Saigon," I said sardonically, "and yet I'm being asked to leave."

"On the contrary, sir," he answered. "The French government knows that you have no connection with the Chinese Communists. They're afraid that the Nanking government will try to harm you. I've come to provide you with plainclothes policemen and bodyguards during your stay in Saigon."

And so I was surrounded by foreigners to safeguard me from my own countrymen! But even with these plainclothesmen, I knew that we were being followed everywhere we went, and I was very uneasy. As close as Saigon is to China, it took an unbearably long time to send and receive messages, so I decided to go to Haiphong — that much closer to China and that much farther away from Nanking's scrutiny.

But evidently not Kwangsi's. While I was in Haiphong, representatives from my home province's military and public service organizations discovered my whereabouts and came to see me. They told me that, after the Northern Expedition, Kwangsi was in turmoil and that the usurpers put there by Chiang were only making a greater mess of the situation. Where before "the Kwangsi Three" was a pejorative, now the Kwangsinese were clamoring for our reinstatement. The representatives told me that Generals Pai and Hwang were already in Kwangsi and were just waiting for my return so that the three of us could reestablish peace and order in the province.

And so I'm home once more. I won't be here that much, though, since the reconstruction of Kwangsi requires my spending a lot of time in Canton and Hong Kong. Do this for our son. Wait until he finishes out his school year, then come back to China. In Canton, there's a school that is famous in all of China for its modern curriculum and progressive educational techniques. I don't want Youlin living and studying in that English colonial outpost any longer than he has to. I want him back where he belongs.

> *May ten thousand of your wishes come true,*
> *Delin*

Bittersweet folded Delin's letter where he had creased it and placed it in her drawer, the one which she had recently emptied of his other letters. No longer did she need her English, Hong Kong Chinese, and mainland Chinese "protectors," just as her husband no longer needed his French protectors. Delin was safe at home and, in less than a year's time, after four years in Hong Kong, so, too, were she and Youlin.

Chapter 13
Lines of Destiny
(1933)

Bittersweet's first decision upon arriving in Canton was to rent a house on a quiet, tree-lined street close to Youlin's new school, Peujing, the one Delin had chosen for him.

Delin had told her, "Ninety percent of the graduates of Peujing High School go on to colleges and universities, most of which are in the United States and England. Its curriculum emphasizes the English language and the sciences, and its educational standards are very high."

Peujing was composed of several buildings in the Western style, each built with money sent by Chinese who had made their fortunes overseas, each named for the country in which the donors had lived — United States, England, Australia, Canada, Cuba. Because only the very well-to-do could afford to send their children to Peujing, the school was often called Youqian, or Moneybags. Though Youlin liked Peujing, he detested the sense of privilege and superiority that many of the students flaunted and assumed was theirs by right.

When Delin first saw his wife's new home near Peujing he had teased Bittersweet. "You're like Mencius' mother who insisted on living next to a school, so she might raise her son in a proper environment."

Bittersweet teased back, "A woman's duties are to cook the five grains, heat the wine, look after her parents-in-law, make clothes, and that is all. A woman's duty is not to control or take charge. Instead she must submit to the 'three submissions.' When she is young, she must submit to her parents. After her marriage, she must submit to her husband. When she is widowed, she must submit to her son. These are the rules of propriety."

Hearing her recite the rules of daughterly duty and feminine virtue, Delin smiled and nodded. "Despite the fact that those rules were first set down thousands of years ago during the Han Dynasty, they're no less relevant today. Here's a quote for you." He scratched his chin,

185

pretending to be struggling with his memory. "From the *Book of Poetry*: 'Serenely she looks and smiles/Without any impatience she delivers her instructions.'"

Bittersweet blushed and laughed into her shoulder like a schoolgirl.

"You're as diligent in your daughterly duties," Delin said, assessing his wife, "as Mulan was in carrying out her filial responsibilities to her father."

Mulan, as Bittersweet well knew from the legend, disguised herself as a soldier and rode to war in her father's place, for he was old and tired. She won many battles in his name, brought much honor to her family, and returned home a hero.

But by Lunar New Year, or Spring Festival as it was also called, the most heroic task before Bittersweet was settling the household accounts. She had to pay merchants and receive money owed her before Lunar New Year, for by dawn of that day, no one could demand payment till the next Spring Festival. During the New Year period, right up to the evening before the big day itself, the city was ablaze with lights. People with lanterns in their hands were out searching for debtors in hiding. Often, the lantern bearers headed for the temples of Canton, for there debtors concealed themselves among the merrymakers watching troupes of actors and acrobats.

Seated at her desk, Bittersweet was studying her ledger while Dashao moved the cedar chests and closets away from the walls and urged Liu-wu, Wenti's second cousin, to help her. Wenti himself had declined Bittersweet's invitation to come to Canton. He had lived too long in Hong Kong to be able to revert to Chinese ways. Instead, he had recommended Liu-wu, who already lived in Canton.

"Old Aunt, why do you sweep each room with inward strokes of the broom?" Liu-wu asked.

"Not to sweep the family's wealth out the door," Dashao answered. "I'll never forget my mother encouraging me each and every New Year, 'Be careful to sweep every inch of the room, my daughter. The speck of dust you miss might fly into your eyes and blind you.' There!" she announced with pride. "The house is spotless. The coming year will be better than the last. Now you can start repainting the red gates, whitewashing the outer walls, and repapering the windows of the house. And be quick about it. They must be finished within a fortnight."

"Do you want me to be as crooked and bent as old Wenti when I'm just a quarter of his age?" the manservant cried. "Have some pity on me!"

"And what of me?" Dashao asked, her hands on her hips. "I must prepare enough food to satisfy the appetites of both man and god for more than two weeks, and I must do it all in the first few days of the Spring Festival, since no knife or cleaver can be used till the festival is over. Do you think I want to be accused of cutting into the family's wealth by wielding a sharp instrument?"

"What you're asking me to do in the time you're asking me to do it would take three men at least," Liu-wu said, sulking.

"A single diligent man would do," she replied. "And while you're about it, console yourself by thinking about my obligations. Making the sweet steamed glutinous pudding, *nian gao*. Stuffing the rice paper skins with chopped pork, shredded scallions, and slivered ginger to make *jiao zi*. And for a few of the dumplings, filling them with peanuts for long life; dates or chestnuts for the imminent arrival of a son; gold or silver coins so that one might never lack money; or perhaps a nugget of jade to bring good fortune to he who finds it in his bowl," she said with a wink, suggesting that he might be the lucky recipient.

She gave Liu-wu an encouraging shove. "Start with the outer gates. Then Li *Tai-tai* can buy pictures of the door gods to protect us against evil spirits. Next, whitewash the walls so that she can hang the red paper couplets over the doorways. The sooner you begin, the earlier you'll be done."

As soon as Liu-wu shuffled out the door, Bittersweet closed her ledger and, together with Dashao, visited the wispy-bearded old man who had studied under a master calligrapher in Peking. He now owned a shop in Canton that sold the finest quality rice paper, sable calligraphy brushes, and inkstones. From him, Bittersweet bought pictures of the two heavenly guardians to paste on both sides of the main entrance of her house and couplets printed on strips of red paper which read: "Ten thousand generations," "May all your wishes be fulfilled," "Happiness, high position and long life." Because Bittersweet was a country girl and wished to be reminded of home, she also bought paper streamers on which were written: "Clear water ripples over the rocks" and "How beautiful are our rivers and mountains!"

"Li *Tai-tai*," Dashao reminded her mistress on their return from town, "in two days, the mat sheds will go up in the center of the city and the flower vendors will set up their wares. Why not ask our landlady, Sze *Tai-tai*, to accompany you to buy flowers? And don't bother asking Yifu if she wants to go. If it involves spending money, she'll be the first in line."

"It will give Liu-wu an opportunity to drive the car and dress in his chauffeur's uniform," Bittersweet said, knowing that was one of the chores Liu-wu was fond of. "Hwang *Tai-tai* might like to join us. We'll make a party of it." Though her husband was governor of Kwangsi and lived in Nanning, Hwang *Tai-tai* had, at his suggestion, set up residence in Canton. The fact that Canton was a far more cosmopolitan city than sleepy Nanning seemed to compensate completely for the geographical separation from Hwang. "We'll go," Bittersweet decided, "the day after tomorrow."

The twelfth month of the Chinese lunar calendar was known as the bitter month, but, on the day that Bittersweet chose to visit the flower market, Canton was filled with bright sunshine. A mild breeze blew through the city, perfuming every street and corner with the fragrance of fresh blooms and ripe fruits. Happy and excited, Bittersweet, Hwang *Tai-tai*, Sze *Tai-tai*, and Yifu piled into the roadster. With Liu-wu at the wheel, they headed for the center of town. But the closer they got to their destination, the thicker the crowds, until the car was barely able to move.

"Oh, this is impossible! Let's get out and walk," Yifu said, throwing her hands up in frustration.

Since they were mere blocks away from the flower market, her companions agreed. Directing Liu-wu to stay where he was so they might find him again, the four women hooked arms and waded out into the sea of people, all pushing and shoving, marching or meandering, shoulder-to-shoulder towards their common goal.

The cries and noises of people of various trades filled the air. Each was hawking his own ware or service, and each had a specific call or sound to distinguish him from the rest. The barber twanged his tuning fork with a short steel rod. The hat seller shook a harness of bells. The puppeteer proclaimed the start of his show with a crash of cymbals and a thunder of gongs. The toy seller shook toys strung from the top of a long stick.

"Buy, little man!" he sang to a child who was being reluctantly pulled away by his mother. "They're life-like! They have eyes and arms!"

"Green-glazed beauties! Old jars in partial exchange for new!" another merchant cried.

And another: "Try my confection of sugar, oil, and flour! It's plaited to resemble a horse's tail decked out for New Year's Day!"

The jar and the horse blossom sellers triggered the voices of the seller of pots, the crab apple vendor, the soup and the turnip vendors. Everywhere there was the cacophony of *renao*, the heat and noise of human relationship and enterprise.

"Only two strings left! Crab apples red and shiny as rubies!"

"Sour prune soup. Just one bowl will quench your thirst!"

"Turnip roots that taste sweet as pears!"

And amid all this, troupes of actors, Cantonese opera singers, and rubber-limbed acrobats demonstrated their skills. Arms still linked, necks straining to catch glimpses of the activities around them, the four women were swept towards the mat sheds of the flower market.

"Chrysanthemums!" Sze *Tai-tai* sighed, overcome by their beauty.

"You're showing your age!" teased Hwang *Tai-tai,* for the chrysanthemum was the floral symbol for the autumn of one's life, signifying longevity and a life spent in quiet retirement.

"You've done the right thing to come here," said the chrysanthemum seller who was anything but retiring. "Come in, come in! Look at my beauties from all angles! Appreciate them for their beauty, rarity, symbolism — and *buy*!" He stretched out an arm before the white, yellow, and purple chrysanthemums. "I love my flowers, and I'm an expert in their every secret and idiosyncrasy," he told the ladies. "Just think! All there is to know about the 133 varieties of chrysanthemum — and I know it all!"

"Madam," he said, noticing Bittersweet's eyes sweep over his floral arrangements, "I can see that you are a connoisseur of floral beauty, and so I will show you only the rarest, only the loveliest, of my chrysanthemums. Look here. Honey-Linked Bracelets. And here. Purple Tiger Whiskers. And there. Eyebrows of the Old Ruler — the Old Ruler being no one else but the venerable Lao Tzu."

"Really?" Bittersweet said, her interest caught as much by the name of the flower as by its beauty. She nodded at the flower vendor's assistant to indicate that she would like a pot of those.

"And there next to Old Eyebrows — Evening Sun on a Duck's Back. And here — Yellow Orioles in the Green Willow. Over there — Golden Phoenix Holding a Pearl in its Mouth."

In other stalls, the women gazed upon branches of white plum blossoms. These signified longevity, since the plum blossom, along with the pine and the bamboo — the "three friends of winter" — bloomed in the winter months. There were also branches of green-tinged peach blossoms, fragrant vellum-like magnolia blossoms, waxen-petalled camellias, and dense, velvety cockscomb. But Bittersweet's favorites were the peonies, *fu-gui hua*, "the flower of wealth and honor." While some were full, feathery blossoms of pure white or delicate pink, she chose to decorate her own house for New Year's with an earthenware pot of the deep scarlet ones. She also bought branches of plum blossoms in honor of her surname, as well as for their calm and simple beauty; a narcissus plant in the hopes that it would blossom on New Year's Day; a kumquat tree heavy with fruit, for kumquats symbolized children; and a bellflower tree since red was the color of good fortune and happiness.

Satisfied with their purchases, the women started to make their way back to where they had left Liu-wu. But, Yifu was distracted by a blind palmist playing his flute. She stopped and tugged at Bittersweet's arm. "Ninth Sister-in-Law, can't we stop a minute?" she begged. "I want to have my fortune told."

Before Bittersweet could answer, Sze *Tai-tai* intervened. "It's so noisy and crowded here. I'll show you a much better place—one away from the flower market where the reader both tells you your past and predicts your future. That way you know whether or not you're getting an honest reading."

"Let's all get our fortunes told," Hwang *Tai-tai* suggested. She looked at the dwarf mandarin orange tree she had just bought at the market. "I wouldn't mind knowing if certain investments I made recently will bear fruit."

Liu-wu had fallen asleep at the wheel, but he quickly righted his cap over his eyes and drove his passengers to Tian Wangliao, the Temple of the Heavenly Gods. When Bittersweet saw the "Temple," she was visibly disappointed. It was nothing but a shopping mall, full of stores and business offices. Still, Sze *Tai-tai* persisted, "The worst-looking restaurants often serve the best-tasting food, do they not? I assure you, you'll get your money's worth."

They entered the building to find a long line of people waiting in the reception area. "This will take forever! Let's go in together,"

Hwang *Tai-tai* suggested. "After all, we're all good friends. What do we have to hide from each other?"

When their turn came, the four women entered a small, well-lit room, barren save for a small desk, two chairs, and a simple wooden bookcase with scores of well-thumbed volumes crowding its shelves. Pasted on one wall of the room was a large drawing of a face covered with dots and Chinese characters. Next to it was a large diagram of the palm of the human hand scored with various lines and marked with Chinese characters. On the opposite wall hung a brush-and-ink scroll of Mount T'ai, one of China's five sacred mountains.

The fortuneteller, seated in one of the two chairs, rose as soon as the four women entered. He bowed gracefully from the waist. Though he didn't resemble Xiao Tzu, Bittersweet immediately thought of her long-haired friend. The physiognomist was probably in his late seventies, but his body was straight and his hair white as the camellia blossoms she had just bought. The skin over his face was smooth and golden, pulled tight over the planes and angles of his face. But what was particularly arresting about his face were his eyes; they had the youth, sparkle, and curiosity of a child's, just like Xiao Tzu's.

"We've come together to save time," Hwang *Tai-tai* explained, "since there are so many people waiting to see you. We don't mind standing and, being friends, we have nothing to hide from each other."

The fortuneteller nodded and extended his hand, indicating that one of the four women should sit down in the chair opposite him.

"You go first," Yifu whispered to Sze *Tai-tai*, giving her a nudge, "since you brought us here. I want to hear what he says about your past and future, so I know whether he's honest or not."

Sze *Tai-tai* sat down. Protectively, her three friends gathered around the back of her chair, while the fortuneteller scrutinized her face and examined her palms. "You have no difficulties or hardships in your life," he told her after several moments. "You have plenty of the four basics of life: food, shelter, clothing, and travel. You had a good beginning and you will have a good end. Though your fortune is not bad, it's not particularly propitious, for though you possess money, you lack position."

Sze *Tai-tai*, satisfied with her fortune, rose from the chair which Hwang *Tai-tai* immediately occupied. "You are a conscientious and diligent helpmate to your husband," the fortuneteller said after looking at her face, her hands, and her general demeanor. "Also, a devoted

191

mother to your son, a loyal friend to those you like, and a fearsome adversary to those you do not. You are astute in money matters and know how to choose your friends depending on their influence and prestige. You have had some suffering in your life which has been caused by your husband and the loss of a beloved family member, but you have been able to turn your suffering to your advantage. For the rest of your life, you may expect good luck and material comfort." Hwang *Tai-tai* rose from the chair with a nod of appreciation towards Sze *Tai-tai*.

"Which one of you remaining ladies would like her fortune told next?" the old man asked when neither Bittersweet nor Yifu sat down in the chair.

Bittersweet looked at her sister-in-law, but the girl shook her head vigorously and motioned for her to be seated. Before Bittersweet could acquiesce, the physiognomist rose from his chair, pressed his palms together at his forehead, and bowed low from the waist. "Madam," he said in a trembling voice, "without looking at your face for more than a few seconds and without looking at your palms at all, I can tell you that your fortune is the best that I have seen in my long life. You are one among millions. You possess love, fortune, position, and long life — the best of what there is to be had on this earth."

Bittersweet grasped the back of the chair and eased herself into it.

"Your husband will stand head and shoulders above the crowd. He will occupy the highest position in the land save one. Had you been born a man, you would have occupied the place I have predicted for your husband. You would have been the number two, perhaps even the number one, leader in the country."

Seeing the confusion and disbelief on her face, he commented upon the features of her face that prophesied the life he had foretold. "You have long eyebrows, the kind called Clear and Beautiful. You have long earlobes, thick, fat and glossy, the kind called Shoulder-Touching Ears. These are very rare and usually belong to a rich and powerful man, to an emperor or a king. Your nose is long, too, strong and well-formed with a rounded tip, a Deer Nose, which means that you are kind by nature, keep your promises, and possess wealth and long life. You also have Elephant Eyes, long and narrow with wrinkles above and below, which signifies kindness, friendliness, and wisdom. Your mouth is a Cherry Mouth, particularly fortunate in a woman. It means that you are clever and wise and possess a gentle nature, that you will always be wealthy, and that you will know a highly-respected person who will help you in times of difficulty."

His clear eyes then dimmed somewhat. "There is, however, a bit of grief in your life. You and your husband do not live under the same roof. You and your husband will never live under the same roof." Bittersweet looked into her lap. Never to live with my husband under the same roof, she thought. Could that be aptly described as a "bit" of grief?

"Oh, *Laoshi*," Sze *Tai-tai* blurted out, "if you only knew how precise. . . ."

Bittersweet put her hand on her landlady's arm to silence her. "What you've said about my life is very interesting," Bittersweet said to the fortuneteller, "but it is also not at all true. In fact, you have misread all our fortunes. The husbands of the two ladies whose fortunes you have told before mine occupy very high positions in the government. My husband is their subordinate and takes his orders from them."

The physiognomist smiled. "People say that fortunetellers make up fortunes at will and at random, without any knowledge of or regard for truth and facts. I have studied books of augury all my life, Madam. The *Ma-i* of the Sung Dynasty. The *Pa P'u Tzu* of the Ming Dynasty. The *Golden Scissors* of the Qing Dynasty. What I say is based on my understanding of these venerable books. If what I have said turns out to be true, come back here and pay me more than what I now charge you. If it is false, come back and recover the fee." He looked into Bittersweet's eyes. "Fortune decides half of your fate. Your efforts decide the other half. Even a woman born under auspicious stars must have a good heart and perform good deeds. Madam, for telling your fortune, I will charge you ten times the usual price, since you can anticipate a ten-fold increase in your fortunes."

"What about me?" Yifu cried, tapping Bittersweet on the shoulder and gesturing for her to relinquish the chair. "You haven't told my fortune yet."

The fortuneteller looked shocked. "Let me see one of your palms." He studied it for several seconds, then put it down on the table. "I'm very sorry to have to tell you, *Xiaojie*, but your fortune is not at all propitious."

Before he could continue, Yifu jumped up from the chair, knocking it over, and began to berate the man. "Liar! Charlatan! You don't know anything!" She then turned to the three other women, her face red, her hands opening and closing nervously. "We should never have come to this place . . . to see this . . . imposter! It's all your fault!" she cried, pointing to Sze *Tai-tai*. "You were the one who brought us here to this . . . this fake!"

"What I have seen in your face and hand is based on my knowledge of the great books of physiognomy that have been written throughout the centuries. What I will say are not my words but the words of the books, and the words are true. In your face and hand, I have gazed upon your future."

"Will I marry?" Yifu asked hopefully, momentarily forgetting her anger.

"You will," the fortuneteller answered. "Your husband will die young. As for yourself, you're comfortable now because of the goodness of others, but you will have a bad and painful end. I advise you to be kind to others and to perform good deeds, and you may alter your fortune for the better. Use the knowledge of your fortune which I have just told you to improve your lot. As for my fee, I charge you nothing."

Yifu's face turned white with fear. "Do you think I'd pay you one cash for hearing a bunch of lies?" she said. "You're nothing but an imposter! I'll report you to the authorities. My brother is very powerful. One word from me and he'll put you out of business!" She turned and rushed out of the room.

"I've read all of your fortunes," the old man told the three remaining women. "Whether they're true or not true, you will find out in the future. I charge you," he said, looking first at Hwang *Tai-tai*, then at Sze *Tai-tai*, "one *kuai*. As for you," he continued, looking at Bittersweet, "I charge you ten *kuai*. And I hope that you will come back and let me know if the fate that I've predicted for you comes to pass."

After the three paid what was asked of them, they found Yifu telling the people in the reception room that they were wasting both their time and money and that they should go home. In the car, they laughed and joked about their visit to the fortuneteller to try to calm Yifu who continued to berate the old man. Still, in their hearts, they knew that the physiognomist was genuine and that his words were sincere.

After dropping Hwang *Tai-tai* and Sze *Tai-tai* off at their homes, Liu-wu drove into the driveway of his mistress's home to find that it was full of limousines and motorcycles. Bittersweet, recalling her "protectors" in Hong Kong, rushed into her house, calling for Dashao.

"The best protector of all, Li *Tai-tai*," Dashao affirmed with a smile. "The general is with the young master in the reception room."

"Delin is here?" Bittersweet said.

"And," Dashao said in a triumphant tone, "he has rented a house in the same district as ours. The general will be living a good part of the time in Canton!"

The news which should have made Bittersweet euphoric cast her momentarily into despair. Yes, in Canton but not under the same roof, she thought, recalling the fortuneteller's prediction. In Canton but with Dejie. What is crueler — that he live far away so that I never see him or that he live on the same block but under another roof?

"Li *Tai-tai*?" Dashao asked, observing her mistress's pale face.

"It's nothing," Bittersweet waved her maidservant's concern away. "The wonderful news has simply taken me by surprise."

Bittersweet walked towards the reception room, but once on the threshold she stopped and stood for a while looking in. Delin was seated in one of the armchairs. Hands on his knees, he was looking up at Youlin who stood, still dressed in his school uniform, before him.

"You're much taller than when I last saw you," Delin said, almost giving in to the urge to seat his son on his lap or to reach up and pinch his cheek.

"The last time you saw me was in Hong Kong, Father," Youlin replied. "That was four years ago."

"Four years," Delin repeated softly. "Still a bit on the thin side," he continued more jocularly. "You must tell Dashao to feed you more."

"Yes, Father."

"You used to call me Daddy," Delin said sadly. "But you're right. You were a boy then, and now you are quite the young gentleman in your Western suit."

Youlin blushed and rocked from one foot to the other. At a loss for words, Delin cleared his throat and looked about the room. "And your throat?" he asked. "Does it bother you anymore?"

"My tonsils were removed over four years ago. My throat is fine."

"Of course, of course. How was the rest of your stay in Hong Kong? Did you like your old school there? Do you like Peujing better? And Canton? Do you like Canton better than Hong Kong?"

"How can your son answer you," Bittersweet said, coming into the room, "when you don't give him a chance to breathe between questions?"

"Ah, your mother," Delin said, rising, visibly relieved.

He bowed to Bittersweet and she reciprocated. For a moment, they exchanged the requisite pleasantries of family members who haven't seen each other for a long time.

"You've asked the young master many questions," Dashao, who had been standing just outside the open doorway, said as a way of ending the protocol. "Now here is one for you: what dishes would you like to eat for dinner tonight, General Li, so that I may go to market and buy the ingredients?"

"I have a better idea," Delin said, turning to his son. "No cooking tonight, Dashao. You see, I haven't forgotten my promise. Tonight I'm taking my son to the best French restaurant in Canton."

Dashao frowned and shook her head. "I've heard all about French food. Not half as good as Chinese. They use dozens of sauces to conceal the fact that they don't know how to prepare what lies beneath them. Too rich, too. I'll see to it that there's a pot of hot tea when you return," she said, turning to go. "You'll need it to settle your stomachs."

"Would you like that?" Delin asked Youlin. "And afterwards, you can come and stay with me for a few days. My driver will take you to school."

Youlin looked at his father, then at his mother. "Why can't we all live together?"

Though a small noise caught in Bittersweet's throat, Delin was the first to break the oppressive silence that followed Youlin's question. "It's very peaceful in this house," he said, avoiding his son's eyes. "The location is very convenient — within walking distance to your school, your mother tells me. From my house, you'd have to depend upon a chauffeur. Then again, I'm obliged to have visitors and conferences at all times of the day and night. Not a very suitable atmosphere for you to study in." His gaze returned to Youlin's face but wavered in apology. "Don't you think?"

Standing halfway between his parents, Youlin looked from one to the other; he was pulled and repelled by each at the same time, torn by simultaneous feelings of love and anger. The words of the fortune-teller came back to Bittersweet now that her husband was verifying them. "You don't have to explain!" she broke down, sobbing. "I have no intention of living with you!"

Youlin rushed to his mother's side and hugged her close. Delin's body, normally martially erect and proud, sagged in defeat, and he slumped back in the armchair. Bittersweet's heart unclenched and turned over in sorrow to see her husband so singularly alone. She lifted Youlin's face from her shoulder and said, "Go with your father. He has so little time to be with you."

Bittersweet's utterance, like the fortuneteller's words at the Temple of the Heavenly Gods, became a prophecy. Not long after Delin and Dejie had settled into their house in Canton, the Japanese invaded Manchuria, and Delin spent much of his time traveling around the country. Contrary to Chiang's wishes, Delin was advocating all-out resistance to Japan.

Anti-Japanese sentiment had risen steadily during the early 1930s. These feelings were enflamed by Chiang's steady concessions to the Japanese and then by Japan's invasion of Manchuria. Kwangsi had taken the lead in the anti-Japanese movement by stirring up national sentiment against the Japanese government and by boycotting all Japanese goods that found their way into the province. The whole nation began to look to the Kwangsi Three rather than to Chiang to lead them out of slow bondage to the Land of the Rising Sun.

When Delin did return to Canton and Bittersweet's house, his visits were almost always in response to some matter regarding the Japanese question. It was now a well-known "rumor" that he and Dejie were not getting along. Dejie's rising social position permitted her to feel that she was qualified to make political or military suggestions to her husband. At times, she was so bold as to make them in public. At times, she even contradicted him in public. It was no secret that Delin was in better spirits when Dejie was in Kweiping or elsewhere — founding a girl's school, fundraising for the Christian missionaries, or giving speeches. When her presence was oppressive and when they were both in Canton, Delin came to Bittersweet to ask for her help, and Bittersweet never had to ask the reason for his request.

One day, he said, "General Fujiwara is coming to Canton in two days. He's agreed to meet with me. No one must know about this meeting. My house is full of guests. Is it possible?"

"Of course," Bittersweet replied. "I'll break my appointment with Hwang *Tai-tai*. I'll say that I'm not feeling well. She'll understand." Bittersweet smiled sardonically. "After all, we are both married to men whose lives are not their own."

Two days later, a limousine drove up to her house, and a Japanese general and his aide alighted from it. Having sent Dashao and Liu-wu out on errands, and with Youlin still at school, Bittersweet welcomed the two Japanese and escorted them to where her husband waited behind a low table set with a pot of chrysanthemum tea, teacups, and a bowl of rock sugar. Though the parlor door was closed, Bittersweet stood just on the other side, her ear pressed against the wood.

"All of China condemns Japan for invading Manchuria," she heard Delin say.

"Not all, General Li. Supreme Commander Chiang has not, and his word seems to be louder than the roar of four hundred million Chinese. And besides, Manchuria's governor invited us to come, as protection against the Russians."

"How can you as a people, a people so similar to the Chinese in written language, social origin, and cultural values, invade our country and infringe upon our sovereignty?" Delin said. "Japan is going the way of the Western imperialists. Such aggression, if not tempered, will lead to a world war. And if it does, you will be defeated."

"Come, come, General. You exaggerate, and you misread our intentions. It's to your benefit that we're here. China is weak and the Russian menace is strong — and it's spreading. If we don't come to your aid, the Soviet Union will use you as a stepping stone into the Pacific, bringing Communism to Southeast Asia. Manchuria was a gateway for Russia's expansion eastward. As China couldn't defend Manchuria, we felt obliged to undertake the task on her behalf."

"I disagree with your evaluation of the situation and with the results you foresee, General Fujiwara," Delin answered. "On the contrary, your invasion of Manchuria is only driving the fish from the waters. That is, driving the Chinese masses — who abhor your recent action and clamor for Chiang to repel your advance — into Soviet arms. With Soviet assistance, the Chinese Communist Party might become powerful enough to eventually control not only all of China but the entire Far East. Admit it, Fujiwara-san, Japan is divided between opposition to the Soviet Union and aggression toward China — between northward and southward expansion. Which is it? Northward or southward? Rumor has it that the aggression will be turned southward — on China."

General Fujiwara laughed. "Rumor! Mere rumor, General Li! And you would believe it?"

"Rumor sometimes has a very substantial basis," Delin replied, "especially when it comes from highly reputable intelligence sources located in Dairen. My own, I might add. I hope you'll return to your country and dissuade your government from readying itself for an all-out attack on ours."

After the Japanese visitors left, Bittersweet could not stop herself from asking Delin, "Will there be war?"

"If the invasion of Manchuria is any clue as to Japan's intentions, then I don't see how war is avoidable. The way Chiang is giving away China piecemeal, nothing will be left. The Chinese people will not stand for it. Already we're clamoring for armed resistance against Japan. What is better: to sap one's strength and life's blood drop by drop, or to stand up and fight, even if it means giving one's life in the end?"

"The question might be better put: which is worse?" Bittersweet said.

A few months after she had received the Japanese visitors in her home, she listened with pride to a radio broadcast in which Delin rallied public opinion against the Japanese colonization of China: "I call China to war. The fate of our country being now in the balance, the question is not whether we can or cannot resist, but whether we should or should not resist. Resist, and we shall stand; submit, and we shall fall. For us there is really no option except resolute armed resistance. If armed resistance means sacrifices, submission entails greater sacrifices, the result of which can be nothing less than the complete destruction of our country. Despite sacrifices, a war of resistance may pave the way for the regeneration of our nation."

Delin's speech was printed in the city's leading newspaper, *The Canton Truth*, an edition which required a second, then a third reprinting. The entire nation was clamoring for resistance against the Japanese aggressors.

In the spring of 1936, when Youlin was finishing up his junior year at Peujing High School, Chiang scheduled a visit to Canton to consult with Delin about the national crisis.

"Now is the time to see if Youlin's career tray was true or not," Delin told Bittersweet. "I requested a meeting between Chiang and Youlin at Whampoa Military Academy, and Chiang graciously accepted 'as your blood brother.'"

Bittersweet sighed inwardly but said nothing, aware that her husband had never given up hope that Youlin would lead a military life.

"Call Youlin in to see me, will you?" he asked her.

"What is it, Mother?" Youlin asked as they walked together to the parlor, sensing that something serious awaited him.

"Your father will tell you."

Youlin listened in silence while Delin told him about the interview he had arranged at Whampoa Military Academy with its director. Now and then, the boy looked at his mother who sat by him in silence.

"You want to use your influence so that I can get ahead in the career which you have chosen for me," Youlin replied coolly.

Delin stared at his son, perplexed. "Don't relatives and friends help each other? Don't parents provide the best they can for their children? They feed, clothe, and shelter them. They provide them with what is necessary and good in life. That is a parent's duty towards his children. I wouldn't be doing my duty if I didn't help you in every way I know how. It's part of my life's responsibility, the equation by which good men live. Responsibility is one half of the equation; the other half is privilege. Every responsibility has its privilege; every privilege has its responsibility. If I now have the privilege of being in a position to help you, why do you question it?"

"I'm not ungrateful for all you've done for me, Father," Youlin answered. "I know that you want what you think is best for me. But I don't think you know what I think is best for me."

Delin looked at Bittersweet with a look that seemed to say, "What is this? We've tried to give him a good education, yet he will soon be graduating from high school speaking words that are barely comprehensible! Is this what comes from sending him to an exclusive Western school — built by wealthy expatriate Chinese and based on a foreign religion called Presbyterianism?"

Reading his thoughts, she said nothing. The best she could do was to listen. Words now would only worsen the matter.

"What *you* think is best for you?" Delin repeated. "What, in your estimation, might that be?"

"I know I'm young and that I haven't had much experience in life," Youlin answered, reddening, "but I am observant and from my observations I've come to certain conclusions. I've observed *your* life — more by your absence than by your presence. You serve the government, but in serving it, you have no time for your family. I also read the newspapers. What it says about the government is that it's corrupt. It corroborates what you yourself have told me about the corruption in the military as well as in the government. Why should I want to work for a government that's corrupt?"

"To change it into an honest government," Delin answered him squarely. "To save China from destruction and to make her strong, to. . . ."

"But it's not the work for me," Youlin interrupted. "It's work for someone like you, who feels as strongly as you do. You feel so strongly about it that you went against the wishes of your parents to pursue it."

Delin's face flushed instantly. "Don't you love your country?"

"Can I love China only by being a soldier? If I want to lead a peaceful life, does that mean that I don't love China?"

"What I am trying to do, Youlin, is to help make China the kind of nation where you can lead a peaceful life."

"I appreciate that, Father. But that's your life, not mine. What I want for myself is to have a stable job, a good career, so I can raise a family and enjoy a peaceful life with them. I've never wanted to join the army or serve the government. Wealth and high position mean nothing to me."

Delin winced as though he'd been struck in the face. "Perhaps not wealth and position, but your duty to your family and the honor you bring to your name should mean something to you, don't you think?"

"It is in duty to my family that I choose to serve my family," Youlin answered, the veins standing out in his neck from emotional strain. "If you must know how I arrived at my decision not to follow in your footsteps, it's because I've walked in the footsteps of my mother. You talk about the government's instability. My mother's life is unstable and insecure and, from what I've observed in living with her, it's been a lonely and unhappy one."

"Youlin!" Bittersweet cried, forgetting herself. She looked at Delin. "Our son is young. It is not he who speaks but his youthful inexperience."

Delin pulled himself quickly out of his chair and came to his full height in a single motion — a signal that the meeting was over. Youlin followed suit, but his mother struggled slowly to her feet.

"I've spoken to Chiang about you," he addressed his son. "He's asked to meet you and will send a car for you tomorrow morning to drive you to Whampoa. Please be ready to leave at six-thirty sharp."

Youlin bowed from the waist to his mother, then dropped to his knees before his father and performed the traditional kowtow. Never in his life had he performed this gesture of complete subservience. Youlin then rose to his feet and walked stiffly out of the room.

When Bittersweet went to Youlin's room after seeing her husband out, the door was closed. She opened it and entered. Her son was standing by the window, staring out onto the cobblestone courtyard.

"I'm not going tomorrow," he said, without looking around.

His mother came up beside him to look at his profile — for one's face is so often a clearer indication of one's state of mind and the truth of one's words.

"But the arrangements have been made. You must go."

"Why must I go? Did I make the arrangements?" he said, looking at her. "They were made by Father and the Son of Heaven. I must do it, yet I am the last to know about it. And Father despises Chiang."

"What your father feels about Chiang personally has nothing to do with the fact that he must work with him for the good of the country," Bittersweet said. "In such matters, a man must put his feelings aside."

He is no longer a boy, Bittersweet thought, studying Youlin's face. When did he stop being a boy?

"There's a rumor circulating around Peujing that Chiang's cronies are thugs and gangsters, members of the most notorious *tong* in the whole country. If Chiang himself isn't a member of the Green Gang, surely he comes close. They're his bank account while Whampoa is his power base. He handpicks the cadets, not for their loyalty to China but to him. They're his personal lackeys. And Father wants me to be one of them!"

"Your father wants you only to attend the meeting with Chiang tomorrow. He won't be accompanying you. What you say and do there is your affair."

Youlin's eyes filled with sudden insight and his face relaxed.

"If you don't go," Bittersweet continued, "your father loses much face. That would be to Chiang's advantage. For better or for worse, your father is Chiang's sworn brother."

"How could he possibly . . . !?" Youlin began but was too enraged and frustrated to finish.

"It wasn't his own doing," his mother replied. "The bond was established nonetheless. Nothing can change that. If your father

202

doesn't honor the bond, the public would be sure to learn of it and public opinion would turn against him."

Youlin looked back out the window. Bittersweet turned to go. She was just at the threshold of the room when she heard him speak. "Would you please tell Dashao to wake me before six tomorrow morning?"

Though her son's back was to her, Bittersweet nodded.

All that night, unable to sleep, she tried to imagine what would transpire at Youlin's interview with Chiang. All the next morning and into the evening, she sat at the window in her room, looking out onto the courtyard, trying to visualize what was happening across the Pearl River and how it might affect not only her son's future studies but also his relationship with his father. At almost eight o'clock that evening, Bittersweet saw Youlin open the front door. She heard quick, light footsteps coming toward her room. She opened the door even before he knocked.

"Now that I've met the Son of Heaven, I'm more determined than ever not to work in the government."

At Bittersweet's urging, Youlin sat down and described his meeting with Chiang. The trip had taken nearly two hours: first, in Chiang's official limousine, then in a motorboat — again one of Chiang's "personal effects" — bound for Whampoa Military Academy.

"I was led into the large reception room of an imposing building and told by an orderly that Commander Chiang would be along shortly. There were no less than six dossier-toting high government officials and generals who had arrived before me and who were also waiting to see Chiang. They all sat stiffly, looking straight ahead of them in their crisp, uncreased uniforms and suits. Obviously, they'd been told that the Son of Heaven hated any kind of sloppiness — in thinking or dress. I sat in a chair away from them all.

"At precisely nine o'clock, the orderly reappeared, clicked his heels together and shouted, 'Li Youlin!' I jumped to my feet, red with shame and embarrassment. Here I was — a schoolboy who had been announced before three-star generals and ministers of state! They stared at me with annoyance, even outrage, as the orderly ushered me into Chiang's office. Not a minute later, Chiang appeared. I rose from my seat and bowed as propriety dictated, and said, 'Commander Chiang.'

"'Call me Uncle,' he said, motioning for me to sit in the stuffed armchair beside his. 'Your father and I became sworn brothers over a dozen years ago. That makes you my nephew.'

"'Your *sworn* nephew,' I answered.

"Chiang grinned slowly, then laughed too heartily to be sincere or even amused at my remark and rang for some tea. He asked me to join him in some breakfast, but I declined, saying I'd already eaten. When the tea arrived, he took a sip, then said in a self-congratulatory voice, 'I drink only tea. Not a spot of alcohol. It warms the blood too much. Dulls the senses. Impedes the brain.'"

"Then, Chiang asked me my age and about my present education and future aspirations. Hearing that I want to be an engineer, Chiang opened his gray eyes wide. Gray," Youlin repeated with a shudder, "but more opaque than if they'd been the darkest brown. Then, he grinned.

"'An engineer,' he said, nodding to himself. 'A very praiseworthy profession. I commend you on your determination, your independent spirit. And I wish you the very best of luck in your studies and an illustrious career — one that will make my sworn brother, your father, very, very proud. If there's anything that I can do to help you to attain your goal, you'll let me know, won't you? And now. . . .' He stood up and extended his hand towards the orderly — who gave him a book with his left hand while his right hand never moved from the gun in his holster! 'Please accept this unworthy token of our memorable meeting — the first, but not the last, I hope, and one which has made me very, very happy.' He scribbled something on the inside cover and gave it to me, smiling and bobbing his head up and down. I read the inscription. 'Be diligent and thrifty,' it said. I looked at the outside of the cover. The book was the St. James Bible! We both bowed and then the orderly showed me out. I've never been so happy to leave a place in my life. And I've never been more certain of anything as not wanting a political career."

"Your father will want to know what happened at your meeting with Chiang," Bittersweet said.

Youlin nodded and his mouth hardened.

"If you don't want to go to Whampoa, where do you want to go to school?"

"To a university in the United States — to get a degree in engineering. Most of Peujing's graduates go on to colleges or universities in America or in England."

"Let me speak with your father before you tell him about your interview with Chiang," Bittersweet suggested. "He knows that the best universities and colleges are in America and England and that they offer a much broader curriculum than Whampoa. As for a career in engineering, how might a nation be built without engineers? You will still be very useful to China."

Youlin smiled. "Thank you, Mama."

Bittersweet smiled at her son. She knew how much Delin hoped that Youlin would follow in his footsteps, especially now that the anti-Japanese resistance movement was gaining momentum. She also knew what her son wished for himself. And she worried that the difference in their desires would lead to an emotional impasse between them. As for the fact that Youlin wanted to leave home for America, she tried not to think about it.

That winter in Xian, Chiang was kidnapped by two of his own officers — his chief of bandit suppression forces in the Northwest and his pacification officer for Shensi. Their aim was to force him to stop bowing to Japanese territorial demands and to declare war on Japan. The so-called Xian Incident proved to be the turning — and the breaking — point in the strained relationship between the two countries. After Chiang managed to convince his kidnappers that his placation of the Japanese was really patriotism — merely a strategy to gain time to organize the army, strengthen the nation, build roads, and prepare for the inevitable retreat into the interior — they set him free. In a complex game of face-saving and counter-face-saving, the kidnappers were sentenced to ten years imprisonment but were, in fact, merely placed under disciplinary observation. In the meantime, Chiang apologized to the Chinese nation for the whole ordeal he'd been through and decided, finally, that the time had come to wage war on Japan.

Every day, it seemed, China and Japan edged that much closer to armed conflict. In late 1936, when Delin wrote his treatise, "Scorched Earth Resistance," war was imminent. "China is an old and a backward country," his piece read. "It possesses neither modern communications, nor modern infrastructure, nor modern industry. We must compensate for our shortcomings by developing our advantages. What are they? Our land is vast; our terrain is hilly; our people are many. We must use them all to harass the enemy. We must not only expect, we must actually plan for, a long tiring war. We must lure the Japanese into the interior of this huge country of ours, until their lines of communication and supply from the coast snap from the strain, then strip the land — scorch it barren — leaving them with neither sufficient manpower nor adequate material resources. Then we must begin guerrilla warfare behind the enemy lines, disrupting their communications, wearing them down both physically and morally. Rather than leave anything that the Japanese might use to their advantage, we must sacrifice everything. Only through sacrifice will victory be ours in the end."

In the midst of these turbulent events, Youlin prepared to leave Canton for the United States and the University of Chicago. As a compromise, to appease his father who wanted Youlin to have an English, rather than an American, education, Youlin grudgingly agreed to abandon his plans for engineering and major in political science.

On July 7, 1937, the Seven Plus Seven Incident, so named for it occurred on the seventh day of the seventh month, a Japanese private went AWOL from maneuvers at the Marco Polo Bridge some ten miles outside of Peking. He had apparently slipped away from his regiment to visit a brothel, but the Japanese accused the Chinese of abducting him and holding him in the town of Wanping. The following day, in spite of the fact that the missing soldier had returned to his troops, the Japanese opened fire near the east gate of the old northern capital. And so, undeclared, the War of Resistance began.

For Delin it meant constant meetings and conferences, the training and deployment of troops, the implementation of strategies, the planning of tactics, and the transfer of the capital of Kwangsi inland from Nanning to Kweilin. Kweilin would be far safer than Canton, and Delin urged Bittersweet to move there both for her own safety and to be close to his family in Dragon's Head.

Dashao, in response to the Seven Plus Seven Incident and Delin's prediction of a long, hard war, shook her head and insisted, "The *T'ui Pei Tu* — the prophecy as stated by two of the Eight Immortals — has come to pass. 'The dragon has lost its teeth; both men and women have cut their hair.'"

It was true that the Qing Dynasty was gone and that there was no new ruler on the Dragon Throne. Sun Yat-sen had died over a decade ago and the Boy Emperor Pu Yi was now the Puppet Emperor of Manchukou. Hair, a part of the body passed down from one's ancestors, symbolized people's continuity. If hair was cut short, then so was continuity.

"The prophecy continues," Dashao went on, "that Peking will be destroyed by a steel wind air, by a great many bombs."

"You must never say such things in front of General Li," Bittersweet told her. "You know what he thinks of ancient prophecies — that they're nothing but silly superstitions, a vestige of China's feudal past. As for the dragon having lost his teeth," she chuckled, "it was Chiang who couldn't get his false set in fast enough when his kidnappers abducted him. No wonder he was so stiff-lipped in the photos his captors took of him!"

But she could find no humor in the relationship between her husband and her son. Ever since the interview with Chiang, the tension between Youlin and his father had mounted. Youlin was, if anything, more courteous to his father than he had ever been, but it was a civility that bespoke of estrangement. The breach was further aggravated when Delin left Canton to meet with Chiang and begin preparing for war — all this before Youlin's ship sailed for America, even before his passport and visa had arrived. On Delin's subsequent visit to Canton, Bittersweet appeared unannounced in his office.

"I know that as a general, particularly in these times, your duty is to your country. But as the father of your son, you owe him a certain amount of concern nevertheless. He needs a passport and a visa. Without them, not only is he unable to go to America, *we* cannot evacuate Canton, because *I* will not budge until I have them in my hands! Every few days, Japanese planes drop their bombs closer and closer to the city. I've heard the explosions. I've seen the black smoke rising in the distance. The sooner I have Youlin's passport and visa, the sooner I can leave for Kweilin, and the less you'll be bothered with family matters."

At the end of the month, one of Delin's orderlies arrived on Bittersweet's doorstep, Youlin's passport and visa in hand. Two days later, Bittersweet watched from the dock, her lower lip held between her teeth, as her son boarded the S. S. *Empress of Japan* bound for America.

BOOK TWO

I was, being human, born alone;
I am, being woman, hard beset;
I live by squeezing from a stone
The little nourishment I get.

In masks outrageous and austere
The years go by in single file;
But none has merited my fear,
And none has quite escaped my smile.

From *"Let No Charitable Hope"*
Elinor Wylie

Chapter 1
The War of Resistance
(1937)

In the fall of 1937, Bittersweet, together with Dashao, Liu-wu, Solin, and Yifu, moved into the house she had built in Kweilin. She had previously entrusted the inheritance she had received at Baba's passing to Old Uncle Bagong and asked him to purchase a plot of land on which she planned to build a large house, designed by a *feng-shui* man — a Master of Wind and Water. Two years before war broke out between China and Japan, the five-*siheyuan* house was completed. The *siheyuan* were square courtyards surrounded by a two-story house on each side. The entire home stood on the banks of the Li River not far from Kweilin's business district and between the city's foremost peaks — Wave Restraining Hill and Folded Brocade Mountain. The first *siheyuan* fronted the street and was rented out to silk merchants; the second, fourth, and fifth *siheyuan* were rented to families; and the third was for Bittersweet's own use. The Master of Wind and Water had promised her a personal retreat, complete with gardens of supple bamboo, fragrant osmanthus trees, and fruit-bearing palms. With the outbreak of war, Bittersweet's home became just that.

Early one morning, soon after she had set up residence in Kwangsi's new capital, Bittersweet woke to excited pounding on her bedroom door. As she fastened the frogs of her *cheongsam,* she heard Delin scolding Dashao for waking his wife, for he was content to wait in the courtyard below, where he was enjoying the pre-dawn peace and the tranquil setting.

When Bittersweet found him, he was standing by the goldfish pond, one foot resting on its rocky ledge, one hand throwing steamed bread to the fish. "*Zao, zao,*" Bittersweet said. "You're up very early."

He looked up, smiled, and threw the rest of the steamed bread into the water. "It's my military training. I couldn't break the habit if I tried. I specifically asked Dashao not to. . . ."

"It's all right," Bittersweet interjected. "No doubt you have many

211

appointments to keep in Kweilin before you return to Nanking. I'm honored to be the first."

"You've become a mind reader as well as the owner of a fine house." Delin looked about, nodding appreciatively. "It's well-designed and well-built, and your gardens are beautiful. One can almost forget that a war is beginning."

"Let me take you on a short tour," Bittersweet offered. "Come."

Rectangular and uncomplicated, her house, she explained, was an auspicious shape. Though it was close to the center of Kweilin, it was also far enough away that no tall buildings cast shadows upon it. Having tall buildings nearby, Bittersweet learned from the Master of Wind and Water, could oppress a smaller house's *ch'i*, or vital energy, and hinder the occupant's personal and financial development. Her house, however, was open to the sun and sky and good currents of the earth's energy. Since water augured wealth, her house faced the river. Her prospects for prosperity were further increased by the ponds and fountains she had installed.

"And my tenants, the silk merchants, also benefit by being the occupants closest to the river. They're doing a brisk trade and can well afford to pay me the rent I charge."

The front door to her house was good and wide, allowing a healthy stream of *ch'i* to enter, and the windows opened outward and completely, permitting maximum *ch'i* inside.

"The Master of Wind and Water advised me to think of my house as though it were a person," Bittersweet told her impressed husband. "A house, like a human being, has its own metabolism. *Ch'i*, like blood, must flow evenly from room to room. Windows and doors are the house's noses and mouths, inhaling the *ch'i* and channeling it from space to space. The occupants of a house, like the organs of the body, function at their best when they're nourished by a sustained, balanced flow of *ch'i* — not too strong, not too weak."

The tour concluded, Bittersweet and Delin arrived back in her courtyard which Dashao was sweeping with rhythmic strokes of a twig broom.

"You've created a very fine home as well as a good source of income," Delin said, inclining at the waist in a respectful bow. "But you're not the only woman in the family who has built a house for herself. My mother's had a mansion built — four courtyards deep — in Dragon's Head."

"General Li, why don't you build yourself a house in Kweilin?" Dashao suggested. "You could use it as your residence and as a place to hold meetings, accommodate guests, and entertain associates." She cocked her head to one side and wagged it slightly. "Everyone needs a place to call home."

"I haven't come to Kweilin to build a house, Dashao — after all, all of China is my home — but to mobilize the province for war." Turning to Bittersweet, he continued: "And to ask you to visit my mother in Dragon's Head for a few days. The day after tomorrow is the anniversary of my father's death, and I hope you will, as you've done so capably in the past, serve as my personal representative. Unfortunately, I cannot discharge my filial duty, since I must be in Nanking starting this afternoon."

"Of course, I'll go," Bittersweet said.

Though her nod denoted submission, she was pleased, for she thought she might take a side trip to Village Village during her stay with her mother-in-law. She hadn't seen her own mother or Xiao Tzu in a long time.

"I'll send a car for you tomorrow at eight o'clock," Delin said. "And don't worry about Youlin's finances. I'll send him money for his tuition and living expenses every six months."

Bittersweet nodded again, this time in acknowledgment and gratitude.

"I hope you'll write to me," he said, his expression almost imploring. "Once a month? Just to let me know the news from home."

"Once a month," Bittersweet repeated in affirmation.

"After we defeat Japan," Delin said with forced gaiety, "I just might return to Kweilin and build my retirement house. What do you say to that, eh, Dashao? Or maybe I'll go back to Dragon's Head and resume my life as a farmer." He looked at Bittersweet warmly. "How peaceful that would be!"

Bittersweet walked her husband back through the moon gate with its incised marble spirit screen — more effective against the prying eyes of curious passers-by than in keeping out the wandering evil spirits for whom it had ostensibly been built.

"*Zai jian,*" they wished each other, though they both knew that they would not see each other soon, and that when they did — perhaps even *if* they did — would be determined by the length and the ferocity of the war.

As Delin had promised, a car came for Bittersweet, Solin, and Yifu the next morning. As they traveled past karst peaks, standing like sentinels about patchwork plains of rice paddies, Bittersweet wondered whether or not her mother-in-law had changed over the dozen years since Baba's funeral. And she wondered if Da Mama would notice the change that had come over Solin who, after separating from Emma, had taken up smoking opium and visiting the House of the Wide Gates. He appeared satisfied to do nothing but live off Delin's good fortune and generosity. How true, Bittersweet thought, that "bad" and "good" have no meaning in and of themselves. Here was a worthy example: money for some means prosperity; money for others means ruin.

But it turned out that, though Solin had changed, his mother had not. The woman who greeted Bittersweet and the others in front of her new home in Dragon's Head was kind, generous, and considerate, as always. Time had inflicted its heartaches, but time had also granted Da Mama majesty and the strength to bear her troubles.

Here is a truly whole person, Bittersweet thought, taking Da Mama's hands in hers. And she remembered one of the *Tao Te Ching*'s sayings, one that was as easy to read as it was difficult to put into practice. How ironic, she thought, that Da Mama, who is illiterate and has never read the *Tao Te Ching*, should be the very embodiment of one of its teachings.

> *The supreme good is like water,*
> *which nourishes all things without trying to.*
> *It is content with the low places that people disdain.*
> *Thus it is like the Tao.*
>
> *In dwelling, live close to the ground.*
> *In thinking, keep to the simple.*
> *In conflict, be fair and generous.*
> *In governing, don't try to control.*
> *In work, do what you enjoy.*
> *In family life, be completely present.*
>
> *When you are content to be simply yourself,*
> *and don't compare or compete,*
> *everyone will respect you.*

"What a big, beautiful house you've built!" Bittersweet exclaimed as her mother-in-law showed her around the compound.

Like Bittersweet's property in Kweilin, Da Mama's personal residence comprised several *siheyuan* which, unlike her daughter-in-law's, were used by her family alone. She had planted a large garden where she grew her own vegetables and several fruit trees, and she had dredged a pond, large as a small lake, which she kept stocked with carp, Delin's favorite fish, and, ironically, a symbol of scholarly aptitude. Da Mama also had three deep wells dug between the third and the fourth courtyards — one for washing clothes, one for washing dishes, and one for washing vegetables.

"So I *must* be kind and fair," she joked, "for if I mistreat any of my daughters-in-law, there are three wells, not one, into which they may throw themselves to take their revenge on me!"

The house was so spacious that even when occupied by all the family members and servants, it was only one-quarter full.

"It's for the extended family that I built such a house," Da Mama confided to Bittersweet. "And now that Solin and Yifu are home, they'll each have full suites of their own."

Her youngest son and daughter glanced anxiously at each other. They preferred to live in Kweilin, but to go against their widowed mother's wishes was unthinkable.

That evening, Da Mama arranged for a huge banquet and invited all her neighbors to celebrate the return of Delin (as represented by Bittersweet), and the return of her youngest son and daughter.

Throwing herself into the festivities, Bittersweet took great pleasure in the good, simple country food that was prepared and the gusto with which the villagers ate it, wrapping what they didn't finish in lily pads to take home to their families. How different this banquet was from the ones she had attended in the city. There, great quantities of the most expensive delicacies were habitually thrown away to show how wealthy the hosts were.

Bittersweet had never seen her mother-in-law happier, except perhaps when she held Youlin for the first time. And yet she knew that under Da Mama's joyfulness lay sadness, for Delin was again to do battle, this time against a foreign and a most formidable enemy.

There was a second reason for Da Mama's underlying sadness. First Outside Sister-in-Law had failed to bear her husband a single child, let alone the all-important son. As a consequence, Demin had taken a second wife with whom he lived in the third *siheyuan* of Da Mama's grand house. This second wife had borne him two sons. But when his second wife was pregnant with their first son, First Outside Sister-in-Law, at Da Mama's urging, adopted a four-year-old boy whose mother had just died in childbirth.

"It is proper that the first wife be the mother of the first-born son," Da Mama had told her. "He guarantees her status as the first wife and that there will be someone to care for her in her old age."

As if that rationale wasn't enough to secure First Outside Sister-in-Law's place in the household, Da Mama rearranged the hierarchy of rooms around the third courtyard so as to accommodate her first daughter-in-law and adopted grandson in a suite of rooms directly across from her own apartment — proof of the young woman's favored position and exalted status.

At dawn the morning after Bittersweet's arrival, Da Mama handed out walking sticks and led her family along the winding dirt roads and up the steep, grassy hill to where her husband was buried. As Bittersweet represented Delin, and as Delin didn't believe in the old ways — in burning bundles of incense in front of the tombstone, in knocking his head on the ground three times, or in wailing about his shortcomings in performing his filial duties while his father was alive — she bowed her head so that her chin touched her chest and murmured sadly and softly, "During my adult life, while my father was still alive, I didn't visit him often enough. Now he is gone, and I can only visit his grave. While he was alive, and I was a young man, I didn't serve my father as a good son should. Now he is gone, and I can serve only his memory."

Da Mama, in deference to Delin's wishes, did not burn bundles of incense or weep, wail, and kowtow before her husband's grave. But she went against custom and broke her silence to comfort her "son."

"On the contrary, you have been a good son," she said to Bittersweet. "Your father was very proud that you became a good man and embarked upon an illustrious career. That you have been successful in your endeavors is due to your having taken your father's teachings and counsel to heart. You have done your duty as a filial son."

Her family was shocked by the words. But as head of the clan she had the right to speak, and, as subordinate members of the clan, they dared not question her but continued to listen.

"The life of a general is not his own," she went on to Bittersweet.

"Your duties and responsibilities are to your country. Be brave in battle. Secure the final victory. I pray for your safe return."

The third day of her visit to Dragon's Head, when the sun was merely half an orange disk above the horizon, Bittersweet left the house of her mother-in-law to walk to Village Village. When she entered the *hutong* where she was born, her mother was sitting on a stool outside the house — just as her husband had done when he was alive. Age had bent her back even further and clouded her eyes, but seeing her daughter, her dull stare brightened, and she rose with difficulty from the stool and hobbled towards Bittersweet, crying her childhood name.

Hearing their mother, Bittersweet's two brothers ran out to greet her, patting her to make sure it was their little sister and not a ghost from the past. "This isn't Bittersweet," they teased, "but a city woman. Where is her old tunic of dark blue homespun? Where are her home-spun trousers?"

Bittersweet, who was wearing a smoky blue silk *cheongsam* and a matching padded *siming* jacket, held out the skirt of her dress. A glossier pattern resembling tiny grains of rice was woven into the matte fabric.

"Look closely," she teased back. "Isn't this proof enough of my country origins?"

While they laughed and joked, Bittersweet kept looking around as though for someone missing. Finally, as the family moved into the kitchen, she said with her old straightforwardness, "Where is my old nemesis, my sister-in-law, Sao-Sao? I'd like to see her again after all these years. How that woman tormented me for failing to find a husband!"

"Little Sister," Bittersweet's elder brother said, "the woman you knew as your sister-in-law died many years ago of smallpox. I remarried two years after her death. The woman standing before you is my new wife." He pointed to a woman, who wiped her hands on her apron and smiled bashfully. "We have a son, Jiaqiu, who is studying new farming techniques in Nanning."

Bittersweet drew the hesitant woman into the parlor, smiling and nodding to indicate her happiness at meeting her. Still, she felt regret that Sao-sao was dead. Bittersweet had lived long enough in Da Mama's house to have learned the value of tolerance and forbearance, forgiveness and family harmony. After Sao-sao had refused to attend her songs-blessing-the-bride party, they had parted enemies. Now it was too late to mend the breach. As Bittersweet inquired after her new sister-in-law — which village she came from, how many brothers and sisters she had — she thought of Sao-sao, and the memory, rather than evoking anger, reminded Bittersweet of the time when she had been happiest, when she had been young and free.

That afternoon the family walked to a spot just beyond the walls of Village Village, to the grave of Bittersweet's father. Unlike Baba's, it wasn't set high on a hill for optimal *ch'i*, for her family, though poor, was satisfied to till their own soil and refused to accept anything but small tokens of affection from Bittersweet — or anyone else. Still, Bittersweet felt proud to be her father's youngest daughter standing before his simple grave, as proud as she had felt to stand before Baba's *feng-shui* grave as his most honored son.

That night, the family sat down to a table laden with food such as Bittersweet had never seen in her mother's house: chicken, duck, beef, pork, fish (which Bittersweet supplied), frog's legs, several kinds of vegetables and a great pot of soup as well as one of boiled white rice. She knew that her elder brother had dipped deep into the family coffer to buy such a variety of food and that her sister-in-law had split much kindling and sweated many hours over the wood stove to prepare the feast.

"These frog's legs cooked in hot pepper and black bean sauce are the best I've ever tasted," Bittersweet said, sticking her thumb up. "*Ding hao*. Without a doubt, the very best."

"They're nothing," her new sister-in-law said, blushing and bringing her rice bowl closer to her red face. "They require no special skill. They're nothing at all."

How different she is from Sao-sao, Bittersweet thought. Elder Brother has done well. She has even given him a son so all is as it should be.

The following morning, knowing that the car that had driven her out to Dragon's Head would be returning in the early afternoon to take her back to Kweilin, Bittersweet woke early to walk back to her husband's village. She took the long route, entering Dragon's Head by the north gate, which was that much closer to the Taoist temple. The *da men* of the temple was open and the priests were already up and about their business when she arrived. A few villagers were in the great hall, burning incense, having their fortunes read, praying, or reading the scrolls that covered the walls. Bittersweet dropped several coins into the earthenware pot at the door, then lit a coil of incense before tetragram 31:

The finest weapons can be the instruments of misfortune,
And thus contrary to Natural Law.
Those who possess the Tao turn away from them.
Evolved leaders occupy and honor the left;
Those who use weapons honor the right.

Weapons are instruments of misfortune
That are used by the unevolved.
When their use is unavoidable,
The superior act with calm restraint.

Even when victorious, let there be no joy.
For such joy leads to contentment with slaughter.
Those who are content with slaughter
Cannot find fulfillment in the world.

While she was contemplating the characters and what they signi-fied, Xiao Tzu's face appeared through the veil of curling smoke that rose from her incense.

"You've come," he said simply and smiled. "I was hoping you would." He looked around the temple at the other seekers of the Way or those who simply sought a moment's peace of mind from thoughts of war. "Let's walk in the courtyard. Thanks to the Japanese, the temple has once again become fashionable."

Though his long black hair was now streaked with white, it was still thick as a horse's tail. His skin was taut and unlined, save for laugh lines at the corners of his eyes, and his body remained slim and flexible as a bow string.

"When I was here the last time, they told me that you were on a retreat with the abbot. Wherever it was you went, you must have found the Elixir of Life there," Bittersweet said.

Xiao Tzu smiled boyishly at the compliment. "I didn't know you had come," he admitted. "I'm pleased to know it now. It wears away the many years since I saw you last. . . ." They walked outside the north gate, outside the north wall of the village, and found themselves strolling along the banks of the stream.

". . . just like the stream wears down the rocks in its path," he continued. "After all, it is only time." They walked on in silence, enjoying their wordless companionship.

"I came today to pray for my husband," Bittersweet said after a while. "He commands the Fifth War Zone. I was praying for his safety."

Xiao Tzu picked up a flat stone and skipped it across the stream — one, two, three, four hops.

"He thinks prayer to the gods, to the Eight Immortals, is silly superstition, but in these times, it comforts me so to pray, superstition or not. I was praying for you, too . . . praying that you wouldn't be away this time."

"And you see?" Xiao Tzu said, turning in place to verify his presence. "Your prayer was answered."

"And will it be answered for my husband's safety as well, do you think?"

"I'll add mine to yours to see that it is."

Before she knew what she was doing, Bittersweet flung her arms around Xiao Tzu's neck and felt his arms enfolding her. "I'm so unhappy. I'm so happy. I don't know what I feel!" she moaned, burying her face in his neck.

"I know what *I* feel, Bittersweet. I've loved you for a long time."

"And I. . . ."

Feeling her stiffen, he released her. Her arms dropped limply to her sides. "But you know what I feel. You *must* know," she said, searching his eyes for what she herself was afraid to acknowledge, "and that it is out of duty that I withhold any expression of it." She shook her head vigorously, fighting with herself. "I mustn't say any more," she chided herself. She lowered her eyes. No sooner did she drop them than she raised them to look again into his. "But this I must say, for this I want you to know: it is *solely* out of duty."

When they walked back to the temple, one of the priests came up to Xiao Tzu to deliver a message.

"He called you Abbot," Bittersweet said when the young priest withdrew.

"That's what I am. The abbot you knew as such died several years ago, and I was chosen to be his successor. My efforts and those of all the priests here are directed towards a just solution to the War of Resistance. Just as your husband has his methods for driving the invader from our land, we who do not bear arms have means of resisting oppression and countering destruction. Together we will not fail."

When the sun was high over Dragon's Head, the car returned to take Bittersweet back to Kweilin. Now and then, she noticed, the driver stuck his head out the window and gazed up at the sky. Finally, in jest, she asked him if he was afraid it was going to rain.

"No, Li *Tai-tai*. Rain would be a blessing. The crops would welcome it. It's the Japanese I fear. The sky is clear and blue today — the perfect kind of sky for an air attack."

It wasn't until they were at Kweilin's city limits and crossing the bridge that spanned the Li River that they heard the sound of air raid sirens going off. The car screeched to a halt and the driver craned his neck out the window and searched the sky.

"Look!" he cried, pointing at the horizon directly in front of them. Ten airplanes, two sets of five aircraft in V-formation, were flying towards them. The driver beat the steering wheel and cursed his bad fortune to be, at that crucial moment, in the middle of a single-lane bridge, unable to turn around and speed back to the countryside and the safety of cover. He got out of the car and opened the back door. "Quickly!" he told Bittersweet, grabbing her hand. "Under the bridge! Hurry!"

No sooner had they run down the embankment than they were waist-deep in sluggish green water. They pressed themselves against the concrete spandrels of the bridge, then they heard the ung-ah! ung-ah! of bombs dropping and exploding, the drone of swooping planes, and the tat-tat-tat of machine gun fire. The sounds were deafening — the "steel wind air" of Dashao's prophesy — and shook the very ground where they stood. When the noise diminished to a hum, the driver led Bittersweet back up the embankment to the car. The windshield and roof were pockmarked from machine gun fire, but the engine sputtered to life when the driver turned the key in the ignition. At the end of the bridge, a large crater-shaped depression lay in the road, and in the distance, in the direction of the city, black smoke spiralled upward, obscuring what had moments before been a blue sky. Bittersweet caught a faint but acrid whiff — the smell of melted metal, charred wood, and burning chemicals.

In Kweilin proper, sirens wailed from fire engines and ambulances. Moans rose from the wounded and cries from the mourners. Dazed parents carried the limp, crumpled bodies of their children in their arms, or frantically dug at the rubble for missing loved ones. Others sat at the edge of the disaster, their faces locked in expressions of disbelief or helplessness. Older siblings, their eyes glazed over with shock or anguish, carried children or their own wounded parents on their backs away from the wreckage. A small girl pulled at the lifeless limbs of her motionless mother, imploring, "Wake up, Mama! Wake up!" For the first time in her life, Bittersweet saw up close the full-blown madness that was war.

When she arrived at her own house which, thankfully, lay far enough outside of the city center to have escaped the bombing, Dashao came running out and grabbed her by both hands. "Li *Tai-tai!*" she cried. "You're alive! We can't stay in the city! We must move to the country! The Japanese will strike again!"

All that night, Bittersweet listened to the wail of sirens competing against the wail of the wounded and the mourning. Denied sleep, she stood on her balcony, staring at the night sky, glowing from fires that would not be put out. How beautiful the rosy view would have been had it meant just the end or the beginning of another uneventful day.

Early the following day, Hwang *Tai-tai*, who had also moved to Kweilin from Canton for safety from the Japanese, called on Bittersweet. She was on her way to the town hall to speak to the person in charge of the city's defense.

"I'll come with you," Bittersweet said, grabbing her *siming* jacket.

When they arrived, hundreds of people, petitions in hand, had already gathered in the courtyard. Two military police, recognizing Hwang *Tai-tai* and Bittersweet, parted the jostling crowd and led the two women through to the office of the director of public works. Scores of people, seeing that the two women were to be admitted, surged forward and through the doors of the office before they could be shut.

"How is it that the Japanese planes were already over Kweilin when the air raid sirens went off?" Hwang *Tai-tai* demanded to know. "We citizens must be alerted *before* the bombs are dropped. What good is an early warning system when the warning comes too late?"

The harried director apologized. The air raid sirens had been neglected, he admitted, but air raid shelters, he insisted, were in abundance. Kweilin's limestone caves were perfect hiding places and bomb shelters. There were also man-made shelters in the basements of government buildings. As for the early warning system, granted the sirens were too few, as were the air raid lamps, but they both cost money — money that hadn't been earmarked for that particular purpose.

"May I make a suggestion?" Bittersweet said. "I don't think you'll have any trouble raising the money needed for new sirens and lamps. We Kweilinese are civic-minded. We'll gladly donate our valuables for their installation. Better that than our lives." Bittersweet was wearing a gold brooch, a pearl hairpin, and an apple-green jade and gold filigree ring. She unclipped the brooch from her *siming* jacket, slid the hairpin out of her bun, slipped the ring from her finger, and laid them all on the director's desk. The people who had crowded into his office behind her began to unfasten their tie clips and pins, slide off their rings and bracelets, and unload their pockets of cash. Hwang *Tai-tai* reluctantly pulled a bracelet off her wrist.

As they thrust their valuables into the hands of the director of public works, they shamed him, saying, "Do your duty and protect us! You're a public servant! Do you need a private citizen to tell you how to do your job?"

Students who had witnessed the incident or were told of it formed "air raid safety brigades" to march from house to house and take up a collection to make their city "defense-worthy." In a few months, air raid warning lamps crowned the limestone peaks and sirens were installed in every neighborhood. Now that the early warning system was efficient, and because they lived in a house between two hills with deep caves, Bittersweet, Dashao, and Liu-wu needed only go a hundred feet or so to either peak for safety.

But the rest of the city was not so fortunate. Sometimes the Japanese planes came twice a day; sometimes they struck at night. Thousands of people were killed or wounded, and the destruction inflicted upon the city rose until it reached the hundreds of thousands of *kuai*. Some Kweilinese abandoned their homes to live with friends or relatives in the countryside; others left the city for the country in the morning and returned at night when conditions were safer. When the planes appeared in the sky, many Kweilinese took refuge under trees, but the gunners opened fire at the treetops, killing or wounding those who sought shelter there.

Just when Bittersweet was ready to capitulate to Dashao's pleas to flee to Dragon's Head, the bombings subsided. As "occupied China" was still far to the north, Kweilin as part of "free China" became, except for a strafing now and then, not only peaceful but prosperous. Ever since Delin had ordered the provincial government moved from Nanning to Kweilin, the small and quiet riverside town had begun to thrive. Schools, factories, businesses, and merchants followed the provincial government officials and their families as they left Nanning. As cities to the north and on the coast fell to the Japanese, refugees streamed into Kweilin. Poets, playwrights, artists, writers, and educators came for safety. Entranced by the haunting, almost mythical, landscape, they stayed on for Kweilin's beauty. The population swelled from one hundred thousand to three hundred thousand in the span of several months, and Kweilin, once a provincial backwater, became a center for commerce and the arts.

When she wasn't busy buying up the best properties to be had in the city, Hwang *Tai-tai* often came to Bittersweet's house to share the latest projections about Kweilin's economic boom. "Give me a few thousand *kuai* and I'll buy you property that will make you a wealthy woman for the rest of your life," she promised Bittersweet. "In a few months property values will skyrocket. Inflation will make money worthless. Invest in what is eternal — land, property. Offices, shops, hotels, theaters, restaurants, teahouses will all spring up overnight. The supply won't be able to keep up with the demand. You'll be able to sell for ten times what you paid. You can charge whatever rent you wish. It's a buyer's market, and when you're ready to sell in a year or two, you can name your own price."

With all the new shops and stalls, sprouting like mushrooms all over the city, Kweilin came to resemble one great fair. Streets were strung with electric and neon lights. Roads were elbow-to-elbow with people walking, eating, chatting, laughing. Life was lively, noisy, and good — despite the air raids, despite the war, despite the Japanese presence on Chinese soil.

But life was kinder to some than to others. There were refugees who came to Kweilin because they had relatives there with whom they could live, and there were refugees who came to Kweilin because they knew it was far safer than the cities they had left and because they had nowhere else to go. It was the latter who brought with them little more than what they could carry on their backs, who needed to find work right away, and who often found nothing. When their meager savings were exhausted, they sold their few belongings for food.

An open market was erected at the edge of the city — rows and rows of stalls selling second-hand merchandise. Clothing, furniture, jewelry, household articles, personal belongings of every type and description were bought from, and sold to, the refugee hordes. With the threat of a Japanese advance on Kweilin, some refugees sold all their possessions for passage elsewhere; when peace reigned and a threat of attack was unlikely, refugees who could afford to, and Kweilinese like Hwang *Tai-tai*, came to the open market to buy expensive items for one-tenth their intrinsic value. Other refugees or Kweilinese who needed household items came to stock up. Buying and selling on the open market made some very rich; others became destitute overnight.

The very poor became beggars who lived in the streets. Men, women, children, entire families followed those more fortunate than themselves and pleaded for a few cash. They went from house to house asking for a scrap of vegetable or a mouthful of rice. When they gathered outside the *da men* of Bittersweet's house, Dashao opened it and, according to her mistress's instructions, distributed pennies and leftover food from the previous meal. Soon Bittersweet set up a soup kitchen managed by both Dashao and Liu-wu. It operated three times a day, but, then, the trickle of the indigent and homeless to Bittersweet's door became an overwhelming flood and she was unable to satisfy even their most meager needs.

Hearing of the people and excitement that animated Kweilin, and bored with the slow pace of the country where nothing ever happened, Solin convinced his mother to let him live with his sister-in-law in the big city. Knowing that he was unhappy and that she was powerless to stop him, Da Mama let him go. No sooner did he arrive in Kweilin than his pent-up desires and old frustrations found release. He was young, Bittersweet told herself; he had seen the ways of the West and of the big city in Hong Kong and Shanghai. Still, she worried when he went out in the evening and didn't come back till late that night or, sometimes, the following day. When she questioned him, he refused to answer or he replied in a surly tone that he was thirty years old, that he owed an explanation of his activities to no one.

"I want to live before I die!" he told her. It was the declaration that always ended their heated conversations.

Bittersweet couldn't understand such talk. Didn't one live *until* one died? Solin was only thirty years old. Didn't he have his whole life ahead of him?

Within a few months of her brother-in-law's arrival in Kweilin, one of the many refugees of the city came knocking on Bittersweet's door. When Dashao informed the visitor of the soup kitchen's hours, the haggard woman said, "It's not food that I want but to speak to the mistress of the house."

Bittersweet, who was sitting at the edge of the goldfish pond, lifted her head.

"My mistress is resting now and cannot be disturbed," Dashao said.

"But I understand that her brother-in-law is looking for a second wife."

"Then you should know idle gossip when you hear it. Good day to you."

"Please," the woman begged, "if she would just agree to meet my daughter. . . ."

The closing of the *da men* cut off the rest of the woman's words.

Bittersweet envisioned Solin frequenting the teahouses that flourished, like rice seedlings after a heavy rain, all over the city. Some of these houses had red lanterns hanging over the gateway. This is what he means by living before he dies, she thought: escaping the inevitable disappointments and setbacks of life. His marriage to Emma was a failure. He couldn't bring himself to find a job or pursue his studies. Now in Kweilin, he goes to the teahouses and the houses of the wide gates to forget his unhappiness in drink and in women. But the more he goes, the more unhappy he becomes and the more he feels compelled to return.

"Dashao," she said, "call the woman back."

"But, Li *Tai-tai*, she's but a beggar woman," Dashao protested. "She can come back when I ladle out the soup."

"Please do as I say and call her back."

Dashao scowled out of protectiveness. "Hwang *Tai-tai* is right," she said, reluctantly opening the gate. "You're too kind. You let people take advantage of you."

"Why do you say that my brother-in-law is looking for a wife?"

Bittersweet asked the middle-aged woman who, though dressed in tatters, demonstrated propriety and decorum in word and gesture.

A young girl, presumably the woman's daughter and only slightly more presentably dressed, stood behind the woman. When her eyes weren't cast upon the ground, she glanced at her mother with concern.

"How can he be looking for a wife when he already has a wife?" Bittersweet asked.

"Not a first wife, Honorable Madam," the woman answered, "but a secondary wife. It is said that his first wife has not given him a son."

"And who says that she has not?" Bittersweet wanted to know.

"The proprietor at the House of the Wide Gates," the woman answered with lowered eyes, "which I visited with great reluctance only yesterday."

She lifted her eyes and Bittersweet saw in them all the despair of a mother forced to sell her only child into prostitution.

"And if you're correct in assuming that my brother-in-law's wife has not borne him an heir," Bittersweet inquired further, "what is that to you?"

The woman called her daughter and stood her in front of Bittersweet. She lifted the girl's head so that Bittersweet could see her face, and pulled back her shoulders so that she stood up straight. She couldn't have been more than sixteen, the same age as Dejie when Delin took her as his second wife. Like Delin at that time, Solin was thirty years old. Bittersweet felt an old, familiar pain. She wanted to send the mother and the girl away, and she recalled the old admonition that a good woman did not arrange a second marriage.

"My daughter and I are from Kiangsu Province," the woman said. "Threat of the Japanese advance forced us from our home. We were heading for Kweichow where I have relatives. What money we had gave out in Kweilin. Look at my daughter, Honorable Madam," she pleaded, stroking the girl's thick, glossy hair and brushing off her dusty tunic. "She's pretty. You can see by her face that she's intelligent. She can read and write two thousand characters. But even more important, she is healthy and strong. Look at her hips — wide as a junk's prow. Surely the sign of a giver of sons!" The woman fell on her knees before Bittersweet and her daughter did the same. "The two of us together will never make it to Kweichow. Alone, with a certain sum of money, I can — that is, if you permit your brother-in-law to meet my daughter and if he decides to take her as his wife."

"It's not necessary to prostrate yourself before me," Bittersweet said, touching the woman's shoulder. "Get up, please."

The girl raised her head and stared at Bittersweet as if both afraid that she would accept and terrified that she would refuse her mother's entreaty. In either case, the girl surely knew that she was about to be severed from the known and cast into the unknown. Her mother's gaze was even more poignant. A man who frequented the House of the Wide Gates often led a dissolute life and abused his wife, much less his concubine. But for her daughter to enter the wide gates of such a house was to be sold into slavery, perhaps to end her life there by her own hands.

Seeing the two women in tatters, sensing their physical and emotional exhaustion, Bittersweet knew that the mother had put off her terrible decision to sell her daughter until all hope was gone. To have discovered a bit of hope when she had abandoned any hope of hope — it was another chance at life, and she must take it.

"I will speak to my brother-in-law about what you have said," Bittersweet told her after a long pause. "Come back in two days at this hour, and if he agrees to meet your daughter, he will see her at that time."

She then instructed Dashao to prepare a packet of food for the two visitors to take away with them. After they had gone, Bittersweet thought about what she had just done and she sighed to no one in particular.

"I'll agree to meeting this girl," Solin told Bittersweet irritably the following day, "out of respect to you, but I won't agree to marrying her!"

"No, I don't suppose you'll want to," Dashao allowed, "seeing that she's the polar opposite of Mistress Emma — young, innocent, and unspoiled."

Bittersweet saw her brother-in-law's pupils dilate at this news. Later, she sent Dashao to buy a set of clothes for the girl, so that she might be presentable when she met her husband-to-be, and a set of traveling clothes for his future mother-in-law.

After the first meeting with the girl and her mother, Solin agreed to a second meeting with the girl alone, and after the second meeting, he agreed to take her as a second wife. The young couple's part in the arrangements having been finalized, the girl's mother and Bittersweet set about bringing the financial aspect of the union to a close. The bride price was negotiated to the satisfaction of both parties, then the mother delivered her daughter at the front door of her benefactress's house with the following words: "A thousand blessings on you and your family for saving both our lives. My daughter will do her utmost to bring happiness to your brother-in-law and increase the harmony and prosperity of your household. With a heart unburdened of care and filled with peace, I can now continue on my way to Kweichow alone."

"It's more than two lives you've saved, Li *Tai-tai*," Dashao told her later, after the simple wedding dinner. "For sure, Master Solin's new bride is a virgin. Master Solin will no longer be passing through wide gates, but narrow ones!"

Bittersweet clucked her tongue at her maidservant's back-handed compliment and off-color remark.

"Still," Bittersweet said, arching an eyebrow in a gesture of mild disdain to conceal how much her kindness had cost her in regret, "isn't it a shame that a girl of sixteen should have to marry a man of thirty!"

Chapter 2
Taierzhuang
(1939)

From the day the undeclared war began, news from the front was discouraging. Occupied China swelled and free China shrank as the Japanese advanced southward from Manchuria and westward from the coast into the interior. Peking fell before the invaders, then Tientsin and Shanghai. In Nanking, thousands of women and children were violated and thousands of civilians executed, so that the fall of the city was known as the Rape of Nanking. *Time* magazine's war correspondent, Theodore White, called it "the greatest sexual orgy of modern times." The Japanese, expecting to win the war in a few months, boasted that the Chinese were fighting Nippon's modern weaponry and warfare with chopsticks. When Tsingtao, the pearl of the Shantung Peninsula, fell before the Japanese Minister of War Itagaki, the claim seemed to be true.

Delin knew that with Japan's capture of Tsingtao, Germany and Italy would expand their borders. When that happened, war would break out in Europe. Then England, France, and the Netherlands would be too busy at home to defend their colonies — Singapore, French Indochina, the Dutch East Indies — in the Pacific. The Japanese imperial navy would head southward to acquire those oil-, rubber-, and tin-rich colonies for their Emperor. When they did, America would be forced to go to war against Japan to protect its bases in the Pacific. The flame of war in Europe and the one in Asia would merge to make one huge fire — one great conflagration. This would be the turning point in China's resistance against Japan.

"Our strategy," Delin had told Chiang, "must be one of using space to win time. The longer we draw out our resistance, the better our chances of winning the war. If we surrender, Japan, Germany, and Italy will become a unified force, one that the Western powers will be unable to check. If we can't hold out against Japan until war breaks out in Europe, we will be slaves to Japan forever."

·✦·

After the Japanese capture of Tsingtao, Delin reappeared before Bittersweet's door in Kweilin. He came directly from Hsuchow, his headquarters as commander of the Fifth War Zone which comprised the whole of the Shantung Peninsula, most of Kiangsu Province, Anhui Province north of the Yangtze River, and the Tientsin-Pukou Railroad — the gateway to the west and China's vast interior.

Delin was back in Kweilin because General Han, the governor of Shantung, and a man long at odds with Chiang's central government, was on the verge of declaring his province independent. A disunified China meant a stronger Japan. Indeed, Chiang considered Han to be defecting outright, and, succumbing to his uncontrollable temper, Chiang was prepared to use his own First Army against Han. But Delin had offered to act as an intermediary and arranged a secret meeting with Han in Kweilin. The outcome of the war and the very unity of China was at stake.

In the privacy of Bittersweet's parlor, Han told Delin, "If I declare Shantung independent and *not* part of China, then Japan has no reason to be at war with me."

"If you declare Shantung independent, you weaken our cause. Then, Japan will overrun China, and with it, Shangtung. Resist the Japanese," Delin urged Han, "otherwise China faces extinction."

"All I want is for the Japanese to stay out of Shantung. Right now, I'm fighting the Japanese and Chiang."

"Manchuria was only their first conquest," Delin reminded Han. "The Japanese won't be satisfied until they control all of China. That means Shantung as well. Haven't they already taken Tsingtao?"

Han drummed his fingers on his knees and nodded in agreement. "Yes, you are right. Tell me what I must do."

Anticipating a Japanese drive from the north, Delin told Han to place his armies in defensive positions at strategic points along the Tientsin-Pukou Railroad. Such a maneuver would prevent Itagaki's Japanese forces, currently marching southward from Tsingtao, from forming a junction at Taierzhuang where they could join other Japanese troops — strung along the northern section of the railroad — and lay siege to Hsuchow, overrunning the entire region.

But if Delin had guessed Itagaki's intention, he failed to foresee Han's. Instead of positioning his troops along the Tientsin-Pukou

Railroad, Han withdrew them to western Shantung, thus leaving the central section of the railway vulnerable to attack. When the Japanese gained control of this section of the railroad, the fall of Hsuchow was imminent.

Delin wasted no time trying to repair the damage. He organized the Fifth War Zone's Youth Corps — a group of displaced students from occupied China — to act as spies, carry messages, produce plays, and disseminate leaflets to bolster morale. He wired Chiang in Canton for more troops to defend the railroad. Delin's own troops had been pitiful — peasants with little or no training and no fighting experience at all — but he had believed that, with proper training and fair treatment, he could transform them into excellent fighters . . . and he had. Now, with Han's betrayal, he needed more men.

"I'll send you *tsai-pai* — miscellaneous unattached units," Chiang wired back.

Miscellaneous unattached units, Delin knew, were troops not under Chiang's direct control. Calling upon their sense of nationalism, Chiang exploited their fighting power while he allowed the Japanese to effectively eliminate them for their unwillingness to pledge their troth to the Son of Heaven. Chiang had long wanted to abolish the nettlesome *tsai-pai*. Here, he felt, was the opportunity to do so. The Szechuanese, "hot pepper eaters," who had long been considered surly vagrants — traveling from province to province, "living off the land," unable to find any army who would accept their services in the War of Resistance — were the units Chiang despised most. They were the troops he offered to Delin.

"Send them to me," Delin wired Chiang back. "I need every man I can get."

Upon learning the origins of the Fifth Army's new recruits, Pai, now Chiang's Minister of Defense, wired his Kwangsi compatriot, "They're not only poor fighting material, they're *huai dan* — rotten eggs! They've been refused by every single army. They're detested by the populace of every city, every *hsien*. Chiang means to crucify you! You're mad to accept his offer!"

Delin calmed his friend by saying, "Chu-ko Liang, one of ancient China's outstanding strategists, a leading figure in the *Romance of the Three Kingdoms*, and a Szechuanese, set up scarecrows to fool the enemy into misjudging the size of his army and succeeded in scaring them away. Surely the Szechuanese are better than scarecrows!"

When the ragamuffin Szechuanese arrived in Hsuchow, Delin supplied them with new rifles and fresh ammunition. He appealed to their regional pride and patriotism, urging them to emulate Chu-ko Liang who had led the Szechuan army north to resist Ssu-ma I. He was confident that he could transform the "rotten eggs" into valiant soldiers.

In early May, 1939, while the Szechuanese were quartered in Hsuchow, the Second Group Army, led by Colonel Sun, one of Delin's best officers, was still trying to hold Taierzhuang against the Japanese. Delin had ordered Tang En-po and his army to draw the Japanese army, led by General Isogai and heading for Taierzhuang, into battle. Tang was to give weak resistance, then flee north to the hills. When Isogai and his men fell on Taierzhuang, Tang and his men would come south, attack Isogai's men from behind, and encircle and annihilate them.

For three days and three nights, Sun's outnumbered Second Group Army fought against the Japanese. When the invaders captured the northern half of the city, Delin ordered Tang to move south immediately and attack the enemy from the north. Tang balked. Delin repeated his order. Again Tang refused, saying, "Sun and I have been rivals for years. What do I care if he dies at Taierzhuang?" Insisting that Tang put personal feelings aside, Delin again ordered Tang to proceed south for the attack. Again Tang refused. Only when Delin threatened him with death did he comply. But the delay had caused the death of three-quarters of Sun's men. The Japanese held two-thirds of Taierzhuang, while the remnants of Sun's troops held only the south gate.

Sun finally phoned Delin. "The Japanese attack is too fierce," he said. "May I request permission to withdraw temporarily to the south bank of the Grand Canal? Allow some men from the Second Group Army to come out of this battle alive."

"Reinforcements," Delin replied, "will reach the area immediately north of Taierzhuang by noon tomorrow. If the Second Group Army abandons its present position, all their efforts will have been in vain. I myself am coming to direct the fighting. We have fought the enemy for one week. Victory will be decided in the final five minutes."

When Sun repeated his plea, Delin reiterated his order, then added another: "I also want you to carry out a raid against the enemy tonight to frustrate their plans for a dawn attack. Then, when your reinforcements arrive, the attack will be on both sides of the city and the enemy will be trapped in between."

"Such a raid is impossible," Sun insisted. "Reserves of both men and ammunition are used up."

Delin was implacable. "I offer a reward of one hundred thousand *kuai*. Every man who can shoulder a rifle — cooks, carriers, buglers — have them join the men at the front in a dare-to-die corps. Victory or defeat hangs on this act."

That night Sun and his rag-tag army executed a raid, attacking the enemy in sections and retaking three-quarters of the city. The stunned Japanese withdrew to the north gate.

At dawn on May 18th, a lucky day for it was Bittersweet's birthday, Delin arrived outside Taierzhuang to direct operations. Late that morning, Tang's army arrived at the enemy's rear as planned. Those Japanese not killed or captured fled. Taierzhuang was won. Delin telephoned Sun offering congratulations by way of an ancient military saying: "Certain defeat for overconfident troops; certain victory for troops forced into deadly struggle." Later that evening, he sent a telegram to Chiang at central headquarters in Canton to tell him the good news. He added as a postscript: "So long as a commander remains impartial and takes into account the talents of all, there are no armies in China that can be called unworthy to serve it."

Taierzhuang not only infused morale into the entire nation, it became a rallying cry, a symbol of national resistance. All over the country, every city and *hsien* celebrated the first major Chinese victory. Delin's hometown of Kweilin proclaimed a three-day holiday — "an extravaganza to equal Lunar New Year," declared Governor Hwang. Parades of lion dancers, stilt walkers, musicians, and people in colorful costumes waved red banners as they wound through every street and *hutong*. Long strings of firecrackers were set off day and night to frighten evil spirits and welcome only good spirits and good fortune. Fireworks in beautiful colors, shapes, and patterns — Peonies Strung on a Thread, Lotus Sprinkled with Water, Double-Kicking Feet — burst over the Li River for three nights running.

No house in Kweilin was busier or happier than Bittersweet's. Friends, officials, and well-wishers came to congratulate her on her husband's victory and on her birthday — a double celebration. Governor Hwang was one of the first to call and, after greeting her with the proper protocol — Bittersweet was now given the honorific *Furen* rather than *Tai-tai* — he couldn't resist giving her the *ding hao* thumb's up sign. Winking, he proclaimed, "A few more victories like that, and we'll drive the Japanese invaders into the China Sea!"

But such victories did not follow in the wake of the great battle of Taierzhuang. Three hundred thousand Japanese soldiers from Manchuria were heading to Hsuchow to provide reinforcements for Isogai's routed troops.

Delin knew that his troops — exhausted as well as exhilarated by the recent victory — and his limited equipment were no match for the best of both Itagaki and Isogai's armies. When Chiang ordered Delin to engage in head-to-head, large-scale entrenched warfare, Delin, disobeying Chiang's directive, ordered a planned withdrawal. Losing the city to the enemy was one thing; losing Chinese lives — both military and civilian — in defense of a hopeless situation was another. Thus, when the Japanese entered Hsuchow, they did not find a single Chinese. Six hundred thousand people had secretly retreated and evaded the Japanese encirclement.

Just about the time that Delin was formulating his planned withdrawal from Hsuchow, the central government was devising its own retreat. With the Japanese capture of the Canton-Hankow railway terminals, the two ends of Chiang's railroad supply line and the route by which he received munitions from Hong Kong were lost. But the victory at Taierzhuang had infused hope in the Chinese people and with it came a new surge of Chinese resistance. Doing what no other people in history had done, they picked up their factories, their government buildings, and their schools, and they walked them to the new capital, Chungking, in China's enormous interior. In the early days of the war, three and a half million dollars of industrial equipment had been transferred out of Shanghai, but that was only the beginning of the mass exodus of manpower, machines, and matériel that now followed.

The migration of government, industrial plants, and colleges lay in the hands of the Minister of National Economy, Dr. Wong Wen-hao, a geologist and mining engineer. By the end of 1938, Dr. Wong had supervised the piecemeal dismantling, removal, and reinstallation of sixty-four machine shops, eighteen electrical plants, twenty-two chemical plants, five glass factories, seven cotton mills, twelve printing plants, and four dockyards. A quarter of a million tons were carried for hundreds of miles, all on the backs of Chinese laborers.

An American war correspondent noted in *Time* Magazine, June 26, 1939: "By Asiatic standards it was an industrial revolution." A *New York Times* correspondent, who had just concluded a 1500-mile trip by car from the French Indochinese border to Chungking in which he covered Kwangsi, Kweichow, and part of Szechuan, wrote from Chungking on January 22, 1939: "The concentration of efforts in the vast 'back' territories of the country is producing dramatic changes which are augmenting Chinese military strength and simultaneously transforming the provinces from a condition of medieval backwardness and isolation into a state of modern organization, enlightenment and ever-growing industrialization. . . . A number of the larger cities, particularly in Kwangsi, have suffered terribly from air bombings. Large sections of Liuchow are destroyed and one-third of Kweilin is in ruins. Nevertheless, the people are carrying on imperturbably amid the ruins, keeping up essential municipal services and living lives of acute danger and discomfort with remarkable cheerfulness. . . . Kwangsi is the heart of the resistance in the southwest. The organization, built up in the last decade by Generals Li Tsung-jen and Pai Chung-hsi, has served efficiently to turn the people's activities into wartime channels. . . . The spirit of the people remains unbroken and if their leaders stay firm and manage wisely there are ample grounds for the conclusion that China is still capable of a strong battle against the Japanese and of resistance sufficiently powerful to bring victory."

Chapter 3
Unpolished Rice
(1940)

With the fall of Suchow and Hangchow, China's best silk production centers were in the hands of the Japanese. Since many of Kweilin's better-shod refugees hailed from those cities, there was a new market, ready and eager, for *cheongsams* and tunics in the elegant fabric. To meet the demand, and to provide extra income for her relatives from Village Village, Bittersweet bought a silk filature and a silk retail store.

"Instead of taking your thick, hard, snowy-white cocoons to the wholesale buyer in Nanning who's always complaining about your 'inferior' cocoons and always threatening to close his doors," she told her silkworm-raising relatives, "bring them to First Cousin Li. He manages my filature, and I can promise you that he'll buy them at a fair price."

Bittersweet had charged First Cousin Li with overseeing all the operations necessary to manufacture silk — the soaking of the cocoons to soften them, the separating of the downy filaments, the spinning of the silken threads, and the dyeing of the unfurled bolts of cloth. Together, First Cousin Li and Bittersweet read manuals on silk manufacture and studied women's magazines for the latest fashions. These journals were easy to obtain now that publishing concerns had come to Kweilin, the locus of free China. Also, First Cousin Li and Bittersweet visited existing silk filatures to examine machines. The old crude machines could only reel and interweave threads, while the new machines could produce high-grade jacquard weaves. It was the latter type of machine that Bittersweet bought for her Li & Li Silk Manufacturers, and she insisted that the tussah silk be reeled through hot spring water so that it shimmered with a soft sheen.

"A Chinese opera house!" Bittersweet exclaimed, when Hwang *Tai-tai* came to try to convince her to buy yet another piece of real estate.

"A gem of a building. Two stories. Sound structure. In the center of town in the middle of a small park," Hwang *Tai-tai* enthused between

237

sips of tea and bites of melon cake. "I thought, 'This is just the project for Li *Furen* and me. We'll be partners!'"

"What will I do with another property?" Bittersweet asked with a sigh. "I have enough right now." In addition to the compound where her house was located, Bittersweet had bought, at Hwang *Tai-tai's* recommendation, a hotel of twenty rooms, the silk filature, and the silk retail store.

"Have I ever recommended a property that hasn't proven well worth the price? The opera house is a better investment than you think —in good will and in hard cash. Because of the war and all the refugees who have flocked here, Kweilin has become the artistic and cultural center of China. The best poets, artists, and writers are here. Connoisseurs of the arts are also here. And yet we have no opera house. The opera singers are itinerant. They have no place to practice or perform but must go about the city like vagabonds, renting a hall here, a house there. Sometimes things look so bleak. . . ." she sighed, then shuddered.

It was true: the Japanese were rolling up one victory after another. Bittersweet grew despondent just hearing Hwang *Tai-tai* allude to the situation.

"We need something to lift our spirits, to distract us, to make us laugh and cry. What in Chinese culture makes one laugh or cry more than Chinese opera? Besides," she added, narrowing her eyes, "you are one of Kweilin's leading citizens. You, Li *Furen*, should be responsible for giving our fair city its own opera house! And just think — as principal donor, you can attend every performance for free."

Bittersweet smiled, the sign of surrender Hwang *Tai-tai* was waiting for. "I, who don't even like Chinese opera!"

To inaugurate the Kweilin Opera House, a new opera was written by a famous librettist who came to Kweilin all the way from Harbin in Manchuria. Tickets sold out immediately and expectations ran deservedly high. On opening night, just as the lights were dimming and Bittersweet and Hwang *Tai-tai* were being led to their private box, a commotion broke out at the back of the theater. The lights were turned up and audience members turned in their seats to see what the disturbance was.

"Wouldn't you know it!" Hwang *Tai-tai* whispered to Bittersweet. "And here I'm wearing the *cheongsam* I had made for me by a master tailor from the old imperial court and cut from your best silk *shantung*. Look at the color! Pearl gray, a gray that has life and depth to it, a gray that's subtle but lustrous. And here some ruffians in military olive drab and dirty blue jackets are getting all the attention!"

Bittersweet stood up. A score or so of people — soldiers, the unemployed, the indigent — stood at the back of the hall. They were all swearing and shouting.

"What are people like that doing here?" a pearled and powdered matron inquired indignantly. "Aren't there enough beggars and thieves on the streets without giving them the run of the opera house, too?" She poked her husband who had dozed off even before the opera had begun.

"Throw the *huai dan* out!" someone else cried.

"What nerve! Thinking they can get in without buying a ticket like the rest of us!"

When an usher tried to prevent a fist fight between a self-righteous patron and a soldier, a few neurasthenic ladies scurried toward the door and safety.

"Please! No trouble!" the usher begged, trying to separate the two men. "Do you want me to lose my job? This is opening night! Please leave or I'll be forced to call the police!"

But a dozen policemen had already arrived on the scene, and they were knocking heads together, waving truncheons, and leading a few of the soldiers and refugees, their wrists in handcuffs, out the door.

"Is there a problem here?" Bittersweet asked the police officer who seemed to be in charge. "I'm one of the owners of this opera house and the performance is about to begin."

Recognizing Bittersweet as the wife of the hero of Taierzhuang, the officer bowed low from the waist. "I'm sorry for the inconvenience, Li *Furen*, but these men were creating a public disturbance. They entered the premises unlawfully. They have no tickets."

"No tickets, he says!" whined a man whose left leg was missing from the knee down. With the aid of his crutches, he pushed his way between Bittersweet and the police officer. "How true! But we're so poor we haven't the money to pay the admission price."

"That's probably very hard for you to believe," said a disheveled old woman with a Peking accent, "a rich lady like you who lives in a fine house and knows nothing about the war, and cares even less, so long as it stays far from Kweilin and her precious property."

A policeman grabbed the old woman by the scruff of her neck as if she were a cat to be drowned in the river.

"Let her go," Bittersweet told him. "I'll hear her out."

"Look at us, Ma'am," the amputee spoke up in her place. "Those of us here who are soldiers are all war veterans who have left at least one limb on the battlefield. We risked our lives to defend you civilians who stayed behind and got rich from real estate investments and speculation."

The policeman raised his truncheon towards the old soldier's head.

"Put that down," Bittersweet said calmly.

"We see it all around us," the old woman added, encouraged by Bittersweet's willingness to listen. "People hoarding goods against the mounting inflation. People speculating in gold and silver, because paper money is becoming the cheapest wallpaper you can buy. People buying teahouses, restaurants, hotels, wholesale businesses with money borrowed from banks at incredibly low interest because they have *guanxi* — connections — friends or relatives who work at the banks and who give them inside tips on the currency fluctuations and the hot commodities to buy. And we! We don't have a roof over our heads!"

The amputee leaned forward on his crutches and looked straight into Bittersweet's face. "After several months, a year at most," he said, "these speculators sell out, having tripled their investments. Of course, they have to reward their cronies who lent them the money in the first place, but what's a few thousand *kuai* when you've made a killing? And yet to those of us who fought the battles that made their fortunes possible, they throw a single cash on the ground for us to fight over, like so many dogs!"

"Do you know who you're speaking to?" the police officer asked angrily. "This is the wife of General Li Tsung-jen of the battle of Taierzhuang!"

The one-legged soldier stared at Bittersweet, then backed away in fear. The disheveled woman lowered her eyes and her head.

"You've spoken. Now I will speak," Bittersweet told the two and the group of unfortunates who stood behind them. "There are those of us who do not hoard provisions or speculate in gold and silver. Why? Because it is illegal. Because depreciating the currency debilitates the war effort. Because we, too, love China and want to see her strong and free."

The old soldier crossed his crutches in front of him, as though to conceal the stump of his leg along with his shame.

"The opera is about to begin and all the seats are sold out. If you agree to sitting at the foot of the stage and to assisting in cleaning the hall after the performance, you're all welcome to stay," Bittersweet said.

Having gained their trust and therefore their consent, Bittersweet appointed the disheveled woman in charge of the clean-up.

Hwang *Tai-tai*, who had left her box to accompany Bittersweet to the scene of the commotion, said, "Well done. You are unquestionably the wife of your husband. Who says that the only place that requires quick decisions and correct strategy is the battlefield?"

The disheveled old woman, proud of her new position, fastened her unruly hair into a tight bun and bowed from the waist to Bittersweet. She gestured to the rest of the group to do the same. "A thousand blessings on you, Madam," she said when she righted herself. "And may you have many sons and grandsons. But do not think that because today you give and I take that there is that much distance separating us. And do not think that the life of a beggar woman is the hardest lot in life. My life may very well have more freedom than yours, for freedom begins where face doesn't have to be maintained."

Just then, the deep roll of drums and the clash of cymbals announced that the opera was about to begin.

"Look!" she cried. "Here comes drama on the open stage, and see who gets a first-row seat — me! You ladies have your dignity to maintain. You must sit far from the stage in an enclosed box or in a tea booth away from the common throng. No one but a beggar woman can see the tears run down the face of the actress who has learned that her lover has died."

The opera performed that evening — the première by the Manchurian librettist from Harbin — concerned the trials and tribulations of a concubine of an imperial court official whose wife is barren. The concubine bears the official his first child — a son, whom the wife takes away from her, as is her right. She then has the concubine raped by a supposed eunuch, for which the husband casts the concubine out. That winter, the concubine returns to the imperial palace and begs for a last glimpse of her son, before she dies of cold and starvation in the snow. Throughout the performance, the actors competed with the audience to be heard — so copious were the handkerchiefs the audience used to catch their tears and to muffle the sounds of their sniffling.

"Wonderful! Author! Author!" the audience shouted at the performance's conclusion.

After applauding the Manchurian who came up on stage, they turned to Bittersweet's box and continued to clap.

"Let's go backstage and congratulate the actors," Bittersweet suggested to Hwang *Tai-tai* after acknowledging the audience's appreciation.

Hwang *Tai-tai* shook her head; such a visit was inappropriate. She and her best friend were women of high position and an actress was little more than a prostitute.

"The old woman — the captain of tonight's clean-up team — what she said has its own truth," Bittersweet said, guessing the reason for Hwang *Tai-tai*'s disapproval. "Today I might give and she receive. But who's to say that our fortunes can't be reversed? You and I are patronesses of the arts and the proprietors of this theater. It is our duty to congratulate the actors. They did such a wonderful job of telling so sad a story."

Informed that Bittersweet and Hwang *Tai-tai* were coming backstage to see them, the actresses Little Hot Pepper and Flying Swallow — their names based on their most famous roles — became very shy and, when they weren't completely tongue-tied, giggled behind their hands. Washed of their make-up and dressed in simple dark robes, they looked and behaved like girls barely out of school. Finally, when they regained their composure, they invited their two visitors to sit down and take tea.

"Please forgive us if we seem impolite," Flying Swallow, who had played the desperately unhappy concubine, said. "After all, a visit by the wife of the governor of Kwangsi and the wife of the hero general of Taierzhuang is an undeserved and unexpected honor."

After Bittersweet and Hwang *Tai-tai*'s unqualified praise and the performers' denials of any talent on their part, the two actresses felt comfortable enough to share some of their feelings.

"If we had a choice, we would never choose this profession," Flying Swallow admitted.

"Nonsense!" Little Hot Pepper, who had played the barren wife, countered. "Since when has choice got anything to do with it? Acting is our destiny and we must follow it."

"Is it destiny that our lives should follow the libretto of the tragic operas we perform?" Flying Swallow, made bold by her colleague's remark, asked.

"My husband often tells me that as commanding officer he shares the bitter and the sweet of army life with his men," Bittersweet said. "As actresses sometimes you play comedy, and sometimes, like to-night, you play tragedy. What you play on stage is what we all live in our lives. It's why we come to see you perform. We can accept so much better the bitter in our lives and appreciate the sweet when you actors show us that it is the human condition."

"You're kind to say so, Li *Furen*," Flying Swallow allowed, "but too many people think that our lives are as happy as the comedies and light romances we act in. Rarely do they think that our lives are more akin to the tragedies we play. Few would believe that after a perfor-mance we often return home without enough money to buy food for our dinner."

Little Hot Pepper nodded her head in agreement. "Life for most actresses is more bitter than sweet. There are some who are lucky and do well, much better than others who aren't necessarily less talented or beautiful." She cast Flying Swallow a pointed look.

"But these supposedly successful actresses have to spend much more money on their wardrobes and on their homes — to keep up the appearances expected of them," Flying Swallow said, looking back at Little Hot Pepper. "And so they have no savings."

Hwang *Tai-tai* leaned forward in her seat to listen to the two ac-tresses. The drama taking place backstage was more subtle than, but equally as dramatic as, the one on stage.

"If we want to make a little more money, we have to sing at parties and banquets," Little Hot Pepper said. "We have to accompany men to drink. Some actresses are forced to become a man's plaything. The luckier ones, through either beauty or brains, can become a rich man's concubine."

"A man's plaything or his concubine," Flying Swallow interjected. "Often they're interchangeable. Some of us, the luckier ones, marry."

Little Hot Pepper became as red as her namesake and the tiny jewels that dangled from her hairpins trembled from her contained anger. "Are they the lucky — or the unlucky — ones?" she asked. "From what I know, married actresses have to work twice as hard as the unmarried ones who can live with their own families. They have to support not only themselves, but their lazy husbands as well!"

Flying Swallow gazed sadly into her lap. For a few moments, she looked like the concubine she had played in the première. "It's true that we're often mistreated by our husbands. It's ironic, isn't it, that the more we support them and do their bidding, the more they beat us, steal from us, and even mock us in front of our own children."

When Flying Swallow apologized to her visitors for complaining, Bittersweet refused her apology, saying, "My friend and I have listened not out of politeness or sympathy but out of genuine interest. Are we not all women and do we not all harbor a woman's feelings? You as actresses are able to express them better than most of us. I'd like to hear more of what you have to say." Rising to go, Bittersweet extended an invitation to the two young women to come to her house for tea the following week. Graciously, the two actresses accepted.

A few days before their visit, Yifu, bored with village life in Dragon's Head, insisted on paying an extended visit to her sister-in-law in Kweilin. When she learned that the famous Chinese opera stars, Flying Swallow and Little Hot Pepper, were coming to call, she invited herself to tea. Awed by their beauty and their gorgeous clothes, she barely heard their stories of hardship and heartbreak. Instead, she idolized them for the glamorous life she believed they led. Thereafter, she went nightly to the new opera house. Not one month after Yifu first set eyes on Flying Swallow and Little Hot Pepper, Dashao came to Bittersweet with a note she'd found on Yifu's pillow.

"She's run away to join the Chinese opera," Bittersweet said after reading it, shaking her head in dismay.

Dashao, in contrast, burst out laughing. "So the spoiled brat who's never opened her mouth in her life but that a peacock's shriek emanates from it wants to be an opera star, does she? With your permission, Li *Furen*, I'll send Liu-wu to bring her back — but, again with your permission, I'll be the one to give her a spanking."

"She's no longer a girl but a woman," Bittersweet replied. "She'd only run away again . . . perhaps into bad company. No, I have a better plan. I'll ask Flying Swallow and Little Hot Pepper to take her in for a few days and initiate her into the life of the opera singer. If they live the life they say they do, then Yifu will be home of her own accord before the week is through."

Just as Bittersweet predicted, Yifu waited five days then sent for Liu-wu to pick her up in the limousine.

"Just think!" Yifu grumbled to her sister-in-law. "They wanted me to get up at five in the morning to throw my voice against a brick wall to strengthen it for singing — and all on a glass of weak tea! They starved me till lunch time and then served me *tsuk*. Can you imagine? Plain rice porridge — and soupy at that. Then calisthenics and singing and dancing lessons all afternoon, then rehearsal for the evening's performance and dinner at midnight. Not even served, I'll have you know. After the performance, I had to do the food shopping with Flying Swallow and help her cook the meal at her suburban home which we reached by rickshaw. Rickshaw! And we couldn't even sit down at table until all the others had finished — her belching husband, her cross-eyed son, and her shrewish mother-in-law. What they left us wouldn't have satisfied a bird! Flying Swallow — a very appropriate name, considering — fell asleep at table, she was so tired, but her husband woke her because his feet needed massaging. *His* feet needed massaging! He sits at a desk in an office all day, while she's on her feet from morning till night. And they sleep on straw mattresses. Have you ever heard the like? Straw . . . like in a stable! And I thought opera stars led glamorous lives!"

"You should have sent Liu-wu after Yifu the moment you read her note," Dashao told Bittersweet after hearing the young woman's harangue. "Better she run away again than we have to suffer the presence of a girl of so little heart!"

During Yifu's visit — a stay which extended into fortnights, then months — Delin appeared at Bittersweet's door in the middle of one night. He came accompanied by several officers and aides who carried a one hundred-pound sack of unpolished rice and bushels of fresh vegetables bought from Liangjiang market. He intended to stay for so short a time that he didn't bother to take off his cape. Dashao was rushing about the house to wake everyone for a quick hello when Yifu ran out of her room screaming, "Thief! Thief! Help!"

Opening the door of her room, Bittersweet heard a clattering of footsteps on the stairs and saw Liu-wu and four of Delin's officers race by. From Yifu's bedroom came scuffling, thudding noises, then silence. When Bittersweet entered, all the officers stood in a circle staring at something, or someone, on the floor. Yifu came in, sobbing uncontrollably.

"I'm very sorry for the disturbance, Li *Furen*," the highest-ranking officer, a captain, said to Bittersweet. "He probably climbed over the wall and got into the house by way of the second-floor terrace. Don't be afraid. He's helpless now."

The intruder was bent over, his arms tied tightly behind his back. With the handle of his riding crop, the captain struck the burglar on the side of his head, causing him to fall sideways to the ground. A trickle of blood flowed from the wound at his temple. Bittersweet saw that the thief was very young, barely out of his teens, and terribly thin. Obviously, he was no hardened criminal.

"The impudence to steal from the family of my commander-in-chief!" the captain bellowed. "I'll put the order in myself to have you shot!"

The sound of a second set of footsteps, less frenzied this time, made Bittersweet turn her head. Delin entered and glanced at her, then at the boy.

"Mercy," he pleaded. "Have mercy on a poor beggar!"

"A poor beggar deserves mercy," Delin replied, gesturing to his captain to right the fallen boy. "Far more than a thief does."

"What choice do I have?" the boy moaned. "My parents died long ago, and I have an old grandmother to feed."

Yifu stopped sobbing and took a defiant step closer to the helpless intruder. His face was waxen and pale, and his shallow, labored breathing seemed to require all the energy his gaunt body could muster.

"I have to steal so that both of us can survive."

"With your permission, sir," the captain spoke up, saluting, "I'll issue the order to have this man shot."

The boy's head slumped to his chest and he wept softly.

"No," Delin said, after studying the boy for several seconds. "Release him."

"Release him?" the captain repeated, incredulous.

"Why release him?" Yifu said crossly. "Why let the wild tiger back into the wilderness so he can kill again?"

"He has killed no one," Delin answered his sister. "He barely possesses life's breath itself. Hunger forced him to steal — and love of his grandmother. His crime hardly calls for death."

246

Delin reached into his pocket, and the boy cringed at the gesture. When Delin withdrew his hand, it held twenty *kuai*. He ordered the captain to free the captive, then Delin handed him the money. "Take this and use it well. Work hard to support your grandmother. If you're caught stealing again, you'll be punished severely. Now go, and remember what happened here tonight."

The boy prostrated himself at Delin's feet, then rose and allowed himself to be escorted out the front door. When he was gone, Yifu stamped her feet in front of her brother. "You're commander-in-chief of an entire army. On the battlefield, you take the lives of thousands of men, yet tonight you couldn't take the life of a single one."

"*Xiao-mei*," he addressed his little sister, more saddened than irritated by her outburst, "do you think I weigh the taking of a life — whether it be one or many — lightly? On the battlefield, either we kill the enemy or the enemy kills us. How can you compare the enemy with a starving young man?"

"I thought you had power," she replied petulantly, her hands on her hips. "I thought you were a man of strength and bravery."

"Don't you think that trying to correct or reform a wayward person is better than taking his life?" Delin answered his sister. "The kind of power of which you speak belongs to either a tyrant or a fool." Delin then turned to Bittersweet, apologized for his late, hasty arrival, and said that even if he couldn't visit her when he was in Kweilin, he would see to it that she received rice and vegetables from Liangjiang market.

"I know how much you love unpolished rice," he said with a parting smile. "Perhaps the time will come when there will be peace enough that I can sit down at your table and enjoy your company and the tastes which I associate with childhood."

Yifu had been holding her breath in anger while Delin spoke to Bittersweet. Only when he left did she let it out.

"You held your breath so long, I thought you'd suffocate," Dashao quipped. "Perhaps the next step is holding your tongue. Then progress will have been made."

Yifu replied by slamming her door.

News circulated in certain Kweilin circles that Dejie was back in town. For several years, she had been traveling about the province, working hard to realize her ambition to be a modern Chinese woman. Now that she was back in Kweilin, she gave every indication of resuming long-term residence, arriving not only with enormous trunks and boxes but also with secretaries and servants.

As soon as she was reestablished in Kweilin, Dejie began to court Yifu. She lent the girl her personal maid to do errands and to accompany her on shopping sprees. Dejie also invited Yifu to teas and other entertainments. Yifu readily accepted, for she was eager to see the wealthy and important citizens of Kweilin and, in turn, be seen by them.

One day, Dashao came to her mistress's rooms and asked if Bittersweet would care to accompany her to Liangjiang market. It was an odd request, for Dashao always did the marketing alone, and almost always within Kweilin proper. Besides, produce from Liangjiang market arrived at their house at regular intervals, thanks to Delin. Furthermore, shopping was an inappropriate activity for someone in Bittersweet's high and esteemed position. And yet, because the request was odd, Bittersweet knew that a deeper motive lay beneath Dashao's invitation, so without questioning her, she asked Liu-wu to drive them the many miles to Liangjiang.

"It's very good of General Li to have so much food sent to us from the county market," Dashao said during the trip, "particularly as his time in Kweilin is so short and infrequent. He chooses it all himself, you know. He must spend a fair amount of time there." After a pause and a glance at her mistress, she added, "He certainly doesn't spend it at home with Guo *Yi Tai-tai*."

Bittersweet, noting her maidservant's peculiar behavior, said nothing but gazed at the market's many stalls.

"Is there something we especially need, Dashao?" Bittersweet asked finally.

"Unpolished rice," Dashao said, without the slightest hesitation, though Delin had recently sent a one hundred-pound bag. "There's a certain vendor whose unpolished rice is the best I've ever seen. I'm sure General Li buys the rice he sends us from her. I believe her stall is a bit further along. I'll recognize it as soon as I see her, for she carries a pretty infant on her back."

Before she even knew what she was thinking, Bittersweet felt the blood drain from her face and her hands and feet go cold. She scanned the stalls of produce, feeling both anxious and reluctant to reach the rice stand in question.

"There!" Dashao cried, pointing.

Liu-wu came to a halt and parked at the periphery of the maze of narrow pedestrian pathways and tiny stalls that comprised Liangjiang market. The two women alighted. Not wanting to be recognized for who she was, Bittersweet had dressed in simple cotton clothes and worn a wide-brimmed straw hat. When they were under the canopy of the rice stall, a pretty young peasant woman in ruddy good health stood up behind the counter.

"I hope you haven't been waiting long," she apologized with a smile, "but I had to nurse my little Deqiu."

She turned sideways so her prospective customers might admire the baby cradled in the floral cloth sling on her back. Bittersweet repressed a gasp. What she had suspected she now knew for a fact; the baby was Delin's son. He had the same double-lidded eyes of Da Mama and Delin, the same broad, sensuous mouth, the same narrow, high-bridged nose. And if any doubt remained, it was dissolved by the infant's name — the same as Baba's.

Bittersweet looked at Dashao who seemed both anxious and relieved that her mistress now knew what she had known for some time.

"What a pretty child!" Bittersweet said.

"Isn't he, though?" the proud mother replied. "He looks just like his father."

"Look who's here! Ninth Sister-in-Law!"

Bittersweet stiffened when she recognized the speaker's voice. Tentatively, she turned around and saw Yifu striding towards her. It was too late to hide in the car, too late to scurry to a different stall.

"What are you doing here?" Yifu said in a probing tone.

"We might ask the same thing of you," Dashao said for her mistress.

"I'm shopping for new slippers with Dejie's maid. But it's hot, so I'm waiting under the water chestnut stand across the way while she goes scouting for them. I want red ones, with fancy embroidery on the toe."

She turned and saw the rice vendor and the baby. "What a gorgeous infant!" she cried. "Can I hold him?" The young mother unstrapped the sling and let Yifu bounce the baby up and down in her arms. "Is it a he? Isn't he handsome? In fact, he looks just like. . . ." Yifu suddenly stopped bouncing the child. Her eyes widened and she looked first at Bittersweet, then at Dashao. Her eyes narrowed and a smile spread slowly over her face. "So that's why you're here! This is De. . . ."

"The baby wants his mother," Dashao said quickly, grabbing the child and placing him in his mother's arms. "He was just ready to cry." Then she added, glaring coldly at Yifu, "See how content he is to be where he belongs?"

"Not a word of this," Bittersweet whispered gravely to her sister-in-law. "Not a word of this to anyone."

"A secret child!" Yifu whispered back with glee. "My brother's secret child!"

"Your brother's secret child who will remain a secret!" Dashao warned her.

"No wonder Dejie's been so nervous and irritable lately. No wonder she's been sending her secretaries and servants all over the city, to the strangest places. Now I know what she's been looking for. Or rather, whom. Ha, ha! What she wouldn't give to . . . Of course, it will remain a secret," Yifu murmured, becoming suddenly very reserved. "I like secrets no less than you."

"I trust that means keeping them," Dashao retorted.

The young woman shrugged. "Of course. What else would it mean?"

"We'd better leave," Bittersweet said, afraid that something more might be revealed. Quickly she bought a few catties of unpolished rice from the young mother before heading back to Liu-wu and the car.

"You'll give us a ride back to Kweilin, won't you?" Yifu cried, running up to them, dragging Dejie's personal maid by the hand. "Now we won't have to spend the money on a rickshaw."

"And I know how much you dislike spending money," Dashao said.

All the way home, the women were silent save for Yifu's occasional giggling, a sound which evoked a raised eyebrow from Bittersweet and Dashao and a questioning stare from Dejie's personal maid.

"Oh, it's nothing . . . nothing at all," Yifu replied in answer to the maid's puzzled look, "I'm just tickled, that's all. I saw the most beautiful baby boy at market today. A more beautiful child I've *never* seen." And she lapsed into giggles once again.

Instead of frequenting the more sophisticated boutiques and markets in Kweilin as was her custom, Yifu began to visit Liangjiang, alone or in the company of Dejie's personal maid. When Bittersweet found out about her jaunts to the county marketplace, she called her sister-in-law in to see her.

"You came to Kweilin to escape country life. Why, then, are you spending so much time at a county market like Liangjiang?"

"I like the city and I like the country," Yifu answered with a careless shrug. "And Liangjiang is so close to Kweilin. I can see my city friends and my country friends in the same day."

"Do you have country friends in Liangjiang?" Bittersweet asked.

"I'm making a few." Yifu smiled slyly. "Remember that pretty peasant woman? The rice vendor with that adorable child?"

Bittersweet took Yifu by the arm, pulled her away from the door-way, and closed the door. "Have you told anyone about that young woman?" she asked sternly. "Anyone at all?"

Surprised at Bittersweet's strength, Yifu shook her head vigorously. Bittersweet loosened her grasp. "Good. Then what we saw that day at market is a secret between Dashao, you, and me. It is imperative that it goes no farther than the three of us. Do you understand? And I want you to stop going to Liangjiang. . . ."

"But why shouldn't I see my cute little nephew?" Yifu whined, pouting. "Or my new sister-in-law? I haven't told her who I am or who my brother is."

"You've never been interested in visiting your other little nephews. Why all of a sudden are you interested in seeing this one? You'll do as I say or I'll send you back to Dragon's Head."

"You can't tell me what to do!" Yifu cried, stamping her foot.

"Use your head, Little Sister-in-Law," Bittersweet admonished, "or innocent people may be hurt and you'll be the cause of it."

A few weeks later, Dejie suddenly decided to return to Kweiping to resolve some problem that had arisen at her girls' school. Yifu was unusually quiet after Dejie's departure. "You'll notice," she told Bit-tersweet, "I haven't returned to Liangjiang once."

"It's not surprising that Yifu's given up going to Liangjiang," Dashao told her mistress one evening after dinner. "Her 'friend' the rice vendor is nowhere to be found. Nor is her son. I've inquired about them at the marketplace. Apparently, the woman left in a great hurry. She left no word of where she was going."

When Dejie returned to Kweilin after four months in Kweiping, it was with two new members of her household: a fourteen-month-old son and his nursemaid. Not long afterwards, Bittersweet received an invitation to the boy's completion-of-the-month party. The envelope was delivered by Dejie's new personal maid. The last, who knew too much, had been fired.

"Tell your mistress that I accept the invitation to her son's party,"

Bittersweet told the girl, for it was her duty to attend as it was Dejie's duty to invite her.

Though the invitation verified her assumption about what had happened to the rice vendor and her child, Bittersweet also knew that Dejie's "motherhood" was well within her rights. The buying and selling of children was a regular occurrence. In the past, war and rebellion left many children orphans. Floods, droughts, and famines destroyed people's livelihoods. To ensure that their progeny might live, destitute parents sold their children to families who could feed and house them. To ensure that a male heir would carry on the family name, care for his aged parents, and worship at the family graves, families without a son bought male children from those who could no longer care for them. A wife who was barren, or who had borne only a girl-child, adopted the son borne of the union of her husband and one of his concubines. Because of her higher position, it was her right to take the son in exchange for a certain sum of money. Then, the biological mother was expected to use the money to move far away, to live out the rest of her days without any tie or claim to her child.

As she readied herself for Deqiu's completion-of-the-month party, Bittersweet thought: Truly, there are those persons who are born with good fortune and those who are born with misfortune. The young rice vendor, when she was chosen by Delin to be his concubine, must have thought that fortune had smiled on her. When she conceived his child, and that child was a son, she must have thought that her destiny was indeed propitious. But our destiny is not ours to know. It is fixed by heaven, by the stars in their courses. As the stars are beyond our reach, so too is our destiny beyond our comprehension. We cannot know it, yet we must live it.

At Deqiu's completion-of-the-month party, Dejie was radiant in her *cheongsam* of red silk and in her new role as mother of Delin's second son. When she saw Bittersweet, she took the baby from the wet nurse. "How kind of you to attend my son's party. Doesn't Deqiu look exactly like my husband?" she asked.

When he began to cry, Dejie gave the infant back to the nurse. While she smoothed out her dress, Bittersweet congratulated her on the birth of a son and complimented her on having kept her figure, no small accomplishment so soon after giving birth.

Dejie's eyes narrowed. "It's a shame Delin couldn't be here," she said, "but he must be in Chungking with Chiang. The war effort, unfortunately, is not going well. He would have been so proud and happy to be here with his little son. But after the war is over, there will be time enough for that."

Dejie excused herself to attend to the needs of her other guests. She chatted animatedly with the high officials, family members, and friends that had answered her invitation. The wet nurse and the infant trailed along behind her as she moved from guest to guest. The courtyard was lavishly decorated and boasted only the finest in food and drink and the most expensive gifts for the baby. But there was no career tray for the baby to choose from, as there had been for Youlin. Instead, a Christian minister in a long black tunic was present to christen Deqiu who sobbed bitterly as cold water was poured onto his forehead. Dejie looked on impassively, as proud and sure of her position as Delin's second wife as she was of the elimination of the woman who might have been his third. As strained as their relationship had become, as frequent as their separations had grown, Dejie need not fear that Delin would abandon her; she was the mother of one of his two sons.

But motherhood itself, particularly as it involved her husband's child by another woman, held no appeal for her. She spent no time at all with little Deqiu. She left him in the care of his wet nurse when he was an infant, and she was already planning for faraway boarding schools. Delin disapproved of these arrangements. He wanted Deqiu to be nurtured within the family instead of cared for by strangers. But he could only bow to Dejie's wishes, for she was his wife and the mother of his son. Domestic matters such as this, as he well knew, were firmly in her hands.

"Why do you look at me as though I'm the one to blame!" Yifu cried, looking alternately at Bittersweet, who had just returned from Deqiu's completion-of-the-month party, and Dashao, who was darning some of her mistress's stockings.

"We haven't said a word," Dashao said.

"That's just it — you're ignoring me, ostracizing me!"

"You might go to Guo *Yi Tai-tai* for some sympathy," Dashao suggested. "Just see what a friend she's turned out to be! All she wanted was to use you as one of her spies. When she found out what she wanted to know, she dropped you faster than a poisonous snake.

She didn't even invite you to her son's party — the son you found for her."

"I didn't tell her. Why won't you believe me?"

"No, you didn't, not in so many words. But you returned time and again to Liangjiang. And you took her personal maidservant with you. With Deqiu's resemblance to General Li, with your giggling and carrying on, and with Guo *Yi Tai-tai*'s knowledge of the rumor that General Li had taken another concubine, weren't those clues enough?" Dashao asked. "And what did the girl get for sharing her knowledge with her loyal employer? Fired! Knowing too much is often more of a curse than knowing too little."

"And what about me? Haven't I suffered, too? Now that she sent the maidservant away, I have no one to go shopping with."

Bittersweet who had mastered her tongue at Deqiu's completion-of-the-month party was unable to restrain it now. "You're missing only a shopping companion," she said, her eyes full of anger. "A young mother is missing her flesh and blood."

"Why do you blame me for everything that's happened?" Yifu moaned. "Hasn't it all ended happily? My brother now has two sons. Dejie is all smiles. Her servants don't have to creep around on tiptoe anymore. The rice vendor was handsomely paid, and she has the satisfaction of knowing that her child will be more than well-provided for."

"If you had a child, you wouldn't speak as you do," Bittersweet answered.

"And what if I don't have a child?" Yifu said, considering the remark an insult. "Is that my fault, too? You're just jealous because now Dejie has a son and can compete for your place."

"Ingrate!" Dashao cried, raising her hand to strike Yifu. "This time your mouth has taken you too far!"

Realizing too late what she had said, Yifu lifted her arm to protect herself, then she fled upstairs to her room to begin packing for Dragon's Head.

Chapter 4

The Funeral

(1940)

Now that war had broken out in Europe, Chiang summoned Delin to Chungking to attend the Wartime High Command Strategic Conference. There, Chiang appointed Delin director of Hancheng headquarters. This meant that, from now on, Delin's duty was to oversee the military operations of three war zones. On hearing the news, Delin bowed to Chiang, but he knew that the appointment was designed to separate him from his men, to make him a general without an army, a leader without power.

At the Strategic Conference, Delin also met up again with an American whom he had first known as a military attaché at the outbreak of the Sino-Japanese War. Joseph Stilwell was a West Point graduate fluent in Chinese, a noted specialist in infantry tactics, and an expert in Chinese military affairs. Vinegar Joe, as he was called, was also honest and outspoken, intolerant of corruption and diplomatic double talk. He was what Delin thought a military officer should be — a warrior-statesman as epitomized by the quintessential military strategist, Sun Tzu. Clearly, Stilwell preferred the battlefield and the gritty company of his soldiers to the luxury of an office job. He believed in the fighting ability of the Chinese peasant soldier, and he knew that the Chinese would fight like men if treated like men. Nevertheless, at their first meeting, he was pessimistic about Chinese resistance and disagreed with Delin's prophecy that war would break out in Europe and that America would enter the fray.

"France," Stilwell had told Delin then, "established the Maginot Line and Germany lacks the strength to cross it and start a war. Japan won't march on Southeast Asia only to take on Britain and France."

Delin had shaken his head. "I hope you'll advise President Roosevelt to take advantage of the fact that the Japanese have not yet blockaded the Pearl River and the Indochinese coast, and that you'll suggest that he issue a loan to us to buy arms. If America is smart, it will use another man's sword to kill its own foe. Otherwise, you'll soon find yourselves fighting shoulder to shoulder with a people that some say are fighting with chopsticks."

"General Li, you overestimate the value of American aid," Stilwell had replied. "No infusion of American money, no currency reform, no amount of American training of your armies can revitalize China. A modern army can function only in a modern state. When China frees itself from the venal corruption and nepotism coming from Nanking and actively embraces democracy and efficiency, then American aid to China will achieve the desired results."

"I reiterate," Delin had said, "the outbreak of war in Europe and Japan's southward march is only a matter of time. Though outwardly it looks as if Japan and China are the two adversaries, this is really a war between the world's aggressive and non-aggressive blocs. The only way for the United States to reduce the number of American casualties on the Far Eastern battlefield is to extend a large loan to China."

"If I were President Roosevelt, I'd seriously consider your proposal," Stilwell had answered. "But being a simple military attaché, I can do nothing."

When the two met for the second time in Chungking, Stilwell gave Delin thumbs up. "You were right," he admitted.

After the first few days of the conference when the most crucial matters involving the outbreak of war in Europe were discussed, Delin requested a leave of absence to visit his mother whom he hadn't seen in years. When his ten days in Dragon's Head were up and he was waiting at the airport to fly back to the conference in Chungking, storm clouds gathered in the west. "The black clouds of Europe's war are gathering momentum and moving eastward," Delin quipped to his aide. "When they collide with our own, the thunder and lighting they produce will shake the world."

When the ominous clouds prevented his plane from taking off, he saw them as a more personal portent, especially since, early the next morning, an urgent telegram arrived: his mother was seriously ill. Wiring Chiang the bad news, Delin requested a few more days leave and sped back to Dragon's Head — but not before he stopped at Bittersweet's house.

"My mother is very ill," he told her. "The doctors don't think she has many more days left. I'm on my way to Dragon's Head right now. Can you join me in a day or two?"

Bittersweet's face clouded over at his words. A day later Liu-wu drove his mistress to Dragon's Head. When they arrived, scores of villagers were already milling near the *da men* or squatting in the shade along the white-washed walls of the compound. At the sound of a car, the gates creaked open and Demin stepped out.

"*Ni hao*, Ninth," he greeted her.

"*Ni hao*, First Brother-in-Law," Bittersweet replied. "What news is there of your mother's health?"

He lowered his head slightly and told her that it had deteriorated steadily since she first fell ill, that she had been unconscious since the previous evening. "At least she seems to be in no pain, thanks to the acupuncturist and the herbalist who've been at her side night and day," he said in a tired, grateful voice.

Together they crossed the quiet first and second *siheyuan* and came to the third where the immediate family lived and where all was *renao*: men chatting and smoking their long-stemmed pipes or cigarettes, women preparing food, children playing tag among the red columns of the portico. In the fourth *siheyuan*, Yifu oversaw servants who were netting carp from Da Mama's pond. Their gleaming bodies lay twitching and gasping on a heavy wooden table in the outdoor kitchen. Next to the fish, a huge mound of freshly unearthed ginger lay, waiting to be sliced. On the wall above hung great bunches of spring onions. A cauldron of rice bubbled on the stove. Children continuously fed straw and twigs into the fire, for the crowd that had gathered in the third *siheyuan* was large.

Demin led Bittersweet inside to Da Mama's room. Delin was seated by the head of her bed while the two healers, Solin, his second wife, First Outside Sister-in-Law, and Demin's second wife stood at the foot. Delin raised his weary, bloodshot eyes and glanced at Bittersweet. He looked as if he hadn't slept since he had arrived. First Outside Sister-in-Law walked quietly up to Bittersweet. "It's good to see you again after all this time," she said with a wan smile. "Unfortunately, the reason for your coming is a sad one. Thankfully, she doesn't suffer."

That evening, Da Mama passed out of the world without regaining consciousness. The men wept silently while the women loosened their hair, as was customary, and began to moan and wail. Hearing their screams, the extended family in the other *siheyuan* gnashed their teeth and also released their tears.

When he had regained his equanimity, Delin stood at military attention over his mother's body and publicly upbraided himself as was expected: "I left home young to start my career. I didn't spend time at my mother's side to serve her as a filial son should. I thought I might retire early, return home to be near her, and wait on her till the end of her days. Who would have known that my mother would die before I could carry out my duty towards her?"

His elder brother, as was required, answered: "You're wrong to castigate yourself. Mother always told you to place your military and governmental duties above all else. Isn't that what you've done? You've followed her words to the letter. Isn't that being a filial son? You've made her happy and proud. What more could a mother ask?"

Delin looked at Bittersweet. "My mother's funeral must be well-planned. It must not be like funerals of old, but as decorous and dignified as she was."

Bittersweet acknowledged her husband's wishes with a slight bow.

But the Li family was no longer a simple or a private family. Since Delin's victory at Taierzhuang, it occupied an important social position, not only in Kwangsi Province but in all of China. Before Bittersweet could meet with her family to discuss funeral arrangements, the central government had sent a Funeral Arrangement Committee to Kweilin. Within days of Da Mama's death, central and provincial government leaders, authors and artists, and directors of civilian and military organizations came to Dragon's Head to pay their last respects. Meanwhile, a storm of telegrams and elegiac couplets poured into the compound.

Chiang himself sent the following words of praise: "Battles of resistance against the foreign invasion rage all over the country. We depend on your son to assist us in defeating the enemy. From far away, he bows his head and thinks of your kind and loving face."

From the famous author and playwright Tian Han's calligraphy brush came words comparing Delin with warrior-statesmen of old: "Since the victory at Taierzhuang, he makes his way homeward with gray hair. Over five thousand years, he hurries back, wearing warrior's garb, to be at his mother's side. In battle, his orders throw the enemy into confusion. His soldiers overrun and defeat the oppressors.

Throughout the land, there is praise for his military prowess. The invading army will be destroyed. His mother who has traversed the Yellow Springs can be proud of her son's outstanding achievements."

To receive the multitude of guests, Bittersweet had sent for relatives to help prepare the house and cook the meals. Under her directives, huge white muslin canopies and curtains were hung throughout the compound, and a dozen women relatives set up two extra kitchens. Here, they were kept busy cooking several huge cauldrons of noodles, so no visitor went hungry or without thanks for coming. During the three days of mourning before the burial, no one who wished to offer condolences was refused entry to the compound, and many of the guests left with bushel baskets of food to take home.

Amid the activity, Bittersweet stopped one morning in the hall where the elegiac couplets were hung. Grateful to be alone, she stood amid the scrolls and telegrams that filled the walls and she wrote down the names of the senders, for each would require a note of thanks after the funeral. She heard footsteps in the room and, turning, saw that it was Delin.

"Dejie has arrived," he said. "You needn't go greet her. First Outside Sister-in-Law is seeing to that."

"They all speak of your astuteness and bravery in battle," Bittersweet said, indicating the hundreds of couplets and telegrams with her eyes.

He looked around the room and walked over to one that had been written on simple, white paper.

"Yet this one is my favorite, for it offers a far greater truth about war than the astuteness and bravery of one man," he said solemnly. "Who sent it?"

Bittersweet examined the chop mark in one corner. "The abbot of the Taoist temple, but it was composed by Wang Pi as a commentary on the *Tao Te Ching*."

Surprised by his wife's knowledge, Delin made no comment but began to read aloud.

> *On the left, undertakings bring good fortune.*
> *On the right, undertakings bring misfortune.*
> *The second in command occupies the left;*
> *The commander occupies the right.*
> *That is, they arrange themselves as in rites of mourning.*

For the slaughter of many,
Let us grieve with heartfelt sorrow.
For a victory in battle,
Let us receive it with rites of mourning.

"I'd like to go to the temple and thank the abbot personally," he said after several moments. "Would you care to come with me? There are enough relatives here to take care of our guests. It will do us good to leave the compound."

When they arrived at the temple, Delin introduced himself as the son of the deceased woman to whom the abbot had sent Wang Pi's words. He then introduced Bittersweet as his wife. Upon hearing her husband say her name, the one he had given her, Bittersweet bent at the waist, as did Xiao Tzu. "I come here to express gratitude," Delin said to the black-robed abbot, "not to pray. My father was a firm Confucianist, and I have never before visited a Taoist temple."

"You are welcome, whatever your reasons for coming," the abbot said. Then, looking at Bittersweet, he added without changing his expression or his tone of voice, "Both of you. Confucianism and Taoism are not mutually exclusive. On the contrary, they're complementary. Confucianism is the observation of the social order; Taoism is the observation of the natural order."

The two men stood under the dynamic symbol of the Tao, the Diagram of the Supreme Ultimate, one half black and the other half white. Xiao Tzu — slim, graceful, and dressed in his priestly black robes — stood under the black half, while Delin — martially erect, solid as an uncarved block of wood, and dressed in the white robes of mourning — stood under the white half. The meaning of the image was clear to Bittersweet. Yin was the dark, the receptive, the female; yang was the bright, the male, the forceful. Yin was Xiao Tzu: the quiet, contemplative stillness of the sage. Yang was Delin: the strong, creative action of the warrior-king. Together, yin and yang represented the whole, the dynamic reality of the universe, the implicit unity of opposites, the highest truth that was paradox. Together Delin and Xiao Tzu were *her* universe, the two men she loved. Her love was not shared by two but made whole by each.

"It's very peaceful here," the grieving army general remarked. "I've changed my mind. I'd like to burn incense and pray for my mother."

260

"And I will command my priests to do weaponless battle," the Taoist abbot replied. "Thoughts and words are forces equal to bombs, tanks, or artillery. We send our thoughts and words out into the world so peace will be won and maintained as vigorously as war is now being waged."

Bittersweet looked alternately at her husband who prayed the prayers he once disparaged and the abbot who fought with forceless force. She recalled a quote from the ancient sage Wang Chung: "The yang having reached its climax retreats in favor of the yin; the yin having reached its climax retreats in favor of the yang."

For three days and three nights, nearby villagers and officials from as far away as Peking continued to arrive with lit candles and smoking incense sticks. Two waiting rooms — one for men and one for women — were set up, one on each side of the funeral hall. When each visitor finished paying last respects, Bittersweet or another member of the grieving family greeted him, thanked him for coming, and led him to the dining hall where he was given food and drink.

One evening, exhausted from seeing to the needs of her guests, Bittersweet went into the women's waiting room. She knelt down wearily and closed her eyes. Suddenly, she felt hands cradling her head. Turning around, she saw Dejie. Knowing that the outwardly compassionate gesture was, in truth, a ploy to attract attention and praise, Bittersweet pushed Dejie's hands away from her head and said, "Watch where you put your hands." Dejie's mouth hardened and her face reddened. She turned and rushed out of the room. Five minutes later, First Outside Sister-in-Law knelt beside Bittersweet. "Word is going around the compound that you beat Dejie," she whispered, unable to repress a smile. "Now she's taken refuge in the men's waiting room. She's weeping and wringing her hands to elicit their sympathy. The only thing red on her body . . . from your beating, of course . . . is her face! Whatever you said to her made her lose quite a bit of it!"

"I've been married to Delin all these years," Bittersweet whispered back, "and Dejie only several years less than I. Yet she still finds it hard to accept the fact that I'm the first wife and she the second. It's bad form when she calls attention to herself and tries to usurp my position. It's always been bad form, but at so grave an occasion, she has a doubly good reason to wear a red face."

The funeral procession, which was led by a sumptuous horse-drawn carriage sent by the central government, took place in the late afternoon of the third day. It was the longest, grandest, and most solemn procession ever seen in Dragon's Head. For dignity's sake, only two musicians were hired: a man who played a bugle's evening serenade, in deference to Delin's military calling, and a man who beat out a slow, decorous drum roll. Hundreds of people walked from their villages to line the route from the Li compound to the gravesite and to witness the majestic ceremony. Some of the mourners rode in limousines; others walked the few miles to the burial ground. Those who harbored more traditional beliefs carried paper replicas of gold coin, clothes, servants, animals, sedan chairs, cars, furniture, and houses — all to be set aflame, the smoke ascending to the skies along with their prayers, so that Da Mama might never want for the things of the material world she had left behind.

Situated three-quarters of the way up a gently rolling hill and overlooking the plain of Dragon's Head and a tributary of the Li River, Da Mama's *feng-shui* grave lay between her husband and her father-in-law's graves. Long before Bittersweet had entered the Li family through the door of marriage, the family burial ground had been chosen by a Master of Wind and Water renowned for his ability to select auspicious sites. If the deceased were not properly buried, their descendants would suffer; and if the burial ground was well-oriented, the offspring would be rewarded with position, health, wealth, and many sons.

The Li family plot fulfilled the classic *feng-shui* tenets for good placement and therefore ensured maximum harmony with the natural order. It sat on the south side of a Tortoise mountain facing the Li River and was embraced on the left by a green Dragon Mountain, on the right by a lower white Tiger Hill, and in front by an even lower vermilion Bird. It was the ideal "armchair" or "dragon protecting pearl" site. It was also high up enough on the hill to receive good drainage, yet low enough to avoid the ravages of strong winds and foul weather. The grave plot itself was square — the best shape — with a narrow inner chamber and a wide entrance.

At the foot of the hill, the long procession stopped and the bugle and drum roll with it. The heavy wood coffin that had come from Liuchow was removed from the horse-drawn carriage and placed on a carved platform to be carried by thirty of Da Mama's close relatives — sons, daughters, cousins, aunts, and uncles, all dressed in unbleached, un-hemmed white sackcloth. They moved slowly up the hill to her final resting place.

How lovely it is up here, Bittersweet thought to herself, after the body was placed in the grave and final respects were paid. She turned about in a circle and gazed at the mountains and the river that had nourished her mother-in-law in this life. She felt sorry for city people who could only wander among mountain peaks and along river banks by contemplating Chinese landscape scrolls.

"The state may fall, but hills and streams remain," Delin murmured, quoting the eighth-century poet Tu Fu.

Bittersweet looked at her husband. Was it discouragement with the war effort, sorrow over his mother's death, comfort in the beauty before him, or regret at the futility of man's efforts in the face of the natural order of things, that unearthed the poet's words from her husband's memory? She bore good news that might comfort him, and now that news swelled her heart so that she placed her hand over her left breast. Patience, she told herself. The right moment will present itself.

As the funeral procession headed back to the family compound in Dragon's Head, the hills began to change from a tint of green to a shade of blue. Though the carriage no longer contained the heavy coffin and the travelers' footsteps flowed with the river's current, the return trip seemed much longer than the trip out.

With the interment, the funeral was officially over, though well-wishers continued to pour into the Li compound to pay their last respects, and it was many days until the family began to put the house back in order. Finally, exhausted by caring for hundreds of guests, and by her many sleepless nights, Bittersweet lay on her bed doubled over with stomach pain. Later that afternoon, Delin would be leaving for Kweilin, and, from there, for Chungking and the military conference. She wanted to be entirely well when she said her good-byes and shared with him the good news that might make his leave-taking and his mother's death easier to bear.

"Xuewen."

Bittersweet lifted her head from the pillow. Delin, dressed in his military uniform, had opened the door and now stood in the doorway.

"Ah, it's you," she said. "Are you leaving already?"

"You're ill," he said, coming to her bedside.

"No," she reassured him. "Just nervous stomach."

"Ulcers?"

Bittersweet shook her head.

"I've had ulcers for years now," Delin admitted, sitting on the bed beside his wife.

She rose up onto her elbows. Delin's grandfather, the herbal medicine doctor who had saved her life as a child, had died from bleeding ulcers, and several other relations suffered from nervous stomach as well.

"You like to worry," she teased to conceal the fact that she was concerned. "Are you doing something about them?"

"I've stopped eating spicy food and drinking alcohol," he replied. "I do miss your *la-jiao*, though. I take some medicine, too, but the doctor advises an operation for a complete cure."

"Then you must have it."

"Yes, yes, I will. When the war is over."

"Then the war must be over soon," Bittersweet insisted, adding, more softly, "so you can take care of your health."

He looked at her and smiled sadly. "First, the health of China. None of us can be healthy without that."

"And no family can be healthy and happy without a son, Bittersweet said. "You haven't asked me about Youlin."

Ever since Youlin had left for America, Bittersweet served as the bearer of news between him and his father.

"Well?" Delin said, noticing Bittersweet's eagerness. "What news, then?"

"Good news. Very good news," Bittersweet replied, sitting up. "Youlin has taken a wife."

She was surprised to see her husband's blank stare immediately change to one of perplexity. "But he has another year of college left. Couldn't he wait till he graduated?"

"I suppose he fell in love with Madeleine and wanted to marry her on the spot. He still intends to finish college and graduate."

"If the dean finds out that he's married, Youlin could be expelled," Delin said. "Is he so foolish that he would risk that? And, Madeleine . . . ," Delin repeated, tripping over the word. "His wife has a Western name. Is she not Chinese?"

"Yes," Bittersweet answered quickly, seeing the anger in her husband's face. "She is. Her father is Cantonese."

"And her mother?"

"Her mother was born in Paris of French parents. Both Madeleine's parents, however, are naturalized American citizens, and she is American by birth."

"Then she is not Chinese!"

Bittersweet stared at her husband, aghast that she could have so misjudged his feelings.

"To think that Youlin has gone against my wishes! Not once but several times! To marry without asking my permission. To marry when he hasn't even completed his studies. And to marry a woman who isn't one of us."

"She *is* one of us!" Bittersweet countered. "She's our daughter-in-law!" She brought her hand to her mouth and closed her eyes. She had miscalculated; she had spoken out of turn; she had defied her husband. When she opened her eyes again, Dejie stood silhouetted against the open doorway. Bittersweet's heart sank.

"She's no daughter-in-law of mine! And Youlin is no longer my son!"

"Delin!" Bittersweet gasped, placing her hand on his arm as he started to turn away. "Isn't losing one loved one enough?"

Instantly, his rage subsided and was replaced with shame. "My words just now. . . ." he began.

"Delin!" Dejie's voice rang out.

Delin stiffened and stood up from the bed.

"The car is waiting. If you don't come now, the plane back to Chungking will leave without you. You simply cannot miss any more of the conference than you already have."

At Dejie's last words, Delin was transformed into his professional self. Bittersweet knew that it was useless to appeal to his personal feelings now.

He bowed to her stiffly from the waist, as did Dejie, slightly and with a small but superior smile. In turn, Bittersweet bowed only her head, more in resignation than in farewell.

Chapter 5
The Mountains
(1944)

Squatting on her haunches while she cut back her peonies and prepared the soil for her chrysanthemums, Bittersweet recalled Da Mama's words: "A flower cannot bloom for a hundred days. A person cannot enjoy good fortune for one hundred years." They weighed heavily in her mind for they lay heavy on her heart: she had lost her beloved mother-in-law; her son had lost his father's love; and China was losing more ground in the war with Japan. Headlines in every newspaper spoke of the imminent invasion of Changsha, the capital of Hunan Province, only three hundred miles away.

Since coming to Kweilin, Bittersweet had been blessed by prestige and prosperity. She was a respected citizen known for her civic- and cultural-mindedness; she was also a wealthy citizen, owner of several of the city's best properties. When people spoke her name, it was not only as the wife of the hero of the battle of Taierzhuang. Bittersweet was a person in her own right. But a person's good fortune doesn't last forever, she recalled. Da Mama's funeral and Delin's angry parting words not only proved this but seemed to indicate more misfortune to come.

She clipped a final peony, the delicate pink color reminding her of the inside of a conch shell, and placed it in her basket to take inside. She bent her head and brushed her cheek against the downy petals. Peonies signified the springtime of one's life. She looked at the earth that she had prepared for her chrysanthemums and wondered if she would still be in Kweilin that autumn to see them bloom. Chrysanthemums signified the autumn of one's life and a life spent in quiet retirement. She had thought that she was in the lotus, or summer, stage of her life, but her longing for peace, for an end to the war, made her believe that she had already entered the fall season. Why else did she forego the amusements of the city, preferring to plant, cultivate, and care for living things, finding pleasure in almost nothing but seeing them become flower then fruit?

The war had entered its seventh year. Refugees, young and old, filled the streets. The casualties of the battlefield wandered the lanes and *hutongs*. Not a section of the city was without its demented and its dispossessed. The soup kitchen that Bittersweet had set up with Dashao and Liu-wu's help had served as a model for other private citizens and public institutions. Still, she could accommodate only a fraction of those who arrived at her back gate. Daily, the line of the hungry and the homeless grew longer, and the rice Dashao and Liu-wu scooped into the begging bowls gave out long before the last in line had been served. With the horrible plight of the refugees and war veterans in Kweilin, with the discouraging news from the front, and with the storm clouds of discord hovering on the horizon of Bittersweet's family, she ventured into town only to go to the temple to pray and burn incense for the safety of her country and her family.

"What would General Li say?" Dashao teased her mistress. "You know how he feels about silly superstitions."

"The war has made me a silly and superstitious person," Bittersweet answered, unapologetically.

The domestic war also made Bittersweet Youlin's sole benefactor. She sent her son his tuition and living expenses — to which she added an extra sum for Madeleine. That the money came through her and not directly from his father was due, she wrote Youlin, to the same circumstances that caused his words to come through her letters; mail sent from Hancheng headquarters was less certain to reach its destination than mail from Kweilin.

"Youlin will never know that his father had disowned him or why," she told Dashao, handing her an envelope to post, "and I'll mend the breach between them before he returns home with his new bride."

"That the general was bitterly disappointed by his son's initiative is undisputable," Dashao said, "but it was compounded by the death of his mother. General Li loves the young master. His rash judgment was, in fact, due to that love, for he has high, perhaps overwhelmingly high, expectations of his son."

Bittersweet nodded in agreement. I must wait for the right moment, she thought. I must position myself and be watchful and patient.

One sultry August afternoon, when not a leaf stirred on the osmanthus trees, Hwang *Tai-tai* came to call on Bittersweet. Her breathlessness was not entirely due to the weather, and there was an anxiety that Bittersweet had never seen before in her friend — not even in July when newspaper and radio reports confirmed rumors that Japanese troops had taken Changsha and were headed for Kweilin. Just as quickly as Kweilin had become a center of commerce and the arts in free China, it had become a ghost town. Prosperity and gaiety disappeared as the hundreds of thousands of refugees who had come to the Forest of Osmanthus Trees fled for safer spots.

Hwang *Tai-tai* waved a piece of paper in front of Bittersweet's eyes.

"If you hold it still, perhaps I'll be able to read it," Bittersweet teased, though she had guessed what news it contained and knew that her friend would tell her soon enough.

"Evacuation orders," the governor's wife wheezed, pulling a silk and sandalwood fan from her sleeve and snapping it open with a flick of her wrist. "Calamity is closing in. Many refugees have seen it coming and have already left. Like they say, the little animals feel the tremors of the earthquake first; the bigger ones take note of the smaller and follow suit. Others continue to hope for a miracle — a Chinese victory in battle. But we haven't seen that since Taierzhuang. I'm afraid we've run out of miracles."

Soon Bittersweet's house was full with visitors asking questions: Had she heard from her husband and would Kweilin be lost to the Japanese?

"What will you do if the Japanese march on Kweilin?" Solin, on a visit from Dragon's Head, asked her.

"As Delin's wife, I'll await instructions from my husband, your brother," she answered.

"The whole family plans to take refuge in Dragon's Head," Solin told her. "If the Japanese come too close to Kweilin and the village becomes unsafe, then we'll hide in the mountains. You may want to come with us."

"I'll await instructions from Delin. He'll know what's best for me to do."

"What will you do if the Japanese come to Kweilin?" Hwang *Tai-tai* also asked her friend.

"I'll wait for instructions from my husband," Bittersweet answered.

Hwang *Tai-tai* pursed her lips together and drew her eyebrows down over her eyes. "Many high provincial officials are taking refuge in Chungking. That's where my husband and I will go. Others are heading for the Yunnan border."

Bittersweet gripped the armrests of the chair where she sat and prepared herself for what she knew was coming.

"You're my closest friend. Come to Chungking with us. A lot of Kweilinese are coming. You'll have friends around you. After family, what's more important than friends?"

Bittersweet rang for Dashao to bring some tea and some melon cakes.

"Your husband is far away on the battlefield," Hwang *Tai-tai* continued. "And your son is even farther away in America. Who is to make this most important decision regarding your safety? Come with us to Chungking."

"I plan to wait a while for word from Delin."

Hwang *Tai-tai* sat forward in her chair, a judgmental look in her eyes. "Your husband never knows where he's going to be from one day to the next. If he can't plan his own whereabouts, how can he plan yours? He has no time to think of your welfare."

Bittersweet sucked in some air with a gasp. She had scalded her hand pouring the tea, but it was her friend's words that had caused her pain. "I will hear from Delin," she said and resumed filling her friend's cup, "and I will do what he suggests."

The two women drank in silence for several minutes.

"How can I join you?" Bittersweet said, finally. "You and other provincial officials are going to Chungking with your families. I am alone. If I must, I can stay with my brothers-in-law in Dragon's Head or move with them to the mountains if the Japanese come to the village."

Hwang *Tai-tai* wagged her head disapprovingly. "You're a person who holds a very important position. If you go back to the village, you have only your two brothers-in-law for protection. And if the Japanese should come? If they should find you and hold you for concessions from the government? Just imagine what those concessions might be — not to mention the compromises your husband would have to make." Hwang *Tai-tai* rose to go, aware that she had made her point. "If you won't think of your own safety, then think of your husband's honor. My husband and I are leaving in two days. I hope you'll join us."

Two days later, Hwang *Tai-tai* was back. "Well? Are you coming with us?" she asked, dispensing with the usual preliminaries.

"Do I look like I'm dressed for traveling?" Bittersweet asked. She was on her hands and knees in her gardening clothes, weeding her chrysanthemums, and tying the long-stemmed flowers to bamboo stakes for support.

"Granted, a good woman listens to her father when she's young, to her husband when she marries, and to her son when she's widowed," Hwang *Tai-tai* said. "But when word from them is only silence, then she must put her own words in their mouths. To what lengths will you go to maintain your propriety? Surely there is no more proper wife in all of Kwangsi!"

Hwang *Tai-tai's* last sarcastic words were drowned out by the roar of a motorcycle, followed by a chauffeur-driven car, pulling up in front of Bittersweet's house. An orderly in military uniform and goggles ran into the garden and asked for the mistress of the house. When Bittersweet told him he had found her, he handed her a letter.

"It's from Delin," she told Hwang *Tai-tai* after reading it. "He asks me to follow those provincial officials headed for Bose. He says to leave Dashao, Liu-wu, and my older brother to take care of my house until the enemy arrives at the outskirts of Kweilin; then, they should go to the mountains along with his brothers. He's sent a car to take me to Bose."

Hwang *Tai-tai* nodded her head, happy for her friend's security.

The motorcyclist saluted and addressed Bittersweet. "General Li has charged me with escorting your car out of Kweilin until you reach open country. From there, you should be able to proceed with ease. Kweilin's streets and even those in the suburbs are swollen with people abandoning the city. I must ask you, Li *Furen*, to pack as quickly and as lightly as you can. The sooner we leave Kweilin, the more confident I'll feel about assuring your safety and the quicker I can report to General Li that I've fulfilled my duty."

"You won't have to wait but one minute," Bittersweet told him. "Come with me. You come, too," she said, motioning to Hwang *Tai-tai*.

Dashao was taking down and rolling up landscape and calligraphic scrolls when Bittersweet led them into her bedroom. At the foot of her bed lay two suitcases and a cedar trunk.

"If you'll take the two suitcases to the car, I'll send for Liu-wu to come for the trunk," Bittersweet told the orderly. "We can leave immediately. I'll just change my clothes."

"How long have you had your things packed and ready to go?"

Hwang *Tai-tai* asked, wide-eyed. "And where were you planning to go? Chungking or Bose?"

She lifted the lid of the trunk and saw thickly padded *siming* jackets, a squirrel-lined coat and snow boots — clothes that were appropriate for the country and a bitter winter in mountainous Bose.

"If you hadn't received word from your husband today, how much longer would you have stayed in Kweilin, risking your life, but never your wifely virtue?"

Bittersweet laughed bashfully. "Delin's been disobeyed by one member of his family. I won't risk becoming the second one! If it meant staying longer in Kweilin than was healthy, then I'd have left it to providence to see me to safety."

Her friend growled happily and shook her finger in mock scolding. "You're the clever one! Too intelligent to take a step that might be construed as an act of disobedience, but too wise not to prepare for it!"

"One may act independently and still be decorous," Bittersweet noted.

"Indeed!" her friend crowed. "Independent actions and proper actions aren't mutually exclusive — if you know how and when to use them!"

With a quick but heartfelt farewell to Hwang *Tai-tai*, with last minute instructions to a tearful Dashao and Liu-wu, and with her luggage strapped securely onto the roof of the car that would take her to Bose, Bittersweet signaled the driver to leave Kweilin.

Her car, bringing up the rear of five busloads of government officials headed for Bose, inched its way among the refugees that filled Kweilin's streets. Some people walked; some rode in rickshaws; some drove donkey carts. Some pulled their children along; some pushed wheelbarrows piled high with belongings. Everyone, even those fortunate enough to ride in a bus or a car, looked frightened and confused. Only those lining the streets — too old or too weak to leave home, too tired or too hungry to go on — bore faces of apathy or resignation. Perhaps they were alone in life, or perhaps they did not want to slow down family members whose sturdier constitutions allowed them to leave the doomed city.

The route out of Kweilin followed the railroad tracks. For days, fleeing refugees crammed its platform. They huddled around the fires they made at night and slept one against the other for warmth and protection. When a train pulled in, the crowd surged forward in a frenzied rush, trampling anyone or thing that stood in its way. Sometimes the trains stood in the station for days, and those fortunate enough to get on relieved themselves right where they stood for fear of losing their place. Those who could not get aboard clung to the roof or tied themselves to the underside of the cars. As Bittersweet watched the multitude disintegrate into a mob — yelling, crying, pushing, pulling, fighting for space, and covering literally every surface of the train — she learned of yet another aspect of war: the loss of one's dignity.

When a train finally left and as it picked up speed, she heard the cries of six or seven people who lost their grip and toppled off the roof. But even more pitiful were the horrible shrieks of those who lay strapped beneath, whose ribs were crushed by the rocks that protruded from the railroad bed, or who were dragged to their death because their bindings came undone.

"Is there no other route to take? This is too terrible to bear!"

"No, there is no other route, and yes, it is too terrible to bear," the driver answered Bittersweet, "yet we bear it. We bear it because we must, because as powerful as death is, life is an even more powerful force."

All along the route to Liuchow, Bittersweet's thoughts dwelt on death and so she barely spoke. Her heart was clenched in suffering and bitterness — the suffering she had witnessed along the railroad tracks, and the bitterness she felt toward her husband who had left her alone. The more she blamed Delin for her misery, the more she upbraided herself for her selfishness. From Kweilin to Liuchow and from Liuchow to Nanning, the resentment she felt for Delin and the disgust she felt for herself were like two evenly matched adversaries. It was only when Bittersweet was exhausted by them both that there was a truce, and her anger towards Delin and her shame for herself began to subside.

In Nanning, the entire entourage rested for three days before continuing the final leg of their journey to Bose. For Bittersweet, it was a respite for the body as well as the mind. She was exhausted from the trip, exhausted with the struggle within herself, and for the first time in days, she slept the sleep of peace in the midst of war.

Not everyone was traveling to Bose. While many government officials were to stay there, some were ordered to continue on to Lunyun, a town closer to the Yunnanese border, higher into the mountains, and therefore safer from the Japanese.

Bittersweet had heard that the closer to Yunnan and the higher into the mountains one traveled, the more likely one was to encounter aboriginals — tribes of people indigenous to the area who, through generations of isolation and ignorance, were uncivilized, backward, and often barbaric — people like the Yao, the Miao, and the Nasu. In Kweilin, she had met several people of Zhuang origin, but because of frequent intermarriage and the predominance and superiority of Han Chinese customs, they had dissolved into the Chinese mainstream and now could hardly be separated out. As for the others, such as the Yao, the Miao, and the Nasu, though Bittersweet had never met any, she had heard that they were very different from Han Chinese, more different even than the Western *da bizi*. Supposedly, they worshipped bulls and ate human flesh. Now she need fear not only the approach of the Japanese but also the presence of hill tribes.

For three days, Bittersweet, and the rest of the party that had not stayed on at Bose, made pitifully slow progress. They left towns, then villages, then hamlets behind. Now, along the narrow mountain path, they saw trees whose tops were hidden in the clouds and flowers the size of tables. Here the air was so cold, pure, and thin, it hurt to breath.

On the fourth day of the journey from Bose, a score of houses, a single stone road, and a handful of people appeared. Informed of the entourage's arrival, the townspeople had fashioned themselves into a welcoming committee. The mayor of Lunyun served as their spokes-man. "We hope you will be comfortable in Lunyun," he said to Bittersweet with a gracious bow. "As comfortable as someone of your prestige and position can be in a tiny backward town like Lunyun," he added in apology.

Bittersweet thanked him for his kind welcome and told him that she had been born and raised in a small village and that she should have little trouble adapting to her new home.

"Field Marshal Li," the mayor continued, "was informed that you will stay in Lunyun and not Bose. I have orders to make sure that you're well cared for. If you'll just follow me, I'll show you to your house."

"It was thoughtful of my husband to have anticipated my needs," Bittersweet replied, feeling grateful and resentful at the same time. "And it is kind of you to have realized them."

He showed her to a well-kept and spacious house, not far from the main square, and introduced her to her cook, maidservant, and 24-hour guard. Bittersweet soon learned that she was in a uniquely privileged position in having a house equipped with such a staff. But then, she was also the only refugee in Lunyun to have come alone — a uniquely unfortunate situation.

Contrary to what she had told the mayor and what she herself believed, Bittersweet did not adapt well to her new home. Just as the mountains isolated Lunyun from the outside world, the absence of family or close friends isolated Bittersweet in loneliness. Though Lunyun was the county seat, it was very small and backward. Transportation other than by donkey or sedan chair was non-existent. Once a month the mail came by donkey from Bose. There were no doctors or nurses, and what medicine there was had been brought by the refugees themselves.

A bitterly cold and windy season followed quickly upon the last days of autumn. Winter settled down as heavily as the first snowfall.

Every day Bittersweet asked her guard to go to the main square, where the citizens of Lunyun gathered, to see what he could find out about the war and the disposition of the nearest Japanese troops. And so, she learned that days after she had left, Kweilin had fallen to the Japanese. Even the fact that the United States had entered the war — after a bombing raid on their Pacific military base, Pearl Harbor — did not alleviate her moodiness. As Delin had predicted, the flames of war in East and West had met in a world-wide conflagration. American participation in the fighting was China's only hope, but in Bittersweet's mind, it only made for a bigger war, greater destruction and devastation — human suffering and despair on a global scale. She thought of Xiao Tzu and his war with peaceful words and positive thoughts and shook her head at his naïveté; at the same time, she admired him for his affirmation of life. She recalled being told of the atrocities committed by Japanese soldiers — pillaging, plundering, raping. She remembered hearing about methods of slow torture so horrifying that Chinese took their own lives by throwing themselves into wells or by hanging themselves rather than allowing themselves to be captured. When she received a letter from her elder brother letting her know that her mother had died — peacefully, in her sleep — Bittersweet grew even more despondent.

"Rumor has it that the Japanese are advancing southward and westward on Bose," her guard told her upon returning from the market square one day.

The discouraging news of the war effort, the fearful rumor of Japanese troops close to Bose, the bleak winter, and most of all, her terrible loneliness made more acute by her mother's death caused Bittersweet to withdraw even further into private, unhappy thoughts. When she spoke with her staff, it was only to delegate responsibilities. She neither sought out her refugee neighbors — all of whom had families — nor did she venture out.

Finally, one day in early spring, when the deep snows began to melt and the sun released the brooks from their icy yoke, her guard returned home from the main square with a broad grin and good news. "Now that they occupy Longan and Pinguo, the Japanese have stopped advancing on Bose."

For the first time since she arrived in Lunyun, Bittersweet smiled and felt her spirits lift somewhat. "Now that the Japanese are not a threat, and now that it's spring," she said, wiping the condensation off a window pane so she could see outside, "I think I'll go out and take a look at this town where I've been living for several months."

She put on her thickest padded *siming* gown and her fur-lined jacket and called her maidservant to accompany her for a walk to the main square. The weather was still quite cold, but the sun was shining and the air was sweet. They walked along Lunyun's principal street. Paved with blue-gray slate, the road, smooth and shiny from constant use, shone like smoked glass. Casting her eyes about, Bittersweet noticed that a great many changes had taken place since her first days in the village. Hundreds of people thronged the street and square. New shops and houses had been built. The marketplace was crowded with people haggling over chickens, ducks, fresh fruits, vegetables, bolts of cotton cloth, swatches of embroidered silk, cooking utensils, and machine parts. Lunyun had become a lively and a prosperous village.

"That's because of the influx of so many war refugees," Bittersweet's maidservant told her.

The girl's name was Siri and though Bittersweet had called her by that name since arriving in Lunyun, only now did she notice that it was an unusual Han Chinese name.

"It isn't Han at all," Siri replied. "It's a Nasu name. It's both my first name as well as a general title denoting a woman relative. In the Nasu language, it means 'of the same root.' I'm a mixed blood. My father is a Han Chinese. My mother is a Nasu."

"Oh, I didn't know!" Bittersweet gasped, then to conceal her surprise at Siri's barbarian status, and not to seem impolite, she added, "You didn't tell me."

Siri smiled. "You didn't ask me."

Again, Bittersweet found herself surprised by the girl's reply. Though not rude, it was forthright — not a response a Han girl would have given. A Han girl might have said essentially the same thing, but she would have used indirect language and a deferential manner. Here she'd been living with Siri in her house for half a year and she hadn't known that the girl was an aboriginal. Now that she knew, Bittersweet was curious.

As winter had enervated her, the approach of spring energized Bittersweet. She would wake up in the middle of the night, open her window, and fill her lungs with deep breaths of mountain air. One night, when a full moon shone in an ink-black sky, she pushed her shutters open till they touched the walls of her house. In the white moonlight, the slate road seemed paved with mercury, and the square glowed with a supernatural blue light. Leaning farther out the window, she detected the fading sound of rapid footsteps and saw Siri, bathed in an otherworldly glow, walking quickly and purposefully towards the village square. But the girl turned off into a *hutong* before reaching it and disappeared from view.

The next morning, as usual, Siri was up early, making breakfast for her mistress, having already gathered the clothes together for washing and mending. When Bittersweet sat down to the meal of *tsuk* and tea, she told Siri what she had seen in the light of the previous night's moon.

"Yes, I was on my way home," Siri said simply as she began to darn a pair of Bittersweet's stockings.

"Couldn't you have told me that you wanted to go home?" Bittersweet asked. "As your mistress, I'm responsible for your welfare. I worried about you the rest of the night."

Siri lowered her eyes apologetically. "I didn't mean for you to worry. But I didn't think you'd understand."

"Understand your desire to go home?" Bittersweet said.

"Our ways are different from yours. My last mistress, also a Han

Chinese, said we lacked propriety and forbade me to go home nights. So I ran away. Even if we work in the homes of others, it's not our custom to spend the night in another's home but in our own bed."

"Chinese homes have servants' quarters so that servants may stay the night," Bittersweet told the girl, "but if you want to spend the night at home, you may. I'm not sickly and don't need you at night. As long as you return early in the morning, you may return home after you complete your evening duties." Bittersweet shrugged her shoulders. "I can't imagine why your previous mistress objected to your returning home on the grounds of impropriety. What could possibly be improper about spending the night with your family?"

"Oh, she didn't mind my spending nights with my family," Siri replied. "What she didn't like was the fact that I was spending them with my boyfriend as well."

Bittersweet's eyes opened wide in amazement. "Do you mean your father and mother allow such . . . such. . . ."

"Impropriety?" Siri said.

Bittersweet nodded her head yes, then shook it no. She blushed, speechless.

"Not only do my parents allow it, they expect it," Siri replied. "We Nasu don't have husbands the way you Han Chinese do. We have *azhu* — partners who are both friend and lover. And our parents don't arrange our *azhu*-type marriages. We're free to choose our own partners. We don't have weddings or marriage ceremonies in the same sense you do. Instead we have coming-of-age ceremonies after which we can meet at dances, fairs, or anywhere else we like. I met my latest *azhu* at the marketplace here at Lunyun. He took a fancy to me and came to my mother's house and asked to exchange sashes with me. I'd taken a fancy to him, too, so I gave him my sash. That meant that we were serious in our feelings towards each other and that he could spend the night."

"Your latest *azhu*?" Bittersweet stammered. "Does that mean that you've had other husbands, *azhus*, that is?"

Siri nodded. "Not many. Only three others. After all, I'm only sixteen. *Azhu* marriages can be temporary or permanent. We don't feel any disgrace to end a relationship, which Han Chinese often feel . . . Han women, that is. There's no shame either in having the succession of relationships of which Han men are so proud." Siri shrugged her shoulders in bewilderment. "All this shame and disgrace is very strange!"

"You think that it's strange?" Bittersweet asked.

"Oh, my, yes! Just as it's strange to us that a Han bride goes to live in the house of her father-in-law. Unlike you Han Chinese, *azhu* wives and husbands don't live together. I'll continue living with my mother, and my *azhu* will continue living with his mother. He'll come to my mother's house and stay the night. Then, in the morning, he'll return to his mother's house. That's how it's done in our culture."

Bittersweet shook her head slowly. How can these people live in the same country, she thought, and yet in a way so contrary to our own?

"But why do you keep saying 'my mother's house'?" she asked. "Isn't it your father's house as well, and even more so, as he's the head of the household and the provider for the family?"

Siri smiled and shook her head. "In the Nasu language, we don't even have a word for father. We're a matrilineal society. The house where we live, the property we own, our surnames — everything — is inherited by, and passed down through, the female line."

"And if no daughter is born into a family to be able to carry on that line?" Bittersweet inquired.

"Then the family adopts a daughter."

Bittersweet nodded slowly. "Then, in Nasu custom the role and status of men and women are the reverse of what they are for Han Chinese," Bittersweet said.

"Just so," Siri answered. "The polar opposites."

"Incredible!" Bittersweet muttered. She shook her head rapidly, as if to unlock her mind. "I can hardly believe my ears!"

"Then perhaps you'll believe your eyes," Siri replied. "Would you like to come home with me sometime?"

"I? To your house?"

"I've told my mother about you. After all, it's not everyone who's employed by the wife of the hero of Taierzhuang. She'd love to meet the wife of a famous Han Chinese. She doesn't speak *putonghua*, however, only Nasu. But that should pose no problem, for I'll serve as translator."

Curiosity overcoming her reticence, Bittersweet accepted Siri's invitation.

"In a few weeks," Siri suggested, "when spring has come to Lunyun. Then the rhododendron will be in bloom — and the camellia trees.

There's no greater diversity of rhododendron anywhere than around Lunyun—violet, pink, coral, yellow, orange, red. And the camellias!"

On a fine, sunny, spring morning, and with assurances to the guard that they did not need his protection, Bittersweet and Siri started off for the tiny Nasu village above Lunyun.

"It's not far on foot," Siri assured her mistress when Bittersweet asked if they should hire sedan chairs. "We'll be there in no time."

"Perhaps it's not far horizontally," Bittersweet said, after an hour of struggling up the steep grade, "but vertically, your village is straight up!"

Siri, showing not the least sign of fatigue, slowed her pace. Bittersweet watched her as she walked, fluid and straight-backed, with a long stride and gently swinging arms—a walk so different from that of Chinese city women who, even though foot-binding had been abolished long ago, still took tiny, mincing steps to affect a certain social status. Most of the villagers in Lunyun, Bittersweet had noticed, had wiry bodies, strong from living in the mountains and working outdoors. They walked as quickly up mountain paths as she did on level ground. Their skin glowed, their hair was thick and glossy, and their teeth healthy and white from drinking from mountain streams and eating the unpolished rice they grew and the wild rice they gathered.

When they arrived at Siri's village, Bittersweet saw little that distinguished it from any other Chinese village. The communal buildings were of stuccoed stone with slate tile roofs. It was just like Dragon's Head and Village Village, but because of the plentiful forests, the residences were built of wood. A cistern fed by a mountain spring served as the center of the community, the village meeting place. Several women and a few children — all of them wearing blue and black homespun tunics, the yokes of which were embroidered with colorful, geometric designs and appliqued with stylized flowers — had congregated around the well. Ropes of twisted or braided silver wreathed their necks, and silver hoops, so heavy and long that they touched the women's shoulders, hung from their earlobes.

"They've dressed in their best for your visit," Siri told Bittersweet. "My mother won't be among them. She'll be waiting outside our doorway."

Just as Siri said, when they finally arrived at her home, a woman stood outside the doorway of a large wooden house. In welcome, she extended a basin of water and a clean cloth so that Bittersweet could wash her face and hands after the long climb. Then, she led her inside where she served Bittersweet a glass of hot tea — though it was more like a hearty soup, for floating among the tea leaves were peanuts, bits of salt pork, and grains of glutinous rice. As she sipped the brew, Bittersweet looked about her, and Siri, following her eyes, explained the workings of a Nasu home.

"Every house contains two buildings — one for humans, the other for domestic animals. The main hall, which is the room we're sitting in now, is the center of all family activities. In this room, we cook and eat our meals, entertain guests. . . ." She bowed to Bittersweet, indicating her as her honored guest. ". . . discuss farm and family matters, and offer sacrifices to our ancestors and to the gods."

She turned around and extended her arm towards the huge stone hearth in the center of the room and, beside it, the equally huge stone altar.

"Elderly women and young girls also sleep in this room, over there, on the wooden floor around the hearth."

"And young women?" Bittersweet asked. "And the men in the family?"

"The young women each have their own room where they can receive their *azhu* men. As for the men," Siri said, "elderly males and very young boys sleep in the communal room."

Just then, three old men, three young men, and three young boys entered the main hall and lined up on the left side of the hearth. Siri, her mother, her three aunts, and her younger sister lined up on the right side of the hearth. Siri motioned for Bittersweet to join them.

"To be seated on the right," Siri told Bittersweet, pointing to the thick wooden pillar that supported the right side of the hearth, "is the greater honor. It is thus proper that the women occupy the right side of the hearth."

The men had entered the main hall from a room on the left. This room was the old men and young boys' communal sleeping quarters; it faced the grain-grinding room which contained a large millstone. Parallel to the main hall and between the men's quarters and the grain-grinding room was a storeroom with baskets of threshed grain and earthenware jugs of wine and oil.

Bittersweet sat between Siri on her left and Siri's mother on her right.

By the deference everyone paid Siri's mother, Bittersweet deduced that she was head of the clan. As if she had guessed her thoughts, Siri leaned over and told Bittersweet: "Not only is my mother head of our clan but of the entire village. She's what your culture calls a mayor. If disputes arise between households, it is she who settles them. If the construction of a new communal building has been suggested, she hears the arguments for and against it, gives the final decision and, if it's to be built, raises the money for it in taxes. If someone is accused of wrongdoing, she listens to the accused, to those who accuse, and to those who defend. She passes final judgment and, if warranted, metes out the appropriate punishment."

After Siri's mother gave a short speech welcoming Bittersweet to her village and her home, all the men stood up and filed out of the room. When they returned a short while later, they carried platters of roast pork, a cauldron of steaming unpolished rice, bowls of a variety of pickled vegetables, and jugs of sweet mountain water and homemade wine. The wine loosened Bittersweet's tongue, even though it was only Siri and one of her brothers who could understand her words. For the first time in months, Bittersweet talked happily.

"It's been so long since I've enjoyed the company of others," she told Siri. "Your family is as hospitable to me as if it were my own — you, who are not only not my family but not even my people! And imagine — men serving women!"

She clapped her hands and laughed when the men reappeared, this time with *pipa* and *lusheng* in their hands. When they began to play the simple instruments, the women started to sing and clap. Bittersweet raised her wine cup before her face and offered a toast to Siri's family. Then she drained her cup dry.

Is the difference that separates their lives from my own so great, Bittersweet asked herself. Here, a woman is head of her clan, even the village! Because Delin must serve the war effort, haven't I been head of the Li clan in his absence? Haven't I received members of his family at the house that I maintain with money I earn through investments that I make? Haven't I found them jobs in businesses that I started and made profitable? Haven't I even found them appropriate wives and husbands so that the chain of life and the name of Li might continue and prosper? A Nasu woman chooses her *azhu* as her birthright. Didn't I, a Han woman, go against custom and tradition to choose Delin as my husband?

Her thoughts were interrupted by the music and before she knew it, she was dancing in a circle with all the others — she who had never danced in her life! The sounds of the *pipa* and *lusheng* entered her arms and her legs and moved them in spite of herself. Everyone danced and sang till dinner was done, and then they danced and sang some more. The last notes plucked on the *pipa* and blown through the *lusheng* and the final refrains of the folk songs reverberated in Bittersweet's head as she stepped outside the house and breathed the night air. Then, she realized, with a start, that it was very late — too late to head for home.

"You must stay the night with us," Siri insisted. "Hours ago, I sent my brother who speaks *putonghua* to tell cook and guard that you will stay with me in my village and that you'll be back in Lunyun tomorrow. It would be a great honor for me if you would have my room. I will stay with my mother for the night."

Before she could object, Bittersweet recalled an aphorism Baba had told her many years ago when she first became his daughter-in-law. Now she repeated it to her maidservant who was also her hostess. "When you are in someone else's house, you must bow your head."

"I'll prepare your room as it should be prepared for an honored guest," Siri said with a smile, leaving Bittersweet to her thoughts.

Was her life so different from the life of a Nasu woman, Bittersweet asked herself again, looking up at the moon as if the Jade Rabbit who lived there might tell her the answer. Yes, it was very different, Bittersweet acknowledged, lowering her head. For every responsibility, there was a corresponding privilege, she recalled. And for every privilege, there was a corresponding responsibility. Such was the equation of life. When a man shouldered a responsibility, it was an achievement, and he gained the praise of others. When a woman shouldered a responsibility, it was her duty and she was expected to fulfill it. A responsible man increased his authority. A responsible woman increased her responsibilities. Authority, if indeed she had any, came secondhand: permitted by her father, bestowed by her husband, granted by her son. So it was for a Han Chinese woman, Bittersweet thought, and otherwise for a Nasu woman. And yet the Nasu were considered backward, if not outright barbarians, because they were poor in material goods, because the women held the power and the men obeyed. She recalled Xiao Tzu's words about morality and propriety being social inventions, not inherent laws of nature — social inventions that favored some people and were detrimental to others. It wasn't a question of wrong or right, good or bad, but of who had formulated the rules, who were bound by them, who were liberated by them. Perhaps the Nasu bore the same prejudice toward the Han; perhaps they thought that the Han were backward and barbarian because they were poor in spirit, frugal in song, and because the men held the power and the women obeyed.

When Bittersweet was shown to her room for the night, she found Siri standing in it, while a young man knelt beside her. When Bittersweet entered, he lowered his head till it touched the floor, and when he lifted it again, Bittersweet recognized him as her dancing partner throughout most of the evening. Blood rushed to her face and she blushed and turned away.

"I hope you'll spend a pleasant night here," Siri wished her. "Toma will keep you company."

"That won't be necessary," Bittersweet said quickly. "I'm used to sleeping alone."

"Oh, but it's Nasu custom!" Siri said. "Toma would be very hurt if you refused him, and my family would lose much face. We will have been remiss in our hospitality to a guest — all the more so as you are a very honored guest. We could not live down the disgrace." She looked at Bittersweet reassuringly. "I'm half Han so I somewhat understand your reluctance. But you're in a Nasu home, and what happens here will stay here. It will go no farther than the threshold of this room. The saying of your people," Siri recalled, "I have indeed heard of it, and I agree with it completely. 'When one is a guest, one must abide by the rules of the host.'"

Bittersweet raised her eyes to look at her handsome young dance partner, her companion for the night. She then lowered her eyes, unafraid.

Taking one of the two lit candles, Siri left the room and closed the door behind her. For a few moments, Bittersweet stood motionlessly. Then the young man, the excellent dancer who had been able to move her body to the rhythms of the music and thus sway her mind, stood up in front of her, a candle in his hand. He held it before him at chest level so that it illuminated his face and hers as well. He looked at her, seeing, searching for . . . what? Bittersweet wondered as she returned his gaze. But she knew exactly what she saw in his. She saw Delin's face as it had appeared soon after their wedding night in the light of the tung oil lamps. She lifted her hand to the young dancer's cheek.

The dancer did not vanish at her touch, as Delin had seemed to, years ago. As she had once stood before Delin, Bittersweet now stood and lowered her eyes. Feeling her companion's warm breath on her cheek, she blew out the flame that hovered in his hand.

That summer, Bittersweet's garden flowered profusely. She had planted red peonies, her favorite flower, and they competed with the beauty of the camellia and the rhododendron trees that grew wild about Lunyun. On her walks into the hills, she would break off branches of the flowering trees, so she could bring wild Nature into her house to complement the domesticated Nature she had coaxed from her small backyard garden. She drank directly from the cold mountain streams, and the water quenched her thirst faster than the water her guard brought home in earthenware jars. She stopped to listen to the stream as it darted around rocks and boulders in its path, and its whisperings reminded her of Xiao Tzu's words: softest water wears away hardest rock; receptivity overcomes force; there is power in being low; the flow of time wears away the most hurtful of ills.

Her daily walks muscled her legs and stretched her spine so that her body began to resemble the lean, hard bodies of the villagers. Her skin and eyes glowed from her simple diet of unpolished rice, mountain herbs, vegetables, and little meat. She walked fluidly, with swinging arms and a resilient step, and now she could walk for miles uphill without getting winded. When she was indoors, she spent hours writing to Delin, whose letters were more hopeful, now that the War of Resistance had become a World War. With the United States in the conflict, the Japanese were suffering defeats in the Pacific, as were the Germans in Europe, and the Italians in Africa.

One day in early autumn, Bittersweet's writing was interrupted by a barrage of short, sharp, rapid bursts that sounded like machine gun fire coming from the marketplace. Had they been misinformed, she wondered. Were the Japanese advancing on Bose after all, and were they already in Lunyun? Throwing a shawl about her shoulders, she ran outside.

"Do you think . . . ?" she started to ask her guard.

"Shall I run to the marketplace and find out?"

"No, stay here. I'll go," she told him and quickly joined her neighbors running towards the square.

When Bittersweet arrived, she saw some people crying on their neighbors' shoulders. Others were sobbing into their hands and still others were calling out to latecomers, who, on hearing their words, also burst into tears. But the machine gun fire was unremitting, and she couldn't make out what they were saying or why they were crying. She grabbed a weeping woman by the shoulders. "The Japanese. . . ." she began anxiously.

The woman heaved a huge sigh and blubbered into her handkerchief. "Surrendered! Just listen to all the firecrackers going off!"

Bittersweet shook her head in disbelief. "Did I hear you correctly? The Japanese have surrendered?"

"Unconditionally!" the woman wailed, bursting into tears again and throwing her arms up into the air. "We've won! We've won this brutal war!"

Bittersweet hugged the sobbing woman to her, and, like her, began to laugh and cry in relief and gratitude. Then, both women turned to congratulate everyone who passed them.

Chapter 6

A Family United; A Nation Divided

(1946)

Bittersweet left Lunyun as abruptly as she'd left Kweilin. The going, like the coming, was slow and arduous, but her excitement about returning home diminished the journey's hardships. During a three-day rest in Nanning, Bittersweet and her fellow travelers learned that Liuchow, their final stop before Kweilin, had been ravaged by a cholera epidemic. And, sure enough, when they arrived in Liuchow, they found that it was a city of the dead. There they learned that they could expect to find Kweilin struck by the same disease and equally desolate.

As Bittersweet was driven into her city, she saw with both relief and heartache that Kweilin's devastation was not due to cholera. Instead, entire neighborhoods, along with her hotel, her silk filature, and her silk shop, had been reduced to rubble. Her house on Folded Brocade Road was gone — the entire five-*siheyuan* compound demolished. Nothing but bits of charred wood and scorched stone remained.

Just as she was about to despair over the loss of her house and her city, she saw something in her courtyard that hadn't been destroyed. It was something that hadn't even existed before — a little wooden house.

Bittersweet got out of the car and picked her way through the debris. When she opened the door to the little cottage, she saw a young man examining a set of blueprints. He introduced himself as Jiaqiu, her elder brother's son. Overwhelmed to see a family member, Bittersweet broke down weeping, then started laughing through her tears as she patted her nephew on the arms and shoulders. The pain she had felt about her house immediately disappeared when she learned that all her relatives were safe. Jiaqiu reassured his aunt that though many of them had suffered from hunger, malnutrition, and theft, no one in the family had been badly hurt.

"Just after peace was declared, Father sent me to Kweilin to make sure you had a roof over your head when you returned home. Though your house has been destroyed, it can be rebuilt around you while you live in your temporary home. You've come just in time. The laborers are just about finished," he said, nodding at their handiwork with pride.

"Do you know what I'll call my little wooden cottage?" Bittersweet asked, glancing about the three little rooms. "I'll call it Xuelu — Xuewen Manor. What do you think of that?"

They laughed and Jiaqiu agreed that it was the perfect name for his aunt's temporary new home.

"Oh, I almost forgot!" he said. He rummaged in his jacket pocket and then withdrew a telegram. "From the United States," he said, pointing at the postmark. "It arrived about a week ago."

Bittersweet sat down on an empty crate that served as one of the room's four chairs and began to read. When she looked at her nephew again, her eyes were again full of tears. "It's from Youlin. He and Madeleine and their children sail from San Francisco next month. Youlin's coming back to China and bringing his family with him."

"Children!" Jiaqiu exclaimed. "Congratulations, Auntie — you're a grandmother. What are their names?"

"They're twins," she said. "A boy and a girl. Eighteen months old. The boy is named An-ruh," Bittersweet said, pronouncing the Chinese phonetic equivalent for Andrew.

"Warm Peace," Jiaqiu translated, nodding his head. "Very fitting, now that the war's over."

"And the girl is called Lei-shi," she said, pronouncing the Chinese approximation of Lisa.

"Thunder Poem. . . . Such imaginative names your grandchildren have," Jiaqiu remarked, though his own name meant Add-a-Ball.

"They'll be arriving in Shanghai in less than three weeks. Three weeks!" Bittersweet repeated. "I must wire Delin! I must rent a house for them in Shanghai. And furnish it the way an American woman would. And buy toys for my grandchildren." She opened Xuelu's single door and looked out on the rubble of her old house. "No," she decided, recalling Solin's marriage troubles and Emma's cravings for all things English. "I won't rebuild my old house. I'll build a new house — a house a Western woman will feel comfortable living in — a Western-style house. I know a Kweilinese architect who studied in America and has built such houses. And I'd like you to oversee the building of it and live in Xuelu in the interim," she told her nephew.

"If you agree, then I can leave for Shanghai just as soon as I place the commission with the architect."

When Jiaqiu immediately accepted her offer, Bittersweet held her head between her hands as if to keep it from exploding with all the plans and arrangements she had to make. Still, her face showed nothing but happiness. "There's so much to do, now that my family is returning to China! My big family!"

Her first stop was to the post office to wire Delin about his family's return. On the way, she stopped at Hwang *Tai-tai*'s residence to see if her friend had returned from Chungking. Hwang *Tai-tai*'s elegant estate had also been burnt to the ground, but its reconstruction was already underway. Bittersweet found her friend living temporarily in her own "manor." "Not a single building I own is standing," Hwang *Tai-tai* complained crossly, then declared, "but I mean to rebuild every single one, regain my former prosperity, and reconstruct Kweilin in the process."

"And I mean to mend the breach between my husband and my son," Bittersweet told her friend. "Delin won't be able to withstand the lure of not just one but two grandchildren — truly a double happiness!"

When Bittersweet arrived at the post office to send off the telegram to Delin, she found a letter from him waiting for her. Its postmark read Peking.

"I wish I could be as happy as the Chinese people about the war's end and our victory over Japan. Instead I am troubled," Delin wrote. "The War of Resistance united us as a country. Kuomintang and Communist fought side by side against a common enemy and for a common cause. Now that the enemy and the cause have disappeared, so, too, I fear has the unity. Already dissent is growing about how the country should be governed — and by whom — and Russia gazes greedily upon Manchuria as at the spoils of victory.

"The war is over, and for that I am thankful. Yet eight years of bloodshed have left tens of millions of Chinese dead and created an uncertain future. The central government remains what it always has been: selfish, greedy, and corrupt. In the winds of our victory over Japan are the seeds of a post-war struggle and a conflict that may well be worse than the war itself. To the inner trouble of our corrupt government will be added the outer menace of the Soviet Union. Should the Russian and the Chinese Communists unite, we will have an enemy even more formidable than Japan. Two wars will then take the place of the one that's just ended: a civil war that will pit brother against brother, father against son; and a cold war that will break out between East and West, threatening both hemispheres for years to come."

A few days after sending off her reply to Delin, Bittersweet took the train from Kweilin to Shanghai. She was accompanied by Dashao who had taken refuge in Dragon's Head during the war, while Liu-wu had returned to Canton. For the three days that it took for the train to steam north to the great port city, Bittersweet thought of little else than what she had to do to prepare for her family's homecoming. Renting a house was one thing she did not have to worry about. As Bittersweet had predicted, the eight-year-old wound between father and son had healed — literally overnight — now that Delin was a grandfather. As a welcoming gesture, Delin had rented a Western-style house on Haight Road in the former British concession of Shanghai. It was a large house with plumbing, an inside flush toilet, and an inside kitchen — just like the two-story Western-style house Bittersweet was in the process of building in Kweilin. Delin also had a house in Peking ready for the moment Youlin and his family were settled in Shanghai and could come to visit him in the northern capital.

Even as Bittersweet and Dashao spent their first two weeks in Shanghai buying Western-style furnishings — carpets, overstuffed armchairs, lamps, a stove, a refrigerator, pots and pans and "china" made in England, brass beds, blankets, sheets, draperies, even a vacuum cleaner, an article neither of them had ever seen — Bittersweet wondered if she was doing her best to provide a familiar environment with which to welcome her American daughter-in-law.

The day that the ship carrying her family pulled into Shanghai harbor, Bittersweet stood on the dock, anxiously craning her neck for a glimpse of Youlin, his wife, and their children. She clasped her hands at her breast when the gangplank was lowered.

Is that my son, she thought, raising her fingers to her lips in uncertainty. Of course not, though the handsome young man in the well-cut, double-breasted suit is coming towards me, his arms outstretched.

"Mama . . . Mama," Youlin murmured, hugging his mother to him.

Ten years since she had heard his voice or held him in her arms. And yet, now that he was home, when she released him to gaze at his face, she could only say, "Has it really been ten years?"

Then Bittersweet saw her — Madeleine, her American daughter-in-law. She released Youlin from her embrace and clasped her hands together at her breast. No, Bittersweet thought, this couldn't be Madeleine. She's much too young to be the mother of two children, much too slender, much too beautiful.

Though she was American, Madeleine wore an elegant *cheongsam* with the pattern of the eternal knot — a Buddhist symbol and one of Bittersweet's favorite designs — woven into the silk fabric. Circling her neck was a double-strand of pearls. She had stayed back, waiting for Youlin to introduce her. At his beckoning, she approached Bittersweet, not rushing forward aggressively as Bittersweet had seen so many Westerners do, but not hanging back timidly either, as so many Chinese did when meeting someone for the first time. Truly, this Eurasian daughter-in-law of mine is half-Eastern and half-Western, Bittersweet thought. And I don't have to be a physiognomist to know that my daughter-in-law is blessed with good fortune.

Madeleine's brows were of the type called "new moon" which signifies kindness as well as a large family, which, in fact, was the kind of family she came from: five sisters and a single brother. Twins, Bittersweet thought, was a promising start.

She took Madeleine's hands into hers and welcomed her into the family and to China and hoped that she would be happy in both. By the expression in her daughter-in-law's eyes, she knew that Madeleine understood, if not her words, certainly her intent. In a gentle and refined manner, the young woman thanked her in very simple Mandarin and called her "Mother." Youlin motioned to the *amah* who stood slightly behind Madeleine with a small child in each arm. The children were as physically different as could be: Andrew was fair-skinned, long and lanky, with stick-straight dark blond hair and almond-shaped blue eyes, while Lisa was round and small, with rosy cheeks, huge brown eyes, and masses of curly brown hair.

"They're too beautiful for mortal eyes," Bittersweet gushed, taking now one child into her arms, then the other.

Andrew immediately began to cry and reached out for Madeleine, but Lisa just stared curiously at her grandmother.

"*Nai-nai, ni hao?*" Madeleine was able to coax Lisa into saying, but Andrew just pouted and clung to his mother.

"An-ruh doesn't resemble Youlin physically," Bittersweet laughed, "but they definitely have similar characteristics."

All the way home in the chauffeured limousine that Delin had hired for his family, Bittersweet held and patted Madeleine's hand and tried to make simple conversation with her. To everything Madeleine said, Bittersweet leaned over to Youlin and remarked, "She speaks Chinese very well, doesn't she? And to think — she's only just arrived!"

When she asked her son whether or not he thought his wife would enjoy their first meal together at one of Shanghai's elegant French restaurants or an opulent Chinese one, Youlin said, "Let's eat at home. How I've missed Dashao's good home cooking! As for Madeleine, have you forgotten?" he asked. "She might be an individualistic American by citizenship and one-half sophisticated French by blood, but the other half is homespun Chinese."

That evening, over a lavish banquet that Dashao prepared in Madeleine's honor, Bittersweet watched with admiration as her Western daughter-in-law tried to unshell salt-fried prawns with discreet nibbles. Unsuccessful, she finally ate the tasty crustaceans, armor and all! With increasing approval, Bittersweet also noticed that Madeleine held her chopsticks correctly, which no one in her own or Delin's family was able to do.

"Is Mother laughing at me?" Madeleine, blushing in embarrassment, whispered to Youlin.

"Here I am, a full-blooded Chinese," Bittersweet confessed when Youlin asked her to share what she found so humorous, "and yet I've never learned to hold chopsticks the right way. And here's my daughter-in-law, newly arrived in China, yet she holds them properly! When I was a child," she recalled, "my index finger always stuck up while eating and my mother, who sat diagonally across the table from me, always scolded me for 'pointing my finger' at her."

"Look at me, *Nai-nai*," Andrew piped up after his father translated his grandmother's words. "I use chopsticks the best."

In a few days, huge boxes and crates began to arrive at the house on Haight Road. Inside were furnishings Madeleine had shipped from America, including a stove, a refrigerator, even an automobile.

"It demonstrates Madeleine's great foresight to have prepared so thoroughly to come to China," Bittersweet told Youlin. "But did she think that our country didn't have cars?"

Bittersweet soon realized that almost all the furniture she had bought for the house — items which she had believed to be the latest in Western fashion — were unsuitable. Even the toys she had purchased for Andrew and Lisa were inappropriate — wooden puzzles in the shape of cubes and spheres, whistles in the shape of birds, porcelain dolls from Japan with life-like eyes, real human hair, and exquisite brocade kimonos, rice paper kites with reeds in their frames so they whistled in the wind. Her grandchildren preferred the American toys that their mother had shipped over: a rocking horse made with real pony-skin, a child-sized piano, building blocks with the letters of the alphabet on the sides, picture books and coloring books, drawing pads and crayons, and dolls made of plastic and rubber whose eyes blinked and who said "Ma-ma" when their stomachs were squeezed. Those dolls, Bittersweet was astounded to discover, had wardrobes as complete as Madeleine's, and she had come to China with three dozen suitcases, two of which were completely filled with shoes.

"I can understand her need for many shoes," Bittersweet said to Youlin. "Having been a dancer, she must have gone through many shoes. Now she doesn't have to worry: when one pair is worn through, there are so many others to take its place."

Though she was proud that her daughter-in-law made almost all her family's clothes, Bittersweet could not understand why Madeleine sewed so many clothes for Lisa's dolls.

"Why would little dolls need so many clothes?" Bittersweet asked her son. "And why does Madeleine make these tiny garments as earnestly as she does her own?

Youlin laughed. "Madeleine's following in her mother's footsteps. Someday she hopes to be a dress designer. So when she's sewing clothes — even when it's for dolls — she's also designing them. She's perfecting her skills."

"Ah!" Bittersweet said, nodding her head. "A deep purpose, and yet such a light-hearted means! I appreciate that."

But what she couldn't appreciate were Madeleine's views on the care of children.

"Our Shanghai house isn't very large," Bittersweet had Youlin tell Madeleine, whose Chinese was improving but still rudimentary. "Only a living room, a dining room, four bedrooms, three baths, a kitchen, a playroom, and servants' quarters. Yet my daughter-in-law wishes the children to each have his own room. Might they at least share a room so they have each other's company?"

But Youlin said that Madeleine felt the room arrangements were just as they should be.

"Perhaps you'll explain my daughter-in-law's reasoning to me," Bittersweet persisted a few weeks later. "For one, if the children slept with her, she wouldn't have to scurry to their rooms in the middle of the night when they cried. Isn't that more efficient? For another, the children are so small, it pains me to see them sleeping in their big rooms all alone. In all other ways, Madeleine is so kind. Isn't it somewhat cruel that she allows her children to sleep alone?"

This time, Madeleine was fluent enough in Mandarin that she could reply to her mother-in-law's inquiry herself. "Da Mama," she explained, "it's not cruel at all for the children to sleep in separate bedrooms. It's healthy."

Bittersweet nodded diplomatically, but she was not convinced.

"I understand that when a Westerner gets sick, he goes straight to the hospital," she told Madeleine a few days later, trying a new tack. "If my grandchildren get sick, you'll send them away to the hospital to get well, and I simply can't bear the thought. People need to be with their families when they're not feeling well, and little children all the more so. Let them stay in my room."

But Madeleine shook her head from side to side and muttered, "*Bu hao. Bu hao.*"

Bittersweet sighed but said nothing. No longer did she insist, for she recalled how miserable her three sisters had been in the house of their heartless mothers-in-law. She also remembered Da Mama, her forbearance, and her tolerance for ideas other than her own. Nevertheless, Bittersweet worried about her grandchildren. When Andrew came down with a bad cold and sore throat, the same ailment that Youlin had been prone to as a child, she feared his mother would send him away. But when Madeleine cared for the boy herself, rising several times in the middle of the night to see to his needs, Bittersweet realized her fears were unwarranted.

Still, there were other aspects of Western living that continued to perplex her. Americans, it seemed, were very particular about their bathrooms. The bedrooms could be rudimentary, but immaculate and comfortable bathrooms with flush toilets and hot and cold running water were essential. And if the bathrooms were important, the kitchen was even more so.

"Why?" Bittersweet asked her daughter-in-law one day.

"Because hygiene is essential to food preparation. One's health depends on it," Madeleine answered in slow but correct Mandarin. "A proper kitchen must have good circulation, lots of sunlight, and spotless utensils."

One of Madeleine's first tasks as mistress of the house had been to teach Dashao to wash dishes in very hot water to which was added a special liquid soap called dish detergent. She told Dashao to rinse them well, and to wipe them dry with very clean, soft cloths called dish towels.

"Never have I ever seen a kitchen such as this," Dashao murmured with both admiration and skepticism. "It's even more luxurious than the living and dining rooms, and the master bedroom is almost primitive in comparison. In Chinese houses, the public rooms shine, but in Western houses, the most opulent rooms are the ones most visitors never see."

One evening, Madeleine prepared the evening meal — a French meal. She went back and forth from the refrigerator to the stove to the toaster to the electric oven to the cake mixer to the ice cream machine. She had planned hors d'oeuvres on toast triangles, a *gigot d'agneau* with julienne vegetables, roast potatoes, a chocolate layer cake, and vanilla ice cream. On this day, Dashao was allowed to clean up afterwards but not to prepare a thing.

"It's surprising to me," Dashao said, "how many machines, big and little, foreigners need in order to cook a good meal, while we Chinese need only a wok and a cleaver."

Madeleine raised her head from the oven where she was basting her leg of lamb.

"For example?"

"For example, Mistress, that great big refrigerator. I can see the purpose of it if the weather is hot all the time, but there are seasons in Shanghai when the weather is very cold. Yet foreigners, I hear, rely on their refrigerators all year round."

"It's true," Madeleine replied. "A foreign family would be lost without a refrigerator. We don't shop as you do — once, even twice, a day. We don't have the time and so we shop once or twice a week."

"Foreigners say that a refrigerator keeps food as fresh as just-picked or fresh-killed." Dashao shook her head. "But I don't believe it. Can you honestly tell me that a box that's cold inside is the same as a plot of earth enriched with a layer of night soil? Or that a chicken that lies in the electric winter of an icebox will be as tender as a still-warm one whose neck has just been slit? I don't mean to criticize, Mistress," Dashao said, "but despite all your fancy machines and exotic ingredients, the things you can·make are proportionately few."

"That sounds like a challenge, Dashao," Madeleine said with a smile. "Remember, though I'm American, I'm also French, and French cuisine is among the best in the world."

"As is Chinese cuisine," Dashao was quick to reply.

"And justifiably so," Madeleine concurred. "Perhaps we should put our theories to a test — a contest."

Dashao wasn't surprised. She had heard that Westerners were competitive and confrontational, always eager to play games that pit one person against the other.

"There's no question that you're a better cook than I am," Madeleine said, diplomatically. "However, national cuisine is the question here, not personal cooking skills. You say that, with all the ingredients and all the machines I have at my disposal, I can cook only so many dishes. Let me cook them, then. You, as the better cook, will be limited to as many vegetables as you care to prepare, but as far as meat goes, solely chicken."

"Not just any chickens," Dashao qualified. "Only freshly-killed, unrefrigerated chickens."

"*Certainement.* The contest will last ten days. We'll each cook for five alternating days. Agreed?" Madeleine asked, extending her hand in anticipation of the handshake that would confirm the arrangement.

"Agreed!" Dashao boomed, taking her hand and pumping it.

Youlin and Bittersweet soon learned of the game that Madeleine and Dashao had devised for their own amusement and the family's pleasure.

"It's Madeleine's Chinese sense of protocol," Bittersweet proudly told Youlin. "To defuse a possible rivalry, she uses the means of rivalry — a challenge — the result of which will be that Dashao will become her loyal servant and unwavering ally."

"It's more likely her French charm and her Gallic rigor," Youlin said. "A blend of Western spiritedness and seriousness."

"Whatever it is," Bittersweet said, "we'll never eat better meals than those concocted over the next ten days."

Madeleine made her meals with the aid of her many machines and a variety of meats and poultry, rare vegetables, fruits, and dairy products — including a cheese board which, she assured the prospective diners, was something the French preferred to any sweet dessert. (She convinced no one, however, about the virtues of the pungent-smelling conclusion to the meal.) Dashao remained well within her limitations of chicken, common Chinese vegetables, a few condiments, and her wok and cleaver. But such wizardry she worked, nonetheless! Cold shredded chicken, salt-baked chicken, General Tso's chicken, *see-yow gai* chicken, paper-wrapped chicken, and the drunken chicken that Madeleine liked to eat with her fingers. At the end of the trial period, Madeleine graciously conceded that Dashao was not only the better cook but also that Chinese food was the better cuisine.

"I may be a somewhat better cook than my culinary adversary," Dashao replied diplomatically, "but I understand that my young master's wife is an excellent dancer."

Bittersweet blushed. "I told Dashao that Madeleine was a professional dancer before she married you," she said sheepishly to her son, "and that photos of her appeared in American newspapers as frequently as your father's appear in ours. Do you think Madeleine would consent to dance for us?"

Madeleine stood up and left the room. "Where is she going?" Bittersweet asked, afraid her request had offended her daughter-in-law.

"To change her shoes," Youlin replied. "The type of dancing she does is unique and requires special shoes. You'll see."

When Madeleine returned, not only had she changed her shoes but her clothes as well. She wore a dress with a tight satin bodice and a very wide skirt made of layer upon layer of diaphanous pink tulle that floated from her waist to her ankles in one great, airy cloud. Her shoes were the same pale pink satin of her bodice, with ribbons that criss-crossed along the top of her foot and tied around the ankle.

"What is that soft knocking on the floor?" Bittersweet asked when Madeleine walked across the room.

"The rectangles of wood in the toes of my shoes," Madeleine said.

"Why would anyone want to put pieces of wood in the toes of her shoes?" Bittersweet whispered to Youlin.

"Just watch," he advised as he and Dashao moved the dining room table to one side of the room and rolled up the carpet. Madeleine put a record on the Victrola in the adjoining living room.

"See how strangely she walks!" Bittersweet whispered to her son. "Those strange shoes have deformed her feet. She's obviously in pain!"

"They're called toe shoes," Youlin told his mother gently, "and Madeleine can do amazing things in them, as you'll soon see."

He sat his mother down in one of the dining room chairs and took another for himself, as did Dashao.

"The Sleeping Beauty Suite by Prokofiev," Madeleine announced as the music began.

Then she rose up onto her toes and began to dance weightlessly on them. Bittersweet and Dashao let out an astonished gasp. When she beat her feet in the air several times in *entre chacottes* and landed on them in a splayed position, they oohed and ahhed, but when she performed a few jetés and pirouettes and balanced for what seemed like an eternity on a single toe point, her audience was speechless. Dashao, who was enjoying the performance enormously, alternately patted her knees and clapped her hands in time to the music, but Bittersweet was too moved to follow suit. She ached for her daughter-in-law. How could Madeleine not be in pain? And how could she, a Western and an enlightened woman, put on those debilitating shoes? Chinese women had given up the feudal practice of foot binding decades ago, yet here was an American woman instituting a foreign version of essentially the same thing.

"I might have won the cooking contest," Dashao said, applauding wildly when Madeleine took her bows, "but Mistress has won our hearts with her gravity-defying toe dancing!"

Bittersweet clapped, too, but less enthusiastically as she eyed her daughter-in-law's waist. It was less than the span of a man's hand.

Now that she had ceased worrying about her grandchildren, she began to be concerned about Madeleine's health. For a woman as particular about the number of clothes in her closet, Madeleine was not at all particular about the quantity of food she ate.

"Do you think your wife might be ill?" Bittersweet inquired of Youlin, a few days after the dance performance. "Madeleine's appetite is not very hearty."

Youlin laughed. "Don't be concerned about your daughter-in-law's health. She eats very little because she doesn't want to gain weight. Chinese women might want to be fat, but not Western women. Western women want to be slim, so they're always dieting. Slender women are considered feminine and attractive. In the West, if a woman gets fat, she feels she's lost all her charm."

"Is that so?" Bittersweet replied, crossing her arms over her chest and tilting her head to one side. "In China, a lot to eat signifies good fortune. When we see someone growing plump, we know that her luck has changed for the better. When we see a woman getting thin, she's down on her luck for sure."

Several weeks after Youlin had returned to China from America, Bittersweet came upon her son reading a telegram in the living room. When he finished reading it, he began to tear it.

"What are you doing?" Bittersweet cried.

"My father has invited me and my family to Peking. Everything has been prepared for us, including the former residence of Foreign Minister Yan Hui-ying, an opulent compound within the Imperial City, not far from Father's headquarters in the Forbidden City."

"And this makes you angry?" Bittersweet asked.

"There's no mention of your going to Peking in the invitation," Youlin replied, tearing the telegram a second time. "My father talks of national unity, but where is his sense of family unity? If you're not going, none of us are going."

"It's natural that your father wants to see you and his new daughter-in-law and grandchildren alone first," Bittersweet said. "I will follow in a few days."

"It's Dejie who doesn't want to see you at all," Youlin replied.

"A woman not to be taken lightly," Bittersweet murmured with a smile. "But you're wrong to blame your father. How many adversaries does he need? The Communists, Chiang and his cronies, and you, too?"

"Yes, yes," Youlin allowed. "I suppose you're right."

Both Youlin and Bittersweet knew that, as director of Peking Field Headquarters, Delin's jurisdiction extended over the Eleventh and the Twelfth War Zones. Theoretically, he possessed the power to supervise the military, financial, political, and party affairs of Hopeh, Shantung, Chahar, Suiyuan, and Jehol Provinces, as well as the cities of Peking, Tsingtao, and Tientsin. But the power he wielded was empty. Severed from his troops, he was where Chiang wanted him — suspended in mid-air, his feet not touching the ground, his head not touching the heavens. And China was where Delin had predicted it would be — engaged in a civil war that was tearing the nation apart, a civil war that was really a war of revolution where the people were clamoring not just for a new government but for a new social order.

"I will follow in a few days," Bittersweet told Youlin. "You've been away ten years. I bore your absence for that time without complaint, but I will not bear being separated from you and my new family now that you're home. Besides," she added, "I've never been to Peking. Rumor can't do it justice. I must see its size and grandeur myself to believe that such magnificence exists in this world."

Bittersweet had read that in the reign of the emperor Yung-lo, the eminent astrologer Lu Po designed the plans for the new capital based on the principles of magic. Peking was to have three heads and six arms and represent the mythical creature, No-cha. The three heads were Chienmen, the principal gate of the Tatar City; his large intestine was the once-open gutter in the West City; his navel was a certain well in the western section of the Forbidden City; his feet treading the Wind and Fire Wheel were the two gates facing the Black Temple and the Yellow Temple; and his red silk stomach protector was the vermilion walls of the Forbidden City.

Several days after Youlin and his family left for Peking, Bittersweet received a long letter from him.

> *My dear Mother,*
>
> *To say that the house that my father has rented for us is a mansion is almost to insult it. Servants quarters alone take up a dozen rooms. It's all very grand but so big that it's hard to feel comfortable here — all the more so since the general population is wanting in the bare necessities of life. There are shortages of both coal and food. Students, university chancellors, the commander of the Japanese prisoners of war — they all come to my father asking for rations. It's true that Chiang has sent officials from Nanking 'to help reorganize the city,' but they, in reality, grow fat on what they can steal from public funds. Then, they spy on Father and report back to the Son of Heaven. Father isn't the director of Peking Field Headquarters, but manager of Peking Rations Operations!*
>
> *He does, however, have his consolations. Many people who seek his help are educators, students, writers, and artists. Father gave the*

noted painter, Chi Pai-shih, a portion of his own personal rations, and the 80-year-old artist repaid him with food for the soul; he painted him a scroll of two red peaches, signifying a long and happy life. I know you'll find this hard to believe, but Father also holds a salon once every two weeks and invites people in the art and academic worlds to his office for informal conversation and tea. I well remember you telling me that Father was never one for formal education, of how he was always the red chair sitter in school! But now that his school days are behind him, he is eager and curious to learn.

There are, however, unwanted visitors in Peking. Terrorism is rampant in the old northern capital and 'midnight callers' — in truth, secret service police who like to extort money from their victims — arrest locals at will, accusing them of treason or collaboration with the Japanese or the Chinese Communists. Students at Peking Normal College are particularly vulnerable. There was one incident where plainclothesmen climbed through windows at the college, arrested several students, tortured them before killing them, and then threw their bodies into the streams outside the city.

When Father heard of this barbarism, he called the chief of police and informed him that such injustices must be stopped, or he would bear full responsibility for any such incidents in the future. The police chief had the audacity to smile but not the courage to speak. Clearly, he not only reports to Chiang and to Chiang alone, but he also takes his directives from him and from him alone.

As a result of student harassment by the secret police, many students, as well as professionals, are switching loyalties and going over to the Communists.

On a happier note, I must tell you how Father received us the moment we arrived in Peking. He came to the railroad station in a bullet-proof car! A gesture of politeness towards his new daughter-in-law, he told us, but I'm sure it was also out of fatherly protectiveness. He took us to the Peking Hotel for the most lavish banquet I've ever eaten. You'll be proud to know that salt-fried prawns were on the menu, and Madeleine shelled every single one that was on her plate. She did it with her teeth only and spit out the spanking-clean shells onto her plate as though she'd been doing so all her life.

But it was by serendipity, or wu-wei, that she captivated Father. Remember the heavy gold chain you sent her as a wedding gift?

When she was introduced to Dejie just before the banquet, Dejie gave her a jade pendant, in the form of a cicada, as a welcoming present. Madeleine was wearing your chain and thought that the pendant would go with the cheongsam *she was wearing, so she slipped the jade piece onto your chain. When Father saw your chain and Dejie's pendant around her neck (of course, Madeleine didn't realize the significance of the pairing she'd made), he was astounded by his daughter-in-law's subtle diplomacy! Whenever he could, he held her hand and patted it, saying, 'Hen piaoliang. Hen congming! Not only beautiful, but intelligent and wise!'*

As for me, however, I've been less successful in getting along with my father. A few days ago, I told him that I wanted you to come to Peking. He intimated that your being here would offend Dejie, and that it was better to wait till summer when Dejie would escape Peking's oppressive heat by heading for their country retreat in the Western Hills. I replied that it offended me that you hadn't come with us and to know that it was at Dejie's behest that you were still in Shanghai. I told him that if you weren't in Peking within a week, my family and I would return to Shanghai. So — I count on seeing you soon in Peking. If not, then I'll see you soon in Shanghai.
> *Your son,*
> *Youlin*

Three days later, a messenger delivered an envelope to Bittersweet. Inside was a first-class train ticket to Peking and a note from Delin. He said that he was anxiously awaiting her visit and was sorry that Dejie would not be on hand to greet her, since she was obliged to visit one of her girls' schools far from Peking.

When Bittersweet boarded the train the following morning, she smiled to herself and then snuggled back into her seat. She was already anticipating her destination. She closed her eyes and saw Delin, whom she hadn't seen for nearly four years, Youlin, Madeleine, Andrew, Lisa, and herself. All of them together — a family reunited.

Chapter 7
The Battle for Vice President
(1947)

"Such long corridors! So many huge empty rooms to pass through!" Madeleine remarked, when they finally reached her father-in-law's headquarters.

"One straight line through five hallways," Youlin said, as they neared yet another couple of sentries who opened the giant double doors for them. "A house built for ordinary mortals would have zigzagged from room to room to deflect evil spirits who can travel only in a straight line. The old belief was that only the deified emperor was powerful enough to withstand such spirits, and so the hallways leading to his throne room were arranged on a straight north-south line."

Bittersweet walked beside Youlin, keeping one eye on her two grandchildren and the other on Yifu and her new husband, a whining, weedy dolt of a man with stooped shoulders and a concave chest. He followed his flighty wife around as though chained to her and seemed always ready to do her bidding, though he wore an unrelieved expression of martyrdom in his soggy eyes.

Perhaps it would have been better if Delin chose offices other than these, Bittersweet thought, dwelling on Youlin's words as they passed through another set of sentries who uncrossed their bayonetted rifles and let the party pass through to the next long corridor. Delin might be a war hero but he was also a mortal. Evil spirits or no evil spirits, the times were such that it was foolhardy to tempt the living, let alone the spirit world. But to broach the subject was inappropriate, and even if she did bring it up, her husband would surely have told her that, as director of Peking Field Headquarters, he needed such an office within the Forbidden City to symbolize his authority — empty though that authority was.

"Ah!" Delin sighed with obvious pleasure, when they finally arrived. "So you've accepted my invitation to spend the day at the Summer Palace, have you?"

He stood up at his desk and opened his arms wide for his grandchildren. Despite the cajoling and admonitions of their parents, Lisa and Andrew hung back, for their grandfather, in his zealousness to show his affection for them, tended not only to squeeze them too tight but to pinch their cheeks hard enough to bring tears. Just the mention of the trip to Grampa's office had been met, earlier in the day, with sobs of protest, especially from little Lisa, whose cheeks were chubbier than Andrew's and thus easier to grab onto. But the promise of a mango ice cream cone had changed her mind.

Before going to the Summer Palace, Delin had his chauffeur stop at the Temple of Heaven where the emperor used to go to pray for good harvests and thus for a firm grip on the Mandate of Heaven.

"Not a single nail," he told Madeleine, who was absorbed by the beauty of the building, "and yet the building stands firm."

"Celestial is exactly what the Temple of Heaven is!" she murmured, enchanted by the color of the glazed tiles on the roof. "I must make myself a *cheongsam* that shade of heavenly blue."

A half-dozen children carrying colored flags in their hands raced around the circular building. Above them flew six pigeons, each following the flag of its master.

"Where is the music coming from?" Bittersweet asked, looking up and shading her eyes with one hand. "Certainly not from those pigeons. Pigeons don't sing so merrily."

"Indeed, they do," Delin countered. "Boys in Peking tie tiny bamboo whistles together, then tie them to the pigeons — the small whistles are called *hu-lu;* the larger ones are called *shao-tzu.* They're made of as few as three to as many as thirteen pipes clamped together and capable of sounding just as many notes. When the pigeons follow their master's flag, they play the tunes you're hearing now."

"How very clever! Look!" she said, naming one type of pigeon, and then another. "A Square-Edged Unicorn! And there! A Striped Sandal! And the rest seem to be Magpie Flowers."

"Clever in more ways than one," Delin continued. "Pigeons carried messages through enemy lines for us during the War of Resistance and carry them today against the Communists. An eminent historian I know told me that in imperial times, particularly in times of famine, birds like these were taught to fly to the imperial granaries where they swallowed as much of the finest rice their artificially-distended crops could hold. Back home, doused with alum and water, they disgorged their bounty which was then washed and sold . . . no doubt at black-market prices!"

"Clever enough," Bittersweet said, suitably impressed. "But we Kweilinese have taught our cormorants to catch fish, and because they can't swallow their prey for the ring around their neck, there's no disgorging or cleaning necessary."

Delin chuckled appreciatively and slipped his arm through Bittersweet's.

"You haven't forgotten your old hometown, have you?" he said. "Nor I my dream of returning to Dragon's Head to take up farming again when our nation's no longer at war."

"Is it a possible dream or an impossible dream?" Bittersweet asked, half-joking.

Though she would never say so, Bittersweet longed for her husband to renounce politics and return home to a more peaceful life. And though he would never admit it, she knew that he knew. They walked in silence, looking up now and then at the singing pigeons wheeling overhead. It was clear to her that Delin's position was a precarious one, that he was fighting two enemies on two separate fronts, that to one of them, who was blood brother and leader of the nation, he owed his allegiance, and that, of the two enemies, certainly the Son of Heaven was the more treacherous. Most of the generals under Delin's command were Chiang's lackeys and would never fight under Delin's orders.

For several months, Delin, who enjoyed national popularity, had wanted to resign from his ineffectual Peking post. Chiang had put him there to garner praise for himself when things went well and to lay blame on Delin when things went awry. Lately, there was much more to criticize than to praise: Kuomintang troops were bogged down in Manchuria, the north China plain was in Communist hands, and inflation was the worst it had ever been, even during the War of Resistance. The hills outside Peking were crawling with Communist guerrillas, and Delin could almost count the days till the old northern capital fell to the revolutionaries. As a Chinese patriot, to surrender the historic city to the Communists was unthinkable; as Director of Peking Field Headquarters, to abandon it was unlawful. Two paths lay open to him: either he defy Chiang and take a more active part in the government, or he withdraw from the political arena entirely.

"You've told me yourself that you're powerless in your present position," Bittersweet said after a long and thoughtful pause. "Your son has returned to China and brought with him his beautiful family. Haven't you done as much as any man can do for his country? Haven't you done more? Your entire adult life has been lived on the battlefield. Even the most valiant warrior takes off his armor, leaves the battlefield, and returns home."

"You're right," he said, taking from his wife's words what he chose to understand of them. "There are only two choices open to me: get out entirely or play a more important role in governing China."

At the Summer Palace, Delin seemed lost in his private thoughts, though the scenery was as beautiful as could be found anywhere in China. The setting was a man-made lake meant to resemble West Lake in Hangchow, the spot which, for centuries, was the favored destination of literati in search of inspiration. His reverie, however, was cut short by the antics of Yifu who had ducked under the velvet rope, climbed up the steps leading to the magnificent throne in which the Dowager Empress used to sit, and plunked herself down.

"Someone come take a picture of me!" she shouted, assuming an imperious pose. "How I'd love to live the life of Old Tigerwhiskers!"

"Get up from that throne this instant!" Delin called up to her angrily. "Behave like the proper young lady you were brought up to be, or I'll climb up there and bring you down myself!

Pouting, Yifu did as her brother commanded and left her perch to rejoin her family.

"This girl has been spoiled," Delin scolded Bittersweet. "You must manage her. The highest praise one may give to a young woman is silence. A young woman's reputation is unblemished when no one has a single word to say either for or against her. Now they may say that Yifu assumed the license to misbehave because of our family's status. Not only is Yifu's reputation at stake, but that of the entire family."

"Don't you think that your comments are better directed to your sister's husband?" Bittersweet replied courteously but firmly. "It is he who must manage her now. My duty towards your sister was while she was a maiden. My duty is done."

Delin lowered his eyes. It was a gentle rebuke, but one with a deeper meaning. In saying that her familial duty towards his sister was done, Bittersweet intimated that his military and political duties towards China were also done, that he was obligated no more.

Yifu tiptoed up to Bittersweet when Delin had wandered on ahead and whispered, "From now on, Ninth, wherever we go in Peking, let's leave my brother at home. He spoils all our fun."

Yifu's concern was unnecessary, for Delin spent little time with his family as it was, and even that time was about to diminish. After an absence of more than two weeks, Delin appeared at their door, dressed for travel, with two bodyguards beside him and a chauffeured limousine outside in the driveway. Quickly, the entire family was roused to say their farewells. Andrew and Lisa cried to be awakened and were taken straight back to their beds once their grandfather had held them, kissed them, and pinched their cheeks.

"I'm going to Nanking and Kweilin for a week or so. When I return, I'll have very important news to tell you — news that will affect us all. I have only a few minutes," he said, looking at his watch, "and I'd like to spend them with my son."

Bittersweet and Madeleine immediately withdrew, but Bittersweet lay awake in bed, listening for the sound of a motor revving up. Hearing the crunch of gravel under the car's tires, she went to the window and saw Youlin standing at the edge of the driveway, his eyes following the limousine out the courtyard and into the quiet *hutong*. His shoulders and chest rose then fell in a great sigh, and she wondered what Delin had said to him to provoke such resignation.

The next morning, she found her son waving goodbye to Madeleine and the children who were going to picnic in the Western Hills.

"Why aren't you joining them?" Bittersweet called to her son.

Youlin walked over to the artificial pond and began to feed the goldfish bits of steamed bread.

"We've survived Peking's broiling summer sun, and today's the first autumn-like day," Bittersweet noted, coming up beside him and tearing off a piece of the bread, then breaking it into bits and feeding the fish, "a perfect day for a picnic in the country."

"Or for feeding goldfish," Youlin replied.

They both smiled.

"Peking is certainly a beautiful city," Youlin said, "with many sights to see. But Madeleine, the children, and I have seen all there is to see as visitors, for visitors are what we are here. Madeleine and I have a family to raise and I, a family to support. We feel we should return to Shanghai and settle down. Here, we're merely guests of my father. We want to live our own lives."

Bittersweet nodded her head sadly. Her son's words sounded familiar. They rang of Solin's former sentiments.

"When are you thinking of returning to Shanghai?"

"Just as soon as Father returns from Kweilin," Youlin said with a finality which he emphasized by vigorously brushing the crumbs from his hands. "An Import-Export Control Commission has just been established in Shanghai. He'd like me to supervise it."

Bittersweet recalled the depth of Youlin's sigh the previous night.

"Father's always wanted me to work in government, and now . . ." Youlin sighed again, this time in an effort at self-control, ". . . he'll have his wish."

"Is it not also your own?" his mother inquired.

"I'm grateful to Father," Youlin said.

But the hard expression in his eyes and the rigidity of his body told Bittersweet that the commission in Shanghai was not his wish. "Your father tells me that China will be saved by science and technology," Bittersweet said, "and by commerce and industry. Certainly he is right. By working for the commission, you'll be honoring your father's wishes, doing your duty towards your country, and earning a good livelihood for your family."

"That would all be fine, Mother," Youlin replied, his voice rising, "if it were my choice, not my father's, if I had taken the initiative to obtain the position, not my father. It's my father who has done everything! Paved the way for me so that it's the only path I can tread! Don't I have a say in what I do, or do I only acquiesce to what others decide for me? Can I both stand on my own two feet and hold my head up high as a man, and drop to my knees and knock my forehead against the ground as a filial son?"

Bittersweet looked at Youlin with alarm. These were Solin's words, Solin's sentiments, but this time they were coming from her own son. "What father doesn't try to help his children on their path in life?" she said. "That is his paternal obligation."

"Remember that story you told me when I was a child?" Youlin asked.

"There were many stories I told you as a child," Bittersweet recalled with a smile.

"The story about the farmer's son and the fish he caught in the dead of winter that saved his father's life."

"Yes, I remember!" Bittersweet cried with pleasure. "The story was

307

about filial piety! Actually, I'd forgotten until you just now reminded me of it."

"Had you? It's one I've never forgotten," Youlin replied with a sardonic smile, as he walked towards the house, "though it would have been better for me if I had. In fact, it would have been better for me if you had never told it to me at all."

Bittersweet started to reach out to him but, thinking better of her action, she dropped her arm to her side and let her son's name die on her lips.

As the Kuomintang cause in the War of Revolution worsened, so did the situation in Peking regarding the violence and abuses of Chiang's secret police. Even Delin was not exempt. In fact, as the Communists encroached upon the city with every passing day, Delin's movements became more and more guarded, until finally, to escape the surveillance of Chiang's henchmen, he visited his family only late at night.

In addition to the incidents of political harrassment, there was widespread social unrest. Riots broke out at shops which were out of merchandise or those charging exorbitant prices for what items remained on their shelves. There were runs on all the banks, and people, when they went out shopping, carted their money around in wheelbarrows. The gold and silver notes piled high within had become that worthless. The streets teemed with people who, with the last devaluation, had lost their enormous fortunes or their meager savings. The Beggars Guild — which referred to the old and time-honored profession as "living off the streets" and whose motto was "aggressiveness in begging and strength in numbers" — found a great pool of people who, if they did not seek membership, were certainly eligible for it.

Theirs, the beggars insisted, was not only a profession like any other, with strict rules and regulations, protocol and hierarchy, but also a tradition with imperial roots, for one emperor was a beggar before ascending to the Dragon Throne. Once this beggar had risen to imperial status, he bestowed his blessing on the beggars of Peking and granted them special dispensations, such as the right to beg at every door and elect a leader-for-life whose obligations included commanding those beggars under him and mediating any disputes among them. Beggars had to be trained properly, learning to appraise a potential benefactor on the spot, to determine his status, and to address him by the correct title, such as "Great Master" or "Your Ladyship." Women and children beggars had to weep in a certain pitch and rhythm, while male beggars had to shout wildly and demonstrate their sores and deformities. There were certain streets and street corners for Sword Slappers, who hit their chests with the broad side of two long swords until their flesh was red and welted; Nail Headers, who tapped nails into their skulls with a brick if their chosen patron refused to give money on the spot; One-Eyed Dragons who pretended to be totally blind but who had the use of at least one eye; Rollers, whose hands and feet were totally deformed and who would lie howling and thrashing about in the mud; Moving Carts, who, being paralyzed, lay on wooden carts which were pulled along by more fortunate beggar companions; and Rock Carriers, male beggars who carried female invalids on their backs.

Madeleine who, at the beginning of her stay in Peking, had wandered about the narrow *hutongs* and along the broad avenues at will, now only went out when it was absolutely necessary, so as to avoid the heart-rending sight of the many beggars. Unlike her daughter-in-law, Bittersweet accepted the beggars as part of city life. In fact, she enjoyed hearing their well-wishing songs of "Turtle, crawl to your door; your wealth will soon soar," and "Madam took pity on me; sons and grandsons you'll soon have." And she grimaced to hear verse such as, "Don't give me money? I don't care! Save it for your coffin!" Curse or blessing, begging was part of Peking's way of life, part of life itself.

Amid spiraling inflation, Communist control of the countryside, and the breakdown of negotiations between the Kuomintang and the Communists, news of a national election was announced in the capital, then throughout the country. The contest infused a new sense of hope in the dispirited nation. Chiang was assured of the presidency and quickly announced his candidacy. The real contest lay among the candidates for the vice-presidency.

Late one night, Bittersweet was awakened by Dashao informing her that "the General" was waiting to see his family in the reception room. Within seconds, all the members of the household were awake, their robes sashed about their middles, their faces washed of sleep. After Delin kissed his grandchildren and exchanged greetings with his daughter-in-law, he asked everyone in the room, including his body-guards, to withdraw except Bittersweet and Youlin.

"I've decided to run for vice president," Delin announced to them both. "That's why I went to Nanking and Kweilin — to hear Chiang's response to my decision and that of my colleagues Pai and Hwang."

Both Bittersweet and Youlin remained silent.

"Surprisingly, Chiang didn't oppose my decision," Delin continued. "He said that the upcoming election was the first step towards democracy in China and that he had no prejudices against or preference for any candidate — so long as the candidate was eligible according to the Chinese constitution.

"But when I arrived in Kweilin, Pai was less encouraging. 'Chiang will never support you,' he told me. 'No matter what he tells you to your face, he'll work against you once your back is turned.'

"'Go into regional politics,' Governor Hwang advised me, when I finally got a chance to speak to him. 'That's where you have friends working for you, not adversaries working against you. Why should you be covered with the stench of the goat without getting a bite of the meat?'

"To both Pai and Hwang, I argued that the Kuomintang government is reactionary to the core. The Chinese people might fear the Communists, but they despise the Kuomintang. It's not a change of regime they want: its reform from within." Delin sat back in his chair. "And reform is what I mean to give them. We did it in Kwangsi. It's time to extend it to the nation. The more pressure Chiang, his Whampoa boys, and his CC Clique put on me, the better chance I stand to win. On January 8th, I plan to announce my candidacy for the vice-presidency. I know for certain of four others who'll announce their candidacy as well: Yu Yu-jen, president of the control *yuan;* Cheng Chien, former commander of the Sixth Army and former favorite of Chiang; Mo Te-hui, a senior politician from Manchuria; and Hsu Su-lin, the Social Democratic Party's nominee." Delin sat forward in his chair, gripping its arms and looking intently at Youlin. "All of them will converge on Peking to announce their candidacy. But I will announce mine from Shanghai. Shanghai is the center of the country's communications system, and Shanghai is where you'll be heading up the Import-Export Control Commission. I plan to hold a press conference, a press conference such as this country has never seen, a press conference such as you've described to me from your years abroad. I want it to be in the American-style, and I hope that you, with your background in political science and government, will help me organize and orchestrate it."

"I'll do whatever I can to help you," Youlin answered unhesitatingly. "China clamors for internal reform."

Having received the reply he anticipated, Delin stood up. Youlin and his mother also came to their feet. "If the coming election is conducted according to due process of law, then I stand an excellent chance of becoming the first duly elected vice president of a newly democratic, reform-minded China."

Within a matter of days, Bittersweet, Youlin, and his family headed home to Shanghai to prepare for Delin's vice-presidential campaign. Before they left, Delin received his son's promise to manage the Import-Export Control Commission which would be inaugurated soon after the elections; and Youlin in return had obtained his father's reluctant consent that, after a trial period of six months, if he found the post unsatisfactory, he could leave it without explanation. Before he flew to Shanghai, Delin received another promise — this time, from Chiang who flew to Peking to personally deliver the message that Delin would never be vice president under him.

"The party controls the government," Chiang informed Delin. "The party therefore sets the guidelines for the election, including those regarding the eligibility of candidates."

"Under the Chinese constitution, any male citizen is eligible to run for any office," Delin reminded Chiang. "Since the constitution contains the laws of the land, my candidacy is perfectly legal."

Chiang smiled, but his red face indicated just how furious he was. "But your candidacy will divide the party and throw the country into chaos," Chiang said. "If you truly love your country, you'll withdraw from the race and save both the Kuomintang and China from disintegration. I tell you this for your own good as your blood brother, and for the good of the nation as a true patriot."

"The party is already a shambles. The country is already in chaos," Delin answered. "I genuinely believe that if I am elected vice president I will make some order of this mess. And have you forgotten? You, my blood brother, gave me your blessing to enter the race in Nanking weeks ago. Had you tried to dissuade me then, I might have abandoned the idea. Now it's too late. My campaign's already begun."

"If you were able to put a halt to it then," Chiang said, "you're able to stop it now."

"You've been to Peking opera," Delin said. "Then you know that once the curtain is raised, the performance must play to its conclusion."

Chiang's smile hardened into a grimace. "I will not support you, and without my support, you'll never win."

"I may win," Delin replied calmly. "Three factors will be decisive. First, we're at a critical stage in our dealings with the Chinese Communist Party. Second, they now control not only most of the countryside but major cities. They're even tightening their grip about Peking proper. But the most decisive factor may well be popular support. I've been called a *chun-tse* — an *honnête homme,* as the French say, and I have friends in all circles. If you don't support me, other people will."

"We'll see about that," Chiang declared, clicking his teeth to emphasize the point.

True to his word and knowing that there was only one potential candidate who stood a good chance of defeating Delin, Chiang appealed to Sun Fo, Sun Yat-sen's libertine son, to enter the vice-presidential race. Sun, a Kwangtung native, would steal away some of the southern votes that Delin would otherwise be assured of. The only obstacle Chiang faced was the fact that Sun had no intention of running for vice president, a position he referred to as a "cold bench" with no real political power.

"To accept the position of vice president, I'd have to step down from the presidency of the legislative *yuan*," Sun told Chiang when the latter came to see him. "Why would I want to do that, when the presidency of the legislative *yuan* is the more powerful position? Besides, organizing and financing a political campaign is an expensive proposition. I hardly have the funds to conduct the kind of campaign it would take to beat Li."

But Chiang *Tai-tai,* whom her husband sent in his place for a second appeal, had a solution for Sun's predicament. "On my husband's behalf, I've come to tell you that he'll gladly provide the funds necessary to mount your campaign," she promised, "and that, if elected to the vice-presidency of the nation, you need not relinquish the presidency of the legislative *yuan.*"

"Madam, I am honored by your husband's magnanimity," Sun answered with an obsequious bow, "but a certain document containing the laws of our land is less generous. According to the constitution, I may not hold both positions simultaneously."

But when Chiang came to see Sun for a second time, he assured the reluctant candidate that the constitution would pose no obstacle; the weight of Chiang's endorsement and the campaign money he would supply would override it.

"Enter the race as a dark horse," Chiang suggested to the suddenly pliant Sun, "and as my favorite. You're sure to win."

From the moment Sun Fo announced his candidacy and joined the five others in the vice-presidential race, the newspapers and radio stations, almost all of which were controlled by Chiang, carried interviews and articles extolling Sun's virtues. They likened him to his illustrious father — whom he resembled neither physically nor morally — while they denounced Delin as a regionalist renegade who was bent upon destroying party and national unity.

All the negative publicity worried Youlin, but Bittersweet felt oddly reassured. "You might view the negative articles and broadcasts about your father as a bad sign," she told her son, "but I see them as a good omen. His popularity and chances for winning must be very great if Chiang is going to such lengths to ensure his defeat."

Only one publisher — Pao of the *National Salvation Daily*, who was nicknamed "Big Cannon" since his surname was pronounced like the Chinese word for cannon and his opinions were known far and wide — dared to support Delin's candidacy. Several generals, Sun Fo supporters, irritated by his praising of Delin and criticism of Sun, broke into his newspaper offices late one night. They hacked away at his printing presses with axes, upended the ink pots, and tore the newsprint to shreds. In the midst of the destruction, Big Cannon suddenly appeared on the second floor landing with a loaded pistol.

"Any one of you vandals who dares mount these stairs," he announced, cocking the trigger, "be prepared to meet your ancestors."

The "Letter from the Editor" which appeared in the following morning's edition of the *National Salvation Daily* apologized for the paper's brief format, a format necessitated by "intruders in the night bringing the will of the highest authority."

"These generals," the editorial continued, "who had, by their own account, fought so gallantly against the Japanese Imperial Army, failed to subdue a single Cannon, contenting themselves with muttering insults before slinking back to general headquarters to file their report."

The Peace Hotel in Shanghai was another target for Chiang's disciples. In the hopes of bribing the national assembly delegates staying there to vote for Sun, they gathered in the lobby and outside the building. With those who were willing to exchange their vote for money or the promise of a political post, they struck a bargain; to those who were reluctant, they made veiled threats. Cognizant of these tactics, Delin decided to hold his press conference in the hotel right across the street from the Peace Hotel. Here, with print journalists and news broadcasters gathered from around the country, he declared to the nation and to the world: "If the coming election is conducted according to due process of law, I will be the first vice president of a newly democratic, reform-minded China."

Together with Youlin, Madeleine, and Dashao, Bittersweet listened to the press conference on the radio. She sat at the edge of her chair, leaning forward to catch Delin's words between the intermittent bouts of static from the vibrating box.

"You spoke very well," she congratulated her husband when he passed by her house a few hours later.

"Did you think so?" he asked enthusiastically. "It was like addressing my men — calling them to action."

On April 19, 1948, Chiang, running unopposed, became the first elected president of China. A day later, the national assembly announced the names of the six candidates for vice president. Three days after that, the first ballots for the position were cast. It was the first democratic national election in Chinese history. When the ballots were counted, Delin had garnered the most votes — 754. Sun Fo was second with 559. None of the six candidates, however, polled enough votes to constitute a majority but, as if to provide a second cause for celebration, April 23rd also marked Delin's grandchildren's second birthday.

"Andrew and Lisa are children of good fortune," Delin said in a telephone call to Madeleine. "Raise them well."

The following day, after the results of the second ballot were known, the three candidates who had garnered the fewest votes dropped out of the race. Delin still led among the remaining three by a slight margin — 1,163 votes to Sun's 945.

"Close . . . too close," Delin worried aloud.

Fearing the potential for violence, he called a meeting of his aides where he proposed a strategy of "advance through retreat." He then called a press conference where he told a shocked nation, "I hereby announce my withdrawal from the vice-presidential race due to invisible but tangible pressures which are jeopardizing these free elections and threatening them with violence."

By withdrawing from the race, Delin hoped to coerce Sun Fo into doing the same. Were Sun to do otherwise, he risked being accused of indifference to a rigged election. The public outcry against Delin's withdrawal would not only force Sun Fo and the third, and badly trailing, candidate to issue similar statements and drop out of the race, it would also force Chiang to halt his campaign of payoffs and veiled threats to the national assembly delegates. Then, the elections would have to proceed along legal channels. Still, with no vice-presidential candidates running, the bewildered national assembly ordered a temporary recess. Beaten, Chiang phoned Delin and asked him to re-enter the race, this time with his full support.

On the third ballot, the one candidate unable to garner the minimum number of votes dropped out, leaving Delin and Sun. A day later, April 29, 1948, on the fourth and final ballot, the vice-presidency of China was decided: Delin — 1,438 votes; Sun — 1,295.

When Chiang heard the results, he kicked the radio he was listening to, shattering it to pieces. Out of frustration, he then ordered his chauffeur to drive him to Sun Yat-sen's mausoleum outside Nanking. In the heat of his anger, Chiang barked contradictory orders at his driver, making him go this way and that, and leading his fleet of would-be protectors on a bizarre chase that concluded with one of the cars plowing into a tree.

In Kweilin, on the other hand, the day following the vice-presidential election was declared a holiday, and the fireworks intended for Lunar New Year's Day were set off in wild celebration of the hometown hero's victory.

And in Shanghai, as happy as Bittersweet was for Delin, her euphoria was tempered by the anxiety she felt during the past few weeks and by her understanding that the political arena was merely a different kind of battleground. Only the weapons are different, she thought, and they are no less lethal.

Chapter 8
Pillar to Post
(1948)

Reluctantly, Delin closed his office in Peking. He was loathe to leave the northern capital, since the Communists were drawing close and there were no Kuomintang forces to stave them off. Indeed, three days after his departure for Nanking, the enemy besieged the city. To prevent the destruction of the majestic old capital, the mayor surrendered on the spot.

Delin's sense of foreboding was further substantiated upon his arrival in Nanking. The vice-presidency, in which he had placed all his personal hopes and his hopes for the nation, was a powerless position. Not only did Chiang keep Delin from participating in affairs of war or state, he made sure that Delin never even knew about them. Every official in the new 'democratic' régime was a disciple of the Son of Heaven. These disciples paid Delin's directives lip service, but, at Chiang's behest, refused to carry them out.

Even more discouraging, his own son wasn't following his orders. On his way to Nanking, Delin stopped in Shanghai to visit Youlin and his family. His happiness at the reunion was dampened by his son's hesitancy to take up his post as "an official in this corrupt government," as Youlin called it.

"I'm hardly asking you to be a government official," his father answered, "only to manage the Import-Export Control Commission, only to observe and take note. If you do, I'm sure you'll uncover sources of corruption. Their discovery will be the first step towards their elimination." He put his hand on Youlin's shoulder and looked into his son's eyes. "I've never given up hope that you would contribute to China's welfare, if not in the military, if not in government, then in commerce and industry. Business and enterprise will be China's salvation. It would mean so much to me, especially now that I'm in a position to help the country, if you would work in her behalf as well."

Youlin turned his eyes aside.

"I'm asking you to do something for China, something you promised to do. I'm asking you again. Still you refuse me?"

Youlin continued to evade his father's gaze.

"How then, when my own son refuses me, can I ask anyone else to do the job?"

Youlin looked back at his father. "I was thinking of a story my mother told me when I was a little boy . . . the story about the boy, his father, the frozen river, and the fish. Do you remember the story?" Youlin asked.

Delin shook his head slightly — mostly in annoyance that his son should interject a fairy tale into so serious a discussion.

"I must have forgotten it," he said, dismissively.

"I won't refuse to do what you ask of me, Father," Youlin said finally. "I keep my promises. But my promise to work for the Import-Export Control Commission also contained a qualification. If after six months I'm dissatisfied with the job, I can quit. If we agree on that point, then I'm ready to begin work tomorrow."

Youlin spent his first two days as manager of the Import-Export Control Commission in enforced, and almost complete, idleness. On the morning of the third day, he went to see the director of the organization: perhaps they had no record of his employment? On the contrary, the director informed him, grinning and bowing, everyone at the commission knew that the son of the Vice President of China had joined the staff. Rest assured, the director told him with a servile smile, he would be given an assignment any day now.

A week passed and still there was no assignment, thus Youlin had plenty of time to "observe and take note" as his father had asked him to do. As far as Youlin could make out, the work being accomplished at the commission consisted of sitting around the office, smoking cigarettes, drinking tea, reading the papers, and chatting. Some of the employees sifted through piles of papers on their desks and produced routine correspondence, but the great majority merely waited for the day to end so they could go home and the week to finish so they could collect their paychecks. Their sloth and indifference infuriated Youlin.

"It's clear why I haven't received any assignment," Youlin phoned his father after a month had passed, "and why no assignment will be forthcoming. My colleagues, if I can use the term, have no intention of allowing, let alone helping, me to uncover sources of corruption in the office when they are the very ones perpetrating it. They smile at me and are extremely courteous and correct with me — a mask for their sabotage and subterfuge. They're excluding and isolating me. For a month now, I've merely been wasting my time. I wish to submit my resignation."

"Resign and you play into their hands," Delin told his son. "Be patient. Remember your promise: six months."

But after another five months had passed, Youlin was only more convinced of his ineffectiveness at the commission. He'd become so miserable that his unhappiness was beginning to undermine his family life, his prime source of contentment. Nothing, he vowed, could be allowed to do that.

Finally, he wired his father: "I've kept my promise. There's still no assignment. I'm tendering my resignation and devoting my best efforts to the welfare of my family."

Delin wired back a terse: "I accept your decision."

On his next visit to Shanghai, Delin called on Bittersweet. Youlin, he was both relieved and disappointed to know, was in Hong Kong.

"I accepted our son's decision," he told his wife, "but I don't understand it."

"You and Youlin are so different," Bittersweet said. "As different as a father and son can be."

"We're the same flesh and blood," Delin protested, "two interconnected links in the same chain of life."

"But made of different metal," Bittersweet noted, "each strong in its own way and weak in another. Your first love is China. Youlin's first love is his wife and children. Which love is weak and without merit? Which is strong and to be commended? You would have relished the chance to take on the Import-Export Control Commission, to expose and punish the corruption there. You'd have laughed at the subversive tactics that wounded Youlin. You would have welcomed the opportunity to outlast your adversaries, to unmask your enemies. But Youlin thrives on peace and must have it. You strive for peace but can live surrounded by adversity."

Delin drummed his fingers on his knees, unable to refute Bittersweet's words.

"So what does our son want to do now?" he asked her irritably. "Now that he's free to decide for himself," he added.

"Youlin went to Hong Kong for business, not pleasure. He's interested in buying a factory that manufactures electrical parts. He thinks Hong Kong might serve not only as a market for the parts but as the assembly point for the finished products. These products could then be sold to America, around the world . . . even to China."

Delin's lips parted, and he smiled slightly. "Is that so?" he murmured, somewhat chastened. "My son . . . an entrepreneur?"

"Youlin believes that Hong Kong is the perfect place to set up a factory," Bittersweet continued, encouraged. "It's right on China's doorstep; it's politically and economically stable. What's more, Youlin won't have to contend with being the vice president's son, with the accusations of nepotism and *guanxi* that have burdened him so. He'll be free to run his enterprise relying solely on his own merits and abilities."

Delin started to say something, but Bittersweet was not done with her explanation.

"There are other pluses. Labor is cheap in Hong Kong. Youlin understands the Chinese mentality and way of doing business. For all these reasons, he wants to open a factory and an office there."

"And abandon China," Delin said, saddened by the thought.

"And leave China," Bittersweet corrected him. She reached forward and placed her hand on Delin's sleeve. "Ever since Youlin was born, your hope has been that he'd work for the good of the country, if not in the military, then in government, if not in government, then in industry or commerce. And here he is, leaving for the British crown colony of Hong Kong, the very island your father so detested as a bastion of Western imperialism! It's ironic, isn't it? But isn't it also just possible that by leaving China, Youlin might be doing China good — and precisely in the fields of industry and commerce that you suggested for him? His factory, once established, will bring foreign investment to China. That is our son's wish and intention. In his own way, Youlin is doing what he can for China. Be happy for our son — and be proud."

"Then you, too, will be leaving China?" he asked, after mulling over his wife's words. He slipped his arm from under her hand and placed his palm on top of her wrist.

"As the general of an army, you must follow your men in order to lead them. As the mother of my son and the head of my household, I must follow Youlin and his family wherever they go."

But Delin, though still a general, was the vice president of his

319

country, and no longer led his army or even followed them, though there were innumerable times when he wished he could. Rather, like Youlin at the Import-Export Control Commission, Delin continued to be isolated from the responsibilities of his office as Chiang and his lackeys built thicker and thicker walls around him, cutting him off from his former colleagues and the affairs of the nation.

By the spring of 1948, the Chinese Communists controlled not only all the countryside but three isolated cities. When they threatened Mukden, Chiang flew there personally to command its defense.

"Any area where Chiang directs our troops, rest assured it will be lost to the Communists!" Delin had muttered in frustration to his aide.

Days later, not only were Kuomintang troops forced to abandon Mukden, but all of Manchuria was lost, and with it 300,000 of the KMT's best soldiers. It was the worst defeat in Kuomintang history.

Emboldened by their latest and greatest victory, the Chinese Communist Party (CCP) issued their list of first-class war criminals: Chiang's name headed the list; Delin's name appeared right after it. Soon afterwards, in an unprecedented show of humility, Chiang, dressed in a simple black Chinese gown, arrived on Delin's doorstep. Heretofore, the Son of Heaven had preferred to send for his subjects and wear his bemedalled military uniform at all meetings.

"What should we do, now that we've lost Manchuria and Suchow?" Chiang asked his vice president.

Delin took a breath. Manchuria needn't have fallen to the Communists, he thought, but Chiang divided the three northern provinces into nine provinces to prevent any single Chinese governor from becoming too powerful. His plan had worked: the entire area was weakened — to the benefit of the Chinese Communists. On another occasion, before the fall of Suchow, Chiang decided to establish two war zones instead of one between the Yellow and the Yangtze Rivers. Delin had told Chiang that, from a strategic point of view, the region between the two rivers formed one continuous plain — a geographical unit whose communications were facilitated by three railroads. To cut the plain in two was contradictory to its innate topography and would hamper transportation. But Chiang had, of course, disregarded Delin's advice.

"Months ago," Delin began, tired even as he started to speak, "I proposed the reunification of the two war zones between the Yellow and the Yangtze Rivers."

"No, no, no," Chiang interrupted, agitated. "That was then. This is now. What should we do now?"

Delin raised a weary eyebrow; the situation must be very bad for Chiang to be asking for advice.

"Resist the Communists to the end," he answered. "What other course is there?"

"Ah!" Chiang exclaimed, his gray eyes lighting up. "But there is another course. Negotiate with them for peace."

"But you've attempted that," Delin reminded Chiang, "and they refused to sit down at the negotiating table."

"With *me*," Chiang emphasized, "but with *you*, the situation will be different. The Communists would accept a cease-fire with you."

"Is there that much difference between first-class war criminal #1 and first-class war criminal #2?" Delin asked. "I think not."

"As much as there is between president of China and vice president of China," Chiang replied, narrowing his eyes. "Therefore, in the name of the Kuomintang Party and in the interests of the Chinese people, I will resign. You shall take my place. . . ." He smiled, and when his false teeth loosened from his gums with the gesture, he clicked them back into place with a grin. "You, Brother Delin, shall be president of China."

The situation, then, must be past saving, Delin thought. The Son of Heaven hasn't come to discuss war strategy at all, but to place on my shoulders the overwhelming burden of the Kuomintang defeat and the surrender of China to the Communists.

"I must humbly refuse your offer," Delin said, his eyes downcast, ostensibly in humility but actually to conceal his awareness of Chiang's treachery. "Surely I am incapable of accomplishing what you have failed to achieve."

Chiang stiffened and his eyes widened in feigned surprise. "You refuse the office? Previously I tried to dissuade you from running for the vice-presidency, but you chose to disregard my advice. You said that your candidacy was legal under the constitution. Now I'm going to resign, and under the constitution you will have to succeed me — whether you like it or not!"

Delin sat forward in his chair, holding Chiang firmly in his sober gaze. "This is not the first time that you've resigned from office," he said, "temporarily. If I recall correctly, the first time was in 1927 with the collapse of the Wuhan front during the Northern Expedition. The second time was. . . ."

"Why dig up history, Brother Delin? This time not only am I resigning from office, I am retiring from politics for five years — a full term of office. I'm surrendering the presidency to you." He sighed wearily and rolled his gray eyes before looking back at his blood brother. "I want only to be an ordinary citizen. What do you say, then? I've conceded all that you could possibly want of me — even the highest position in the land. And what with the nation praying for peace negotiations between the KMT and the CCP, and you the only one who can obtain peace for them, what can you say?"

As Spring Festival and the beginning of another year approached, there was little merrymaking. The entire country prayed for peace, yet peace depended on the Communists, and the Communists weren't interested in talk or compromise. Instead, the CCP sent the *Eight Demands* to the Chinese people. The *Eight Demands* included punishment of all war criminals; annulment of the bogus constitution; abolition of the present "legitimate" Kuomintang government and its institutions; confiscation of bureaucratic capital; introduction of agrarian reform; abolition of treaties that betrayed the nation; convocation of a political conference without the participation of reactionary elements; and establishment of a democratic coalition government.

Given these impossible demands and the Communists' swift occupation of all of central and eastern China north of the Yangtze, the outlook for the new year looked very bleak. Inflation was the highest it had ever been. Riots broke out in the major cities where people clamored for government reform, an end to corruption, peace negotiations with the Communists, and Chiang's immediate retirement. In response, Chiang called an emergency meeting in Nanking where he delivered his final speech as President of China. Invited to be present at Chiang's farewell address, Delin listened to the words by which the position of the highest office in the land was transferred to him: "In the hope that the Communists may be moved by my earnestness and that the people's suffering may be relieved," Chiang read tearfully from a document, "from January 21, 1949 Vice President Li will succeed the president to exercise his duties and powers in accordance with article 49 of the constitution which provides, 'In the event the president is for any reason unable to perform his functions, his duties and powers shall be exercised by the vice president.'"

While high officials wept aloud, Chiang handed Delin the document for his signature.

"But where did you mention your retirement or even your resignation?" Delin whispered.

"How can you quibble over incidentals at a time like this?" Sun Fo, who stood behind Chiang, hissed vehemently. "Just sign the document! Where is your sense of propriety — your sense of *li?*" he asked, emphasizing the last word and taking great pleasure in doing so. "Didn't you hear him say that you were succeeding him as president? How many guarantees do you need?"

"Yes, but article 49 of the constitution states. . . ," Delin began.

The wailing resumed with even greater pitch and intensity. Article 49 of the constitution stated, "in the event that the president's office becomes vacant," and not as Chiang had read, "in the event that the president is for any reason unable to perform his functions." Chiang, after all, was hardly incapacitated. Still, putting his concerns aside, for China's situation was critical, Delin signed his name to two copies of the document and pressed his personal seal to them. Only after he left the conference did he read what he had signed, a document which differed critically from what Chiang had read. The following day Chiang held another news conference. Delin was not told of this conference and thus was absent.

At this public gathering, Chiang read a substantially different document than the one he had read the day before. In place of the phrase "from January 21, 1949, Vice President Li will succeed the president and exercise his duties and powers in accordance with article 49," Chiang now announced to the entire country: "From January 21, 1949, Vice President Li will *act for* the president in exercising his duties and powers in accordance with article 49. . . ."

All the newspapers, Delin was soon to discover, as he sped towards Chiang's residence, carried the same erroneous phrase. When he arrived at the presidential palace, Chiang had already left for Formosa, aboard his private plane — *Meiling,* named after his wife. Delin sent off a wire to him. Despite Chiang's prompt response — a honeyed promise to reissue the statement in its corrected form, disclosing his resignation/retirement before Delin was sworn in — the statement never arrived. On January 21st, just before the ceremony, Delin refused to be sworn in. "On the grounds that without the proper title — president, not acting president — I can neither continue the war nor negotiate for peace effectively," he told the president of the judicial *yuan* who was eager to administer the oath of office.

Hwang, his old colleague, stepped close to Delin and said, "My friend, be aware of your immediate environment. Nanking is full of 'special service men.'"

Delin looked around him at the numerous bodyguards newly assigned to protect him in his post. He recognized the men as disciples of the Son of Heaven. His very physical safety, he realized, was threatened.

"If you want to be president," Pai, the other member of the former triumvirate belatedly warned, "make sure it is as an authentic, not a quasi-, president."

Delin looked at his former cohorts. "Do I have your full support?" he asked them.

"You do," Pai answered solemnly. "Without reservation."

"And all of China's," Hwang affirmed. "The nation is behind you."

Delin looked at the statement by which he would act in Chiang's stead. "When the country stands on the brink of disaster," he said, "what good is it to quibble over acting or succeeding president? My task is to avoid further suffering."

Thus, in a simple ceremony held during the weekly memorial service for Sun Yat-sen in the National Government Building, the president of the judicial *yuan* administered Delin the oath by which he became the first acting president in China's history.

At the time that Delin was formulating official policy regarding matters of grave urgency — negotiating with the Communists for a peaceful settlement and an end to the war; preventing them from crossing the Yangtze; consolidating his troops; carrying out democratic reforms to regain popular support; and seeking American aid to halt inflation — Bittersweet was seeing her family off to Hong Kong from the dock in Shanghai. Only later would she be joining them in the villa she had rented for them in Happy Valley. First, she had to return to Kweilin to arrange for the stewardship of her properties and the management of her possessions in her absence.

Because of the war effort, each Chinese could take only two ounces of gold and a single piece of jewelry out of the country. Friends laughed when Youlin and his family — relatives of the acting president of China and thus people who could have escaped the restrictions —

carried out the government directive to the letter. Youlin wore his mother's thick, 24-karat gold chain, hung with ancient Chinese gold coins. Madeleine wore a double strand of large and perfect pearls. Andrew wore a gold chain with a carved jade pendant. The stone was a translucent cream color, the kind of jade which the Chinese call "mutton fat" and honor above all other colors of jade. And Lisa wore a similar chain bearing a gold locket in the shape of a book, each of whose six picture frames carried a photo of a family member — Delin, Bittersweet, Youlin, Madeleine, Andrew, and herself. The "front cover" was inscribed with the Chinese characters for Bittersweet's name, for the chain and locket had been Youlin's gift to his mother on her last birthday.

"I want Lisa to wear the locket," Bittersweet told Youlin. At first, he refused the temporary return of his gift. But Bittersweet insisted. "The gift," she said, "will lock Lisa into this world and serve as a link connecting me with my departing family."

"Make sure that the jewelry is concealed under their clothes," Youlin reminded Madeleine yet again, as they neared the water. "The dock will be swarming with people, not all of them there to sail for Hong Kong but to pick the pockets of those who are."

The crowd on the dock was far worse than Youlin predicted. Police with truncheons had to rope off an area past which only ticketed passengers could go. The armed officers formed a human barricade between the travelers and those who had come to see them off. It was here, just on the other side of the dividing line, that Bittersweet, protected by her chauffeur and her manservant, had to wait, bobbing and weaving among the other well-wishers, to try to get a view of her family.

"That tiny boat can't possibly hold all these people!" Madeleine exclaimed, linking arms with Youlin whose free arm carried Andrew, while Lisa sat in the crook of her mother's free arm.

"And it won't," Youlin yelled above the din as he surged forward, pushed towards the gangplank by the crowd behind him. "Some of these people are regular passengers. Others will travel in steerage, having sold every article they own for a ticket to leave the country. A great many more won't even make it aboard."

"Youlin!" Madeleine cried in alarm.

Several people pushed headlong into the couple. Madeleine's arm unlatched from the crook of Youlin's elbow.

"Madeleine!" he called back, trying to catch sight of her. "Madeleine! This way! Madeleine!"

She bore into the people who had dislodged her from her husband's side. But she needn't have even tried. Just then, the entire throng gave a sudden, great, and sustained thrust in the direction of the boat, and Madeleine could have gone no where else but where the people carried her. Lisa began to cry, as she was jostled this way and that, even though her mother held her close. In the pushing and shoving, Lisa's cardigan had come undone, and her gold chain and locket flew out onto her white blouse. Not daring to take both arms from about her child, Madeleine allowed the necklace to remain where it was, fully exposed.

"Madeleine," she heard Youlin yell to her. "The locket! Watch out!"

When Madeleine turned her head, she saw a pair of arms reach out towards Lisa's neck.

"No!" she screamed.

Just as she reached out to ward off one of the approaching hands with one of her own, she felt something hard at the side of her head; she felt her grip dislodge from about her daughter's buttocks and legs; she felt herself gasping for air, her torso pitch to the side, then down into the dark where knees and elbows struck her body. When she surfaced, fighting for air, a trickle of blood running down the side of her face, she felt Youlin's arm around her. Her ribs hurt where he held her and she couldn't get enough air. Youlin and the crowd carried her along. Andrew was in Youlin's other arm, crying. Youlin, too, was crying.

"Lisa!" Madeleine screamed, looking frantically about. It hurt her to scream. It hurt her even to breathe.

"No, no, keep moving forward toward the boat," Youlin begged her. "We'll be crushed to death if we try to fight the crowd. They'll find her. They'll find her. Don't think of her now. Don't think at all! Just lift your feet. Let the crowd carry you."

But Madeleine didn't hear her husband. She had fainted. Youlin continued to hold her and their son as the crowd carried them toward the gangplank.

From where she stood, Bittersweet witnessed the incident and she cried out Lisa's name. She waved frenetically when she saw Youlin on the gangplank. A stretcher had been brought for Madeleine who was still unconscious. Youlin looked exhausted and despondent. Andrew continued to cry and clutch at his mother. Suddenly, there was the sound of several volleys of pistol fire. Bittersweet's chauffeur and manservant grabbed her by the arms and ran for the car.

"What's that?" Bittersweet called from out of the backseat window to a passing guard.

"The police are firing into the crowd. People without tickets are trying to get on the boat. If they do, they'll swamp it. Perhaps it's better that they don't get on — those who do will only stay on deck with a heavy iron-link net thrown over them instead of in a comfortable stateroom under a warm blanket. It's so they don't break into the cabins and start a riot. Poor fools! Those who don't get pitched over-board and drown at sea will come down with pneumonia or hepatitis. Even those who do make it to Hong Kong — how long will they survive? Better to die in your own bed than in a strange land. Without family, a person is nothing but a piece of dog meat!"

An hour later, the ship pulled out of Shanghai harbor and the final hangers-on trickled away from the dock. Only when the armed guards began dismantling their human barricade could Bittersweet rush though the spotty line to look for her granddaughter. The bodies of four adults, trampled to death in the rush for the boat, were being carried away on stretchers. Another six adults and one young child who had been wounded were also placed on stretchers and taken away. But the child wasn't Lisa. Three stretchers were unfolded for those who were shot while trying to rush the gangplank. Two had been killed. Other people had been hurt in the riot, but not so seriously that they warranted stretchers; instead, they hobbled off, leaning on the arms of friends or relatives and moaning or sighing softly.

"Honorable Madam," her manservant said, catching her attention with what he held in his hand.

It was the little red cardigan Lisa had been wearing, but it was so trampled and mangled, it looked more like a filthy brown rag. Bitter-sweet shivered, but she fondled the pearl buttons, all intact, save for one, which was broken and dangling by a single thread.

"I'll sew it back on good and tight," Bittersweet said, holding the sweater to her chest.

"We're unable to find the little mistress," her manservant confessed. "Surely someone else has — someone with a good heart, who'll take good care of her until he can locate her family."

The manservant and the chauffeur looked at one another, trying to conceal their anxiety by nodding hopefully to each other.

327

"Then we must help that person locate us," Bittersweet said, folding the matted sweater carefully. "We'd better go to the central police station and file a missing person's report. We'll offer a substantial reward for Lisa's return or any information regarding her whereabouts. And, of course, I shall have to inform my husband."

Bittersweet had no desire to contact Delin, to add personal misfortune to Delin's mounting professional problems. Still, as acting president, he might arrange for a thorough search not only of Shanghai but the entire region, the entire country if need be.

Though she wanted to remain in Shanghai until Lisa was found, the Communist advance made her wish impossible. Youlin wired her from Hong Kong, urging her to come as quickly as possible, since Shanghai's fall was imminent. "Also, we need you here — especially Madeleine," he wrote. "She's hysterical about Lisa, though her own health is improving — her rib is mending, as is the punctured lung. Thank god Andrew requires almost all of her time and attention. We're doing all we can to find Lisa. Your remaining in Shanghai won't improve our chances; it only keeps you far away from us. Come. Come soon."

The very day she received Youlin's wire, Bittersweet booked passage for herself and Dashao on the train to Kweilin. Leaving Dashao in Kweilin, she would then travel by train, then by boat, to Hong Kong. But Bittersweet's heart was divided as cleanly as if it had been severed in two, for with every mile that passed, she came that much closer to her son and grew that much farther away from her husband and her missing granddaughter. With every mile closer to Hong Kong, she was that much nearer to a temporary cutting of ties with her family in Kweilin. In Dragon's Head, in Village Village, and in Kweilin, she would have to say her farewells, and though she had said them so many times before, this would be the first time that she would be leaving China altogether. Still, she knew that she must put aside these thoughts about her departure and simply resolve immediate, practical matters.

She had given long and hard thought as to how she wanted her properties and possessions managed and by whom, and she had decided that her nephew, Jiaqiu, the son of her elder brother, should oversee the running of her hotel, which she had rebuilt after the War of Resistance, as well as the maintenance of her house on Folded

Brocade Road. Her other restored properties — the opera house, the silk factory, and the silk retail store — would also come under Jiaqiu's stewardship. Her valuables, her gold, pearl, and jade jewelry would be put in Jiaqiu's wife's hands for safekeeping until Bittersweet returned.

Having settled in her mind her household responsibilities, Bittersweet settled back in the plush seat of her train compartment and watched the fertile plains of the central Chinese coast become the limestone backs of the inland southern dragons of her home province.

Chapter 9
Ends of the Earth
(1948)

Now that Delin was acting president, the CCP agreed to a temporary cease-fire and the renewal of peace negotiations. Just as the skirmishes along the lower reaches of the Yangtze quieted, Sun Fo decided to move the executive *yuan,* whose presidency he had assumed after his vice-presidential defeat, from Nanking to Canton.

"All the better to thwart my peace initiative," Delin said on learning the news. "And all the better to be closer to the Son of Heaven in Formosa. Divide a house between Nanking and Canton and how long can it stand?"

When Delin flew to Canton to insist that Sun move the executive *yuan* back to Nanking, his former rival refused, explaining, "The roaring of the cannons is too loud in my ears."

"During our eight-year war with Japan, did a single day pass that you didn't hear the roar of cannons in your ears?" Delin countered.

Though Sun did return the executive *yuan* to Nanking, he left the CC Clique and the headquarters of the Kuomintang Party that the clique controlled in Canton. As for Sun himself, no sooner did he arrive back in the capital than he resigned.

But Delin knew that a handicap might be turned into an advantage. When he was vice president, Chiang had isolated him from Chinese officials in power. In retaliation, Delin had begun to cultivate the foreign diplomatic community. Now it was time to renew and intensify those connections. He began by summoning the Soviet ambassador to his headquarters and requesting Russian assistance in ending the civil war.

"President Li, if I recall correctly, your predecessor made a similar attempt towards peace in 1946," the ambassador replied. "We informed him then that we were willing to consider his request, the stipulation being that China remain neutral in the event that the Soviet Union ever went to war. Based on that condition, Chiang backed out of a proposed trip to Moscow to discuss the matter further. It is now

1949, my dear Mr. President, and too late. China will never cut her ties with the United States. What, then, do you expect the Soviet Union to do for her?"

News from Delin's peace delegation was just as discouraging; negotiations had broken down. Things were at a stalemate. Meanwhile, the Communists were standing on the northern shore of the Yangtze and looking south. For months, Delin had been summoning the American ambassador to his office in hopes of negotiating a loan. Now that the situation was so urgent, Delin went to the American ambassador's office to repeat his request.

"A billion dollars to stop the spiraling inflation . . . ," Ambassador John Leighton Stuart pulled at his chin and repeated Delin's words. "As you are well aware, we've extended financial aid to China in the past. Most of it, unfortunately, went to line the pockets of corrupt officials."

"That was when my predecessor was president," Delin said. "Now I am president. The situation is completely different."

"President Li," the scholarly ambassador began reluctantly, "Chiang's 'retirement' to Formosa was planned well in advance of his taking it . . . well enough in advance that he could issue secret orders to transfer the entire reserve of silver dollars and United States gold bank notes — $335 million worth — from Chinese to Formosan banks. On the very day that he made his farewell address, not far from where you and I are sitting, he withdrew $10 million from the Bank of China and deposited it under a colleague's name in American banks. If you want to stop inflation in China, there is a countryman of yours in America and one in Formosa who have the money to do it."

"Mr. Ambassador, when all is lost," Delin said after a brief but ponderous silence, "what's left but to spread all one's cards on the table, as you say in your country. There's no more face to save, as we say in ours. The financial market is bankrupt. All activity is at a standstill. The people's confidence has never been lower." He took a deep breath before continuing. Only then did he realize how tired he felt, how vastly older than his years. "Allow me to make a prediction, one I'd rather not make, one I would hate even more to see come true. But as a loan is not forthcoming from your country, China has no alternative but to fall to the Communists, and I have no alternative but to warn you of the consequences of this for your country.

"If the United States doesn't give China one billion dollars now to stop inflation and Communist expansion in China, it will have to spend ten billion to stop the Communists in the Far East in the future. Not only that, American blood will be spilled, if not in China then elsewhere in Asia ... Korea, perhaps ... or Indochina. Then, when the United States acts to halt Communist aggression, America, instead of being considered the harbinger of democracy, will be accused of imperialism."

When this final request for a loan failed, Delin asked the American ambassador at least to co-sign a joint communiqué, a document from the international community that would express concern over the Kuomintang and Communist debacle and sincere hope for successful negotiations in China and the Far East.

But instead of the joint communiqué Delin was hoping for, Stuart reported his meeting with Delin to the United States' State Department which then published an erroneous White Paper, including allegations that eventually helped erect a Bamboo Curtain between China and the United States, similar to the Iron Curtain that existed between the Soviet Union and the United States.

"On January 23, [1949] the Acting President called on Ambassador Stuart to request a public statement of support from the United States," the White Paper read. "From the visit we are led to believe that General Li had been in touch with the Soviet Embassy and had worked out a tentative three-point draft agreement between China and the Soviet Union which the Soviet Ambassador had taken with him to Moscow a few days earlier. The three points were: (1) strict Chinese neutrality in any future international conflict; (2) the elimination of American influence to as great an extent as possible in China; (3) the establishment of a basis of real cooperation between China and Russia. General Li had agreed to these three points in principle and felt that his hand would be strengthened in negotiating on them if he had a statement of American support."

According to the White Paper, Delin had sold out to the Soviet Union and betrayed the United States.

With the Kuomintang troops heading towards Formosa and pulling away from the Yangtze, the Communist takeover of Nanking was imminent. Time running out, Delin flew to Hangchow where Chiang was calmly orchestrating his return to power. Before withdrawing to Formosa, Chiang had set up seven radio stations within China. From these stations he continued to direct the country's military and administrative operations.

"Transfer the silver dollars and the U.S. gold bank notes back to the Chinese treasury?" Chiang asked in sorry surprise, "and Kuomintang troops back to the mainland? Would that I could, Brother Delin, but I'm an ordinary citizen. By what authority can I carry out such an order?"

"Yet you as an 'ordinary citizen' assume the leadership of the country," Delin said. "How can I possibly govern China, end a war, and negotiate for peace, when orders are coming from Formosa as well as Nanking?"

"Whatever you do, I will support you," Chiang assured him. "Whatever you do, I shall support you," Chiang repeated. "You should assume complete responsibility, of course. . . ."

Responsibility, Delin thought, for the Kuomintang defeat, but not authority over the Kuomintang Party or the Chinese government.

". . . and if I've done anything in the past that has infringed upon that responsibility, tell me now. I am a man who is willing to correct his mistakes," Chiang said, eyeing his watch.

Delin shook his head hopelessly.

"No? Nothing?" Chiang replied, rubbing his hands together. "Then, good day to you," he said, rising abruptly, "and remember — you have my full support to the very end."

"Is it that near?" Delin asked, stopping in the doorway.

"Just a figure of speech, Brother Delin." Chiang smiled. "Just a figure of speech."

When Delin returned to Nanking, he found the capital almost deserted in anticipation of the Communist advance. He also found two telegrams waiting for him. One was from the peace delegation, headed by Hwang Shao-hsiung, that Delin had sent to Peking. The document was a joint communiqué, actually — for, it was signed by Hwang as well as by Chou En-lai and Lin Piao.

"Nanking unsafe," it read. "Request that you fly to Peking where you will be welcomed as an honored guest."

Delin closed his fist over the telegram. In other words, he realized, the peace delegates that I sent to persuade the Communists to sign a peace treaty have instead defected to them. Hwang included.

The second telegram clamored for Delin to step down from the presidency so that Chiang might reascend to the throne. It was signed by Sun Fo and members of the executive *yuan* and the CC Clique.

Delin called an emergency meeting of his cabinet and informed them that, since the Communists were thirty miles from Nanking, the central government should immediately proceed to Canton. When they reached Canton, however, the situation there was as untenable as the one they had left behind. Meanwhile, Nanking fell to the Communists who were also making a clean sweep of the southeastern course of the Yangtze. Delin ordered the Kuomintang troops to move towards Canton, but, on Chiang's orders, they headed instead to Amoy, so they could be closer to Formosa.

Delin considered the situation. The Kuomintang armies were in revolt. Pai's plans for the defense of southern China were a shambles. Though Pai and Delin had appealed to Chiang to transfer troops, currently stationed on the southern island of Hainan, to the mainland, the appeals had been ignored. Delin had no choice but to order all government departments to the interior and Chungking.

"We're following the same route we took against Japan," Delin wired Pai, "only this time, I fear, the outcome will not be to our advantage. We've met with a far greater adversary than the Japanese — our own brothers, fathers, uncles, and sons. We say that the Yellow River is China's sorrow. Today, it is China's people who warrant that title."

When Delin arrived in Chungking, he found that the city was entirely garrisoned by troops whose commanding officers were disciples of the Son of Heaven. They immediately suggested that Delin retire voluntarily and join them in a campaign to restore Chiang to power.

"Leave Chungking," Pai wired him. "Chiang flying to Chungking to compel you to sign document begging him to resume presidency. If you don't — and perhaps even if you do — you will be detained and placed under house arrest."

The telegram slipped from between Delin's fingers and he doubled over, clutching his stomach.

"Duodenitis. Bleeding ulcers," the examining doctor told him at the army hospital. "Half of your stomach's eaten away."

"Take my place in Chungking," Delin wired Pai in return. "I need to leave temporarily for the United States to have a stomach operation and to make a final appeal for last-minute aid."

In Hong Kong's Yanghuo Hospital, on Delin's first leg of the trip to America, he learned that all of China had fallen to the Communists and that Pai had followed Chiang to Formosa as his minister of war. There, Chiang declared the Kuomintang government the one true government of China and vowed to win back the mainland from across the Straits of Formosa.

"Hwang has gone over to the Communists. Pai has gone over to Chiang. And I am going to America," Delin said to himself. "After thirty years of working together towards a common goal, this is what has become of the Kwangsi Three."

"Li *Furen?*" the nurse asked.

Bittersweet stood up and looked questioningly at Youlin and Madeleine.

"Your husband would like to see you alone, if you don't mind, and your companions may visit him in just a few minutes."

When Bittersweet entered Delin's room in Yanghuo Hospital, he smiled to reassure her that he felt fine, but his face twisted unwittingly into a grimace.

"The doctors tell me that you must have an operation, and that you must go to America for it," Bittersweet said, trying not to dwell on her husband's condition and the reasons for it.

"America possesses the best medical facilities and technology in the world, so that's where I'll go. But I want to go there for another reason," he confided. He smiled, as though recalling a secret. "Remember many years ago when we were first married? When I said half in pride, half in sorrow that my home for all my adult life was the battlefield? Well, now that all of China is lost, I'm without a home, aren't I?" he said, his index finger raised in the air. "But, I am not without a cause. Perhaps my weakness has always been that I could never press my advantage. I could employ deception in battle, but I couldn't utilize deceit in office. Nor could I ever get over the notion of face. But my strength lies in my ability to find an opportunity in any crisis, and the present crisis is this: the Communists have overrun our homeland. But I have not given up hope of receiving American aid. Chiang thinks it's from across the Straits of Formosa that he'll win back the mainland. He's mistaken. It will be from across the Pacific Ocean — from America."

"Then," Bittersweet began uncertainly, "do you mean to live in the United States?"

"Only until such time when it is possible for me to return to China to live," Delin said. "I know the American government will welcome me. And I want you and Youlin and his family to live there, too."

"But Youlin's plans to work in Hong Kong," Bittersweet replied. "His factory, his. . . ."

"Hong Kong is out of the question," Delin told her, "for all of us. I'm war criminal #2 on the CCP's most-wanted list. With Hong Kong so close to China, it's too dangerous for me, or any member of my family, to remain here. By the same token, Hong Kong is too close to Formosa. Youlin will understand, and he'll agree."

The next several days Bittersweet and her family spent applying for visas in anticipation of moving to America, the Flowery Flag Nation. Madeleine and Andrew, as American citizens, had no worries other than Madeleine's reluctance to leave China and her still missing daughter. But Youlin, Delin, Bittersweet, Dejie, and Deqiu required an American visa. While Delin's English-speaking interpreter spent many hours filling out visa applications for his employer and his family, Youlin filled out applications for himself and his mother, arranged for his father's operation in New York City, and rented an apartment there for himself and his family. When all the applications were completed, the interpreter delivered them to the American consulate. It was decided that Youlin would accompany his father, Dejie, and Deqiu on the flight to America as soon as they obtained their visas so that the operation could be performed as soon as possible; Bittersweet, Madeleine, and Andrew would follow by ship after they had finalized family matters and moved out of their rented villa in Hong Kong.

When the visas arrived the day before the flight, Bittersweet's was missing. A private plane had been sent by the American government to fly Delin to the United States. It could not wait, nor could his operation. Reluctantly, Youlin bade his mother good-bye and instructed Madeleine to press the issue of Bittersweet's visa with the consulate and to discover the reason for its delay.

"The reason for its delay?" the consulate officer replied to Madeleine's inquiry when she appeared before him the day after her husband left for America. "You mean the reason for its denial." He handed her a document. "This came in just this morning."

"Denial? But we were assured that visas would be issued to President Li and every member of his immediate family."

"And they have been, Mrs. Li — to President Li, his two sons, Youlin and Deqiu, and his wife Guo Dejie."

Madeleine's eyes widened first in alarm then, almost immediately afterwards, in understanding.

"Guo Dejie is President Li's second wife," she told the officer. "My mother-in-law, Li Xuewen, the woman requiring the visa, is his first wife."

"The United States recognizes only one wife, Mrs. Li," he answered, pointing to the document he'd just given her. "Guo Dejie was recognized as wife of President Li when she left with him for the United States yesterday. I'm sorry, but those are the rules. Your mother-in-law can apply for a visa on her own, however — as a Chinese citizen and a refugee."

"Instead of for reasons of political asylum?!" Madeleine said. "Along with the millions of other Chinese who are doing the same? That will take years! Maybe decades — maybe never! There's a strict quota on Chinese immigrants entering the United States. With China in Communist hands, immigration may be restricted even further."

"I'm very sorry, Mrs. Li," the officer said, "but I have no better news to tell you. I can only advise you to have your mother-in-law start applying for an American visa as a Chinese refugee as soon as possible. The number of applicants will only swell."

When Madeleine returned home after visiting the consulate, Bittersweet was waiting to hear her news.

"There isn't much time," Bittersweet reminded her daughter-in-law when she learned her visa was still delayed. "The S.S. *President Cleveland* sails for San Francisco in two weeks. Will my visa arrive before then?"

A small technicality, Madeleine told Bittersweet. The visa would be finalized in a day or two, a few days at most.

"My daughter-in-law's words are sweet," Bittersweet murmured to Dashao as the two women watered the hibiscus blossoms that grew in the blue and white flowerpots that dotted the sunny terrace of the villa, "but her heart is sour with something she is withholding. Her mouth says certain things, but her pale face and downcast eyes say other things."

Later, when Bittersweet overheard Madeleine's anxious voice on the phone as she spoke to her husband in New York or to Kwok Lan-shing, his lawyer in Hong Kong, she was convinced that her visa was not forthcoming. Madeleine could not meet her eyes, nor could she sustain a smile on her lips without an expression of apology.

Dashao came into the kitchen to prepare some breakfast. She looked out the window to where the yellow sun was balancing on the horizon.

"My young mistress is trying very hard to save face," Dashao told Bittersweet. "Everyday she goes to the consulate, and everyday she returns looking more weary than the last."

"It's time I make a trip to the consulate on my own," Bittersweet said. "Don't you agree, Dashao?"

"Today is a good day for you to go," Dashao answered.

Bittersweet smiled. "It may be the only time I stand on a patch of American soil in a long, long while."

Though Dashao wanted to accompany her old mistress — an affirmation of her support — Bittersweet insisted that she stay at home and find a pretext to keep Madeleine from going to the consulate that day, for she must never learn of Bittersweet's own visit there.

And I must accustom myself once again to being alone and doing things on my own, Bittersweet thought to herself.

The rickshaw ride home from the American consulate seemed interminable, which was as Bittersweet wished it. For her daughter-in-law's sake, for her grandson Warm Peace's sake, she needed the time to compose her face, her words, and her voice so that they would never suspect that she knew of her abandonment nor the reason for it.

With unseeing eyes, Bittersweet looked straight ahead of her as the rickshaw driver trotted past the great banyan trees overgrown with orchids, and the oleander and the hibiscus that climbed up the white-walled homes. Dejie was Delin's second wife, but Dejie was first in his heart. Bittersweet acknowledged this with rancor in her own heart. It was Dejie who, for thirty years, had stood at his side, shared his house, shared his bed. How could he not have chosen her to accompany him to America when he had to choose only one of them, when one of them would have to be left behind? Had it not always been so? Why now should she feel abandoned when in fact she had been abandoned throughout her married life? Still, in all these years, though Dejie had taken her place, she had not taken her position. But now she had taken even that. Now, safe in the Flowery Flag Nation, she was not only the first, she was the only wife.

"No, not yet," Bittersweet called out to the driver when her house on Link Road came into view. "Take me anywhere but there."

The wiry young man came to a standstill, scratched his unkempt head of hair, and asked over his shoulder, "Anywhere, Madam? Today is the Seventh Day of the Seventh Moon, the day when the Spinning Maid crosses the Bridge of Magpies over the Silver River to meet her husband, the Cowherd, for their yearly visit. It's the day when young girls pray to the gods to find them a good husband," the rickshaw driver continued. "The temples will be full of gorgeous young girls dressed in their best and burning incense so the gods hear their prayers and answer them."

Bittersweet said, "That might be just the place for you, young man, but it's hardly the place for me! On the other hand," she said after reconsidering, "a temple—a Taoist temple—sounds like a fine choice. Might there be one in Hong Kong where the festival won't be celebrated?"

The rickshaw driver shook his scruffy head.

"A Buddhist monastery, perhaps," he replied, "if it's peace and quiet you want. There's one on Lantau Island. My first cousin started his own *sampan* business rowing customers back and forth between Hong Kong and Silvermine Bay. Po-Lin Monastery's just above the bay, in the shadow of Lantau Peak. A short rickshaw ride will take you there and back."

"Yes," Bittersweet decided, "that's exactly where I want to go. To the Buddhist monastery."

A short *sampan* ride took Bittersweet from Hong Kong Island to the fishing village of Mui Wo on Lantau Island. From Mui Wo's dock, a rickshaw carried Bittersweet to Po-lin Monastery — a score of pavilions whose yellow-tiled roofs gleamed in the noonday sun. When Bittersweet arrived, several saffron-robed monks and nuns were serving a vegetarian lunch to the faithful who had just participated in religious services. She found an empty spot at one of the long wooden communal tables and sat down while two monks — or perhaps they were nuns, for their shaved heads made it hard to tell — came by with bowls of steaming white rice topped with a variety of tofu and vegetables. One was a youth and one was past middle age but not quite old. Most of her fellow diners were either women or elderly, and Bittersweet realized as she looked at their wrinkled yet serene faces that she had indeed reached the winter of her life, if not in years, then certainly in terms of her prospects for peace and happiness.

"Some tea?" a wizened old woman asked, grinning a brown-toothed smile and holding the teapot towards Bittersweet's empty cup.

Bittersweet acknowledged the woman's kindness by turning her tea cup over to receive the fragrant, hot liquid. As the tea filled her cup, she felt warmed by the woman's kindness. Indeed, tears came to her eyes, and she felt both relieved and shamed by them.

"Some food for the body after food for the soul?" the older monk asked.

He'd come over to Bittersweet and extended a bowl as if it were a precious gift and its recipient an honored guest. Something in the monk's voice made Bittersweet look up, though her tears blurred her vision.

"Bittersweet!" she heard him say.

Though she couldn't make out his image clearly, she recognized his voice.

"Can it be? After all these years? In Hong Kong? At a Buddhist monastery?" Her tears evaporated, and she saw Xiao Tzu with a clarity intensified by the joy she felt to have found her old friend again and at such a difficult moment in her life.

"Minus the long hair and minus the black robes," he said in a teasing voice. "A Buddhist monk must have his head and his eyebrows shaved. And the color of the robe he wears is saffron yellow. And if you want to be orthodox about it, which, thankfully, this monastery is not, he must also refrain from looking at a woman," he said with a smile, "let alone speak to her. But just for today, let me be less than a good Buddhist!"

"But how do you come to be here — a Taoist abbot in a Buddhist monastery?" Bittersweet asked.

"They're not mutually exclusive. Buddhism and Taoism are actually perfectly compatible, perfectly complementary. Yin and yang. Compassion and wisdom. But I must finish serving lunch," Xiao Tzu told her. "Come to the vegetable garden behind the kitchen after you're done. I'm on weeding and watering duty today. We can talk there."

Amid clumps of thin, bumpy Chinese string beans and tangled vines of red, ripe tomatoes, Bittersweet recounted the events of her life since she had last seen Xiao Tzu at Da Mama's funeral: her escape from Kweilin during the War of Resistance; her year in the mountains of

Lunyun; Youlin's return from America; her new status as a grand-mother; Delin's election; her upcoming voyage to America to be reunited with her family.

"How fortunate you are," Xiao Tzu said. "Not many families are intact after the War of Resistance and the War of Revolution."

Bittersweet looked away. "Yes," she said, "I've been very lucky."

"When do you join your family?" Xiao Tzu asked.

Bittersweet dropped her eyes. "The ship sails in less than two weeks."

Xiao Tzu nodded. "Then, I, too, am fortunate—fortunate that it isn't sailing sooner and fortunate that you chanced to come here."

Bittersweet looked up into the sky where the Spinning Maid and the Cowherd met just once a year. The two stars would never be closer than they were today.

"And you?" Bittersweet said, turning back to Xiao Tzu. "You haven't told me how you come to be here."

Xiao Tzu described the Japanese occupation of Kweilin, of how the horrors inflicted on the Chinese populace forced him to question his beliefs. "It was a crisis of faith," he said simply. "I thought I'd found a truthful view of the universe, but I discovered that I didn't have a view about — or a feeling for — humankind. Taoism adequately explains the universe's energy systems, but Buddhism delves into its very consciousness."

He looked at Bittersweet, squinting against the sunlight. "I'd never felt the emotion of love for anyone but you. And then I saw people being tortured and killed by unimaginable means, people committing suicide out of despair, people dying of exposure and starvation. My world view vanished. It only returned when it was complemented by a view of humankind, when love, in the form of compassion, was added to it — when in my desperation I thought of you. My love for you as an individual was transformed into an identification with all of humanity — with no one, no single one but all of us — with no-thing, no single thing but all there is."

Before Bittersweet took the rickshaw back to the dock, she accompanied Xiao Tzu to the great hall where it was time for him to join the others in meditation. After they said their good-byes, Bittersweet lit a bundle of incense in the vestibule in the back of the hall and gave thanks, for she was indeed fortunate to have spent this day with her old friend.

· ✦ ·

"*Nai-nai*, guess where we've been?" Warm Peace cried, when his grandmother arrived home. "To the horse races! Mommy, too. Dashao made her come with us. And I ate two ice cream cones. One mango and one coconut."

"I was worried about you," Madeleine said, standing up from the wooden puzzle she was assembling with Warm Peace and Dashao on the floor, and coming over to her. "Where have you been all this time?"

"I'm sorry if I caused you concern," Bittersweet said, "but did you know that today is the Seventh Day of the Seventh Moon — Maiden's Day — when the Spinning Maid makes her annual visit to her husband, the Cowherd, and young girls pray to the gods to be good to them."

"The strange look on your face, Li *Furen*," Dashao said, narrowing her eyes, "tells me that you are one to whom the gods have been good today. Am I right?"

"Not in the way you imagine," Bittersweet replied.

Dashao looked at her mistress.

"But the gods have been good nonetheless."

Twelve days later, Bittersweet boarded the S. S. *President Cleveland*, bound for San Francisco, to see Madeleine and Warm Peace off to the United States.

"I wish you were coming with us," Madeleine said, fighting back her tears, "but your visa is bound to be issued soon."

"*Nali, nali*," Bittersweet consoled her daughter-in-law, patting her hand. "I'm sure the problem will be cleared up, and then I'll come to join you in America. And don't worry so much! Worry is bad for your health!"

Bittersweet promised to keep in touch with Kwok Lan-shing in Hong Kong who was working, as feverishly as Youlin in New York was, for her visa's clearance.

"With two such able men working in my behalf, it will be no time before I'm with my family again," Bittersweet told Madeleine.

Then, she took Warm Peace in her arms and sang, "Row, row, row your boat, gently down the stream; merrily, merrily, merrily, merrily: life is but a dream." The English words had been easy to learn because their meaning, if not their pronunciation, was familiar, both Taoist and

Buddhist. True, it was a children's song, but in its innocence, it spoke a profound and, for today, appropriate truth.

Visitors were ordered to disembark, and the ship pulled into the waters of the Pacific. Bittersweet waved goodbye. Still waving, she watched her daughter-in-law and grandson grow indistinct then merge with the other travelers on the great ship that itself soon became a tiny black speck on the great ocean. Bittersweet and Dashao waited until even the speck disappeared.

"I'm totally alone now!" Bittersweet, no longer able to maintain face, said to Dashao.

"And what am I?" her maidservant asked, struggling with her own tears, hoping to shame her mistress into doing the same. "A ghost? A fox fairy?"

"You well may be," Bittersweet said, linking arms with Dashao, coaxing a little smile to her lips. "You're too clever to be a mere woman. And you assume too many disguises to be merely one woman!"

"Life is never so cruel, Li *Furen*, that it leaves a traveler in the world with no path to tread," Dashao reminded her mistress as she led her away from the desolate dock.

No sooner had Madeleine and Warm Peace left for America than members of Bittersweet and Delin's families came flocking to Hong Kong, fleeing the victorious Communists. First came Bittersweet's great aunt from Village Village. Then came Delin's aunt and her four grandsons from Dragon's Head. With nothing but the clothes they wore and comforters slung over their shoulders, they looked and acted like frightened birds carrying their nests upon their backs.

As they had nowhere else to stay, and as Madeleine and Warm Peace were no longer living in the villa, Bittersweet invited her relatives to stay with her. They accepted but remained anxious; surely the Communists would overrun Hong Kong, or kidnap, or harm them. Bittersweet couldn't help but laugh at their fear.

"Look at you," she said one day when their terror was particularly acute. "Why are you so afraid? What could the Communists possibly want with a household of terrified, harmless peasants? During the war with Japan, weren't things even worse? We survived, didn't we? Great Aunt, we lived through the warlords who trampled our crops, raped our women, kidnapped our men. We lived through the provincial wars, through Kwangsi fighting Kwangtung, through the Northern

Expedition. And, Old Auntie," Bittersweet said, picking out the next oldest member in her brood, "you lived through the Sino-Japanese War, didn't you? And you, my second cousins, you endured the War of Revolution. Yes, we're tired of all of this. But haven't we all lived on? Now the Communists are the victors, and that is a fact, whatever we wish. Enemies they were, but they are Chinese, like us."

"They are not like us," Great Aunt spoke up, wagging her arthritic index finger at Bittersweet.

"Whatever they are, I understand that the poor and the oppressed under the Kuomintang were not only unafraid of the Communists," Bittersweet answered, "they welcomed the Communists. It's well-known that the Communists couldn't have gained power without the peasants' help. If the peasants weren't afraid, why should we be?"

"We are not peasants!" one of her second cousins declared, having taken offense at Bittersweet's earlier reference to the family as a "household of terrified and harmless peasants."

"I beg your pardon, you with the wisps of straw still sticking out of your ears," Bittersweet said, "but whatever I am now, I still remember my early years on the family farm. I remember them as happy ones, and I think of them with great longing."

And with greater clarity, as the years go by, Bittersweet thought to herself, repressing the urge to sigh. So it is that the older I get, the more vivid the memories of my youth become and the happier they seem. Perhaps it's because I'm no longer in the autumn of my years, but the winter, which the plum blossom symbolizes. In the depths of winter, the plum tree puts forth new blossoms from leafless and seemingly dead branches. And here are my little blossoms of family members bursting upon me, giving life to my dead branches, demanding to be nurtured. Here I am, taking care of them, providing a roof over their heads, food for their stomachs, so I have no time to think of my future nor even weigh it against my past. I must live in the moment, she told herself, for in the moment lies eternity.

She looked at her family squabbling among themselves, whining at their plight. Family, she thought. Dashao is right; life, if one allows it to flow unimpeded, does not leave a person with no path to follow.

Before the year was out, Bittersweet, with Kwok Lan-shing's help, applied as a private citizen and a Chinese refugee for an American visa. Two years went by. Her application was being "reviewed," and then she received word from the American consulate that her request for a visa had again been denied. While her first application had been turned down on the grounds that she was not her husband's wife, the denial of the second request, according to a letter from Youlin, had to do with an American senator who was accusing every Chinese — and many Americans — of having Communist sympathies or of being Communist spies.

"Then, Kwok *Xiansheng,* how will I obtain a visa," Bittersweet asked the lawyer, "if not in the way we've gone about it for the past four years? Is there another way?"

"There may be," he told her, "but it doesn't depend on you or me."

"On this McCarthy *Xiansheng,*" Bittersweet said, her spirits dropping along with her voice. "Then the way is blocked."

"On Youlin," Lan-shing replied.

Bittersweet looked at him with surprise.

"You see, your daughter-in-law and your grandson are American citizens."

"As is my granddaughter," Bittersweet interjected.

"Yes, and your granddaughter," Lan-shing said. "But Youlin is not."

"Of course not," Bittersweet said, as though it were obvious. "He's a Chinese national."

"Precisely," the lawyer affirmed. "Your son is not only not an American citizen, he is a Chinese national. There are, however, two Chinas now, each claiming to be the legitimate one. The China of which Youlin is a citizen is the China the United States believes is now 'lost.' These days, the government that controls China is hostile to the United States, and the feelings of the United States towards this new China are mutual."

"And this mutual hostility prevents my son from obtaining a visa for me," Bittersweet said.

"Not prevents, but presents an obstacle," Lan-shing told her. "That obstacle could be removed. . . ." He looked at Bittersweet tentatively. ". . . by Youlin's becoming an American citizen."

"Kwok *Xiansheng,*" Bittersweet began after a pause, "as a young man, Youlin's grandfather was rabidly anti-colonial and anti-Western. His vehemence was only somewhat tempered in his son, Youlin's father, my husband. Delin was strongly anti-imperialistic, and he received no help from the United States in his darkest hour as acting president. Youlin himself suffered discrimination as a college student in Chicago. When he married my daughter-in-law, he was unable to find a suitable apartment to rent. Only through the intercession of one of his professors was he able to find a decent place. My son, to this day, feels anger at this insult dealt to him in the land of equal opportunity. Do you think he would forfeit his patrimony by becoming an American?"

"If it meant the unity of his family and your safety, Li *Furen*," Lan-shing answered, "I believe he would. That's what I wanted to tell you. As soon as your son heard that your second request for a visa was denied, he applied for American citizenship. He would have done it sooner but we were certain, what with the second application, your visa was forthcoming. But then this McCarthy appeared. It will take a little while longer, but with Madeleine and Andrew — and Lisa — all American citizens, it is just that: a matter of time."

Bittersweet's eyes filled with tears. "His filial duty towards me," she murmured, "but at the cost of his patrimony!"

"The China of Youlin's patrimony is not the China that exists today. You mustn't feel that your son has sacrificed anything for your sake. He himself has only benefited. You must feel that, Li *Furen*. He would want you to."

"What I feel," Bittersweet said, shaking her head, "is that destiny has a strange way of revealing itself to those who try to tamper with it."

Lan-shing looked puzzled.

"Remember the children's story?" she asked him. "The fable that every Chinese boy is told from the moment he can understand the meaning of words — the fable about the boy who lies down on a frozen river to melt the ice on its surface, so that he can save his sick father's life."

"So that he can save his sick mother's life," Lan-shing corrected her. "Or, at least that's the version I always heard."

"Indeed! Indeed!" Bittersweet said. "His mother . . . not his father. But that wasn't the version I chose to tell."

In February 1954, Youlin became an American citizen. Three years later, Bittersweet received a letter from the American consul informing her that her application for a visa had been processed and after her personal interview was granted, the matter would be finalized.

At the prescribed hour, Bittersweet arrived at the consulate on the arm of Kwok Lan-shing. She looked at the high pole at whose pinnacle the American flag fluttered. Here was an American flag planted in a British colony, on an island where 95% of the population was Chinese. Bittersweet recalled Delin's most recent letter. In it, he said he dreamed of the day when all colonialism would cease, when all political boundaries would be erased and all nationalities would live as a single people. "For," he wrote, "the existence and veneration of kings, presidents, separate nations, separate races, national boundaries, and political ideologies have caused the greatest suffering known to mankind by providing the reason and the rationale for war."

Now, Bittersweet said to her lawyer, "A little patch of America lies right at my feet, but the America where I long to be lies ten thousand miles away. The promise of my visa is like this dot of America on Hong Kong island compared to the country that lies on the far side of the earth: at my fingertips, yet beyond my reach."

"You'll know in a few minutes," Lan-shing said. "Just answer the questions truthfully."

In a room with a second and smaller American flag, the consul asked Bittersweet her name, the place and date of her birth, the names of her father and mother, sisters and brothers, her family history. He asked her the dates she married Delin and gave birth to Youlin, and the names of three American acquaintances and how long she had known each of them. Every answer that Bittersweet gave the consul checked against not only her application, but Youlin's as well, and at the end of the interview, he insisted on taking a sample of her blood.

"What, in the name of the Jade Emperor, for?" she wondered aloud.

"To prove that you are indeed Li Youlin's mother," the consul said.

"How could I not be the mother of my own and only son?!" she exclaimed. She turned to Lan-shing. "Have I not done well? If I had passed the interrogation, why should he be so suspicious of me?"

The consul laughed. "You did very well in your 'interrogation,' as you call it. I'm sorry if I appear suspicious. I'm just trying to be thorough."

"It's not that the consul's suspicious of you," Lan-shing reassured her. "It's the United States that's suspicious of China."

Bittersweet nodded her head, suggesting that the matter was settled, but actually wondering if, in finally being able to join her son and his family, she was also going to live in a hostile environment, one that considered her country and her nationality an enemy. Yet she could not return to China, and she did not want to remain in Hong Kong.

Home was where her family was and thus, hostile or not, New York City was where she longed to be.

In April, 1958, Lan-shing arrived on Bittersweet's doorstep, smiling broadly and waving a piece of paper in his hand. "Here it is. Your American visa!"

By the end of May, Bittersweet had settled all her household and family accounts. She had helped her four second cousins find jobs in Hong Kong, and she had signed the villa's lease over to Great Aunt and Old Aunt. Taking leave of Dashao was almost as hard as saying good-bye to her immediate family had been. What money she had she divided equally among the two aunts, the four second cousins, and her long-time, faithful servant.

"You've been more than a trusted servant," Bittersweet told the weeping woman. "You've been more than a family member. You've been a wonderful friend to me, and I will miss you very much."

"Li *Furen*," Dashao said, clasping her hands together and bowing repeatedly, "return to China when we've won it back. Send for me and I will come. I will wait till I hear from you. And I will serve you for the rest of my days."

When all her affairs were in order, Bittersweet felt released from the obligations holding her to her relatives and to her past. A journey of a thousand miles begins with a single step, she reminded herself. She took a deep breath and crossed the threshold of the airplane for a journey that would take her ten thousand miles away.

Chapter 10
Flowery Flag Nation
(1957)

"Bombs away for Tokyo!" Several boys ran down the big hill behind Andrew's home. They were re-enacting China's War of Revolution.

"Bombs away for Tokyo," they shouted again.

"That's World War II when the Allies fought Japan," Andrew told his classmates.

"Japanese or Chinese," one boy shrugged, palms turned upwards. "What's the difference? They both look alike, don't they?"

Andrew recognized this classmate as the one who had called him a "Commie" when he did his report on China for geography class.

"Uh-uh," another said, setting his index fingers at the outside corner of his eyes. "The Japs look like this. . . ." He pulled the corners of his eyes down. ". . . and the Chinks look like this." He pulled the corners of his eyes up. Suddenly he found himself sprawled on his back and seeing only the blue sky. When he righted himself, a trickle of blood flowed from his right nostril.

The other children came running and gathered around him. "What happened?" they asked.

"Gee whiz, Andy," the fallen boy said, "what did you go and do that for?"

"For what you said," Andrew answered, frightened at what he'd done but angry still.

"What did you say?" the other children asked the boy who was twisting a corner of a tissue and plugging up his bleeding nostril.

"I didn't say diddly," he growled, getting to his feet, glaring at Andrew.

"Liar!" Andrew shouted. "It's Japanese and Chinese — not Jap and Chink!"

"Okay, okay," the boy replied. "What are you so sore about, anyway?" He cuffed Andrew playfully on the side of his head of wheat-blond hair and looked into his blue, almond-shaped eyes. "You'd think you were one of them."

"You're one of us," the other children assured him, nodding. "You're an American."

Andrew wanted to scream. He was one of them but he wasn't one of them, and if that's the way they thought, he didn't want to be one of them.

"Don't you know the Commies kidnapped his twin sister," the others whispered to the bloody-nosed boy. "Don't you know they tortured her then killed and ate her? The Commies in China will eat anything."

"Jap frog chink yank," Andrew repeated the words under his breath that night and wished he'd bloodied the boy's other nostril, too.

Not that I'd mind bloodying my geography teacher's nose either, he thought. He hated when she took up collections or held bake sales "for the poor, starving children in China." Were all the starving children in the world Chinese? All his classmates looked at him in pity and alarm, wondering if he had enough food to eat and enough clothing to wear — he who lived in a house bigger and better than any of theirs, whose grandfather lived nearby in a gigantic house in an exclusive neighborhood where only Americans and a few important foreigners were allowed to live. Indeed, his grandfather was so important that a 24-hour guard, who wore a gun in a holster and carried a walkie-talkie, was posted on his property. No other child he knew could claim a grandfather who had been vice president of a country that was lots bigger than the United States and with five times as many people.

Soon Andrew's grandmother would be coming to the United States, too. But she would be living with Andrew and his parents, not in her own house like his grandfather. They'd be three generations living together. It was the Chinese way.

"Don't peek," Youlin admonished his mother. "Warm Peace, hold your hands tighter over *Nai-nai's* eyes."

Reluctantly, Andrew obeyed — not because he didn't want to prevent his grandmother from seeing her new home before they drove up to it, but because he didn't like being spoken to in Chinese. And he hated his Chinese name — not An-ruh, so much as what it meant: Warm Peace. It immediately suggested its opposite: cold war.

"Now — you can take your hands away," Youlin said.

"Ahh!" Bittersweet gasped, clasping her hands together.

It was as if her home on Folded Brocade Road in Kweilin had been transported to suburban New York City. Like her old home, her new house had two floors and was half-timbered, built of stone and brick. To guard against evil spirits and curious eyes, it was raised up on an embankment supported by a six-foot stone wall. For additional privacy and for shade in the summer, it was landscaped with hedges and trees. The grounds were so extensive, it seemed as if the house was located in the middle of its own large park. There were three separate and well-tended lawns and three separate and well-tended gardens to complement them. Red rose bushes and box hedges lined the top of the stone wall. A meandering path, bordered by hyacinths, tulips, daffodils, and jonquils, led up to the house. And there was a circular garden right before the front entrance where fragrant lilies of the valley and, Bittersweet was charmed to see, her favorite flower — peonies — grew. At the back of the house, there was a large sandbox delineated by sky-blue hydrangea bushes, rows of bright orange tiger lilies, a dogwood tree with simple but elegant parchment flowers, and a flourishing bittersweet bush.

"What did you say the name of that bush was?" she asked, walking towards the bittersweet bush.

"Bittersweet, *Nai-nai*," Andrew repeated. "Right now it's green because it's summer, but in the fall it's full of tiny orange-red berries that cling to the branch right through till winter."

"Is that so?" Bittersweet murmured. "It must be an American version of the 'friends of winter' — the bamboo, the fir, and the plum — for they all bloom in winter, too. And how propitious that this bittersweet blooms bright red — the color of good fortune! This sandbox will make a perfect vegetable garden. With the bittersweet nearby, it's bound to grow well."

Because gardening was play for her, and time was plentiful, Bittersweet soon decided to extend her vegetable garden from Andrew's former sandbox to Madeleine's flower beds. Store-bought vegetables in America, she had discovered, were tasteless — refrigeration and chemical fertilizers saw to that. So she uprooted the daffodils, hyacinths, tulips, and jonquils — the peonies and lilies of the valley she left untouched — to make room for *bok-choy* and Chinese string beans. She already grew tomatoes and *guy-lan* in the sandbox. Daily, she replenished the soil of her garden with the family's cocker spaniel's droppings.

Though Madeleine was tactfully silent as the green and white oblong heads of *bok-choy* emerged where formerly flowers bloomed, Andrew — at least, during meals — was upset. He wrinkled his nose and set down his chopsticks beside his rice bowl when he discovered just what it was that made his grandmother's vegetables so flavorful. "Oh, gross!" he'd first exclaimed, twisting his face. "I'm not taking another bite!"

But he soon altered his vow. His grandmother's cooking was too good to refrain from eating it. He just had to stop looking at or thinking about the family dog, or dogs in general, at mealtime. There were other times, however, when Andrew could not be so philosophical.

"I can't bring my friends over," he complained to his mother one day. "I just can't! It's too embarrassing! If we come in by the front door, they'll see her vegetable garden where flowers ought to be. And if I take them around to the back door, they'll see dried-up *bok-choy* leaves hanging on the clothesline instead of laundry, or cookie sheets full of red chili peppers shrivelling in the sun. We don't live in the New York suburbs anymore — we live on a Chinese commune!"

Andrew crossed his arms angrily over his chest, but still he thought of the pickled vegetable and sliced pork that would be the final result of Bittersweet's withered leaves, and the spicy *la-jiao* that she made from the wrinkled chili peppers. Bittersweet made her hot pepper sauce without the burn of the store-bought variety, but it was still potent enough that a pea-sized dab warmed and flavored a whole bowl of noodles.

"The last time I brought a friend home," Andrew continued, "*Nai-nai* was sitting at the edge of the covered porch pouring water on the Chinese cleaver and sharpening it on the edge of one of the flagstones! Why can't she buy a new cleaver or use a knife sharpener like normal people? But this," he said, pointing to the offensive object hanging from the light socket in the middle of the porch ceiling, "is the final straw!"

Bittersweet had inserted a wire hanger into the cavity of a chicken which had come, as all her chickens did, freshly-killed from the Yonkers garage of a recently-arrived Chinese emigré. Once a week, in Youlin's company, Bittersweet would wade through the garage's hundreds of clucking and pecking birds in search of the few she wanted for her table. These would then be whisked off to the chopping block, thankfully out of eyesight and earshot, then home to be cooked.

The chicken that she'd hung on the hanger from the light socket in the porch ceiling, however, had been selected for a different manner of preparation: it was to be air-cured and would receive salubrious northern breezes for maximum taste and tenderness. Now that it had hung for several months, as the object of interest of more than one kind of insect, Madeleine decided that Andrew had a point; her mother-in-law must have forgotten about her air-dried chicken, so Madeleine unhooked the sorry-looking bird and threw it out.

Not long after, the summer pollen from the roses and the sumac tree in the front yard was particularly prolific and exacerbated Madeleine's hay fever. So on their weekly family trip to Chinatown, Bittersweet stopped in a *yao-pu*, a traditional Chinese medicine shop, and explained her daughter-in-law's condition. The elderly herbalist whorled a sheet of paper into a cone and filled it with bits of bark, pods, seeds, roots, and berries which he had crushed with a mortar and pestle. Home again, Bittersweet boiled the concoction in water and steeped it, repeating the procedure several times. She then offered the final bitter brew, which smelled of melting tar, fired gun powder, and curry, to her daughter-in-law to drink. Bittersweet couldn't help but smile as Madeleine gulped and grimaced, for the remedy served two purposes: it cured Madeleine of her sneezing fits, and it made Bittersweet feel vindicated for the loss of her chicken.

One of Andrew's responsibilities was to accompany his grandmother on her twice-yearly visits to the dentist. On one such visit, along the tree-lined streets that led to the dentist's office, among the matted grass and fallen horse chestnuts, Bittersweet saw . . . "*Gow-gay*," she cried, examining and touching a low bush. "How I've wanted to add another leafy green vegetable to our menu! And this one's full of iron!"

She turned to her grandson who hung back from her find. His hands thrust deep in his jeans pockets, his baseball cap pulled down low over his eyes, he was clearly fearful that someone might see his grandmother hugging a bush.

"*Gow-gay*," she repeated, laughing. "As a girl, I used to go to the foothills near our village to pick it. We added it to boiling water or, on special occasions, simmered it in chicken stock into which we slowly added a beaten egg. It makes the most fragrant soup. To think it grows in America — and on the very street where we live!"

After that, every summer weekend, Bittersweet, wearing a broad-brimmed straw hat and carrying a large shopping bag, recruited the recalcitrant Andrew to help gather the week's supply of *gow-gay*. While he halfheartedly assisted her in picking the stuff, he adamantly refused to eat the soup in which it ended up.

"All the more for us," Bittersweet replied, catching Youlin's eye before he scolded his son. "When so much work is required to grow domestic crops, it's a shame to waste whatever food is naturally and freely given."

But if she forgave Andrew his distaste for *gow-gay*, she would not relinquish Andrew's help in gathering it. She recalled how Delin had sent Youlin back to Dragon's Head every summer so that, even though he attended a boarding school in Canton, he would learn how hard the Chinese peasant labored to coax crops from the land. A city boy needed to be reminded that each rice grain left in the bowl was a drop of sweat from a hard-working farmer's brow.

When Bittersweet's usual *gow-gay* patch had been picked bare, Andrew suggested they try a spot further up the inclined road.

"There well may be more up there, but we won't be the ones to find out," Bittersweet said.

Andrew understood his grandmother's reluctance to venture farther afield, for at the top of the hill lay the house Delin shared with Dejie. For the first two years of their life in America, Delin and Dejie had lived there with no less than a dozen people who had followed the Acting President of China to his New York home. In those early years, house guests had been cared for by several cooks and servants. But as Delin's resources became depleted, his guests and staff drifted away to live their own lives. And the great house where Delin and Dejie lived and entertained now became too big, too quiet, and too still. Now, those who were invited were no longer important government officials. Mostly, they were members of Delin's immediate family — Youlin, Madeleine, and Andrew. Deqiu had married and moved away and, remembering the distance and coldness with which his adoptive mother had raised him, he chose, in adulthood, to maintain the same distance and coldness. For similar reasons, Bittersweet maintained her own distance from Dejie and, necessarily, from Delin as well.

As for Andrew, he preferred to stay away whenever visits to his grandfather's house were planned, since, as he now told Bittersweet, he disliked the Pearl Eater.

"The Pearl Eater?" Bittersweet asked.

"Dad and Mom call her Madam, but I call her the Pearl Eater." He leaned closer to her and whispered theatrically, "She crushes pearls in a little bowl, puts the powder in a glass of water, and drinks it to make her skin young again. And she spends hours in front of the mirror, plucking out her gray hairs." Andrew heaved an exaggerated sigh and shook his head in disgust. "And Grampa, I want to talk to him but he's always behind a Chinese newspaper, drinking tea, and arguing about 'the China Question.' And that's what he does all day long, every day. No day is different. All he talks and hopes about is China. He's always telling me that China is better than New York."

It had been years since Bittersweet felt her heart turn over due to her husband, but it turned over now, as Andrew described how he spent his days. She no longer suffered because of Delin; now she suffered for him, for his loneliness and unhappiness. The Chinese idea of happiness is living with four, perhaps five, generations of family. After years of separation, Bittersweet was finally reunited with her son, her daughter-in-law, and her grandson. If only Delin lived with them, she thought, and Lisa, then her happiness would be complete, and her husband might have some of that happiness, too.

"Set another place at the dinner table tonight, would you?" Youlin asked his mother one evening on his way out the door.

"And who is to be our honored guest?" Bittersweet said, bringing her cleaver to a halt and looking up from her chopping board where she was slicing a big knob of ginger root.

"My father will be joining us."

Bittersweet looked at her son.

"All the members of my father's entourage have dispersed, yet Madam still misses her ladies-in-waiting. One of them gives weekly mahjong parties in her home in New Jersey. While Madam's at her mahjong game, why shouldn't Father be here with us?" Youlin asked.

"Why not indeed?" Bittersweet replied, going to the sideboard and reaching for another thin, almost translucent, rice bowl and another pair of ivory chopsticks.

That night, when the screen door squeaked open and she heard her son's voice, Bittersweet untied her apron and felt her bun to see if any stray wisps had escaped. Then she scurried to the front door to greet her dinner guest.

"*Ni hao*," she said, placing her palms together in front of her face and bending forward slightly.

She dropped her eyes quickly, for her husband had aged in the nearly ten years since she last saw him in Hong Kong. He was very thin, almost as gaunt as he had been then in the hospital. Nevertheless, he bore himself with dignity and wore a three-piece navy suit and a dapper gray fedora for the occasion. Delin removed his hat and handed it to Bittersweet with a nod of gratitude. What little hair he still had was completely gray.

"*Ni chi le fan le ma?*" Bittersweet asked, leading him into the parlor. It was the Chinese way of asking how one was, though literally it meant, "Have you eaten yet?"

"I no longer have much appetite," Delin said, answering her literally. After a pause, he added, "For much of anything."

"You must take care of yourself, for if you don't do it, no one else can do it for you."

It was what a mother might say to a child. As soon as Bittersweet had spoken, she wished she could take her sour words back. The silence that lingered did nothing to sweeten them. Finally Delin spoke. "That is just what you have done," he said, gazing around the room in admiration and regret. "Taken care of yourself, for no one else was there to do it for you. Why worry about me? In the past, I've given you too little thought. Now, I'm but a guest in a foreign country, while you are the mistress of your house and home. Finally you can enjoy the peace and happiness that is your due."

For the first time since he arrived, Delin looked directly into Bittersweet's eyes. What face is there to save for either of us at this stage of our lives, his expression seemed to say. As for Bittersweet, she knew that it was not Dejie but a far more beautiful mistress that enchanted him: China. It was China that had also betrayed him and that had finally abandoned him. And yet China lured him still. If Bittersweet harbored bitterness over the years, it was compassion that now guided her words and actions.

"You and I have been through a lot," she acknowledged, pouring Delin a cup of tea and handing it to him. "We've both survived many upheavals. But in spite of them all, here we are, together, without the need to uphold face, able to see each other once more. Is that not something to be thankful for?"

Delin smiled. "And here I thought I would be comforting you, when it is you comforting me."

Bittersweet laughed. "You and I are *lao ren*. Old folks are meant to comfort one another. What else do we have to say to each other? We've had our day, and now our day is done. Better we talk about the younger generations whose day it is and whose day is still to come."

They talked about Youlin whose import-export business was doing well, and Madeleine who had opened a boutique of her own clothing designs.

"Our son was wise, don't you think," Delin said, sitting at the kitchen table, sipping a second cup of tea, "to have chosen business as his profession and to have chosen it early in life. If he'd chosen his father's path and become a government official, could he have stayed afloat, treading the stormy waves of politics? How many have succumbed to exhaustion and been swept under?"

"He did what his heart urged him to do," Bittersweet said. "Fortunately for him, his heart was in tune with a favorable destiny."

"Youlin is headstrong — like his mother," Delin accused her with an admiring nod.

Bittersweet demurred by shaking her head, but the blush on her cheeks showed that she accepted the remark as a compliment.

"Speaking of little rams with growing horns, An-ruh is the one to watch. To watch," she repeated in advice, "and not to be commented upon, as his father's done. To say nothing about his appearance tonight is best, even if his hair hangs well past his ears. Though Youlin has criticized him for looking like a Taoist priest, An-ruh is more akin to a wild horse. His father thinks that tethering him is the way to tame him, but he would do better to offer his son a wide and open field."

Bittersweet silently recalled the incident that prompted her advice. Youlin and Andrew had been watching the evening news on television. A small news item concerned a man from Taiwan who had been discovered living behind the boiler of an abandoned building in Harlem, his home for seven years. His reason for becoming a recluse was that he had failed a course at Columbia University where he was studying for his undergraduate degree in biochemistry. Rather than face his parents with his failure, he had opted to disappear from the face of the earth, leaving no trace of himself.

"*Hen hao, hen hao,*" Youlin had murmured, nodding his head in approval. "A true filial son."

To Youlin's astonishment, Andrew jumped up from his chair, his face livid with anger. "Filial son? Bull! A coward, you mean! A worm! If he had any backbone at all, he would face up to his parents, retake the course, and pass. Does a loving son allow his parents to believe he's dead so that they grieve endlessly for him . . . for a lie? Does a man stop living and exist like a mole because he's failed an exam? Filial son —bullshit! Hypocrite and coward—yes! No wonder they call Chinese the yellow race! The streak runs a mile wide!"

Youlin blanched and his hands twitched. "If you can't understand that he withdrew from the world out of inner strength, out of shame for himself and respect for his parents," Youlin said, shaking in his effort to control himself, "then you're not Chinese — and you're no son of mine!"

At that, Andrew had stalked out of the room.

"And don't expect your grandson to say too much at dinner," Bittersweet continued to warn her husband. "He's rather withdrawn these days, with me, and even with his mother. I believe he has too much on his mind."

"Ah, to be young again!" Delin said, "and to have too much on one's mind rather than too little!"

"Right now it's better to fill your stomach than your head," Bittersweet suggested, carrying a platter of steamed ground pork, redolent of ginger and water chestnuts, into the dining room and setting it down among several other dishes on the table. "Dinner is ready."

But, Bittersweet needn't have warned Delin about Andrew's anticipated silence, for that night it was the *lao ren* who filled the dining room with *renao*, who held the two ends of the cord of conversation, keeping it taut and giving it a tug now and then.

"This wine," Delin said, lifting his glass, whose rosy contents matched the color of his cheeks, "it tastes and even smells like the wine I poured for you on our wedding night almost fifty years ago."

"But this wine is cool. The wine you poured then was warm," Bittersweet recalled, blushing. "Our wedding wine had been heated over an open flame."

"Ah, but what do you expect?" Delin said. "I was a young man then!"

They both laughed, then looked sheepishly at sullen Andrew, at disapproving Youlin, and at embarrassed Madeleine. But, their family's faces only made them burst out laughing again. "Please forgive us!" they begged. "It's the wine! It's been aged too long!"

After dinner, in the light of the waning sun and the waxing moon, Bittersweet took Delin on a tour of her gardens. Looking around him at how beautiful they were, how carefully tended, Delin could only shake his head and say, "I'm sorry. I'm so sorry."

Lifting up the leaves of one of the clambering vines, Bittersweet uncovered a mottled green and red tomato. "In a week's time, it will be ripe," she told him. "I hope you'll return then."

"With great pleasure. It's ironic, isn't it?" Delin noted, seeing Youlin motion him towards the car. Dejie would be returning home soon, and she must never know where her husband had spent the evening. "When we lived in China, we rarely saw each other. Now that we live in a foreign country ten thousand miles away, we can enjoy each other's company regularly."

"Then you never had time. Now you're a free man," Bittersweet said, thinking of her husband's two mistresses, the greater and the lesser.

"Yes, I'm a free man."

But when he came weekly to dine with his family, Bittersweet saw that he wasn't free. Though he sat comfortably in her parlor or dining room, he was thinking of China.

"Delin," she remarked one evening when wishful thinking was obviously carrying him far away, "you've often told me that in the sea of politics, there are those who float with the tide and those who sink beneath the waves. Now, after much treading, you've reached another shore. Why not leave the water and come up on dry land?"

"New York is not as good as China," he said softly.

"China is the past," Bittersweet reminded him, "and New York is the present. We live in the here and now. You must not lose sight of the very fundamentals of life."

Delin didn't seem to hear her. He only repeated, with greater conviction, "New York is not as good as China."

If New York was not good to Delin, it was good to Bittersweet, and she was wise enough not to ask for better: her entire family save for Lisa was reunited. Yet she knew that the nature of life was such that the seeds of misfortune were hidden in the fruits of good fortune; the seeds of good fortune grew in the fruits of misfortune. It was merely a matter of time before one became the other.

A straight-A student through high school, Andrew had been accepted to Harvard on a partial scholarship. As a freshman, he showed, much to his father's delight, a strong aptitude for the hard sciences and had decided to concentrate in physics which he declared as his major in the fall of his sophomore year — the same year that the United States entered into war with Vietnam. Andrew, then, narrowed the subject further to nuclear physics. It was all his father hoped for: a brilliant physicist for a son, an expert in the hardest of hard sciences.

Still, ever since the incident when Andrew and Youlin had clashed over the man from Taiwan who had gone into hiding for a failed grade, both father and son had been more courteous and more distant with each other. Andrew no longer talked enthusiastically with Youlin about his future plans, nor about his new excitement over theoretical physics. These days, each level of the science led him to a deeper, less visible, more essential form of natural law; each layer revealed yet another layer, taking Andrew into the heart and core of physics. Theoretical physics, Andrew was sure, was where his life's work would be.

But, by the summer of his sophomore year, Andrew had decided to switch his major.

"From theoretical physics to Chinese studies?" Youlin asked, stupefied.

"I know," Andrew said sheepishly. "It surprised me, too."

"I don't see the connection," his father admitted, reminding himself to listen rather than to lecture.

"And yet they're totally interconnected," Andrew replied. "In fact, they're one and the same. I can't explain it in words, but the deeper I delved into the nature of matter and energy and into theoretical physics — in the same way I went from physics to astrophysics, to nuclear physics, to theoretical physics — the closer I came to Chinese thought — to Mahayana Buddhism, to Taoism, to Chan Buddhism, or Zen as it's called in Japan. What I'm trying to say is that everything that physicists have discovered in the last thirty or forty years, the Chinese already knew over two thousand years ago. It's mind-blowing. Particle-wave theory. Space-time theory. Quantum theory. Boot strap theory. The works. With experimentation and measurement,

Western physicists came upon the answers that the Chinese knew
intuitively through detailed observation of the outside world and deep
study of their own consciousness."

"How are you going to support yourself on Chinese thought?" his
father asked him, starting to lose his temper.

"I knew you were going to ask me that," Andrew said. "I chose
Chinese studies because it answers the question of how I should live
as close as I can to natural law, which is what physics is, after all, and
how I should live as close as I can to deeper levels of consciousness —
not what I should do to keep myself alive. Isn't that a more fundamental question? And won't the answer to the first question eventually
answer the second?"

"Stop being facetious with me, young man," Youlin ordered.

"That's just it. I'm being perfectly serious, and yet you think I am
joking. It's you who are joking, Dad," Andrew said. "A few years ago,
you said I wasn't Chinese. Well, I didn't want to be — not the way you
meant, not the kowtowing, self-sacrificing filial son, the face-saving
forced-to-be-a-hypocrite kind of China boy. Here I am intent on ma-
joring in Chinese thought and you who accused me of disowning my
patrimony don't want me to."

"And you won't," Youlin confirmed angrily. "I'm not sending you
to Harvard so you can grow long hair, sit on some mountain, and stare
at your navel."

"You don't have to send me to Harvard at all," Andrew answered,
coming to his feet. "I'm on partial scholarship. If I need to, I'll get a
part-time job and apply for financial aid on my own."

"Just see if they give it to you — with a major in Chinese studies!"

"Is it true," Bittersweet asked her son one day soon after, "that you
don't want to pay for An-ruh's last two years of college?"

Youlin looked away and made a motion with his head that was
neither a confirmation nor a denial. "Don't try to defend him," he said,
avoiding her eyes. "And don't try to change my mind."

"Since I don't know what your mind is, it would be foolish of me to
try to change it," Bittersweet replied. "And I haven't come to defend
him, since I don't know exactly what transpired between you two.
What I know comes from Madeleine who is as disturbed as I am by
this disruption in our family harmony. I've only come to ask you to
remember your own dealings with your father at An-ruh's age —

when you were about to marry, and after, when he wanted you to work at the Import-Export Control Commission, and even before, when he wanted you to attend Whampoa rather than go to college in the United States. After you've thought back on those times, I know that whatever decision you make regarding An-ruh will be the right one."

Youlin could only do as his mother asked, not out of filial piety, but because her words naturally reminded him of his youth. In light of his recollections, he had to bow to Andrew's wishes.

But the pendulum, Bittersweet discovered, no matter how she set herself in its path to try to slow its trajectory, had not completed its swing. In his whole-hearted immersion in Chinese studies, Andrew had become a Buddhist and was involved in peace marches at his university and even at the White House. In Boston, in New York, in Philadelphia, he and others sat down in civil disobedience, practicing harmlessness in the belief that peaceful means of dissent were a more powerful alternative to aggressive ones.

Madeleine and Youlin were aghast when Andrew called them from jail one day. Only Bittersweet was philosophical. "But why do we wring our hands at the news? Have you forgotten the May 4th Movement? It unleashed the vanguard of social change in China — the students that have been our country's hope ever since. Isn't most of the blood that flows in An-ruh's veins Chinese? Why, then, should we be surprised or saddened that An-ruh feels the same convictions as the May 4th students for whom we feel nothing but pride?"

As the war escalated, the peaceful demonstrations did, too, sometimes including not-so-peaceful expressions of protest and dissent. There were draft card burnings and American flag burnings in the United States and, in Vietnam, self-immolations of Buddhist priests. When Andrew's draft status was changed to that of conscientious objector, his family was relieved. Now that he was exempt from military service on religious grounds, their fears could be laid to rest. But the pendulum had not finished its swing.

One evening, during the spring break of Andrew's junior year and over a dinner at which Delin was present, Andrew read aloud a letter he'd just received from the Dean of Students. It stated that since his involvement in anti-war activities had adversely affected his academic standing and disrupted his participation as a responsible member of the college community, he had been expelled. After Andrew calmly asked for and was granted permission to leave the table, a long silence filled the dining room. Bittersweet looked at the remaining family members whose eyes were cast down into their empty bowls. Youlin's face was working in an effort to try to understand the news without resorting to anger at either the school or his son. Delin's face expressed disappointment and confusion. Madeleine's face was calm, if sad.

"To be expelled," Youlin finally muttered. "After such a promising beginning. A straight-A student. How could something like this happen? How could he have allowed it to happen?"

"He began to ask his own questions and make his own conclusions," Madeleine said softly to no one in particular. "He began to take responsibility for his own actions."

"Your father was a red chair sitter throughout grammar school," Bittersweet said, in an effort to console her son. She indicated the elderly culprit with a glance in his direction. "Later he was thrown out of trade school for being all thumbs. Yet he became a leader of men, a leader of his country, and the route he took was hardly the one his parents chose for him. It's much too soon to say the sun has set on An-ruh's prospects. Perhaps his sun is only just beginning to rise, and in ways we can't foresee. Do we ever know how events will transform themselves?"

Madeleine, who had slipped away from the table, now quietly returned. "He's asked me to call my relatives in Paris," she said after another long silence. She looked at her husband, trying to anticipate his reaction. "He says he'd like to get away for a while . . . leave the United States for a bit. He says . . ." She stopped, trying to understand the feelings behind the words she now uttered. ". . . he's ashamed to be an American."

One morning in June, at an hour and on a day when he never visited, Delin appeared at the edge of the sandbox garden. Bittersweet was watering her tomato plants in the shade of the budding dogwood tree and the leafy bittersweet bush. Madeleine and Youlin were away at work. Andrew was in Boston.

"How do you come to be here?" she asked, so startled to see him she thought him, at first, to be an apparition.

"I walked," he said. "It's such a glorious day!" He smiled at his evasive answer, and Bittersweet noted that his rosy glow wasn't due to the warm sun, that his flush was one of excitement. There was news he was anxious to tell her. After she invited him inside for a cup of tea and even before she could put the kettle on, Delin blurted out, "I've decided to return to China."

He laughed to see his wife pull a chair up to the stove and slowly sit down. "I haven't decided when. I can go at any time, but it could be dangerous. The American presidents from Truman to Kennedy, the heads of committees, congressmen — everyone to whom I've written my point of view regarding the 'China Question' vis-à-vis Taiwan, vis-à-vis the invasion of China by India, vis-à-vis the Kuomintang-Communist struggle over the islands of Quemoy and Matsu, and vis-à-vis the Vietnam War . . . they've all ignored my memoranda and my advice. They think I'm an old army general playing at foreign affairs."

Delin chuckled. "However, as harmless as they consider me and as doddering as they take me to be, they've never called off their watchdogs, their secret service men, from tracking my scent. If my ideas and viewpoint are dismissible, why not, then, their hound dogs, too? Ah, Westerners! They're still prey to the Fu Manchu mystique!" He shook his head, pleased with the reactions he'd elicited.

"Since the American government will make it difficult, perhaps even impossible, for you to return, why do you even consider it?" Bittersweet asked. "The Chinese Communists will only double the danger. Mao himself labeled you public enemy #2, right after Chiang. Even if you succeeded in eluding the Americans, how would the Chinese receive you — you, whom they once vowed to annihilate?"

"I've thought a lot about Mao and the Communists over the past fifteen years," Delin said evenly. "And I've come to the conclusion that what they've done for China is good. She's no longer the sick man of Asia, but strong and united — a power to be reckoned with. Other nations, instead of pitying, despising, or laughing at her, respect or fear her. The Chinese people stand firmly behind their chosen government. The inequities and the iniquities of the Kuomintang régime, the worst results of the natural calamities of drought and flood — famine, drowning, starvation — they're things of the past. We had our chance, and we failed. What difference does it make if Kuomintang or Communist rules, as long as the people are happy and healthy and the country is prosperous and at peace — finally at peace? Hasn't that been my dream for China ever since I was a child?"

Bittersweet nodded.

"And peace is now a dream I have for myself. I'm an old man," Delin admitted. "Too much older, and I will die here. And if I die here, my eyelids will never close."

"You're right to go back, then," Bittersweet agreed, "but even if you get through the first line of American secret service men, the Chinese government will surely stop you."

"But," Delin said, "it is the Chinese government that's asked me to come. The invitation is extended by none other than the Premier himself. Pai was right to spare his life in the thirties. Zhou Enlai's arranged everything for me — from the first leg of the trip to Switzerland, where I'll be met by a liaison who will then facilitate the second leg of my journey to Pakistan, to the final leg to China. Zhou even promised that I could enter and leave China at will, that I could leave altogether if I was not happy. But such an incentive is unnecessary. Once I return, I shall never leave China again. This may be the last time that we see each other," Delin said gently, "and for safety's sake, I've chosen to tell you about my plan, and you alone. Tell Youlin of my decision only after I'm gone."

"This is not the proper way to say good-bye," Bittersweet protested, pouring Delin a cup of tea. "I should prepare a farewell banquet . . . with all your favorite dishes . . . and unpolished rice."

"Take me on a tour of your gardens," Delin requested. "That will be farewell enough."

In her sandbox garden, Delin surveyed her work. "You've grown Chinese gardens," he said, nodding. "America hasn't changed you. If anything, you've changed America — at least, your peaceful little corner of it."

"One is what one is," Bittersweet replied with a shy laugh. "*Meiyou fazi.* Nothing can change that. There's a saying in America: you can take a man out of the country, but you can't take the country out of a man. I guess the saying holds true for a woman as well."

"*Country* meaning *farm* in your case, and *country* meaning *nation* in mine," Delin noted. "It's like our own saying: even if a tree grows to ten thousand feet, its leaves fall back to its roots. America is ten thousand miles from China," he said, "but my desire to go home is even greater than the distance that separates the two. When I was a soldier on the battlefield, I considered home wherever I took off my boots. I never thought there would come a day when I would miss my home and yearn for my homeland. First I needed to taste the bitterness of exile."

He looked at Bittersweet and his gaze went straight to her heart. "You may taste that bitterness of homelessness one day, if you stay in America."

"My home is where my family is. My home *is* my family," Bittersweet replied.

"Yes, you're fortunate," Delin acknowledged. "You have Youlin to take care of you. Filial son that he is, he spends much time seeing to your needs and desires . . . much more time than an American son would spend with his American mother," he continued with an edge to his voice. "Too much time. But our son must take advantage of his youth while he's still young. One season follows the next in fluid succession. It will not wait. So it is for nature; so it is for man."

Her husband's words made Bittersweet heartsick, but like his grandfather, the good doctor who had saved her life when she was a child, Delin offered her a remedy.

"Wait till I'm settled in China. Then choose a time when you want to return and ask Youlin to send you back. I will arrange everything for you on the other end. I'll be there to receive you." They looked at each other for what seemed a long time before Delin resumed speaking. "In the past, I haven't worried about you or cared for you the way I should have. Perhaps in the future you will allow me to fulfill my obligation." Then he bowed slightly from the waist, turned around, and started down the road for home.

Bittersweet turned her hose on her tomato plants as if nothing had interrupted her gardening, but her mind could not shake itself free of her husband's words. How am I a burden to Youlin? she asked herself. If anything, I'm a help, not a hindrance. I grow, I gather, I cook the family meals. But the mere fact that she defended her place and position in her family troubled Bittersweet. Henceforth, she began to keep a close watch on the number of days each week, the number of hours each day, that Youlin spent away from his office and with her.

Every week, on a weekday when the streets were less crowded, Youlin drove her to Chinatown, so she could restock her larder and eat out in one of the restaurants there. How she anticipated those trips to Chinatown, for as she walked along the narrow, winding streets and made her way past throngs of her chatting, jostling countrymen, it was like being back in Canton. Here she felt free enough to tell the waiters that their *see-yow gai* or drunken chicken was tasty but just slightly overdone, or the shopkeepers that their prices were too high or that their produce was not fresh enough.

On a different day of the week, Youlin drove Bittersweet to the garage of the Chinese emigré for her week's supply of freshly-killed chickens. Was asking Youlin to take her to Yonkers a burden when it meant having the best to feed her family? Wasn't shopping the Chinese way — in a variety of small shops where a person greeted you at the door, asked to show you this and that, helped you make your final selection after a bit of polite conversation, and only then culminated the transaction — so much more pleasant than buying things at a supermarket? She hated the shopping mall that was as broad as the Empire State Building was tall. Its vast size made her dizzy and disoriented. There, the only contact between buyer and seller was at the single moment of the exchange of goods for coin. Bittersweet saw no advantage in convenience or efficiency if the time gained meant a loss in human relations. Wasn't the clicking of the beads on an abacus a friendlier sound than the whiz, whir, clang of a cash register drawer?

On weekends, Youlin drove her to Long Island to visit Auntie Kwok, or drove Auntie Kwok from Long Island to visit Bittersweet in New York. Auntie Kwok, though no relation, was so called because she was a few years older than Bittersweet, had lived in the United States several years longer, and was the mother of Kwok Lan-shing who had helped Bittersweet obtain her American visa. Auntie Kwok lived with Lan-shing's brother, Lan-bo, and his wife who owned and ran a chain of Chinese restaurants.

Even more than her trips to Chinatown, Bittersweet enjoyed the visits with Auntie Kwok, for though in Chinatown she spoke Cantonese with everybody, with Auntie Kwok she conversed with a friend. Indeed, Auntie Kwok reminded Bittersweet of her old friend, Hwang *Tai-tai* — not because Auntie Kwok was a good businesswoman but because, despite the fact that she was a tiny woman, frail and delicate in health, she was opinionated and obstreperous.

Auntie Kwok had fewer opportunities than Bittersweet to know Americans and American ways firsthand. Her entire family was Chinese and spoke Chinese both at home and at work. And, because they put in long hours at their restaurants, they had little time to spend with her — far less than Youlin spent with Bittersweet. But through listening to gossip, watching television, and looking at magazines, Auntie

Kwok learned about America. She was convinced that she was well-versed in the manners and mores of the Flowery Flag Nation.

"Living in America is like being under house arrest," she complained to Bittersweet. "I stay in the house all the time. Living in America is not at all like living in China where family and friends fill every room every hour of the day and night. In America you can have all the gold and silver you want, but one possesses real wealth in China. There, one has family."

"But here, too, you live with your family," Bittersweet reminded her. "Doesn't that make America your home?"

Auntie Kwok chuckled at her friend's naïveté. "I've lived in the Flowery Flag Nation longer than you," she reminded Bittersweet, her seniority allowing her to feel superiority as well. "For us Chinese, family is everything. We put all our hopes, efforts, and dreams into it. Some of us, the most fortunate ones, live under the same roof with four, even five, generations. But that's hardly the American way. I know. I've heard it from other Chinese women who have lived here longer than you or me, women who have had no choice but to succumb to the American way of doing things. Mark my words: what happened to them will happen to us."

On previous occasions, Bittersweet had listened politely to Auntie Kwok's disparaging words, but she had dismissed them. After all, her own situation so clearly contradicted Auntie Kwok's conclusions. But now that she had heard Delin's warning, it seemed to parallel Auntie Kwok's words and augur the same end.

"In America, when the children grow up and the old man . . . which is what they rudely call the master of the house . . . loses his ability to work and make money, that is the beginning of the end," she told Bittersweet. "The children, who, by the way, are not obliged to support their parents, leave home and seldom return to visit. In America, children cut their ties to their parents as soon as they can afford to live apart from them. As for grandparents, they don't live with their family at all."

"I'm a grandparent, and I live with my family," Bittersweet said.

"That's today," Auntie Kwok said. "Who knows what will happen tomorrow?"

"With whom do grandparents live, then?" Bittersweet wanted to know.

"Why, with no one — by themselves, in a small apartment, alone and afraid," Auntie Kwok answered. "They might as well be dead so few people come to visit them. Many have been found dead, you know, and for a long time, for if no one comes to visit them, who knows that they have died?"

Bittersweet shivered.

"If they're not put in a tiny apartment, then they're sent to an old-age home," Auntie Kwok continued. "There, they're surrounded by sad, lonely people like themselves. What is even more unthinkable is that their children are convinced that they're doing their filial duty and proud to be able to send them to such homes!"

Auntie Kwok stretched out a tiny, gnarled hand and patted Bittersweet's arm. "Oh, don't think that my son and daughter-in-law are cruel to me or mistreat me any more than yours do you. Young people lead a different life from us old folks. I live in the same house as my son, but distance is not counted only in *li*. In America, emotional distance between generations increases with age. As time goes by, the older and the younger generations have less and less in common, less and less to share. Your son and daughter-in-law have their work to do and your grandson to care for. In fulfilling the requirements of their jobs and raising their son, how can they stay at home to wait on you? The day will come when old age and its faithful attendant, loneliness, will be your companion."

"You exaggerate," Bittersweet insisted. "It's true we're *lao ren* and perhaps a little lonely, but nonetheless we live with our children and our children's children."

"And how long before they decide that we're nuisances and stick us in one of these old-age homes?" Auntie Kwok said, cocking her head to one side. "Your in-laws are Americans. Tell me now, how often do your daughter-in-law's relatives come to visit?" Even before Bittersweet could speak, Auntie Kwok answered, "I'll bet not very often. Everybody works, even the women, and no one has time. Visiting in America requires a special occasion as well as special permission. Even the closest of relatives might not see each other more than a few times a year, during the American festivals — Thanksgiving, Christmas, New Year, and Easter. Easter — hrumph! Instead of tidying up their ancestors' graves, Americans search for painted chicken eggs! In America, guests have it very tough. Whether you're family or friend, you can't just drop in but must phone ahead and request to come by. You also can't assume that an invitation to visit is the same thing as the right to share a meal. Oh, no! Your visitation rights are limited to sitting and talking only, unless, of course, you've been expressly invited to eat. And even if you are, guests bring their own food. In America, the host evidently doesn't provide an adequate table."

Bittersweet burst out laughing. "It isn't for that! American guests bring food out of politeness and concern for their hostess, so that she won't have to work so hard to feed them."

"It's a strange form of politeness that makes a host and hostess lose face!" Auntie Kwok sniffed. "We Chinese, on the other hand, visit whenever we want — without phoning in advance and without bringing our own food. When we arrive, the host simply puts out one more bowl and one more pair of chopsticks."

Auntie Kwok clucked her tongue against the roof of her mouth. "The winter of our lives is beginning. You may think that the chrysanthemum season has come and gone with little frost because we are both with our families, three generations each. But little frost means deeper snows."

A flower does not bloom for a hundred days; a person may not have good fortune for one hundred years. So Da Mama had said so many years ago. Like petals from that flower, members of Bittersweet's family began to drift away. Soon after his surprise visit, Delin left for China. Fast upon Delin's departure, Andrew left for Paris.

One day, months after Andrew and Delin had left, Youlin returned home from work, flashing a broad smile and waving a letter in front of Bittersweet's eyes. She had just been reading newspaper reports from Hong Kong about a new kind of patriotism that was gaining momentum in China: young students were fashioning themselves into zealous soldiers, sworn to the principles of Mao Tse-tung, now called Mao Zedong, and his Little Red Book. Red Guards, they called themselves. Their purpose was to root out and punish the Four Olds — old customs, old habits, old culture, and old ways of thinking — and any trace of Western corruption.

"That wouldn't be a letter from your father, would it?" Bittersweet asked, putting down the newspaper.

"You guessed right!"

She took the envelope that her son dangled before her eyes and examined it.

"But there's no stamp."

"Of course not," Youlin said. "If it had, it would never have arrived — not a letter from behind the Bamboo Curtain! It's been passed from hand to hand around the world."

Bittersweet slid the letter out of its envelope, then hesitated.

"How is your father? Is he well?" she asked.

"Read the letter instead of trying to read my face," Youlin suggested.

Carefully Bittersweet unfolded the two sheaves of thin rice paper and began to read. Her husband had been welcomed back to China with great pomp and ceremony. Premier Zhou Enlai — along with the mayor of the city, Teng Zhen — had greeted him at Beijing's Dadu Airport. The Great Helmsman Mao Zedong had received Delin, as had President Liu Shaoqi and Marshall Zhu De. An interesting functionary named Deng Xiaoping had also been on hand. He was a diminutive man who had greatly impressed Delin, a man whose physical stature belied a keen, possibly brilliant, mind. Delin had then been taken on a tour of the country to witness for himself the great achievements the Communist Party had made since 1949. Continuing in a guarded and propagandistic tone, Delin wrote that he had been especially happy to revisit his home province of Kwangsi, now known as Guangxi, where he had met Bittersweet's nephew, Jiaqiu, now a teacher at the agricultural institute in Nanning, and his wife Tanmin. As for Dejie, she had died of cancer only a few months after their arrival in China.

Dejie's illness was already in an advanced stage, requiring immediate surgery, when she received the diagnosis in America. But the night before the morning of the operation, Dejie had had second thoughts and had stolen out of the hospital and refused to return. For all her insistence on the superiority of Western science and technology, she still harbored the old Chinese belief that the body was sacrosanct and that "breaking" it deprived it of its wholeness and thus its access to the Shadowy World.

"Chairman Mao has stated that those who have left China are welcome to return," Delin's letter continued in the same stiff prose. "The government will treat them with propriety and courtesy. China has always maintained that overseas Chinese are all close members of the same family. They are free to return and to leave China. Never again will China be divided, and all Chinese will work for continued national unity. The Chinese government sees no difference between those Chinese who loved their country early and those who love it late.

371

Even if a tree grows ten thousand feet tall, its leaves fall back to its roots. All Chinese are welcome home."

As self-censored and woodenly worded as his letter was, the final few sentences held Bittersweet's attention for they echoed her husband's sincere sentiment . . . and his last spoken words to her. We shall see, she told herself, quelling a sudden sense of foreboding, for her eyes had strayed back to the Hong Kong paper she'd been reading. We shall see what the next letter brings.

But a next letter never arrived. Instead, news of Delin came via American newspapers: his obituary appeared in *The New York Times* on February 2, 1969, then again, ironically, on February 14, Valentine's Day, in *Time* magazine at the height of the Great Proletarian Cultural Revolution. The latter stated that Delin had defected from the United States.

"Defected?" Bittersweet asked Youlin who had just translated the obituary notice for her. "But how could he defect from a country not his own? He was simply an old man who wanted to die in his homeland."

"Blame it on the ravages of the cold war," her son said in a somber voice, "that a personal act should be construed as a political one."

The New York Times obituary devoted almost a full page to Delin's life: "Li *Xiansheng*," one Chinese journalist had reportedly asked Delin soon after his return to China, "in your long career in Chinese politics, you were a four-star general and a high-ranking official in the Kuomintang government. You then lived for many years in the United States, whose system is capitalism. The political system under which the People's Republic of China is governed is communism. Which 'ism', then, do you support?"

According to the interview, Delin had replied, "Patriotism."

But the other news devoted to the Cultural Revolution made Bittersweet fear that Delin's press conference had been, in reality, an inquisition.

Youlin, guessing her thoughts, comforted his mother, saying, "Knowledgeable and reputable persons both inside and outside China have assured me that Father was under the protection of Zhou Enlai from the moment he stepped down on Chinese soil to the moment he died. He was seventy-eight years old and ailing. He was taken to a hospital outside Beijing. He died of old age."

But the images Bittersweet watched on television did little to reassure her. In one news clip of a "struggle" session, a man assumed a "take-off" position — standing, his torso bent forward perpendicular to his legs, his hands tied tightly behind his back so that his arms strained painfully at their sockets — a position he had to maintain for hours while he was questioned, mocked, and struck. Finally, he confessed to the crimes against the state of which he was accused. Other clips showed men and women — "running dogs of the capitalists" — wearing tall white dunce caps and being paraded in open army trucks to the jeers and insults of the angry crowd. Still other clips offered images of children not yet out of high school vandalizing the homes of "stinking capitalist pigs," and of youngsters not yet out of grammar school denouncing their brothers and sisters, their fathers and mothers. Here was a country once devoted to family now demonstrating a fanatical love of nation. China was now, Bittersweet thought, a country filled with fear of and hatred for anyone who came from a Mandarin family or a Western background. Hadn't Delin lived in the United States, the most hated of nations, for fifteen years? Hadn't his son become a despised American citizen? Weren't his daughter-in-law and grandchildren Americans by birth? How, then, might he have been spared by the fanatical Red Guards?

Delin's death, besides giving Bittersweet a reason to grieve, was also a stark reminder of his parting admonition and Auntie Kwok's prediction. But Delin was no longer alive to send for her, and China was no longer China but a country without a culture, a nation in the throes of self-destruction.

Chapter 11
The Leaves Fall Back to the Roots
(1971)

Though the worst of the Cultural Revolution was over by the early 1970s, Hong Kong had not escaped its effects. Sporadic riots broke out on the island, necessitating, at one point, the closing of Youlin's factory for a few days. Then, one evening, a homemade bomb went off in his factory, injuring the guard on night duty and destroying equipment. Youlin flew out to Hong Kong to assess the damage and to determine what should be done. He had to consider the condition of his equipment, the shift in the political climate in Asia, as well as the growing economic trend towards investment in new technology. Seeing adversity as opportunity, Youlin and his partners decided to switch from the production of electrical goods to the production of electronic goods.

Such a fundamental change in plans required that Youlin fly to Hong Kong several times a year and stay for weeks at a time each visit. But, inevitably, he returned home to New York after less than a week. Sometimes he even cancelled his flight to Hong Kong at the last minute. Bittersweet understood that her son was divided between his professional obligations and his filial responsibilities. Delin's parting words now sounded like a rebuke. She was occupying too much of Youlin's time.

And too much of Madeleine's. A few years after opening her boutique, Madeleine had opened a second one, and she often worked late into the evening and on weekends. The times when Youlin was in Hong Kong, Madeleine did the food shopping. Driving to Yonkers for fresh-killed chickens was out of the question. It was difficult enough for her to find time to stop at the local grocery store.

Eventually, Bittersweet could no longer convince herself that she was more a help than a hindrance to her son and daughter-in-law. And what help she was — growing her gardens and preparing the family meals — seemed small recompense for the sacrifices they made on her behalf, especially now that Andrew and, frequently, Madeleine weren't at home. Often, Bittersweet cooked meals for Youlin and herself alone and, sometimes, only for herself. Soon, there was no more need for her second garden.

What levity Bittersweet enjoyed in her life was provided by Andrew's letters from Paris. He had enrolled at the Sorbonne and was pursuing two degrees: one in theoretical physics, the other in Chinese studies. At the university, he had met Irina, a Czech student whose father had played an important role in Czechoslovakia's political reform, only to be ousted and self-exiled to France when the hard-line government came to power. It was Andrew and Irina's intention to finish their degrees and then, when the Cultural Revolution was over and political stability was restored, live and work in China for a year or two.

In 1973, the United States officially recognized the People's Republic of China, and the American government began to issue visas to those citizens who wished to travel there. The Bamboo Curtain that had been drawn over China for nearly a quarter of a century was parting.

One day in the spring of that year, Bittersweet received a letter written in Chinese characters and stamped with very official-looking chops. It was an invitation to lunch from the First Secretary of the Permanent Mission of the People's Republic of China to the United Nations. She showed it to Youlin.

"Ah, an invitation from the Chinese Mission," Youlin said. "How does it feel to be asked to lunch by the opposition?"

"I was born at the end of the Qing Dynasty," Bittersweet replied. "I've lived through the Boxer Rebellion, a few provincial wars, the Northern Expedition, the War of Resistance, and the War of Revolution between the Kuomintang and the Communists. I have lived under monarchy, anarchy, Western imperialism, Japanese imperialism, Sun Yat-sen's fledgling democracy, Chiang Kai-shek's personal dictatorship, British colonialism in Hong Kong, and capitalism in the United States. Which opposition do you mean?"

On the appointed day, Youlin accompanied his mother to the Chinese Permanent Mission. When they arrived, the First Secretary, the Deputy Ambassador, and two junior secretaries were standing before the doorway of a large reception room to welcome them. As the guest of honor, Bittersweet was seated between the Deputy Ambassador and the First Secretary. Their mammoth over-stuffed armchairs were separated by small tables over which they traded platitudes and sipped cups of fragrant tea. Then, lunch was announced. In the huge dining room, where their tiny party was swallowed up by empty space, they were served an excellent and lavish banquet, each course punctuated by a round of *mao-tai* and an equal number of *gan bei*.

"And how do you find living in New York, Li *Furen?*" the First Secretary inquired when the fish course was over.

"To live with one's children is the dream of every Chinese mother," Bittersweet replied. "My son Youlin lives in New York. So do I, and so my dream has been fulfilled. I feel very fortunate in that respect, but in another respect, I am less fortunate. I don't speak English, and so my life in the United States is necessarily restricted. I'm completely dependent on my son, but he must work all day to support his family. Though I have my garden to take care of and the family meals to prepare, I have much time on my hands yet too little to do with it."

Winter melon soup, served in its own elaborately carved rind, arrived.

"Li *Furen,*" the Deputy Ambassador said, leaning towards her over his bowl of soup, "I've considered what you've told us about your life in America. I wonder, have you ever thought of returning to China? Do you think that you might be happier there?"

Bittersweet set down her porcelain soup spoon and looked at Youlin who was seated directly across the table from her.

"That was my husband's last wish for me, that I return to China," she said, looking at the Deputy Ambassador, once she was certain that she had her son's ear as well. "His last wish *of* me, however, was to see that our son Youlin realized his full potential." She glanced at Youlin and saw that he well understood the significance of her words. "I am eighty-three years old, Mr. Deputy Ambassador. I think I can safely say that I am a *lao ren*. I think I can also safely say that I have always tried to fulfill the wishes of my husband. In this case, however, it is not merely a question of fulfilling my husband's last wish and serving my son, but of receiving permission to return to China from the Chinese government. If that permission is granted, then it is my sincere wish to return to the land of my birth."

The Deputy Ambassador and the First Secretary looked at each other and nodded. "Li *Furen*, if it is your sincere wish to return to China, then it can be arranged," the Deputy Ambassador told her. "If your son is in agreement," both he and the First Secretary looked at

Youlin simultaneously and, receiving his affirmative nod, the Deputy Ambassador continued, "then rest assured that I will relay your request to the Chinese government."

Just then, dessert — a beautifully molded and glazed *babaofan*, or eight treasure rice — appeared on the table, a fitting finale to the banquet and just recompense for the diners' diplomatic skills.

Months passed in which Bittersweet had no word from the First Secretary, the Deputy Ambassador, or any other member of the Chinese Permanent Mission to the United Nations. In the meantime, Youlin telephoned Andrew to tell him about his grandmother's decision to return to China. Soon after, Andrew arrived in New York for a long-awaited family reunion. He brought with him a new family member — Irina, his fiancée — as well as the news that they had both graduated with honors. Andrew now taught physics at a *lycée* in Paris, and Irina worked as a translator at UNESCO.

At the end of their New York stay, as the young couple was packing to return to Paris, Bittersweet appeared before them, holding something wrapped in tissue paper. Extending it to Irina, Bittersweet felt proud that she didn't have to ask Andrew to translate, for Irina had learned Mandarin as part of her studies in international relations.

"I hope you'll accept this small token of good will," Bittersweet said to her. "Before Warm Peace left home for Paris, I wanted to give him a bit of money, but he refused it. I then tried to give him this." Bittersweet unfolded the leaves of tissue paper from about a thick chain, heavy with Chinese gold coins. "For though it is money, it is also not money; he would not lose face to accept an heirloom. But again, my grandson refused. I've wanted him to have this, for his father wore it around his neck when he left China for Hong Kong during the War of Revolution. I feel it carries good luck. Since Warm Peace won't have it, perhaps you as his fiancée will. I offer it to you as an engagement present. May you wear it in good fortune, good health, and long life."

"You're a wily diplomat, *Nai-nai*," Andrew conceded while Irina hugged Bittersweet.

"Grandmother wisdom," his fiancée corrected him. "Grandmother wisdom."

When father and son embraced at the airport before Andrew's flight back to Paris, Bittersweet felt that her work was done: now she could leave her home in America for the land of her birth.

· ◆ ·

"Here's your visa," Youlin said, handing his mother the document, "and here's a letter from the Deputy Ambassador detailing the arrangements. If they're not suitable, he says they may be changed. And if you've changed your mind, now that you've had more time to think about the matter, if you don't want to return to China . . . ," he continued, his voice becoming gentler as it became graver.

"Not return?" she said, dismissing his concern with an impatient wave of her hand. "What have I been waiting for, then? Only these. And to think — I've waited only a few months for my Chinese visa when I had to wait eight long years for my American one."

She fluttered the papers before her son's eyes. But as soon as he left the room, she fell upon their every word. According to the Deputy Ambassador's letter, her house on Folded Brocade Road had been restored and would be returned to her — the house she had never lived in and had seen only once, the house she had built in the Western style in deference to her then new daughter-in-law. Her nephew Jiaqiu and his wife Tanmin, their son Lizi, his wife Nan-nan, and their four-year-old son, Liqi, had already been transferred from Nanning to Guilin, as Kweilin was now called, for the express purpose of providing companionship and care for her. Also, two doctors from the People's Hospital #2 just across the street from her house would make biweekly visits to ensure her good health. If these arrangements were not to her liking, she should contact the Deputy Ambassador and more suitable ones would be devised.

Bittersweet let her hand and the letter it held drift to her lap. Four generations living together under the same roof. It was what every Chinese dreamed of.

She gave a sudden start and settled her glasses squarely on the bridge of her nose. Four years old, she thought. To start school very soon. To learn to read and write. And she would help Liqi — her great-grand nephew, the fourth and youngest generation of her household-to-be — just as Delin had helped her learn on their wedding night. She would use the very same imagery, the very same word Delin had used. She would start with their surname: Li.

"For Li contains every stroke that is common to all Chinese characters," she recalled him saying. "Horizontal stroke, which must look like clouds forming a thunderhead. Vertical stroke, like a thousand-year-old vine stem, still stout and strong."

Chapter 12
Centennial
(1973)

In early autumn in Beijing, the Chinese government welcomed Bittersweet home. Just as Delin had been greeted upon his return by Premier
Zhou Enlai, Bittersweet was met at Beijing's Dadu Airport by Zhou's
wife, Deng Yingchao. This was a great honor, for Madam Deng, like
her husband, was considered a great revolutionary and was well-
loved by the Chinese people. Again, as Delin had been, Bittersweet
was the guest of honor at a banquet held in the Great Hall of the People
which, along with the National People's Congress, flanked the great
gray expanse of Tiananmen Square.

Madam Deng told Bittersweet, "These two buildings and the Square
of the Gate of the Heavenly Peace, as the square is called, were built at
a time when China and the Soviet Union were staunch allies. They
were built in the Stalinist architectural tradition."

How little the Stalinist tradition has to do with the soul of Peking,
Bittersweet thought to herself, as her limousine passed before the
Square. How different today's Beijing is from the old Peking where I
used to wander blind alleyways filled with curio and calligrapher's
shops, teahouses, and mahjong parlors.

But not everything old had succumbed to the new. There, directly
opposite Tiananmen Square, lay the Forbidden City with its rows of
imperial palaces and pavilions. The former residence of the Chinese
emperors was unchanged but for a single addition: a giant portrait of
Mao hung above the central portal.

For her first few days in China, Bittersweet was taken on a tour of
the Forbidden City, the Summer Palace, the Temple of Heaven, Beihai
Park, Beijing University, and the Great Wall — all of which she had
visited when she had lived in the capital. But the place that impressed
Bittersweet most was a place she had never been before. North of the
city, on a bleak and windswept hill, was Babaoshan, the place where
the ashes of illustrious Chinese patriots — Delin among them — were
kept. Entering House #2 at the top of the hill, and carrying ugly plastic

379

flowers (for real blooms were considered capitalistic and artificial ones could be reused), Bittersweet bowed her head before Delin's funerary box. It lay next to the box of chairman of the People's Republic Liu Shaoqi and was surrounded by scores of similar wooden boxes, all bearing birth and death dates. The year 1969 — the year of her husband's death — was inscribed on box after box, in row upon row, on shelf after shelf. Too often, Bittersweet surmised sadly, to indicate deaths due to natural causes.

Her visit to Beijing concluded, Bittersweet boarded a plane bound for Guilin, her final destination. All during the flight she wondered how her hometown might have changed in the twenty-four years since she had left. How would she be treated there? What would her life there be like? She realized that the questions she was asking herself were the very questions she had put to herself on the eve of her wedding — questions prompted by the same trepidation, the same excitement. Indeed, she felt the same ambivalence on going home as an old woman as she had felt at leaving home as a new bride.

But when the plane finally landed and she stepped onto the tarmac, she immediately recognized her hometown by scent. The osmanthus trees were in full bloom, the tiny parchment-colored buds releasing a delicate orange-blossom fragrance. And when she caught sight of her house on Folded Brocade Road, the house she had just barely seen completed, she was almost certain she had made the right decision. The house bore an uncanny resemblance to the house she had just left in suburban New York; it had the same pleasing shape, the same steeply pitched roof, the same decorative half-timbering that Americans called English Tudor, the same stone and brick façade. I've been living in a replica in America, Bittersweet thought. Now I will live in the original.

Just at that moment, even before she pulled on the bell overhead, the *da men* opened and the occupants of the house ran out to greet her. First Jiaqiu, whom she recognized after all these years, and then his family — Tanmin, Lizi, Nan-nan, and Liqi.

"*Huanying! Huanying!*" they cried, smiling and crowding around her. "Come inside! Come inside your old home," they said, taking her by both hands and pulling her up the porch steps.

✦

(1989)

The red light went on.

"Ladies and gentlemen, please fasten your seat belts," a voice said over the sound system. "We are about to land at Guilin airport."

The words broke Youlin's train of thought, but only momentarily. He fastened his seat belt and smiled nervously at Madeleine beside him. He had looked forward to this day — his mother's 100th birthday and a family reunion, the first one ever in Guilin. But recent events in China made him anxious.

He had been so proud of Andrew and Irina when they became "foreign experts," professors of physics and romance languages, respectively, with one-year teaching positions at Beijing University. Now, he was worried for them, precisely because they were there.

He had been worried about them three years ago, too, in 1986, when they first went to China as tourists. At Beijing University, they had listened to some student leaders calling for reforms, and they had marched with students, hundreds strong, to Tiananmen Square to demand those reforms. Andrew had been especially enthusiastic — as motivated as he had been in his own student activist days.

Soon after the student demonstrations, Hu Yao-bang, the reform-minded Secretary General of the Chinese Communist Party, was stripped of his title for failing to take a hard line against the students. He had been allowed to retain his position as member of the Politburo and, undeterred, he continued to press for reforms.

Three years later, on April 15th, just as Youlin and Madeleine were preparing for their trip to China for Bittersweet's centennial birthday celebration, Hu died. His death was a great blow to the students who felt that they had lost the "Soul of China." But with this loss, they regained their resolve. The student movement of 1986 was revived.

From April 15th on, Youlin watched televised images of hundreds of Chinese students wearing black armbands. To mourn Hu's passing, they hung "big character posters" around Beijing and lay white wreaths at the Hero's Monument in Tiananmen Square. They marched to Zhongnanhai, the exclusive residence of China's top leaders, and called for democratic freedoms, an end to corruption and nepotism, and more state funding for education. Disregarding police orders to evacuate the Square, the students had camped there while the official memorial services for Hu were held in the adjacent Great Hall of the People. As Youlin watched, he could not help but scan the crowds for one blond, blue-eyed Eurasian in his mid-40s, the son he had once accused of not being Chinese.

As the student demonstrations escalated, Youlin called Andrew almost daily to find out what was happening in Beijing and to be reassured that his son and daughter-in-law were safe. He grew especially concerned after reading an editorial in the *People's Daily* which accused the students of "an organized conspiracy to create turmoil" and of a plot to overthrow the government. The editorial prompted 150,000 students — enraged that their democratic, patriotic movement had been deliberately misrepresented by the press — to take to the streets of Beijing and demand the retraction of the insulting editorial and a meeting with Premier Li Peng.

"Don't worry," Andrew told his father over the phone. "Secretary General Zhao Ziyang is urging the State Council to look favorably upon the students' demands. And the demonstrations are well-organized and peaceful."

But on May 4th, when perhaps a quarter of a million demonstrators marched on Tiananmen Square in celebration of the first student movement in Chinese history, Youlin still anxiously scanned his television screen for his son. As he watched, he remembered how, decades ago, his father had explained to him the rationale behind the May Fourth celebration. "On May 4, 1919," Delin had said, "Chinese students discovered that public opinion and mass protest could force their weak-kneed fledgling republican government to reject the Versailles Treaty whereby Shandong Province would be handed over gratis to Japan. May 4, 1919 marked the beginning of national consciousness in China."

The student movement received a new impetus just days after the 70th anniversary of the May Fourth Movement when a thousand journalists in Beijing delivered a petition to the government. The petition demanded talks on freedom of the press, while it denounced government censorship of the student demonstrations, and called for fair and comprehensive coverage of the democracy movement. Some of the journalists carried banners or wore headbands proclaiming, "We refuse to lie anymore." When the *People's Daily* refused to retract the offensive editorial or to recognize the legitimacy of the student movement, several hundred students launched a hunger strike in

Tiananmen. Now when Youlin phoned his son, it was to ask Andrew and Irina to fly to Guilin earlier than they had planned. But Andrew was neither in his office nor at home. He's with the students, Youlin concluded. He's in the Square.

Youlin's airplane touched down and taxied to a halt, but Youlin was still lost in his thoughts.

"They're fine," Madeleine assured him, though she herself looked worried. "We'd have heard something if they weren't."

Youlin looked at his watch. "By this time tomorrow, Soviet Prime Minister Gorbachev will be in Beijing. If the students don't leave the Square, their presence will threaten the Sino-Soviet summit. What Deng Xiaoping had planned as a foreign policy *tour-de-force* could end up as a fiasco." He sighed. "If only I'd gotten through to Andrew. If only he had called. If only I could be sure that they're both safe."

Tanmin stood back from the *da men*, her arms folded across her chest, and surveyed her handiwork. The new coat of paint that she had applied to the door was glossy and bright red and, most importantly, dry. It was the same shade of red as the clusters of berries weighing down the bittersweet bush that stood to one side of the door. And to think that when her aunt had brought it from America it had been no more than a scrawny sprig! It had grown so tall that some of its boughs arched over the *da men*, making a festive entrance for the birthday guests to pass under early this afternoon.

Tanmin heaved a satisfied, if rather weary, sigh and dropped her arms to her sides. Everything, finally, was ready. The house had been scrupulously cleaned; extra chairs had been set out; long-life noodles were ready to be cooked in giant cauldrons; rolls of red paper flecked with gold and bearing the calligraphy of well-wishers hung on the walls of the house; gifts of plastic peaches and cranes, both denoting long life, were set out alongside huge baskets of fabric flowers on long tables. More than a hundred rice bowls had been decorated with her Aunt Bittersweet's name, her venerable age, and the date of her 100th birthday — May 18, 1989.

"Youlin! Youlin!" Tanmin called to her nephew inside. She wanted him to see how attractive the door looked with its new coat of paint. Not surprisingly, there was no answer. She knew where she might find him. If he wasn't with his mother, then he was in front of the television watching the student sit-in and hunger strike in Beijing, or he was on the phone trying to call his son. She had seen the concern on Youlin's face when he learned that the democracy movement had upstaged the Sino-Soviet summit. Because Tiananmen Square had become one vast student encampment, the wreath-laying ceremony at the Hero's Monument, planned for Gorbachev's visit, was cancelled, as was a tour of the Forbidden City and a night of Peking opera. Youlin's concern became even greater when, four days after the hunger strike began, hundreds of students suffering from dehydration and sunstroke had to be hospitalized.

Tanmin heard the phone ring and scurried inside to answer, but Youlin got there first. He was talking excitedly. Madeleine was at his side.

"Andrew!" Youlin closed his eyes in relief. "You can't imagine how glad I am to hear your voice. How are you? And Irina? Where are you?"

"In Tokyo," Andrew said. "The Chinese government kicked us out — for our own safety, they said — for being in the Square and taking part in the democracy movement. We couldn't call you from Beijing. The phones were completely tied up. We've got an hour layover in Japan before heading on to Paris. We just want to reassure you that we're both fine and to say we're sorry we can't make *Nai-nai*'s birthday party."

"I wish you two had flown to Guilin earlier," Youlin said.

"We couldn't." There was a pause. "We just couldn't, Dad. You can't imagine what's going on in Beijing. Irina and I just had to be there. What the students have done is incredible. They've turned Tiananmen Square into a miniature city with its own government. There's a broadcasting station, a sanitation department, a media organization, and a security system complete with passes and security checks. Student police direct traffic in and out of the Square. Doctors have set up a makeshift field hospital in the Square. The Red Cross has donated a hundred buses as shelters from the rain. Ordinary citizens have donated food, quilts, and tents. Daily, hourly, the students in the Square are being joined by their professors, by other professionals, and by workers. The spirit of Tiananmen has become infectious. Some say that it has already spread to over thirty cities throughout China. I myself talked with students from Shanghai and Nanjing who came to Beijing to join the movement and add their support. All of them say that their desire is to improve the system, not to overthrow it. . . . They're calling our flight number. Dad, can you put *Nai-nai* on? We want to wish her a happy birthday. And tell Mom that we're fine, that we'll call again from Paris, and that we love you all."

Bittersweet was napping when Youlin came into her room to tell her that Andrew was calling from Tokyo. Groggily, she shuffled to the phone with the assistance of her cane, but at the sound of her grandson's voice, she was wide awake.

"*Nai-nai*, it's Warm Peace," Andrew said.

"How you hated that name when you were little," Bittersweet said with a smile, as she sat down in her favorite chair. "It seems to fit you these days. You've been with your students in Tiananmen Square, so I'm told. Yes, yes, one must follow one's destiny. One must go with the grain. One mustn't go against the current. As that Buddhist-Taoist-American nursery rhyme says, 'Row, row, row your boat gently down the stream,' not up the stream. So, Warm Peace, are you coming to my birthday party?"

Andrew explained again where he was, why he and Irina couldn't be in Guilin, and how sorry they were to miss Bittersweet's birthday celebration and the family reunion they had so looked forward to. Then, Irina got on the phone.

"*Ma chère grandmère*," Irina said.

Bittersweet smiled to hear the pretty words, the ones she preferred being called by her granddaughter-in-law.

"I hope you will forgive Andrew and me for not being in Guilin on your 100th birthday," Irina continued, "but though we cannot be with you in person, we are with you in spirit. We both wish you *bonne anniversaire* and ask you not to worry about us. We are well and safe. China, too, please the evolutionary process and the Taoist Immortals, will be well and safe and free. This Beijing Spring, unlike the Prague Spring of my homeland, shall not be cut short. We love you, *chère grandmère*, and we hold you close to our hearts."

Bittersweet leaned heavily on her cane to rise to her feet. She shook her head in disgust. Just a few years ago—or had it been several years?—she could get down on her hands and knees to tend her garden. She could ferociously dust the furniture, sweep the floors, and wash the heavy iron wok.

"And now," she said, squinting at her watch, then waving away Youlin and Madeleine's offer of assistance back to her room, "I wouldn't mind a little nap to be fresh and alert for my birthday party. The guests will be arriving in just over an hour."

Bittersweet

· ✦ ·

"Huanying! Huanying!"

Tanmin stood just inside the red *da men*, greeting the guests as they entered the compound, while Youlin, Madeleine, Jiaqiu, and the rest of his family formed a reception line beside Bittersweet. Officials from the city and provincial governments were the first to arrive. Soon after, members of the extended family came. There were some whom Bittersweet hadn't seen in decades, others she'd never met because they lived far away or because they'd been born after she left China for Hong Kong and America. Even a member of the National People's Congress came all the way from Beijing to congratulate her on her one hundred years and to wish her many more. Bittersweet recognized him as Cheng *Xiansheng*, Delin's former secretary and the liaison who met her husband in Switzerland after the first leg of his journey home.

Finally, when the stream of guests had slowed, Youlin led Congressman Cheng off to one side of the room to engage him in conversation about the newest developments in the democracy movement.

"Yesterday," Cheng said under his breath, "the General Secretary read a statement asking the students to return to their campuses. He fears for their health because of the inadequate sanitation facilities and the hundreds of hunger strikers."

"For their health — or for their safety?" Youlin asked anxiously.

He knew that Cheng, aside from being privy to inside information, had been purged during the Cultural Revolution. He might, therefore, be especially canny in interpreting signals from Beijing.

"If he had meant their safety, he would have said so," Cheng assured Youlin. "The students trust Zhao. They know that he sympathizes with them. In his address, he recognized their movement as patriotic and promised not to punish any of the student leaders. Unfortunately, the *People's Daily* editorial has not been retracted, so the students march again today. This time perhaps as many as a million citizens will line the streets to encourage and applaud them. Should that happen, public order will have begun to deteriorate."

"I'm surprised that Deng has allowed the students to go this far," Youlin admitted.

"To save the summit and himself from embarrassment," Cheng said, then added, "and possibly to catch the ringleaders."

"If the students are not to be punished, why do the ringleaders have to be caught?" Youlin asked.

"It's Zhao who has urged leniency, not Deng," Cheng reminded him. "There's a rumor — that Zhao called a pre-dawn emergency meeting with the top leadership today where he continued to push for concessions for the students, including an immediate dialogue with their leaders and an anti-corruption campaign, a campaign to begin with his own family. Everyone knows that both his and Deng's sons have received inestimable favors because of their fathers' positions."

"Speaking of sons, mine, who was in the Square with the students, was asked to leave China," Youlin said. "Otherwise he would have been here today."

"Then your son will be glad to know," Cheng said, "that Premier Li Peng has agreed to meet this very afternoon with the student leaders in the Great Hall of the People."

"It's a concession," Youlin said. "It's that much at least, and perhaps it means more concessions to come."

A joyful commotion behind him made Youlin turn around.

"Delin!" Bittersweet gasped, her hands to her mouth. She rose to her feet. This time she didn't even need the support of her cane. "How very much like Delin you look! What a surprise to spring on a very old lady! You're very fortunate, young man, that my heart is in excellent working order!"

All the guests laughed — the actor who had portrayed Delin in the movie re-enactment of the battle of Taierzhuang most heartily of all. He took Bittersweet's hands in his.

"Not very old, Li *Furen*," he protested. "In years, perhaps, but not in spirit."

"Oh, in spirit, too," she confessed, toasting him and her other guests once more with yet another glass of *san hua*. "But I will tell you a secret: not in my dreams. Oh, no. If in my waking hours I am one hundred years old, in my dreams I am always young."

Bittersweet sat back down in her chair with the actor's help. When her son came to her right and placed his hand warmly on her shoulder, a photographer and film crew gathered around. Tanmin shooed Madeleine closer to Bittersweet for a symmetrical portrait. My son stands to the right of me, my daughter-in-law to my left, Bittersweet noted as video cameras whirred and flashbulbs popped. My grandson is with me in spirit, and I am living in a four-generation household full of *renao* where the rooms are never empty, the tea cups never dry.

She sighed. Suddenly she felt very tired. Her life had been composed of comings and goings, of reunions and leave-takings. Always there had been something left unsaid, someone or something and some part of one's self left behind. Such was the movement and pattern of life, but for now she was secure in the knowledge that whatever life had granted her, both the bitter and the sweet, it had granted in full measure. And she had embraced life's gifts, both the bitter and the sweet, in full measure.

"*Gan bei! Gan bei!*" everyone demanded, raising their glasses of *san hua.*

Bittersweet looked around her. Such honor accorded on my birthday, she thought and realized that she was secretly bored with all this fuss over her — she, who had been a simple farm girl, who was still a simple farm girl in her heart and who was certainly that in her dreams. Perhaps she was dreaming now, for there was Delin's look-alike raising his glass to her and smiling, just as her husband had toasted and smiled to her on their wedding night.

"Speech! A few words from Li *Furen* on this unique and momentous occasion!" Congressman Cheng's voice boomed above the rest.

But Bittersweet had already slipped back in time to when she was living in Village Village, when she was a headstrong old maid who defied tradition and married the man of her choosing, despite her parents' initial objections and the villagers' derision.

"Ungrateful girl! Disobedient daughter!" they had jeered. "To choose your own husband! Do so — and you oppose the gods! Do so — and you tempt fate!"

Bittersweet rose unsteadily to her feet.

"Within the common destiny is the individual destiny. That destiny is fixed in heaven by the stars in their courses. I have not tempted fate," she told her well-wishers, "but followed it. Only as I follow fate will the pattern of my life appear. Only as I live my life will time decide if that pattern is pleasing and harmonious."

Bittersweet sat back down in her chair and blinked in surprise at the applause that greeted her declaration when before it had brought her only censure. Then, along with her guests, she raised her glass once more as they toasted to her long and exemplary life.

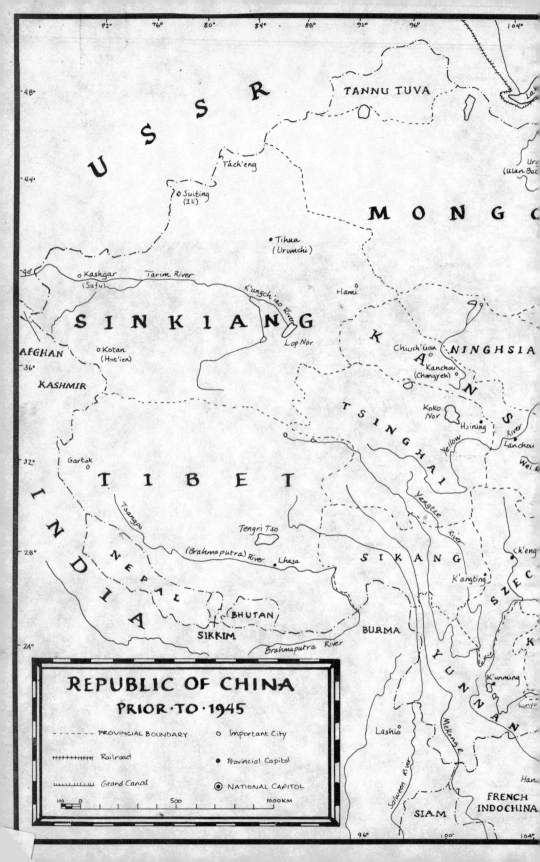

REPUBLIC OF CHINA
PRIOR·TO·1945

- - - - - PROVINCIAL BOUNDARY   o Important City

+++++++++ Railroad   • Provincial Capitol

⊥⊥⊥⊥⊥⊥⊥ Grand Canal   ◎ NATIONAL CAPITOL

100   0   500   1000KM

U   S   S   R

TANNU TUVA

M O N G O

Tách'eng

o Suiting
(Ili)

• Tihua
(Urumchi)

Hami

Urc
(Ulan Bat

o Kashgar   Tarim River
(Sufu)

S I N K I A N G

K'ungch'iao River

Lop Nor

K

Chiuch'üan   NINGHSIA

AFGHAN

o Kotan
(Hot'ien)

Kanchou
(Changyeh) o

A

KASHMIR

T S I N G H A I

N   S

Koko
Nor

Hsining

Yellow   River

Lanchou

Gartok
o

T I B E T

Yellow

Wei k

I
N
D
I
A

Tsangpo

N
E
P
A
L

Tengri Tso

(Brahmaputra) River   • Lhasa

S I K A N G

Yangtze

Ch'eng

River

SZEC

BHUTAN

K'angting

K

SIKKIM

Brahmaputra   River

BURMA

Y
U
N
N
A
N

K'unming

K

Lunyu

Lashio

Mekong R.

Salween River

Han

FRENCH
INDOCHINA

SIAM